HISTORICAL THINKING FOR HISTORY TEACHERS

Edited by
**Tim Allender
Anna Clark
Robert Parkes**

HISTORICAL THINKING FOR HISTORY TEACHERS

A new approach to engaging students and developing historical consciousness

LONDON AND NEW YORK

First published 2019 by Allen & Unwin

Published 2020 by Routledge
2 Park Square, Milton Park, Abingdon, Oxon OX14 4RN
605 Third Avenue, New York, NY 10017

Routledge is an imprint of the Taylor & Francis Group, an informa business

Copyright © in the collection Tim Allender, Anna Clark and Robert Parkes 2019 Copyright in individual chapters with their authors 2019

All rights reserved. No part of this book may be reprinted or reproduced or utilised in any form or by any electronic, mechanical, or other means, now known or hereafter invented, including photocopying and recording, or in any information storage or retrieval system, without permission in writing from the publishers.

Notice:
Product or corporate names may be trademarks or registered trademarks, and are used only for identification and explanation without intent to infringe.

 A catalogue record for this book is available from the National Library of Australia

Internal design by Simon Rattray, Squirt Creative
Index by Puddingburn
Set in 11/14 pt Minion Pro by Midland Typesetters, Australia

ISBN-13: 9781760295516 (pbk)

CONTENTS

Acronyms and abbreviations vii
Contributors ix
Preface: Understanding history and the history classroom xvii
Ruth W. Sandwell

Introduction xx
Tim Allender, Anna Clark and Robert Parkes

PART 1: UNDERSTANDING THE AUSTRALIAN HISTORY CURRICULUM

1   Historical consciousness and the Australian Curriculum 3
       Tony Taylor

2   Understanding the Australian Curriculum: History 18
       Stuart Macintyre

3   A primary history perspective on the Australian Curriculum 31
       David Boon

PART 2: TEACHING HISTORICAL SKILLS AND EFFECTIVE ASSESSMENT

4   Scholarly historical practice and disciplinary method 47
       Anna Clark

5   The role of questions and sources in promoting historical thinking 60
       John A. Whitehouse

6   Developing your approach to teaching history 72
       Robert Parkes

7   Teaching empathy and the critical exam nation of historical evidence . . . 89
       Tyson Retz

8   The nature of values and why they matter in the teaching and
       learning of history 102
       Deborah Henderson

9   The value of direct teaching and historical knowledge 117
       Paul Kiem

10   Inquiry approaches to assessment in the history classroom 129
       Heather Sharp

11   Social history in the classroom 145
       Claire Golledge

PART 3: TEACHING APPROACHES

12 Teacher talk within the history classroom 159
   Tim Allender

13 Personalised narratives of war and teaching engaging history 180
   Jacqueline Z. Wilson and Keir Reeves

14 Using fiction to develop higher-order historical understanding 194
   Grant Rodwell

15 Drama pedagogy in the teaching of history 208
   Kelly Freebody and Alison Grove O'Grady

16 Integrating filmic pedagogies into the teaching and learning cycle . . . 221
   Debra J. Donnelly

17 Using websites to develop historical thinking 231
   James Goulding

18 Digital technology in the primary classroom 245
   Catherine L. Smyth

19 History teaching and the museum 260
   Craig Barker

PART 4: KEY ISSUES IN AUSTRALIAN HISTORY TEACHING

20 Classroom perspectives on Australia's contact history 279
   Nina Burridge

21 Approaches to teaching Aboriginal history and politics 299
   Heidi Norman

22 Teaching citizenship in the history classroom 310
   Yeow-Tong Chia and Kieren Beard

23 Navigating professional identity as a teacher of history 323
   Nicole Mockler

Index 337

ACRONYMS AND ABBREVIATIONS

AACTF	Australia in the Asian Century Task Force
AAPA	Australian Aboriginal Progressive Association
ABS	Australian Bureau of Statistics
ACARA	Australian Curriculum, Assessment and Reporting Authority
ACER	Australian Council for Education Research
ACSA	Australian Curriculum Studies Association
AEC	Australian Education Council
AEP	Aboriginal Education Policy
AfL	Assessment for learning
ALP	Australian Labor Party
AoL	Assessment of learning
ASC	Australian Schools Commission
ATM	Automated teller machine
ATSIC	Aboriginal and Torres Strait Islander Commission
AWM	Australian War Memorial
CHP	Commonwealth History Project
COAG	Council of Australian Governments
CRP	Culturally responsive pedagogies
FCAATSI	Federal Council for the Advancement of Aboriginals and Torres Strait Islanders
GFC	Global Financial Crisis
HaSS	Humanities and social sciences
HiTCH	Historical Thinking—Competencies in History
HSC	Higher School Certificate
HSIE	Human Society & Its Environment
HTA	History Teachers' Association (NSW)
HTAA	History Teachers' Association of Australia
ICT	Information and Communication Technology
IPA	Institute of Public Affairs
K-10	Kindergarten to Year 10
MCEETYA	Ministerial Council on Education, Employment, Training and Youth Affairs
NAA	National Archives of Australia
NAEP	National Aboriginal Education Policy
NAPLAN	National Assessment Program—Literary and Numeracy

NCB	National Curriculum Board
NCHE	National Centre for History Education
NFSA	National Film and Sound Archive
NLA	National Library of Australia
OECD	Organisation for Economic Co-operation and Development
QR Code	Quick Response Code
RAP	Remembering Australia's Past
SCHP	Schools Council History Project (UK)
SHEG	Stanford History Education Group
SOSE	Studies of Society and Environment
TOK	Theory of Knowledge
VHA-VLA	Very high achievement to very limited achievement
YA	Young adult (refers to fiction)

CONTRIBUTORS

Tim Allender is Professor and Chair of History and Curriculum at the University of Sydney, where he has taught preparing history teachers for the past twenty years. Tim has held visiting fellowships at the Universities of Winchester and London as well as visiting professorships in Germany, at the University of Toronto, Canada, at the Institute of Advanced Studies in Shimla, India, and at Jawaharlal Nehru University, India. He has successfully completed two Australian Research Council grants, and his most recent monograph, *Learning Femininity in Colonial India* (Manchester University Press, 2016) won the Anne Bloomfield Book Prize awarded by the History of Education Society UK for best history of education book published between 2014 and 2017.

Craig Barker is the Manager of Education and Public Programs at Sydney University Museums. He has extensive experience in K–12 and adult museum education, and has published and presented on museum education at teacher and academic conferences and in various publications. Craig has a PhD in Classical Archaeology from the University of Sydney and has considerable archaeological fieldwork experience in Australia, Greece, Turkey and Cyprus. He is the Director of the Paphos Theatre Archaeological Project, excavating at the World Heritage-listed site of Nea Paphos in Cyprus, and writes extensively on the archaeology of the Hellenistic and Roman worlds.

Kieren Beard is an English and EAL/D secondary teacher at Georges River College Oatley Senior Campus. Kieren studied at the University of Sydney, where he began to explore his interest in Asia's place in Australian education, particularly in the History and English curricula. This project was inspired by his own educational experience, which led him to feel that there was a genuine void in the history curriculum with regard to preparing Australian graduates as active and informed citizens for an Asia-centred twenty-first century.

David Boon is Principal Education Officer for years K–8 at the Tasmanian Department of Education, having taught all grades (F–10) and held a number of curriculum and professional learning roles over a 33-year career in education. His acknowledged expertise in primary history education led to him being involved in the National History Summit in 2006 and as a presenter at the National Summer School for Teachers of Australian History in 2008, contributing to the development of the framing paper for the Australian Curriculum for history and co-authoring *Place and Time: Explorations in Teaching Geography and History* (with Tony Taylor, Carmel Fahey and Jeana Kriewaldt, Pearson, 2012).

Nina Burridge is an Associate Professor in the Faculty of Arts and Social Sciences at the University of Technology Sydney (UTS). She has been involved in teacher education since 1991 in the Education faculties at Macquarie University, the University of Sydney and, since 2005, at UTS. Her main research interests and publications focus on Aboriginal and Torres Strait Islander education, education for social justice and human rights within Australia and in international contexts. She has published two books on Aboriginal and Torres Strait Islander education and a wide collection of articles and reports on multiculturalism, social justice, women's empowerment and human rights issues.

Yeow-Tong Chia is a Senior Lecturer in History Curriculum Education in the Sydney School of Education and Social Work, University of Sydney. His research interests include history and citizenship education in Singapore and Australia, the teaching of Chinese history in Ontario's high schools, Chinese Canadian history in Canadian history education, and education and developmental state formation. He is the author of *Education, Culture and the Singapore Developmental State: World-Soul Lost and Regained?* (Palgrave Macmillan, 2015).

Anna Clark is an Australian Research Council Future Fellow at the Australian Centre for Public History at the University of Technology Sydney (UTS). She has written extensively on history education, historiography and historical consciousness, including *Teaching the Nation: Politics and Pedagogy in Australian History* (Melbourne University Press, 2006), *History's Children: History Wars in the Classroom* (UNSW Press, 2008), *Private Lives, Public History* (Melbourne University Press, 2016) and *The History Wars* (with Stuart Macintyre, Melbourne University Press, 2003), as well as two history books for children, *Convicted!* and *Explored!* Reflecting her love of fish and fishing, she has also recently published *The Catch: The Story of Fishing in Australia* (National Library of Australia, 2017).

Debra J. Donnelly is a history educator, teaching and researching in the School of Education at the University of Newcastle, Australia. She has a secondary-school background with extensive classroom, school administration and welfare experience across a range of educational settings, both in Australia and internationally. Debra's research focuses on multimodal representations of history in contemporary society, such as museums, films, computer games and virtual-reality experiences. Her research explores the integration of these representations into history pedagogy, and their cognitive and affective impacts on the development of historical understanding and consciousness. It also investigates the relationship between teacher conceptual frameworks of historical understanding and problematic knowledge, digital interactive and performative affordances, and pedagogical practice.

Kelly Freebody is a Senior Lecturer in Drama Education in the Sydney School of Education and Social Work at the University of Sydney. Her research focuses on educational drama, social justice, creativity in education and school–community relationships. Her teaching interests focus on drama pedagogy and teacher education. Recent publications include *Drama and Social Justice: Theory, Research and Practice in International Contexts* (with Michael Finneran, Routledge, 2016) and *Applied Theatre: Understanding Change* (with Michael Balfour, Michael Finneran and Michael Anderson, Springer, 2018).

Claire Golledge is a Teaching Fellow and PhD candidate in the Sydney School of Education and Social Work at the University of Sydney. Her doctoral research concerns the practices of exemplary history teachers in secondary schools, and her broader research interests include teacher practice, curriculum and student voice. Claire teaches a range of subjects to both undergraduate and postgraduate education students in the areas of curriculum, history of education and Aboriginal studies. Prior to commencing her doctoral studies, Claire taught history and legal studies in NSW secondary schools.

James Goulding has a strong research interest in the social practices surrounding technology use in educational settings. Having begun his career as a secondary history teacher, James is now teaching History Curriculum and Educational Psychology at the University of Sydney. His current research involves examining how individuals evaluate the credibility of historical websites, and how the different features of the online medium reshape their historical thinking.

Alison Grove O'Grady is the Program Director (Combined Degrees) and a Lecturer in the Sydney School of Education and Social Work at the University of Sydney. She teaches across a range of subjects, including Pedagogy and Practices; English Curriculum; and Creativity, Learning and Teacher Artistry. Alison's PhD thesis examined the teaching philosophies of pre-service and graduate drama teachers, and how they use language to orient to theories of social justice. Alison is involved in an international research project that examines the effectiveness of drama in professional learning for history teachers. She is currently working on an interdisciplinary project that facilitates a critical consciousness of human rights in personal practice using drama.

Deborah Henderson is an Associate Professor in the Faculty of Education at Queensland University of Technology (QUT) Australia, where she lectures in history curriculum and in social education curriculum. Prior to this, she taught history in secondary schools. Her transdisciplinary research interests include fostering values, intercultural understanding and critical inquiry in the history, civics and citizenship, and social education curriculum; politics and policy-making for Asia literacy; teacher leadership and professional development; and the internationalisation of higher education. Deborah is the editor of *Curriculum Perspectives*, the peer-reviewed journal of the Australian Curriculum Studies Association (ACSA).

Paul Kiem is Professional Officer for the History Teachers' Association of New South Wales and a Research Associate at the University of Technology Sydney (UTS). Formerly a secondary history teacher, he has been Chief Examiner of Modern History in New South Wales, is the author of a number of popular history texts, was editor of *Teaching History* (NSW) for twenty years and regularly presents to teacher and student groups. He was President of the History Teachers' Association of Australia from 2007 until 2012.

Stuart Macintyre is a Professorial Fellow at the University of Melbourne and has served terms as President of the Australian Historical Association and Academy of the Social Sciences. His involvement with history teachers began when he chaired Paul Keating's Civics Expert Group in 1994, which led to the Discovering Democracy Program. In 2008, he wrote the framing paper for history in the national curriculum and was involved in its subsequent preparation. His books include *The History Wars* (with Anna Clark, Melbourne University Press, 2003) and *Australia's Boldest Experiment* (UNSW Press, 2015).

Nicole Mockler is an Associate Professor of Education in the Sydney School of Education and Social Work at the University of Sydney. She is a former teacher and school leader, and her research and writing focus primarily on education policy and politics, and teacher professional identity and learning. Her recent scholarly books include *Questioning the Language of Improvement and Reform in Education: Reclaiming Meaning* (Routledge, 2018) and *Engaging with Student Voice in Research, Education and Community: Beyond Legitimation and Guardianship* (Springer, 2015), both co-authored with Susan Groundwater-Smith. Nicole is currently Editor-in-Chief of *The Australian Educational Researcher*.

Heidi Norman is Professor and Chair of Aboriginal History and Economics at the University of Technology Sydney (UTS), where she teaches in the Communication Program in the Faculty of Arts and Social Sciences, and in the social and political sciences major and Aboriginal Studies elective in the Bachelor of Communication degree. In 2016, she was awarded the Neville Bonner National Teaching Award. She is a descendant of the Gomeroi people of north-western New South Wales.

Robert Parkes (BEd Hons, PhD) is Acting Head of the School of Education and Associate Professor in History Education at the University of Newcastle. He is Convenor of the HERMES History Education Research Network; Founding Editor of *Historical Encounters: A Journal of Historical Consciousness, Historical Cultures, and History Education*; a member of the Editorial Board of *Sungràpho*; a Core Author for *Public History Weekly*; Founding Co-Convenor of the History and Education Special Interest Group within the Australian Association for Research in Education (AARE); and a member of the Academic Advisory Board of the International Society for History Didactics (ISHD).

Keir Reeves is a Professor of Australian History and Director of the Collaborative Research Centre in Australian History at Federation University Australia. He has worked at Monash University as a Senior Research Fellow and prior to that at the University of Melbourne as a Lecturer in Public History and Heritage and also as an Australian Research Council Post-Doctoral Fellow. In 2013, he was a Visiting Fellow (now Life Fellow) at Clare Hall Cambridge and a Visiting Researcher at the McDonald Institute for Archaeological Research. Keir has also been a Senior Rydon Fellow and Bicentennial Fellow at the Menzies Centre for Australian Studies, King's College London. As a practitioner, Keir is the current historian member on the Public Records Advisory Council (PRAC) for the Public Records Office of Victoria (PROV) and a past historian member on the Heritage Council of Victoria.

Tyson Retz is Associate Professor of History Education at the University of Stavanger in Norway. He holds Doctoral and Masters qualifications in history and education from the University of Melbourne and is the author of *Empathy and History* (Berghahn Books, 2018), as well as numerous articles on history education and the philosophy of history. His time as a secondary teacher of history and French saw him win teaching awards in both subjects.

Grant Rodwell has worked as a school principal in Tasmania and in various administrative and academic capacities at Australian universities since the 1980s. He has published over 50 articles in international peer-reviewed journals as well as nine books. He holds five PhDs from Australian universities and is an internationally published novelist of time-slip historical fiction.

Ruth W. Sandwell is a historian and history educator at the University of Toronto, in both the Department of History and at the Ontario Institute for Studies in Education. She was co-director of the history education website series The Great Unsolved Mysteries in Canadian History (www.canadianmysteries.ca) and co-founder of The History Education Network/ Histoire et Éducation en Réseau (THEN/HiER) (www.thenhier.ca). She has written on historical thinking, particularly the use of primary documents in teaching history at all levels, and is the co-editor of *Becoming a History Teacher: Sustaining Practises in Historical Thinking and Knowing* (with Amy von Heyking, University of Toronto Press, 2014). As a historian, she is the author of books and articles on the social history of Canada, particularly rural Canada, and more recently on the social history of energy during the country's great transition to fossil fuels, from 1860 to 1960.

Heather Sharp is a Senior Lecturer in the Faculty of Education and Arts at the University of Newcastle. Heather is a founding member of the HERMES research group. She is convenor of the History Network for Teachers and Researchers (HNTR), Editor of the *Sungràpho* section of the *Agora* journal, and the Special Issues Editor of *Historical Encounters: A Journal of Historical Consciousness*. Her research investigates historical representations in school curricula, particularly around topics of significance to a nation's history. She is currently a recipient of a Swedish Research Council grant as part of a research group investigating historical and moral consciousness.

Catherine L. Smyth is a Lecturer in the Faculty of Education and Social Work at the University of Sydney, where she coordinates and teaches HSIE K–6 curriculum (Human Society and Its Environment) in both the Bachelor of Education and Masters of Teaching primary teacher education programs. Catherine previously worked as a primary teacher in New South Wales, the Solomon Islands and Kuwait, and as a project officer in HSIE curriculum. She was primary adviser for the Australian Curriculum: History. Her research and PhD thesis explore history teaching and learning in the primary classroom, and she is particularly interested in the role of ICT (information and communication technology) and process drama in activating historical knowledge.

Tony Taylor began his career as a history educator in 1967 at a boys' comprehensive school in Brixton, South London. He worked in British comprehensive schools before gaining a research scholarship and history doctorate from Cambridge. From 1981 to 2014, he was a history educator in Australian higher education. In 1999, he headed the national inquiry into history education; he wrote the inquiry's 2001 report and became Director of the National Centre for History Education (2001–7) as well as history education consultant to Australian Curriculum, Assessment and Reporting Authority (ACARA) (2008–12). He is co-author of *Place and Time: Explorations in Teaching Geography and History* (with Carmel Fahey, Jeana Kriewaldt and David Boon, Pearson, 2012) and author of

Class Wars: Money, Schools and Power in Modern Australia (Monash University Publishing, 2018).

John A. Whitehouse is a Lecturer in History/Humanities in the Melbourne Graduate School of Education. A Fellow of the Australian College of Educators, he is the recipient of the Barbara Falk Award for Teaching Excellence (University of Melbourne) and a national Award for Teaching Excellence (Australian Learning and Teaching Council). His research interests include discipline-based pedagogy in history, curriculum studies and historiography. He is the International Consulting Editor for *Learning and Teaching*. His research appears in leading publications such as *Educational Practice and Theory* and Springer's *International Handbook of Research on Teachers and Teaching*.

Jacqueline Z. Wilson is an Associate Professor in the Centre for Collaborative Research in Australian History at Federation University Australia. She is a graduate of La Trobe University, where she was awarded the David Myer University Medal, and Monash University (PhD History). She has authored over 50 scholarly publications and is the sole author, editor and/or co-editor of five books, with research interests that focus broadly on heritage, education and Australia's welfare and justice systems. Jacqueline is currently a chief investigator on several collaborative and interdisciplinary research projects, funded by the Sidney Myer Fund and the Australian Research Council Discovery Awards.

PREFACE
Understanding history and the history classroom

Ruth W. Sandwell

I like to begin each term by giving my history education students the following definition: history is simply an ongoing dialogue about the interpretation of meaningful evidence about almost any aspect of a collective past or pasts. My students' revisions of this definition usually continue right through to the end of term. As they are quick to point out, even if this definition were to satisfy a handful of professional historians, history is never simple in any sense. Even if history is *not* a school-based plot to brainwash the Canadian population (as they sometimes hint) and is instead a way of knowing and understanding collectively, who gets to decide who and what are worthy subjects of investigation and collective understanding—who counts, in other words, and according to whom?

As they learn more about the difference between memorising historical facts and learning how to 'do' their own historical research, students become even more aware of the power imbalances within history, and even more critical of the national (and nationalistic) narratives they were taught in schools. What evidence has been lost, and why? Whose voices have been left out? Why are certain stories told and others forgotten? Is history always written by the winners? Who is the 'we'—the collective—typically implied inside the history classroom? Even as they learn that history is not an averaging out of everyone's individual experience, but instead a series of answers constructed in response to specific questions asked of the past, they still poignantly struggle with the question: how can we teach a history that fully represents, and does justice to, the experiences of *everyone*?

Challenges to the power imbalances so evident throughout history are not new. For almost a century now, Western historians have been challenging epistemological hierarchies that seemed to privilege only the political actions of the powerful, broadening their understanding of *who* counts within a society's collectivity to include the poor, immigrants, the disenfranchised, the sexually marginalised and the young. In their re-evaluations about who is important, historians have necessarily been challenging ideas about *what* counts as historically significant. They now routinely include the people whose decisions and preferences were seen neither as politically relevant nor to be of immediately obvious wider social or economic significance. Historians write now about the lives of working people and the unemployed, families and the homeless, and examine personal, cultural, economic, psychological, intimate and environmental aspects of daily life. In the process, historians increasingly have focused on the intersection of identity, power and autonomy in order to understand and explain the ways that societies worked in past times. How did societies reconcile the needs and desires of the individual with those of society as a whole? What were the systems of governance—formal and informal—that people created, acquiesced to and protested against? How can people in the present comprehend the contours of disempowerment and exclusion that seem, along with narratives of individualism and freedom, to have defined so much of modernising human society in recent decades?

While historians have broadened and deepened the *who* and the *why* of history, my students' questions nevertheless underscore the point that history has never belonged only to historians. Before the profession emerged and long afterwards, most human groups have kept records and maintained explanations of their collective's stasis and change, and through timescales larger than any individual's life. In the last half-century and around the globe, however, there has been an efflorescence of non-professional interest in history—an interest that, while laudable, also highlights just how powerful uses and abuses of the past can be. Whether this new public interest in history has been stimulated by the challenge (and perceived threat) posed to nationalist narratives by globalisation, or by ever-increasing access to education and evidence (and pseudo-evidence) about the past, historical representations seem to be on the increase. Museum visitation and the consumption of historically focused media such as films, books and websites are increasing significantly around the world. People may be looking more actively to the past to find their place in collectivities of the present—whatever those may be, and however varied.

Perhaps less benign are the uses of the past to encourage or discourage particular kinds of beliefs and behaviours for individuals defined within targeted collectivities. For good or ill, though, history arguably is taking a more dominant role in the ways that individuals and societies are imagining themselves.

If history seems to be more prominent locally and in a variety of ways, however, it is arguably in the schools of the contemporary world that the potential of history has been most thoroughly explored, both in theory and in classroom-based practices. Historians of the educational state in twentieth-century Europe, North America and the Antipodes argued with some consistency that history was long taught explicitly to nurture national (collective) pride and other virtues of 'good citizens'—a tradition that (as my students indeed suspect) continues to play some role in most state-funded history curricula. But over the past 30 years and as part of a global trend, education has sparked a variety of intense discussions—and indeed History Wars—about the nature of the individual, society and directions of social change. History education has become a kind of hot zone where teachers, educational policy-makers, politicians and even sometimes students debate with a broadly based public about the roles and purposes of history. To put this in slightly different terms, it is as if the relationships (real and imagined) between individuals and a variety of social, economic and political collectivities are now being worked out partly through discussions about what history should be taught in the schools, why and how.

Situated clearly within the unique context of Australia's own highly politicised History Wars and curriculum changes of the last few decades, this volume explores a range of issues confronting history and social studies educators, from dealing with conflict and difference in the classroom to the nature of historical consciousness and the purposes of historical thinking for humanity generally. Through its focus on the particularities of teaching and learning history in Australia, this collection not only furthers understanding of history education in one country, but contributes to wider discussions about the meanings and purposes of history, and of history education, within human societies around the world.

Introduction

Tim Allender, Anna Clark and Robert Parkes

This book is designed to offer pre-service and early career history teachers a gateway into becoming proficient in their chosen profession in Australia by drawing on the experience and research of many expert academics and teacher professionals. The book is long overdue and serves to add to earlier works in the field. Most particularly, it is a distinctly Australian response to recent international developments in the field of history curriculum. It also fills a gap that exists in providing the profession (at school and at university) in Australia with closer guidance about the orchestration of best practice in the history classroom and how to understand what such practice looks like. The book acknowledges the earlier work of Carmel Young and Tony Taylor (2003), *Making History*, and seeks to incorporate the research of many new and established scholars in the field of history curriculum to enrich our understandings of how school children learn history.

There is a wealth of expertise in Australia regarding the teaching of history and about honing expertise in this discipline in the classroom. However, a consolidated synthesis of Australian practice is yet to emerge that responds to international developments in this area—particularly around *historical thinking* developed from the work of Sam Wineburg and later Peter Seixas and Tom Morton and many other national and international scholars in recent years, who are referenced in the 23 chapters of this volume.

While not designed to offer any single model of best-practice history teaching, this book is informed by the research findings of academics (including already completed Australian Research Council-funded inquiries). It also brings together other experts in the field, drawing on many years' experience of research and teaching at university level and in the history classroom, to offer both preparing and beginning teachers vital insights into their chosen vocation.

The contributors to this book have been encouraged to engage with the current academic literature but also to be reflective about practice and conversational in style, and to include a strong practical element in terms of suggestions offered. The focus is what teachers need in terms of disciplinary expertise when teaching history as a distinctive subject, away from integrated studies approaches that have been a feature of past syllabuses in many Australian states. As a discipline, history occupies a distinctive domain concerning literacy, where historical reasoning is immersed in the complexities of active citizenship in a literacy-saturated society (Allender & Freebody 2016). Yet a troubling feature is maintaining student interest—particularly at senior school levels—in Australian history as a national history worthy of complex contestation and as holding multiple perspectives regarding interactions with Australia's first peoples (Allender 2015).

In part, the motivation for any collection of this kind also lies in understanding the contested politics of national memory. History education is located at a critical juncture in debates over Australia's past and reveals the significance of history education to the nation's narrative and identity. Like contests over museum exhibits and national commemorations (think of the #changethedate discussion and commentary on Anzac Day), contests over history teaching have prompted not only extensive public debate, but also significant research (Clark 2008; Donnelly 2004; Land 1994; Parkes 2007; Taylor & Guyver 2012). Furthermore, they are a global phenomenon, playing out over contested pasts right around the world: the development of the National Curriculum in the United Kingdom, or National History Standards in the United States, or history textbooks in Israel now comprise an entire research field into teaching difficult histories (e.g. Goldberg 2018; Nash, Crabtree & Dunn 1997; Phillips 1998). Such contests confirm the nation-state's dependence on history for the formation of identity, as well as its politically contested capacity to curate and construct that narrative (Bevernage & Wouters 2017). Understanding the role and function of history education in Australia—especially its place in contested national memory and identity-formation—is one important starting point of our volume.

Yet research into history teaching is also much more than a study of competing versions of what's 'in' or 'out' of a particular curriculum, or textbook, or classroom. History is much more than 'the past'. It is an entire practice of reading and writing of that past: sources must be gathered and interrogated, arguments must be synthesised, characters must be examined with both empathy and judgement, competing versions must be teased out, and our own approaches need to be self-consciously critiqued (Tosh 2008).

As such, history *education* adds another layer of complexity: how do we teach not only 'what happened', but also those practices of reading and writing it? Simply locating history education as one arena of the History Wars, and assuming its significance is linked to the nation, fails to account for that methodological and pedagogical complexity. Any debate over 'what to teach', as the American educationist Sam Wineburg (2001: xii) famously intimated, obscures not only why history is so important, but also the components of the discipline and its practice. The 'identification of a structure of historical understanding', Canadian history educationist Peter Seixas (1996: 777) further explains, complicates any assumption of history education as simply a question of teaching 'what happened'. In doing so, it constitutes 'a different kind of historical pedagogy', which raises a much broader and more complicated set of questions and has concomitantly demanded a more diverse and nuanced set of interpretation and analysis.

These historical thinking skills aren't intuitive, however—hence the need for a historical education. In recent years, there has been increasing work done into what exactly constitutes proficiency in the subject. UK history educationist Peter Lee (2001) suggests that, 'Even if the substantive past is "ordinary"', 'the discipline of history is not' (see also Lee & Ashby 2000). The second-order forms of historical thinking—beyond that substantive capacity for 'factual knowledge and grand narratives'—are what Stéphane Lévesque has termed a 'disciplinary form of knowledge', prompted by questions such as: 'What group(s) am I part of? Why is this story important to me? Should I believe it? On what grounds? What evidence do we have?' (Lévesque 2012). As Wineburg insists, those skills of historical thinking are downright 'unnatural': understanding concepts such as historical significance, continuity and change, progress and decline are all vital components of understanding how we *do* history, as are the critical reading of sources and considering the tension between empathy and historical judgement (Morton 2000; VanSledright 2009: 434).

That's not to say we don't need content. Interpreting 'what happened' is a critical component of our historical understanding. Yet clearly history is also much more than trying to understand the past. It is also a leap of imagination, as historians such as Tom Griffiths (2017) and Greg Dening (1996) insist: it's a test of empathy, a capacity for judgement, as well as a practice that involves the use of oral history, critically reading sources, analysing images and film, and producing historical narratives themselves.

In other words, content is only one component of many in the teaching and learning of history. As Lee (2001: 8) contends, the 'point of learning history is that students can make sense of the past, and that means knowing some content'. So that *doing* part of history, which we all strive for in our history classes, requires students to know what they are talking about. But Lee insists that it is only understanding the discipline itself and its practice that enable students 'to do things with their historical knowledge'.

Each of these elements of history education is explored in our book, by historians and history educators who are passionate about their subject. History teaching is difficult—teaching the significance of Australia's federation to a roomful of grumpy teenagers on a Friday afternoon is no one's idea of fun. Yet it is the very skills provided by such a class—of critique, critical engagement and even an understanding of the significance of federation in the first place—that are important, as Lévesque (2012) writes:

> Perhaps in the past it was sufficient for learners to recall memory information of the community, but in today's complex, rapidly changing world, this approach to history is no longer sufficient. We need an educated citizenry capable of orienting themselves in time with critical, usable narrative visions of their world.

This shift to critical engagement with narratives that help a citizenry orient itself in time, which Lévesque calls for, is part of an important supplement to the idea of historical thinking as a set of discrete disciplinary skills that is also raised in some of the chapters in this volume. According to Jörn Rüsen (2005), a key feature of historical consciousness, and thus history education, is the ability to orient oneself in relation to the past, the present and the future. Rüsen writes out of a German-speaking tradition that recognises the importance of understanding oneself as a historical being, with perspectives that are shaped within the historical culture a person experiences throughout their life. This requires us to think beyond history as a set of procedural skills and to explore its function in helping us to acknowledge and navigate the gulf between the past and the present. It also underscores the need for the history teacher to recognise the positionality of all historical accounts, including those we encounter in textbooks, films and other historical media, as well as in the accounts of historians themselves, marked by the historiographic traditions in which they have been trained.

Between the covers of this volume, a range of perspectives on history, historical thinking and history teaching register the influences of the various traditions within which research on historical thinking has occurred, including both the second-order concept approach associated with Lee, and reflected in work by Seixas and Wineburg among others, and this historical narrative orientation tradition, identified with Lévesque and Rüsen.

A wide range of interrelated history themes are contained in this volume, which are referred to in more than one chapter. What we mean by some of these is worth noting here. Historical thinking refers fundamentally to the capacity to think or reason like a historian. Researchers have identified a number of different structural features that make up 'historical thinking', including the capacity to: establish *historical significance* (what we think was important about the past, or why we care about certain events, trends, issues or people from the past); use *evidence* (how to locate, select, contextualise and corroborate primary sources from the past and secondary accounts about the past); identify *continuity and change* (what has changed and what has remained the same over time); analyse *cause and effect* (reason how and why certain conditions and actions led to particular consequences or events); take *historical perspectives* (understand that people and societies think differently in different social, cultural and historical situations, including ourselves—sometimes also understood as 'historical empathy'; and understand the *moral dimension* of historical interpretations (how our values, and the values implicit in the historical narratives we encounter, have consequences for people in the present and future). The Australian Curriculum: History draws on these concepts and skills explicitly (Seixas & Peck 2004).

Historical consciousness is represented in the work of Peter Seixas as: (1) both individual and collective understandings of the past (what we know or believe about the past); (2) the cognitive and cultural factors that shape our understanding of the past; and (3) the relationship of historical understanding to how we think about the present and the future. This makes historical consciousness of great importance to history educators. Jörn Rüsen presents historical consciousness as the tendency or desire of people to orient themselves in time, which is performed through our construction of narratives about the past, their connection to the present and future, and our place within them. In the Germanic tradition of which Rüsen is a member, to have 'historical consciousness' is not simply to have knowledge of the past: it signals that one is aware that one's own perspectives are always socially situated and historically shaped, that there is a temporal aspect to consciousness that we cannot escape, and that this influences our interpretation of any texts or artefacts we encounter (Seixas 2004).

Historical reasoning is a form of inductive analysis in which traces of the past are explored, compared and interpreted in an attempt to understand and explain a historical phenomenon, culture, activity or event. Whenever students draw inferences from, or attempt to make meaning of, historical texts and artefacts using source analysis principles of the discipline of history, or considering sociocultural and political causes of an event, they are involved in historical reasoning (van Drie & van Boxtel 2008).

Presentism is inserting the perspectives and social values of one time period inappropriately into another time period in history. More recently, in Australian history curriculum development, this term has come to mean the poor contextualisation of events in the twentieth and twenty-first centuries by failing to adequately analyse longer-standing precursors that may belong to the eighteenth and nineteenth centuries and before. Historical literacy is the mastery of key words and concepts that have strong disciplinary meaning, such as Industrial Revolution, fascism and pharaoh. Understanding their meaning is a necessary part of embarking on deeper historical inquiry into particular events (Lee 2011). Historical empathy is the capacity to place oneself as the historian, exploring more deeply the feelings and perspectives of people(s) in history. Seen as part of the affective domain of learning, empathy does not necessarily imply sympathy, as non-sympathetic empathy can be used to deepen interpretations of the actions of tyrants in history such as Hitler or Stalin (Yeager & Foster 2001).

Historiography is the study of different schools of thought regarding historical events and how such history is variously constructed using different sources and interpretation of sources, as well as the use of broader and different theorisations and paradigms. For example, the political historian has a different approach to an economic or a social historian. Historiography is interested in the contrasts of these different approaches and also often groups historians (when they have engaged with the interpretations of each other on a particular topic) into separate time periods of research-based debate and interpretation—for example, the immediate post-World War I interpretation of the causes of this war compared with interpretations of those same causes made by different historians after World War II. Revisionist history is a body of work that revises previous historical interpretations and schools of thought—for example, feminist histories have revised Australian historiography in the 1970s.

ORGANISATION OF THE BOOK

The book contains 23 chapters and is organised into four sections, each of which has a specific over-arching theme.

Understanding the Australian Curriculum: History

This first section provides essential context for developments in history curriculum in Australia in recent years. In Chapter 1, Tony Taylor examines historical consciousness as the process of how individuals and groups understand the past and how this understanding may affect the present and the future. The chapter focuses particularly on how the interaction of international influences and Australian political processes has led to the national curriculum in history in ways not unfamiliar in other Western countries. In Chapter 2, Stuart Macintyre, as the key writer for History, outlines the intense political and educational developments that gave rise to the Australian Curriculum: History. This process saw a move away from direct political interference and the transferring of this work to an expert independent body; today, however, new sensitivities have left little provision for a genuinely national approach. Finally, in this section, in Chapter 3 David Boon takes the discussion into the primary school classroom and explores how the national curriculum has opened the door to the pedagogy of inquiry, using examples to show the development of conceptual understandings as well new assessment modalities.

Teaching historical skills and effective assessment

This section looks more closely at history pedagogy, particularly in the context of a focus upon thinking historically. Anna Clark, in Chapter 4, explores the possibilities for teaching historical thinking in the classroom. She argues that not only does history demand that a critical and complex disciplinary approach be taken, but also that is how students learn the subject best. John A. Whitehouse, in Chapter 5, concentrates on the use of effective questioning in the history classroom within the frame of historical thinking. He argues that for students to pursue questions about the past, they need to draw on key concepts including those nested within the historical thinking project to build substantive and procedural knowledge. In Chapter 6, Robert Parkes invites the developing history teacher to locate their own position in relation to important debates that have occurred in the curriculum field, as their position in these debates has significant pedagogical implications. His chapter also offers a framework that articulates four approaches to history teaching, extending and revising earlier work by Peter Seixas, which aims to respond effectively to both conservative and postmodern attacks on history, by outlining an often unarticulated critical pluralist position that can be adopted when navigating the stories of the past that we encounter. Tyson Retz, in Chapter 7, explores the use of empathy in the classroom. He takes the study of empathy beyond its simpler deconstructions in the 1970s and 1980s to posit how empathy's emotional dimension, and empathy as a cognitive act, can, through moderate hermeneutics, negotiate the territory separating the past and the present. In Chapter 8, Deborah Henderson explores the nature of values and why they are central to the teaching and learning of history in Australian classrooms. She argues that historical thinking enables schoolchildren to acquire a vocabulary to engage with values associated with conflicting accounts of the past, a generative process with strong implications for teaching the discipline deeply. Paul Kiem, in Chapter 9, surveys the ongoing impact of the 1980s changes made to history teaching, which emphasised inquiry-based and skills-focused learning. He argues for the teaching of more direct historical knowledge as a priority for history teachers. In Chapter 10, Heather Sharp examines the problematics of assessment—particularly that imposed externally on the classroom. More centrally, the chapter offers discussion of different forms of assessment in the classroom and the multifaceted considerations attached to these, in order to best position students to be beneficiaries of these necessary assessment processes. Claire Golledge, in Chapter 11, explores how teaching social history can enrich the history classroom. The chapter examines the vital implications that exist when teaching social history for other history classroom strategies, including teaching empathy and evidence. The chapter endorses strong student-centred teaching approaches when teaching this kind of history.

Teaching approaches

In Chapter 12, Tim Allender examines the classroom praxis of two experienced senior history teachers. He illustrates how expertise can look quite dissimilar in different history classrooms. However, he argues that 'teacher talk' is the most spontaneous and demanding phenomenon in conveying the disciplinarity of history to school students, in terms of conceptual understandings and in the building of key competencies. Jacqueline Z. Wilson and Keir Reeves, in Chapter 13, offer a model of teaching about World War I that is suitable for both tertiary and secondary school students. Along with other models that they have developed, this project is designed to be hands on, to provide context for teaching areas and to 'personalise' the survey histories often encountered in our curriculum. In Chapter 14, Grant Rodwell develops a strong analysis around teaching history through a well-chosen, relevant historical novel, while comparing historical eras. This is a way to encourage student higher-order historical thinking. Kelly Freebody and Alison Grove O'Grady, in Chapter 15, examine how drama pedagogy can build historical knowledge in the classroom. The chapter sees its uses in many dimensions, including student self-critique regarding value formation and alternative avenues in the formation of historical knowledge. In Chapter 16, Debra J. Donnelly examines the role of film and its favoured pedagogies in the history classroom. Recognising the 'Disney effect' that films can have in the classroom, this chapter explores practical deeper pedagogies (including student formation of values and attitudes) that offer effective historical learning using film. James Goulding, in Chapter 17, examines the use of websites and the importance of treating quality websites as sources, with a broad range of issues identified and approaches provided when teaching using resources found online. In Chapter 18, Catherine L. Smyth examines the use of online digital technologies in the history classroom. These can be disciplinary or generically based, and they provide powerful epistemic capacities to deepen student historical knowledge. Concluding this section, in Chapter 19, Craig Barker examines the issues related to resourcing the teaching of history through the museum. His chapter surveys the ways in which museum educators and teachers can build strong partnerships, striving to achieve the same learning outcomes, but with the museum offering distinctive alternative approaches in pedagogy.

KEY ISSUES IN AUSTRALIAN HISTORY TEACHING

The fourth section of the book deals with more general issues and approaches concerning the teaching of history in Australia. Nina Burridge, in Chapter 20, deals with the incorporation of Indigenous perspectives into the curriculum. Taking a personal perspective, this chapter discusses how key curriculum components can be enriched by taking the Aboriginal clans' perspective along the relatively short history of European settlement in Australia. In Chapter 21, Heidi Norman explores history-teaching strategies that relate to 'truth-telling about our history' at university level (also applicable to history school teaching), writing as a descendant of the Gomeroi people of northwest New South Wales. The chapter examines 'deep history' and the ways in which the multifaceted history of Aboriginal and Torres Strait Islander peoples can be told, away from the strictures of European-predicated narratives. Yeow-Tong Chia and Kieren Beard, in Chapter 22, examine citizenship teaching in the history classroom from an Asian perspective, where Asian history and the history of Asian Australia are not neglected. Most particularly, some of the limitations of historical thinking, when taking only a Western approach, are examined where East Asian conceptions of history and citizenship have a different paradigmatic makeup. Finally, in Chapter 23, Nicole Mockler examines the influential factors that shape history teachers' professional identity. This is from her vantage point as a once early-career history teacher where professional identity is deeply individual.

This collection represents the scholarly expertise of authors from a range of Australian academic institutions, all with a strong interest in history education. Written in a scholarly, yet inviting, tone, the chapters in this collection offer a road map to history teaching for the aspiring teacher of history. The book is aimed at both primary and secondary pre-service and early career teachers. A wide range of terms integral to the history education field—at various levels of schooling—are drawn upon in this volume, including historical understanding, historical consciousness, historical literacy, historical empathy, historical reasoning, historical perspective, historical narratives and historical knowledge, as well as a range of -isms, such as postmodernism, contextualism, relativism, presentism and nominalism, and different forms of history, such as new history, social history, local history, world history, oral history and commodified history. Some of these terms (and their associated traditions) may be very familiar, and some will be completely new to the reader. It is our hope that this helps to make this book a touchstone reference guide for scholarly perspective on history teaching in Australia today.

REFERENCES

Allender, T. 2015, 'History lessons from the Antipodes: Teaching history didactics in Australia', in E. Erdmann & W. Hasberg (eds), *History Teacher Education: Global Interrelations*, Schwalbach: Wochenschau Verlag, pp. 213–28.

Allender, T. & Freebody, P. 2016, 'Disciplinary and idiomatic literacy: Re-living and re-working the past in senior school history', *Australian Journal of Language and Literacy*, vol. 39, no. 1, pp. 7–19.

Bevernage, B. & Wouters, N. (eds) 2017, *The Palgrave Handbook of State-Sponsored History After 1945*, New York: Springer.

Clark, A. 2008, *History's Children: History Wars in the Classroom*, Sydney: UNSW Press.

Dening, G. 1996, *Performances*, Melbourne: Melbourne University Press.

Donnelly, K. 2004, *Why Our Schools are Failing*, Sydney: Duffy & Snellgrove.

Goldberg, T. 2018, '"On whose side are you?" Difficult histories in the Israeli context', in C. Peck & T. Epstein (eds), *Teaching and Learning Difficult Histories in International Contexts: A Critical Sociocultural Approach*, London: Routledge, pp. 145–59.

Griffiths, T. 2017, *The Art of Time Travel: Historians and Their Craft*, Melbourne: Black Inc.

Land, R. 1994, '"Furore over invasion text": Introduction to the politics process and players', in R. Land (ed.), *Invasion and After: A Case Study in Curriculum Politics*, Brisbane: Griffith University, pp. 1–11.

Lee, P. 2001, 'Understanding history', paper presented at the Canadian Historical Consciousness in an International Context: Theoretical Frameworks conference, Centre for the Study of Historical Consciousness, University of British Columbia, Vancouver.

—— 2011, 'History education and historical literacy', in I. Davies (ed.), *Debates in History Teaching*, London: Routledge, pp. 63–72.

Lee, P. & Ashby, R. 2000, 'Progression of historical understanding among students ages 7–14', in P.N. Stearns, P. Seixas & S. Wineburg (eds), *Knowing, Teaching and Learning History: National and International Perspectives*, New York: New York University Press, pp. 199–222.

Lévesque, S. 2012, 'Between memory recall and historical consciousness: Implications for education', *Public History Weekly*, 12 October, <http://public-history-weekly.oldenbourg-verlag.de/2-2014-33/memory-recall-historical-consciousness-implications-education>, accessed 23 October 2017.

Morton, D. 2000, 'Teaching and learning history in Canada', in P.N. Stearns, P. Seixas & S. Wineburg (eds), *Knowing, Teaching and Learning History: National and International Perspectives*, New York: New York University Press, pp. 51–62.

Nash, G.B., Crabtree, C. & Dunn, R.E. 1997, *History on Trial: Culture Wars and the Teaching of the Past*, New York: Alfred A. Knopf.

Parkes, R.J. 2007, 'Reading history curriculum as postcolonial text: Towards a curricular response to the History Wars in Australia and beyond', *Curriculum Inquiry*, vol. 37, no. 4, pp. 383–400.

Phillips, R. 1998, 'Contesting the past, constructing the future: History, identity and politics in schools', *British Journal of Educational Studies*, vol. 46, no. 1, pp. 40–53.

Rüsen, J. 2005, *History: Narration—interpretation—orientation*. New York: Berghahn Books.

Seixas, P. 1996, 'Conceptualizing the growth of historical understanding', in D.R. Olson & N. Torrance (eds), *The Handbook of Education and Human Development: New Models of Learning, Teaching and Schooling*, Malden, MA: Blackwell, pp. 765–83.

—— 2004, *Theorizing Historical Consciousness*. Toronto: University of Toronto Press.

Seixas, P. & Morton, T. 2013, *The Big Six Historical Thinking Concepts*, Toronto: Nelson.

Seixas, P. & Peck, C. 2004, 'Teaching historical thinking', in A. Sears & I. Wright (eds), *Challenges and Prospects for Canadian Social Studies*, Vancouver: Pacific Educational Press, pp. 109–17.

Taylor, T. & Guyver, R. 2012, *History Wars and the Classroom: Global Perspectives*, Charlotte, NC: Information Age.

Tosh, J. 2008, *Why History Matters*, Basingstoke: Palgrave Macmillan.

van Drie, J. & van Boxtel, C. 2008, 'Historical reasoning: Towards a framework for analysing students' reasoning about the past', *Educational Psychology Review*, vol. 20, no. 2, pp. 87–110.

VanSledright, B. 2009, 'Thinking historically', *Journal of Curriculum Studies*, vol. 41, no. 3, pp. 433–8.

Wineburg, S. 2001, *Historical Thinking and Other Unnatural Acts: Charting the Future of Teaching the Past*, Philadelphia, PA: Temple University Press.

Yeager, E.A. & Foster, S.J. 2001, 'The role of empathy in the development of historical understanding', in O. Davis, E.A. Yeager & S. Foster (eds), *Historical Empathy and Perspective Taking in Social Studies*, Oxford: Rowman & Littlefield, pp. 13–20.

Young, C. & Taylor, T. 2003, *Making History: A Guide for the Teaching and Learning of History in Australian Schools*, Melbourne: Curriculum Corporation.

PART I
UNDERSTANDING THE AUSTRALIAN HISTORY CURRICULUM

CHAPTER 1
Historical consciousness and the Australian Curriculum

Tony Taylor

INTRODUCTION

As has been the case in many other nations, the teaching and learning of history in modern Australian schools have endured a controversial past—indeed, arguably more controversial than any other Australian school subject. This is principally because historical interpretation—even at the school level—is frequently tied to politicised versions of national narratives (Taylor & Guyver 2012). Consequently, understanding the contentious nature of the events that preceded the establishment of an Australian national curriculum in history is an important part of a classroom teacher's sense of both historical consciousness and curriculum knowledge. By historical consciousness, I mean more than just knowing and understanding the past: it entails understanding the process by which individual and group understandings of the past are formed, how they affect the present and how they may affect the future. By curriculum knowledge, I mean comprehending the past, present and future contexts of a curriculum. In other words, when teachers of history inspect their latest curriculum publication, they need to ask and be able to answer several questions: what lies behind this document? How and why did the education system get to this place? And where is this history curriculum heading?

This chapter attempts to deal with these questions during the period prior to the 2008–10 drafting of the Australian Curriculum: History (dealt with in Chapter 2). The chapter discusses the importance of the UK Schools Council History Project (SCHP) as an inspiration for history education reformers in Australia, the fall and subsequent rise of historical consciousness in schools during the twenty-year period that preceded the 2010 introduction of the Australian Curriculum, the significance of the 2000–01 National History Inquiry, the Commonwealth History Project 2001–06 and the 2006 National History Summit.

THE BACKGROUND TO TEACHING AND LEARNING HISTORY IN MODERN AUSTRALIA

Prior to the 1980s, much of the history teaching in Australian secondary schools had a traditional look about it. Classes in secondary schools were largely based on chalk and talk, combined with the intermittent colourful anecdote, the reading of textbooks or topic books, the occasional 16-millimetre film shown on a cumbersome Black and Howell projector and, for the more able students, the taking of notes and the writing of essays. Primary school students, often taught by teachers with little or no background in history, tended to work on integrated projects that included historical elements. During the 1970s, though, progressive educators in Australia had become increasingly critical of a subject-by-subject disciplinary approach to the humanities in secondary schools. They wanted a broader, more socially and economically relevant approach to curriculum to help deal with the increased numbers of students staying on to the senior years in secondary schools, and they looked to the other side of the Pacific for inspiration. There, a US-based New Social Studies movement, originally based on the work of American educator Edwin Fenton (1966), offered an alternative vision for Australia in the 1980s. This over-arching social studies approach, based on the use of a facts, concepts and generalisations template for all humanities subjects, came at a time when state- or territory-based curriculum design in Australia was haphazard, localised and built on previous syllabus incarnations.

Australian supporters of the New Social Studies saw value in integrating subjects within themes or topics so that the knowledge and skills used in each discipline could cross over and join with the knowledge and skills acquired in other subjects. For example, if students were finding out about the sixteenth- and seventeenth-century European voyages of discovery, they could use facts, concepts and generalisations gained in studying history, geography and economics, leading to what was expected to be a socially productive curriculum based on knowledge and skills that would, according to one contemporary observer, 'teach the art of cooperative living' (Taylor et al. 2012: 29).

Consequently, at a 1989 annual meeting of Australian education ministers in Tasmania, it was decided that the states and territories would teach humanities by following a fully integrated social studies model, a Studies of Society and Environment (SOSE) K–10 curriculum framework. This decision—part of a federal Labor government push to increase retention rates—was announced in the 1989 Hobart Declaration on Schooling. The integrated SOSE approach would now become the standard way of teaching humanities to students in the K–10 years in most Australian government schools as well as all Catholic diocesan schools. There were to be two additional features added to SOSE. In Australia, Fenton's (1966) knowledge and skills elements were joined by 'values' and, as the framework's title suggests, the new program featured study of the environment. Within SOSE, history's knowledge and skills features were limited to Time, Continuity and Change.

New South Wales was the only state that declined to give up its history and geography lessons at the secondary school level. Major non-government schools also declined to join the SOSE framework, sticking to history and geography as their main humanities subject areas. One consequence was that while a majority of Australian schools in the 1990s followed the SOSE path, a substantial minority did not. Another consequence was that, at the school level, history as a subject and historical consciousness as an educational outcome went into a steep decline.

THE NEW HISTORY MOVEMENT

Meanwhile, a different kind of curriculum movement called New History had begun in the United Kingdom during the 1960s, and it began to flourish there in the early 1970s, dominating secondary school history education during the 1980s. New History was to reach Australia in the late 1980s, eventually playing a part in the formation of the Australian Curriculum: History in 2010.

The British idea of New History was to move the subject along from its early twentieth-century origins as a memorised learning of Ancient Egypt, Greece and Rome (in Year 7), and Medieval England and the Tudor and Stuart eras (in Years 8 and 9) followed by a study of the achievements of Great Britain as the originator of the Industrial Revolution (in Year 10). In terms of student interest, this topic sequence went from the fascinating through to the vivid but concluded with the dull, just as students were about to choose their two-year examination courses in Years 10 and 11. This approach was not a formal national history curriculum but the basis of a patchwork curriculum of common practice and common agreement in the hundreds of local education authorities of the different jurisdictions of England, Wales, Scotland and Northern Ireland.

New History had its theoretical origins in UK education philosopher Paul Hirst's (1966) argument that there were seven 'forms of knowledge', all of which were distinctly different from one another, and one of those forms was history. In 1970, UK educator Martin Ballard (1970) published an edited collection of chapters, *New Movements in the Study and Teaching of History*, which gave UK history educators a theoretical starting point for curriculum design in history. UK history educator Jeanette Coltham (1971) then authored a pamphlet published by the Historical Association in 1971, *The Development of Thinking and the Learning of History*. In the same year, Coltham and John Fines (1971) co-authored a brief but very influential Historical Association pamphlet, *Educational Objectives for the Study of History*. This pamphlet introduced UK teachers of history and UK syllabus designers to the structured curriculum approach of US educator Benjamin Bloom (1956). By this stage, those UK history educators who wanted to develop an informed and systematic pedagogical approach to the subject as a replacement for what was effectively an old-fashioned teacher-centric curriculum now had a great deal of scholarly and professional literature to provide them with support. Accordingly, Roy Wake, a senior government inspector in Whitehall's Department of Education (covering England and Wales), who was concerned that history was being left out of a late 1970s broad curriculum reform movement, pressed for the government to take action, according to inaugural SCHP director David Sylvester (2009).

THE SCHOOLS COUNCIL HISTORY PROJECT

Under pressure from Roy Wake, in 1972 the UK government's Schools Council established a grant of £126,000 (approximately A$250,000) to set up a Schools Council [ages] 13–16 History Project (later the Schools Council History Project, or SCHP, and later again the Schools History Project), to be trialled in 32 schools in England, Scotland, Wales and Northern Ireland. The principal aim of the project was to develop historical thinking by examining mainly primary sources across a sequence of topics in Years 9–11 that focused in turn on detective skills, a study in development over time, a modern world history topic, a depth study and a local history investigation. This was a revolutionary approach to secondary school history. The effect of the SCHP on the teaching and learning of history in the United Kingdom was astonishing. For example, in one large comprehensive school (1700 students), where the author was a new head of history in the 1970s, the number of students taking history as an option in Years 10 and 11 rose from 50 to 420 in a two-year period (Taylor 1980). By the mid-1980s, students and teachers in the United Kingdom were voting with their feet. One-third of all Year 10 and 11 students studying history were taking the SCHP syllabuses, two of a proliferation of regional examination board (age 16+) examination syllabuses. The SCHP is currently in its 45th year. For its current status, see Schools History Project (2018).

A clear indicator of the success of the SCHP was the assessment report written by Denis Shemilt (1980) in his *History 13–16 Evaluation Study*. A social scientist by background, Shemilt had been recruited to carry out an external appraisal of the SCHP. His conclusions were that students and teachers now worked far harder in history lessons than they did in other subjects; they recognised that history was a complex discipline; the inquiry-based and problem-solving approach of the SCHP was pedagogically beneficial; and the clear disciplinary framework provided by the SCHP provided school history with a solid rationale for a subject that more students could relate to and understand.

There were problems with the SCHP, though, many of which were dealt with at school level and through syllabus adjustment. These included too much emphasis on primary sources at the expense of secondary sources, and incoherence issues in a syllabus that seemed fragmented, with no overarching chronology linking the depth studies. Nevertheless, by 1989 when the UK government introduced its first version of a national curriculum, the SCHP was the dominant approach used in teaching history at secondary school level in the United Kingdom, and its influence extended into national curriculum history in three respects. First, the SCHP advocated a new and systematic way of inquiry-based thinking about history founded on the use of evidence, causal relationships and empathy. The latter was a product of the SCHP team's slightly inaccurate version of UK philosopher and historian R.G. Collingwood's work on empathetic re-enactment as a historical understanding (Marnie Hughes-Warrington 2003 deals at length with historical empathy; see also Taylor et al. (2012: 196–9). Second, the idea that history was about running a race through a chronicle of events no longer held true: depth studies were now the norm. Third, the view that school history should lead to a single inevitable conclusion was also no longer valid. The SCHP had introduced students and teachers to open-ended explanation based on sound disciplinary methodology.

THE SCHOOLS COUNCIL HISTORY PROJECT AND AUSTRALIA

In Australia during the late 1970s, a small number of mostly NSW history educators who were looking for a progressive approach to syllabus reform absorbed what was happening in the United Kingdom and began to take a serious interest in using the SCHP as a foundation for their state's history curriculum. Their interest lay in three aspects of the SCHP: first, the project provided an exemplary model of teacher-involved curriculum development process; second, the SCHP offered a sound philosophical basis for the disciplinary nature of history education (the views of Hirst and Collingwood); third, the SCHP syllabus was varied in format (depth studies/local history/contemporary history/studies over time).

In 1977, NSW history inspector John Lambert visited the SCHP team's headquarters in Leeds and negotiated a June/July 1978 visit to New South Wales by the project's then director, Tony Boddington, who conducted twenty successful workshops across the state. Boddington's tour was followed by working visits from other prominent UK history educators. At the same time, NSW history educators Norm Little and Judy Mackinolty (1977) published an edited subject association manual, *A New Look at History Teaching*. Such New History concepts were too late to be included in the NSW overhaul of its 1980 syllabus, but they were included in the radically different and controversial 1992 Junior Secondary Syllabus.

Carmel Young (later Fahey), who witnessed and participated in these events as president of the NSW History Teachers' Association (HTA) and as chair of the 1992 NSW Junior Secondary Syllabus Committee, commented in an email to the author (Fahey 2017):

> The process core of the 1992 syllabus owes a great deal to the SCHP and the National Curriculum UK. However, the 1992 syllabus was also a response to changing local curriculum demands and constraints, as

well as an expression of emerging views about content and approaches to the teaching and learning of Australian history. It was the first syllabus in Australia to mandate Aboriginal history, women's history and environmental history. So, in terms of content—a great departure from the SCHP, but not in its commitment to the inquiry process and all that entails.

In 1999, educationally conservative NSW Premier Bob Carr oversaw the introduction of a Year 9 and 10 history syllabus that rejected the thinking behind the politically contentious 1992 version. The new syllabus insisted on at least 100 hours of Australian history (and geography) in the final two years of compulsory schooling. The history content was a long list of key events, which unfortunately reintroduced the idea of history as a rapid race through a chronicle of events. Meanwhile, in the other states and territories, SOSE prevailed. On the face of it, both authentic historical pedagogy and historical consciousness in Australian schools were now at a very low ebb.

THE LIFE AND DEATH OF SOSE

During the 1990s, the prevalence of SOSE in Australian schools—particularly its dominance of the secondary school curriculum—began to cause increasing anxiety among members of both the academic history and history-teaching communities, the latter represented by state-based HTAs. Their concern was that, beyond New South Wales, history as a distinctly different subject had all but disappeared from the timetable, and the number of students taking history in Years 11 and 12 was in decline. Conservative politicians and media outlets deplored the seeming absence of history in SOSE classes—in their case, because of the apparent absence of a celebratory study of Australian history. However, the traditionalist side of politics could do little at Commonwealth level during a continuing Australian Labor Party (ALP) period of government in the first half of the 1990s. When the Liberal-National coalition was elected to power under Prime Minister John Howard's leadership in 1996, things began to change. At this point, history in schools became a political as well as a pedagogical football.

Although Howard had largely kept out of debates about history education prior to his accession to prime ministerial office, he did have a special interest in Australian history that was ideological and personal.

In ideological terms, the Prime Minister saw Australian history as a chronicle of largely benevolent events that began with an eighteenth- and nineteenth-century colonial past and went on to a late twentieth-century present that was the commendable consequence of steadily developing parliamentary democracy, individualistic commercial endeavour and a firm national identity. It was true, he conceded, that there had been unfortunate incidents; however, these were now in the past, and times and attitudes had changed. Howard's personal interest in history was based on his father and grandfather's military service in World War I. The Prime Minister made his views known publicly four months after taking office when, in a major speech in July 1996, he attacked allegedly leftist academic historians as derogatory 'cultural dietitians' who were guilty of making an 'insidious attempt to rewrite Australian history in the service of a partisan [leftist] political cause' (Howard 1996). This speech was to mark the beginning of Australia's History Wars, a cultural conflict that was to obsess a minority of conservative Australian opinion in the media and in politics for the next eleven years, dragging school history into the melee (Macintyre & Clark 2004).

THE NATIONAL INQUIRY

While the Prime Minister and his allies criticised a supposed leftist 'black armband' (apologetic) view of the history of Aboriginal and Torres Strait Islander peoples in schools, history teachers and academic historians pressed their professional case that history in schools was generally in trouble. In mid-1999, John Hirst and Stuart Macintyre, two doyens of the Australian history community, met Education Minister David Kemp and decided that there would be a national inquiry into school history.

The inquiry amounted to a meeting of differently motivated minds for a common purpose. The professional history community wanted their subject to be given a fair chance in a SOSE-dominated education system. Conservative politicians and commentators were anxious about assumed leftist influence in schools and hoped that such an inquiry might confirm their worst beliefs. That being the case, the Howard government agreed to a national investigation and, in late 1999, the Commonwealth government called for tenders to conduct a national inquiry into the teaching and learning of history in Australian schools. The inquiry, carried out by a team from Monash University, commenced in 1999, and its final report was published in 2000 as *The Future of the Past: The Final Report of the National Inquiry into School History* (Taylor 2000).

The National Inquiry's major findings were as follows. First, history is a unique form of study that requires specialist teachers operating within a disciplinary framework. Second, students engage successfully with the subject if they are allowed to study topics in depth using an evidence-based and concept-led (historical understandings and skills) approach. Third, political interference in school history is counterproductive, as is the imposition of a prescribed, chronologically based syllabus (a reference to the Carr-initiated change of curriculum in New South Wales during 1999) (*The Sydney Morning Herald* 2002). Fourth, primary-school teachers and non-specialist secondary teachers are under-prepared to teach history. Fifth, if there were no clearly identified history classes in what was by now a low-status SOSE framework, the discipline of history would continue to suffer. Sixth, Australian history is unpopular, seen by students as boring and repetitive.

The National Inquiry report led to the setting up in 2001 of a $6 million Commonwealth History Project (CHP) that, among other initiatives, would raise historical consciousness in the school system by funding a national centre for history education, setting up national seminars in history education, organising professional-development workshops and projects for primary teachers, and publishing a guide for all teachers of history—qualified and unqualified. The CHP's emphasis was to be on Australian history.

THE COMMONWEALTH HISTORY PROJECT AND RAISING HISTORICAL CONSCIOUSNESS

The National Centre for History Education (NCHE), a virtual centre found at <www.hyperhistory.org>, had two sequential three-year contracts to do its work in attempting to raise historical consciousness. During its first contract period (2001–03), the NCHE's head office was at Monash University's Gippsland campus. There was also an outpost in LaTrobe University's Bundoora campus as well as two author/editors attached to the centre, one in Queensland and the other in Sydney. During its second contract period (2004–06), Monash University and the editors carried on with the project. The LaTrobe NCHE staff were Dr Corinne Manning, Ms Susan Aykut and Dr Adrian Jones. The two author/editors were Dr Brian Hoepper and

Dr Peter Cochrane. The manager was Ms Scilla Rantzen and the director was the author.

Apart from national-level liaison work, running national seminars and attending Commonwealth and subject association meetings over a six-year period, the NCHE's principal accomplishments in history education were publishing, in conjunction with the Curriculum Corporation, *Making History: A Guide for the Teaching and Learning of History in Australian Schools*, as well as two topic books, an upper primary school volume, *Making History: Investigating Our Land and Legends*, and a middle secondary school volume, *Making History: Investigating People and Issues in Australia after World War II* (Hattensen & Parry 2003; Hoepper & Mirams 2003; Taylor & Young 2003). At the same time, the NCHE published an online journal, *Ozhistorybytes*, and a *Professional Digest*.

The NCHE's goal in publishing the *Making History* topic books was to fill the school-level gap in professional knowledge of history education by disseminating what constituted good practice and by modelling units for teachers of history in all states and territories. The role of the *Professional Digest* was to summarise the latest Australian and overseas research in history education. *Ozhistorybytes* provided background in-depth articles on interesting history topics written by academics for teachers of senior school students. *Making History: A Guide* summarised the latest thinking about history education and introduced teachers to the idea of historical literacy, which was originally devised as a conceptual framework that would supplant SOSE's Time, Continuity and Change, giving teachers a clearer and more sophisticated idea of what was expected of students in terms of historical understandings and skills. The guide's index of literacies was based on a combination of approaches to historical thinking and skills, most taken from the SCHP and the United Kingdom's national curriculum. As for historical thinking, the NCHE's index included use of evidence, continuity and change, motivation (perspectives), significance, empathy and contestability. Of these, empathy and contestability were to become uniquely Australian curricular concepts.

In Australia, the NCHE's approach to teaching and learning history reached a large audience. The Curriculum Corporation, a publisher supported by the Commonwealth, produced 18,000 copies of the award-winning *Making History* books, which were based specifically on the historical literacy approach. The books were sent to schools across Australia.

The idea was each school would get one copy to use as a model classroom source. Clearly one book per school was not enough to resource hundreds of students in a school, so free PDF files of each book, as well as of the accompanying guide, were available for downloading from the NCHE website for photocopying in schools. In the first full year of the NCHE's existence as a resource (2003–04), there were 300,000-plus PDF downloads from the <www.hyperhistory.org> site. In the second year (2004–05), there were an estimated 200,000 PDF downloads, averaging out over that two-year period at 55.5 downloaded copies per school.

The NCHE's second contract ended in mid-2006, its work at an end. The History Teachers' Association Victoria then supported the hosting of the NCHE site—which was still being used as a resource by teachers—until 2009, when it was transferred to the National Library of Australia's (NLA) Pandora archive as a website of national significance; it remains there today (<http://pandora.nla.gov.au/tep/31185>) and is still in use.

THE HISTORY SUMMIT AND A DIFFERENT KIND OF HISTORICAL CONSCIOUSNESS

If the Howard government's Education Department had been fully supportive of the NCHE initiative in raising historical consciousness in a noninterventionist and professional manner during 2001–06, the ideological side of the Coalition leadership took a different approach after having become increasingly involved in the 2003–06 History Wars and following a pre-Christmas 2005 inter-ethnic disturbance in Cronulla. The Prime Minister and the conservative media became concerned that the SOSE framework was leaving students uninformed about the traditionalist view of Australian history as a proud narrative of progress based on Christian values, economic rationalism and the stability of parliamentary democracy. This was a different kind of historical consciousness from that promoted by the NCHE, based as it was on 30 years of professional experience and academic research.

In January 2006, the Prime Minister announced that his government would undertake a 'root and branch' renewal of Australian history in schools. Blaming SOSE, he commented that, 'Too often [Australian history] is taught without any sense of structured narrative, replaced by a fragmented stew of themes and issues' (*The Sydney Morning Herald* 2006). Howard wanted a fact-based approach to the past.

The Prime Minister's Office convened a 'summit' of academic historians, journalists, teachers and other educators on 17 August 2006. Discussion centred on two papers, one of which (Taylor & Clark 2006) was critical of SOSE, while the other (Melleuish 2006) gave a draft outline of a specimen primary and secondary syllabus in Australian history. On the day, opposition from the teachers and academic historians sank the Howard-supported draft syllabus on the grounds that it was well beyond the capabilities of most school students. The summit ended with no substantive recommendation about the teaching of Australian history.

An interesting series of events followed. Six months after the summit concluded, the author was commissioned by Education Minister Julie Bishop in early 2007 to draft a new curriculum guide, a K–10 version based on the historical literacy principles (Taylor 2007). The draft was accepted by the Education Minister and was then referred to the Prime Minister's Office, where it disappeared. In June 2007, the Prime Minister announced that he had convened a panel consisting of Geoffrey Blainey (a conservative historian), commentator and former Howard chief of staff Gerard Henderson, retired private school principal Elizabeth Ward and Nick Brown of the *Australian Dictionary of Biography* team. The panel's job was, in one September day, to construct an Australian history syllabus—but for Years 9 and 10 only. The upshot was *The Prime Minister's Guide to the Teaching of Australian History in Schools,* released on 11 October 2007, which contained a slimmed-down version of the author's pedagogical section in his 2007 draft guide. Following on from the Harvard guide's progressive pedagogical introduction, there came a traditionalist list of 77 essential facts in Australian history and 100 recommended biographies, a harking back to the professionally unpopular NSW 100 hours syllabus of 1999.

The Howard guide was launched in the middle of the 2007 general election campaign, which the Coalition was to lose. Kevin Rudd, the incoming Labor Prime Minister, having already promised that there would be an 'education revolution' complete with an across-the-board national curriculum, immediately appointed Julia Gillard as Deputy Prime Minister and Education Minister. The Rudd government quietly buried Howard's history guide in early 2008 and, in April of that year, Gillard announced the formation of an arm's length National Curriculum Board, later the Australian Curriculum, Assessment and Reporting Authority (ACARA). The process of setting up a professionally designed, consultatively framed national curriculum with history as a core subject then began.

After this long succession of twists and turns, an inquiry-based world history curriculum was published by ACARA in 2010, featuring seven by now very familiar historical understandings: Evidence; Continuity and Change; Cause and Effect; Perspectives; Empathy; Significance; and Contestability. It represented a considerable change from SOSE's Time, Continuity and Change (ACARA 2017). At the early stage of design, ACARA decided to use 'literacy' in conjunction with reading and writing only, so the literacies became Understandings and Skills. As of 2017, they are 'key concepts' in 'learning areas'. The ACARA secondary curriculum also featured SCHP-style depth studies, but in this instance they were linked by overviews.

By now it will have become clear that this approach was not unique. With the exception of empathy and contestability, the 2003 *Making History* version of historical literacy featured understandings and skills that, by the late 1990s, had been arrived at and disseminated in other liberal democracies by history education researchers and by informed practitioners such as Peter Lee and Ros Ashby (UK), Christine Counsell (UK), Linda Levstik (USA), Keith Barton (USA), Sam Wineburg (USA), Peter Seixas (Canada) and Jocelyn Letourneau (Canada). They and hundreds of other prominent history educators worldwide shared common views about the importance of history as inquiry, about the use of sources, about perspectives, about significance and about continuity and change—views that had been maturing in different places and at different tempos over a period of more than 30 years.

CONCLUSION

During the 1990s and the first decade of the 2000s, educational debates in Australia about the nature of history and of history education became increasingly polarised. These debates were based in part on differing and inaccurate views of what the study of history in schools entailed. Such views were based first on a pedagogical, SOSE-derived viewpoint and second on a political, traditionalist viewpoint. Meanwhile, modern history education as a discipline-based form of inquiry was by now conceived around longstanding and apolitical pedagogical concepts that would coalesce to form a single inquiry-based world history curriculum model that, in 2008–10, became the basis for the design and implementation of the Australian Curriculum: History as it stands at the time of writing.

Having said that, the current curriculum framework is not yet immune to future political interference, nor is it yet safe from various forms of tinkering at the state and territory level.

REFERENCES

Australian Curriculum, Assessment and Reporting Authority (ACARA) 2017, *Australian Curriculum: History*, <www.australiancurriculum.edu.au>, accessed 13 August 2017.

Ballard, M. (ed.) 1970, *New Movements in the Study and Teaching of History*, London: Maurice Temple Smith.

Bloom, B. 1956, *Taxonomy of Educational Objectives: the Classification of Educational Goals* (2 vols), London: Longmans.

Coltham, J. 1971, *The Development of Thinking and the Learning of History*, London: Historical Association.

Coltham, J. & Fines, J. 1971, *Educational Objectives for the Study of History*, London: Historical Association.

Fahey, C. 2017, email correspondence with the author, June.

Fenton, E. 1966, *Teaching the New Social Studies in Secondary Schools: An Inductive Approach*, New York: Holt, Rhinehart & Winston.

Hattensen, S. & Parry, A. 2003, *Making History: Investigating Our Land and Legends*, Melbourne: Curriculum Corporation.

Hirst, P. 1966, 'Educational theory', in J.W. Tibble (ed.), *The Study of Education*, London: Routledge & Kegan Paul, pp. 29–58.

Hoepper, B. & Mirams, S. 2003, *Making History: Investigating People and Issues in Australia after World War II*, Melbourne: Curriculum Corporation.

Howard, J. 1996, *Sir Thomas Playford Memorial Lecture*, Adelaide, 5 July, <https://pmtranscripts.pmc.gov.au/release/transcript-10041>, accessed 13 August 2017.

Hughes-Warrington, M. 2003, *'How Good an Historian Shall I Be?' R.G. Collingwood, the Historical Imagination and Education*, Exeter: Imprint Academic.

Little, N. & Mackinolty, J. (eds) 1977, *A New Look at History Teaching*, Sydney: NSW History Teachers' Association.

Macintyre, S. & Clark, A. 2004, *The History Wars*, Melbourne: Melbourne University Press.

Melleuish, G. 2006, *The Teaching of Australian History in Australian Schools: A Normative View*, Canberra: Department of Education and Science.

Schools History Project 2018. 'Schools History Project: Understanding ourselves in time', <www.schoolshistoryproject.co.uk>.

Shemilt, D. 1980, *History 13–16 Evaluation Study*, Edinburgh: Holmes McDougall.
The Sydney Morning Herald 2002, 'Carr's history lesson too dull, teachers say', 10 October.
—— 2006, 'Howard aims to make ancient history of modern learning', 26 January.
Sylvester, D. 2009, Interview with N. Sheldon, Institute of Historical Research, London, History in Education Project, July.
Taylor, T. 1980, 'Teaching modern world studies', in J. Fitzgerald, *History: 13 Year Olds–16 Year Olds. British Schools Council Project. Australian Teacher Handbook*, Sydney: Dominie School Centres, pp. 35–9.
—— 2000, *The Future of the Past: The Final Report of the National Inquiry into School History*, Melbourne: Faculty of Education, Monash University.
—— 2007, Outline of a Model Curriculum Framework: Australian History Years 3–10 (unpublished), Canberra: Department of Education, Science and Training, April.
Taylor, T. & Clark, A. 2006, *An Overview of the Teaching and Learning of Australian History in Schools*, Canberra: Department of Education and Science.
Taylor, T., Fahey, C., Kriewaldt, J. & Boon, D. 2012, *Place and Time: Explorations in Teaching Geography and History*, Sydney: Pearson Education.
Taylor, T. & Guyver, R. (eds) 2012, *History Wars and the Classroom: Global Perspectives*, Charlotte, NC: Information Age.
Taylor, T. & Young, C. 2003, *Making History: A Guide for the Teaching and Learning of History in Australian Schools*, Melbourne: Curriculum Corporation.

CHAPTER 2
Understanding the Australian Curriculum: History

Stuart Macintyre

School education has always been a major undertaking of our states and territories, and each jurisdiction has insisted on control of its own curriculum. Yet as the Commonwealth took on a substantial financial contribution to the cost of public and private schools, it also sought greater influence over them. There have been repeated attempts to establish a national curriculum framework. The most ambitious was the Australian Curriculum, developed after 2007. This chapter relates how history was chosen as one of the first four subjects in the Australian Curriculum, the way history was designed and the difficulties it encountered.

The Australian Curriculum had its origins in a conjunction of circumstances. The first was a change of government in Canberra at the end of 2007 that brought a new Minister of Education, Julia Gillard, to the table. The second was the new Labor government's determination to avoid entanglement in the 'Culture Wars' that John Howard had used to his advantage between 1996 and 2007. The third was its decision to entrust the preparation of a national curriculum to an independent authority.

Julia Gillard brought a particular zeal to the government's goal of leading an 'education revolution'. The eldest child of Welsh working-class parents denied the opportunity to stay on at school, she was imbued with a 'passion for education' and its 'life-changing power' (Kent 2010: 138). As Deputy Prime Minister, she brought an unusual authority to the portfolio, to the advantage of the school sector. She believed a national curriculum was indispensable to her goal of lifting standards and closing the gap between advantaged and disadvantaged students.

Julia Gillard also thought it was vital that the preparation of the curriculum should be undertaken by experts, and not just because of her disciplined, orderly approach to policy-making. The previous government had favoured private schools at the expense of government schools, which it accused of lax standards and a failure to instil values (*The Sydney Morning Herald* 2004; Taylor 2018: Ch. 9). Howard, in particular, was highly critical of the teaching of history on both curricular and pedagogical grounds: he alleged that it slighted the national achievement and neglected a settled narrative in favour of a 'fragmented stew of themes and issues' (*The Sydney Morning Herald* 2006). As Tony Taylor relates on page 13 in this volume, Howard embarked in his final term of office on a 'root and branch' renewal of Australian history in schools. His preferred course of action—commissioning a favoured historian to prepare a draft—came unstuck at an invitation-only 'summit' in 2006 that was meant to ratify it; the efforts of a subsequent working group did not satisfy him, and those of another working group he commissioned were overtaken by the 2007 election (see also Chapter 1).

The Rudd government took a different tack. Its election policy, 'The Australian Economy Needs an Education Revolution', presented an increase in the country's expenditure on education from the low level to which it had fallen by 2007 as an investment in human capital that would yield 'a competitive, innovative, knowledge-based economy' (Kayrooz & Parker 2010). The Prime Minister's emphasis on 'evidence-based' policy design was intended to lift this particularly vexed area of policy above the ruck of competing interests. He had no intention of reopening the debate between educational progressives and those calling for 'back to basics', much less engaging with the entrenched prejudices of the History Wars.

The Global Financial Crisis (GFC) gave added impetus to the education revolution. Between 2008–09 and 2009–10, Commonwealth payments to support the states' educational activity increased from $11.8 billion to $19.4 billion, with special programs for disadvantaged schools, numeracy and literacy, and the provision of computers. Then there was the economic stimulus measure of $14 billion for new primary school buildings (Kayrooz & Parker 2010). The rushed nature of the construction brought criticism of waste, and a similar haste bedevilled development of the My School website to report the outcomes of National Assessment Program—Literary and Numeracy (NAPLAN) tests. The intention here was to lift standards by making schools publicly accountable for the numeracy and literacy standards of their students, a strategy previously adopted in the United Kingdom and United States. Gillard was a strong supporter, influenced by Joel Klein, head of the New York City Board of Education, whose use of such measures as a management tool would soon be discredited (Gillard, 2014, pp. 252–3; Ravitch 2010). One effect of NAPLAN was to narrow the curriculum, as schools responded by drilling students in literacy and numeracy at the expense of a broad-based education; this had implications for the uptake of the Australian Curriculum.

If the education revolution was implemented precipitately, the preparation of the national curriculum was a model of deliberation. Whereas Howard made a clumsy intervention into just one school subject—history—and threatened to impose his ill-conceived curriculum on the states as a condition of Commonwealth funding, Gillard initiated a comprehensive national curriculum with the states fully involved in its design. She obtained agreement through the Council of Australian Governments (COAG) for the establishment of an independent agency, and an interim National Curriculum Board (NCB) operated from early 2008 pending the statutory creation of the Australian Curriculum, Assessment and Reporting Authority (ACARA) a year later. It was governed by a board that consisted of nine senior educational administrators nominated by Commonwealth, states and territories, with two more representing the Catholic and independent schools. The chair was Professor Barry McGaw, a former director of the Australian Council for Education Research (ACER) who had recently returned to Australia from Paris, where he was Director for Education at the Organisation for Economic Co-operation and Development (OECD).

McGaw was instrumental in formulating the principles of the Australian curriculum. It was to be designed afresh rather than being cobbled together as a composite of existing state curricula. It had to meet the needs of all students and provide a clear statement of the knowledge, understanding and skills for each year of learning from Kindergarten/Foundation to Year 12. McGaw was also responsible for the decision to base the curriculum on disciplinary studies, as his own research affirmed the importance of disciplines as distinct domains of knowledge that are foundational to learning. Furthermore, he determined that history, along with English, mathematics and science, was one of the first four subjects to be developed. In keeping with the government's expectations, the curriculum was to be 'world-class' and future-oriented, but we may detect McGaw's hand in the statement that 'The curriculum should provide students with an understanding of the past that has shaped the society, culture and environment in which they are growing and developing, and with knowledge, understandings and skills that will help them in their future' (NCB 2009a: 8).

Barry McGaw asked me to serve as the key writer for history. This involved the preparation of a framing paper to set out the scope and approach, and then my participation in the writing of the curriculum. An initial decision was to use a world history perspective. Here I was influenced by Anna Clark's (2008) finding that students are more likely to respond to encounters with a distant past, partly because of its familiarity, and partly because they seemed to retrace the same ground over the course of their studies; many found Australian history boring.

Leaving aside the complaint of many of Anna's informants that nothing happened in Australian history, I was convinced that the study of history needed to take us beyond our own experience and immediate concerns. Besides, world history would assist a deeper understanding of Australia's past: students would better appreciate the long occupation of this continent by Aboriginal and Torres Strait Islander peoples, for example, if they knew how humans had come to occupy the other continents.

A second decision was to use an inquiry-based approach to develop historical understanding. It was not a difficult choice: as Tony Taylor explained in Chapter 1, the inquiry-based approach to developing historical understanding was developed by leading educators from the 1970s and taken up in a number of countries. I had worked previously with Tony, admired his leadership of the Commonwealth History Project and knew of the guide to the teaching of history that he and Carmel Young had prepared (Taylor & Young 2003). I knew also of similar work done by his colleague Peter Seixas at the Centre for Historical Consciousness at the University of British Columbia, and my framing paper drew on Peter's articulation of the components of historical understanding. The first draft began with the proposition that, 'The fundamental objective of school history is to provide students with the capacity to think historically.' The plan was to introduce the components in primary school for development in Years 7–10 through a sequence of world history that would begin at the earliest time and conclude in the present.

Tony Taylor made valuable comments on the draft framing paper, as did John Hirst, an eminent Australian historian who had played a leading role in the preparation of history materials for the Commonwealth's Discovering Democracy program from 1998. The paper was then exposed to a group of school and university historians, who also offered helpful suggestions, before discussion at a large forum of teachers, curriculum officers and academics in October 2008. That day-long consideration, additional state and territory forums and numerous submissions allowed further refinement. We settled on the organisation of each year into a small number of depth studies along with overview and bridging components; provision was made for choice among the depth studies so long as students engaged with all the major civilisations (NCB 2008). The paper was then released for consultation and, by March 2009, a total of 218 respondents had completed a survey and another 79 had made submissions. There was strong support for the world history approach and the emphasis on historical understanding (NCB 2009b).

The principal concerns were the amount of ground to be covered, the demands it would make on teachers, particularly those who had no training in the discipline, and the challenge this posed for student engagement. The History Teachers' Association of Australia (HTAA), which was fully involved in the preparation of the framing paper, pressed these concerns forcefully and it was fully justified in doing so: the Australian Curriculum: History could not succeed without a commitment of classroom time and provision of teacher support. But staffing, in-service professional development and the timetable all lay outside the remit of ACARA, within the disputed hinterland of Commonwealth–state funding and responsibility for school education. None of the prescient concerns was laid to rest.

We nevertheless proceeded to elaborate the national curriculum for the compulsory years of schooling, Kindergarten/Foundation–Year 10. Teachers and curriculum officers, who were contracted for the task, did the writing under the guidance an advisory group of seven or eight members, including myself, Tony Taylor and Paul Kiem, the president of the HTAA. This proved an arduous task. The writing team of ten was drawn from across the country—as were the ACARA staff responsible for history—with the intention of keeping the states and territories onside, and it was hardly surprising that they tended to draw on the practices of their own jurisdictions. This problem would become more acute when we moved onto Years 11 and 12.

The advisory group met with the writers regularly during 2009 in one- or two-day sessions that tended to lose sight of the forest for the trees. Then there were the workshops and consultations that continued throughout the writing. ACARA was meticulous in ensuring wide involvement and frequent feedback, but the process was highly iterative, with a series of tight deadlines that often required us to redo work we had done before with a frustrating indeterminacy of roles and a tendency to fall back to a bland composite of views.

At certain points, decisions were made in the higher reaches of ACARA that compromised the design. We planned three strands—Knowledge, Skills and Understandings—but it was then determined that there could only be two strands, so Understandings was absorbed into Knowledge, to the curriculum's detriment. We conceived of bridging and overview components that would go beyond linking and contextualising depth studies to draw out their larger implications, but the bridging component disappeared and then (as a result of pressure from one state), an arbitrary limit of 10 per cent of class time was determined for the overviews.

We wanted the Great War to be the first depth study of world history in Year 10, which covered the period from 1900 to the present, for that study would set the scene for so much that followed. We were told the curriculum had to conclude before the present on the grounds that teachers could not be expected to deal with events that occurred after the curriculum appeared. This decision had unfortunate implications for the 'futures orientation' that was a declared objective of the national curriculum, which was intended to prepare students for the changed circumstances in which they would live after completing their education. A cut-off date for modern history would inhibit teachers and students from applying their historical understanding to contemporary issues—or, to put it another way, from seeing how our current concerns have a historical dimension.

Instead, the Great War depth study was taken back to Year 9 and turned into a study of Australia during World War I. Our intention was that students would learn of the causes and dimensions of that prolonged conflict, the scale of the losses among the principal combatants, and the war's momentous political, social and economic consequences. The prospect of newspaper headlines and talkback radio hosts demanding to know why young Australians were denied learning about their Anzac heritage evidently spooked ACARA, for it unilaterally changed our depth study into a tired and parochial study of Australians at war. They would follow the Gallipoli landing with little likelihood of knowing that the Anzacs were outnumbered by British and French troops; they could investigate the discord aroused here by the conscription plebiscites and remain unaware of the revolutions sweeping Europe at the time.

I was convinced that ACARA was jumping at ghosts. I knew my appointment as lead writer would be controversial, since I had played a prominent part in a particularly fraught episode in the History Wars, the assault on historians who had written of the wrongs done to Aboriginal and Torres Strait Islander peoples during the European occupation of this country. When the book I wrote with Anna Clark on the History Wars appeared (Macintyre & Clark 2003), I was described as 'a presiding academic presence over the "black armband" era of Australian historical writing' and a 'godfather' of the historical profession. 'History is too important,' controversialist Janet Albrechtsen insisted, 'to be left to historians like Stuart Macintyre who want to shut down historical debate'—not that the Murdoch press entertained any debate of its prosecution of the History Wars (Albrechtsen 2003; Melleuish 2003; Ryan 2003).

Since Barry McGaw was not in Australia when these accusations appeared, I reminded him of them at the outset. He was insistent that they did not affect his confidence in my capacity to undertake the commission. The news of my appointment was greeted with predictable criticism from *The Australian*. A lead article bore the headline 'History Wars Player Steers Future'; inside the newspaper, Kevin Donnelly (who served simultaneously as an educational consultant, an adviser to the Howard government and the newspaper's authority on school education) stated, 'My Worst Fears Have Been Realised'; an editorial in the same edition was headed 'Rudd Must Not Allow Curriculum Hijacking'. None of this came as a surprise. *The Australian* routinely referred to me as 'controversial', 'left wing', 'left leaning', 'Marxist', even 'the intellectual father to a generation of postmodernists' (Taylor & Collins 2012).

The release of the final draft in 2010 brought a fresh round of hostilities. Back-to-basics Kevin Donnelly thought anyone reading the curriculum could be 'left in no doubt that Australia will soon be forced to teach a new-age and politically correct view of history and Australia's view of the world'. He and others who contributed their criticisms to the *Quadrant Online* website were particularly aggrieved by ACARA's three cross-curriculum priorities—Aboriginal and Torres Strait Islander histories and cultures; Asia and Australia's engagement with Asia; and sustainability—which were described as progressive fads in a 'back to nonsense curriculum' (Donnelly 2010, 2011).

Some of these denunciations were unencumbered by consideration of the curriculum. Mervyn Bendle (2010), a lecturer at James Cook University, had clearly not paid attention to ACARA's intervention when he alleged it was 'proposing to introduce a radical national history curriculum that encourages students to criticise, ridicule and debunk ("deconstruct") the Anzac tradition'. Others were based on that most superficial form of reading a document: the word search. Hence it was claimed that trade unions were mentioned more often than business enterprise, that references to Labor Prime Ministers exceeded those of Coalition ones, that the Magna Carta and the Westminster system of government were absent, and that Christianity only appeared alongside other religions. Apart from confusing words with concepts, these critics laboured under the misapprehension that a curriculum document constitutes a binding and exhaustive statement of what every student will learn and remember. Their assumption that education is no more than instruction found expression in the warning of History Summiteer Gregory Melleuish (2010a) that the national curriculum would become 'a tool of indoctrination'.

Since Melleuish, a Wollongong historian, had prepared John Howard's ill-fated mandatory course in Australian history, this allegation came across as psychological projection. He had been discomfited at the Canberra Summit when John Hirst, a public intellectual who could hardly be accused of leftism, declared it to be inappropriate. The rebuff rankled. In criticising my involvement in the national curriculum, he cast back to my partnership with Hirst in an earlier exercise in school education, the Discovering Democracy program: 'Why were historians such as Stuart Macintyre and his mate John Hirst chosen to deal with such issues as civics and the nature of Australian democracy?' (Melleuish 2010a).

These and other polemics attracted very little attention during the forums and consultations in 2010. Most of the submissions came from within the sector, and were concerned with practical considerations. Teachers criticised the organisation of the curriculum structure in just two strands, conscious that this weakened the attention to historical understanding. They worried about the number and choice of depth studies, the amount of content they contained and the failure to allocate sufficient time to them. While supportive of world history, they were divided about the attention given to Asian history (ACARA 2010).

I shared these concerns; indeed, I shared those expressed by Gregory Melleuish (2010b) about the way the curriculum had changed in the course of the development. The overviews had been weakened and no longer provided an adequate 'map of the past' for students who were confronted in Years 7–10 with long passages of time. The depth studies had become narrower and more constrictive. There were three for each year, and in Year 7 a student had to choose between Egypt, Greece or Rome, and China or India. In Year 8, there were many more choices, some broad (Medieval Europe) and some restricted (the Black Death). Unimaginative surveys of Australian history were accompanied by ambitious world history topics as Year 9 depth studies. I thought the Year 10 ones (World War II, Social Movements, Popular Culture and Migration) failed to capture the transformative changes of the twentieth century.

All of this is to say that the curriculum lost cohesion during its development. Too many writers were involved; too many piecemeal changes were introduced at the expense of consistency and cohesion. With good cause, the HTAA warned against the volume of content and the continuing uncertainty that there would be time to teach it. Above all, it called for ACARA to withstand pressure from the lobby groups to which it too often acceded (HTAA 2010; Ferrari 2010). But these lobby groups were not simply enthusiasts for particular fields or approaches to history clamouring for their special interests to be incorporated; they included the state and territory representatives who sat on ACARA's board. As the fortunes of the Labor government in Canberra declined—Rudd's difficulties culminated in his replacement by Gillard in June 2010—its control over the national curriculum dissipated.

Tony Abbott's overthrow of Malcolm Turnbull at the end of 2009 had brought a sharpening of Opposition rhetoric. Here, as in the United Kingdom and the United States, conservative politicians have repeatedly intervened in school history to demand that it inculcate patriotic pride. None of Keating's successors has shown any inclination to contest that version of the national past; they prefer to stay out of the debate and leave determination of the curriculum to the educators. Teachers are not inclined to respond to the wild accusations of subverting young minds, nor well placed to engage with their critics in the press and on talkback radio (Taylor 2013).

Abbott and Christopher Pyne, his Shadow Minister for Education, took up several lines of criticism of the history curriculum from right-wing commentators. The first was that it neglected the constitutional history that marked out Australia's system of government. Hence the absence of the Magna Carta and the lack of attention to the English Civil War meant that students would not appreciate the virtues of our Westminster system of government. The choice of these two episodes was puzzling. My predecessor as professor of history at the University of Melbourne liked to say that he had a large collection of allusions to the Magna Carta by Australian politicians, 'all of them eloquent and all entirely wrong', and it is doubtful that these conservatives admired Oliver Cromwell's dissolution of the Long Parliament, let alone regicide. Besides, the makers of our Constitution blended the British system of responsible government with American federalism and our own advanced democracy (Howard 2012; Macintyre 1994: 106; Pyne 2011).

A second criticism was that the curriculum failed to enshrine the Judeo-Christian tradition. Tony Taylor (2013: 232–5) has explored the changing meaning of this collocation, which began as a term of biblical interpretation, became a rallying cry in the Cold War, was revived by Ronald Reagan and the Moral Majority, and is now a constant theme of neoconservative rhetoric. Taken literally, it seems to exclude the Hellenic component of what the critics call Western civilisation, the absence of which from the curriculum is a further complaint. But throughout the secondary school years of world history, the Australian curriculum specifies studies of that civilisation. The complaint here is 'moral relativism': that it is taught alongside other civilisations as if they were all equally deserving of consideration. As Kevin Donnelly (2013) put it, 'The history curriculum, in addition to uncritically promoting diversity and difference instead of what binds us as a community and a nation, undervalues Western civilisation and the significance of the Judeo-Christian values to our institutions and way of life.'

It thus came as little surprise, after the Coalition was returned to office at the end of 2013, that Christopher Pyne ordered a review of the Australian Curriculum and entrusted it to Donnelly and Kenneth Wiltshire, a professor of public administration. Their report appeared in August 2014. It found ACARA at fault in both design and execution, and it criticised the Australian Curriculum overall and in every subject area. The assessment of history was predictable. Criticism commissioned from Melleuish was set against its support from the History Teachers' Associations. Complaints from the neoconservative Institute of Public Affairs (IPA), the Catholic Education Commission of New South Wales and supporters of religious education were preferred to 85 submissions that rejected any claim of ideological bias ('apparently being orchestrated as part of a campaign'). Donnelly and Wiltshire recommended that the curriculum be revised 'to properly recognise the impact and significance of Western civilisation and Australia's Judeo-Christian heritage, values and beliefs' (Australian Government 2014: 176–81).

The state and territory Ministers of Education were not interested in pursuing that folly. By this time they were implementing the Australian Curriculum according to their own preferences. Some states, such as New South Wales, Victoria and Western Australia, adapted it to their own curricula; others adopted it as a framework while allowing their schools to determine how it was used. They were much more responsive to another recommendation of the review: to reduce the content to a narrow core, especially in the primary-school years. ACARA was accordingly requested to reorganise the Kindergarten/Foundation–Year 6 curriculum for history, geography, civics and citizenship, and economics and business into a new 'learning area': humanities and social sciences. History retains its own content strand, Knowledge and Understanding, but shares a skills strand with geography, civics and citizenship (from Year 3) and economics and business (from Year 5).

The compression did not stop there. All four subjects were similarly grouped into the same unwieldy learning area in Years 7–10. History retained its identity within humanities and social sciences, with three depth studies specified for each year and very little change in their specification and design—despite Christopher Pyne and his review, the history curriculum remains essentially intact. But its use is less clear. Some states, such as New South Wales, have maintained history as a subject in its own right; others use the new learning area and leave schools to determine what subjects they will teach within it. Back in 2000, when Tony Taylor conducted the inquiry into school history, there was a dearth of information about how many schools were teaching history during the compulsory years of education. Nearly two decades later, after a concerted effort to make it available to all students, we are back at the same state of patchwork provision.

The story of history in the Australian Curriculum is thus one of good intentions imperfectly realised. Chosen as one of the foundation subjects, it was meant to recognise history as a distinctive form of knowledge and way of understanding the world, only to see it reduced to a strand in a composite area of learning. It was premised on the expectation that history teachers would be trained and supported with the same respect accorded to teachers of mathematics and science, but the level of professional support is still patchy. It was intended to provide a rich sequence of world history within which Australian history could be better understood, but it has been weakened by fragmentation. And it was meant to overcome the practice of political partisans telling students what they should learn, only to be subjected to repeated intervention.

For all that, I think it gives teachers and students more than they had before the Australian Curriculum was created: a clear framework with depth studies that provide opportunities to engage with the past and develop historical understanding. In the end, any curriculum is dependent on the commitment and skill that teachers bring to the classroom, and I hope those entrusted with history will use it to the benefit of their students.

REFERENCES

Albrechtsen, J. 2003, 'Revenge of the nerds', *The Australian*, 24 September.
Australian Curriculum, Assessment and Reporting Authority (ACARA) 2010, 'Issues for history identified from feedback', ACARA internal document, 15 May.
Australian Government 2014, *Review of the National Curriculum: Final Report*, Canberra: Australian Government, pp. 176–81.
Bendle, M. 2010, 'Declaring war on ACARA', *Quadrant Online*, 1 October.
Clark, A. 2008, *History's Children: History Wars in the Classroom*, Sydney: UNSW Press.
Donnelly, K. 2010, 'Left dictates history curriculum', *Quadrant Online*, 1 June.
—— 2011, 'A back to nonsense curriculum', *Quadrant Online*, 1 March.
—— 2013, 'Our colonial classroom', *Quadrant Online*, 29 October.
Ferrari, J. 2010, 'Keep out the lobby groups, history teachers say', *The Australian*, 18 May.
Gillard, J. 2014, *My Story*, Sydney: Knopf.
History Teachers' Association of Australia (HTAA) 2010, *Interim Response to Draft K–10 History Curriculum*, 15 May.
Howard, J. 2012, The Paul Hasluck Foundation Inaugural Lecture, <http://resources.news.com.au/files/2012/09/27/1226482/801957-sir-paul-hasluck-foundation-inaugural-lecture.pdf>, 27 September.
Kayrooz, C. & Parker, S. 2010, 'The education revolutionary road: Paved with good intentions', in C. Aulich & M. Evans (eds), *The Rudd Government: Australian Commonwealth Administration 2007–2010*, Canberra: ANU Press.
Kent, J. 2010, *The Making of Julia Gillard, Prime Minister*, Melbourne: Viking.
Macintyre, S. 1994, *A History for a Nation: Ernest Scott and the Making of Australian History*, Melbourne: Melbourne University Press.

Macintyre, S. & Clark, A. 2003, *The History Wars*, Melbourne: Melbourne University Press.
Melleuish, G. 2003, 'Propaganda decides history winners', *The Australian*, 3 September.
—— 2010a, 'The dubious future of history', *Quadrant Online*, 1 May.
—— 2010b, 'History in the National Curriculum: No focus, no story', in C. Berg (ed.), *The National Curriculum: A Critique*, Melbourne: Institute of Public Affairs, n.p.
National Curriculum Board (NCB) 2008, *National History Curriculum Framing Paper*, Melbourne: NCB.
—— 2009a, *History Framing Paper—Interim Consultation Report*, March.
—— 2009b, *The Shape of the Australian Curriculum*, May.
Pyne, C. 2011, 'Teaching history with no regard for civilisation', *The Australian*, 2 February.
Ravitch, D. 2010, *The Death and Life of the Great American School System: How Testing and Choice are Undermining Education*, New York: Basic Books.
Ryan, P. 2003, 'Fighting words', *The Weekend Australian*, 6–7 September.
The Sydney Morning Herald 2004, 'PM unfurls his patriotic schools agenda', 22 June.
—— 2006, 'Howard aims to make ancient history of modern learning', 26 January.
Taylor, T. 2018, *Class Wars: Money, Schools and Power in Modern Australia*, Melbourne: Monash University Publishing.
—— 2013, 'History in politics: Neoconservative progressivism, knowledgeable ignorance and the origins of the next History War', *History, Australia*, vol. 10, no. 2, pp. 227–40.
Taylor, T. & Collins, S. 2012, 'The politics are personal: The Australian vs the Australian Curriculum in History', *The Curriculum Journal*, vol. 23, no. 4, pp. 531–52.
Taylor, T. & Young, C. 2003, *Making History: A Guide for the Teaching and Learning of History in Australian Schools*, Melbourne: Curriculum Corporation.

CHAPTER 3
A primary history perspective on the Australian Curriculum

David Boon

INTRODUCTION

As an early childhood and primary teacher, I first discovered my passion for teaching history in 1989. Having researched family and local history for my own interest, I realised that local sites, primary sources and oral history were things I could explore in and with my students. I soon discovered that in some areas children have more finely honed skills than many adults. This was brought dramatically to light when, after looking at the different architectural styles of housing in the local area with a class of six-year-olds, we went on a walk around the local area. Cries from those six-year-olds of, 'Look ... a primitive Georgian', 'There's a Gothic revival' and 'That must be a Californian bungalow' soon had passing adults turning in amazement at the perceptual powers of young children. This has been reinforced further in the professional learning I have run for teachers after taking demonstration lessons with their classes, consistently demonstrating that students often outperform their teachers when it comes to things such as analysing change over time in a local area from photographic evidence. For some teaching staff, the local area may as well have been a foreign country, as many had never taken the time to look around them for evidence of the past. The old store in one photo was the supermarket where they bought their groceries at the end of the working day, but they had simply never taken the opportunity to shift their gaze much wider than the frame of the self-opening supermarket door.

The release of the Australian Curriculum: History in 2011 saw not only the introduction of the study of history as a distinct discipline outside of a broader social sciences/humanities curriculum in Australian primary classrooms, but also a nationally accepted framework for the teaching of primary history in Australia. Having been a member of the History Advisory Group that developed the framing paper for the history curriculum, I was pleased to see that the inquiry skills I had been so passionate about developing in students for two decades were now to be a key focus of the curriculum. Perhaps now all teachers might have reason to shift their gaze beyond the narrow frame of the 'self-opening curriculum content door' and broaden their focus to a pedagogy of inquiry.

Although more recent changes to the Australian Curriculum have seen history placed within the F–6/7 humanities and social sciences (HaSS) curriculum, and states and territories have adopted a range of implementation models, the teaching of history in Australian primary classrooms has experienced a period of positive change and development. Yet, while the introduction of the Australian Curriculum and the work of primary educators has improved the teaching and learning of history in Australian primary classrooms, there is a continuing need for research to capture the significance of this practice in bringing to life the major international theoretical frameworks of researchers such as Wineburg and Seixas, which underpinned the development of the Australian Curriculum: History (ACARA 2008).

This chapter explores some of the major implications of the Australian Curriculum for the teaching of history in primary classrooms in a way that considers broader trends within primary teaching in Australia, such as the nature of both formative and summative assessment, the Australian Curriculum's general capabilities, and pedagogical approaches to the teaching of thinking and understanding.

THE IMPORTANCE OF CONCEPTUAL UNDERSTANDING

The introduction of an integrated F–6/7 Australian HaSS curriculum, which resulted from the additions of both civics and citizenship and economics and business, has reignited divisions over disciplinary versus integrated/interdisciplinary approaches to history. Debates on whether to use a disciplinary or interdisciplinary/integrated approach to the curriculum have tended to see them viewed as polar opposites. In reality, students must fully understand the discipline of history in order to effectively apply any inquiry context. Whether teaching history as a stand-alone discipline or including it as part of an interdisciplinary or integrated approach, inquiry must focus on the concepts of disciplinary thinking outlined in the Australian Curriculum. In primary history, these concepts—drawn largely from the work of Seixas (2006)—are:

- sources
- continuity and change
- cause and effect
- significance
- perspectives, and
- empathy (ACARA 2015).

While some of the concepts used by Seixas in his framework for assessment of historical thinking have been used directly in the Australian Curriculum, the terms 'evidence', 'cause and consequence' and 'moral dimension' in his framework correspond respectively with the concepts of sources, cause and effect and empathy in the primary Australian Curriculum: HaSS.

The use of both primary and secondary sources is an essential component of the Inquiry and Skills strand of the Australian Curriculum: HaSS. By Year 6, students 'locate and collect relevant information and data from primary sources and secondary sources' (ACARA 2017). They analyse those sources to determine origin and purpose, which in turn requires students to consider *perspectives*. This analysis of sources is also used to examine *continuity and change* in the aspect of history under investigation, such as experiences of democracy and citizenship over time, which requires students to apply *empathy*. In undertaking a historical inquiry into something such as Federation, students investigate the events that led to Federation and their impact; they investigate both *cause and effect*, and they make decisions about the *significance* of Federation in shaping Australian democracy (ACARA 2017). These concepts, as they apply in different levels of primary schooling and within different structures of the Australian Curriculum, are further explored in other sections of this chapter.

THE ROLE OF FORMATIVE AND SUMMATIVE ASSESSMENT IN ASSESSING THE KEY HISTORY CONCEPTS

The introduction of the Australian Curriculum: HaSS has resulted in a shift in focus of assessment, largely as a result of the Inquiry and Skills strand. While, prior to the introduction of the Australian Curriculum, teachers planned history learning sequences that focused on skills, knowledge and understanding, far greater emphasis was placed on summative assessment of knowledge and understanding. This largely came about around the turn of the twenty-first century, due to the combined influence on Australian education of the culminating performances component of Harvard's Teaching for Understanding framework (Blythe and Associates 1998) and the Coalition of Essential Schools exhibitions (Coalition of Essential Schools 1990).

Culminating tasks or performances of understanding in a learning sequence were often used as the major form of summative assessment evidence, and tasks earlier in the learning sequence were more often seen as providing formative assessment evidence to guide and modify teaching and learning later in the sequence. This focus on summative assessment of a final product and final understanding did not fully consider the role of the inquiry process in developing and demonstrating both skills and understanding. The disadvantage of such an approach is that students received a message that only the final piece of work was considered important enough to count towards a final assessment. Communication of understanding was given far greater emphasis than development and ongoing demonstration of understanding, or the level of independence in the use of inquiry skills throughout the stages of an inquiry.

While the Australian Curriculum provides guidance that might support greater use of formative and summative assessment throughout an inquiry, we must always be aware that the 'achieved curriculum'—or what teachers actually *do* with the curriculum—is of far greater importance than curriculum *content* (Wiliam 2011: 13). It would be possible to teach both strands of the history curriculum, but for assessment not to capture or support all aspects of student skills, knowledge and understanding. Rather than seeing formative and summative assessment as distinct categories of assessment, it might be better to think of them in terms of *process*. It is not whether an assessment is formative or summative, but how an assessment is used, that determines whether it is formative or summative (Wiliam 2011: 39). The same assessment could be used to guide future learning for the student, but also provide evidence for summative assessment of the inquiry process within an inquiry.

With the explicit inclusion of inquiry in the Inquiry and Skills strand, as well as in the achievement standards for each year-level, it is important that teachers gather assessment evidence at all stages of the inquiry process for both formative and summative purposes. For example, in a Year 3 inquiry into change in the local area over time run with a former class, I utilised photographs and paintings of the area as an introductory activity to stimulate observations by students, which demonstrated prior knowledge; these images were also used by the students to develop their own inquiry questions. The observations and the connection to the types of questions asked by students provided opportunities for formative assessment and evidence that contributed to summative assessment of elements within the Inquiry and Skills strand. A student who posed questions about the absence of something in these images, such as electricity poles, and went on to wonder when electricity was introduced to the area, was already making comparisons between the present and past at the outset of a unit. Another student identifying what was actually in the image, such as a semaphore signal station, wondered what it was used for and whether it was still there. Such observations and questions demonstrated students' capacity to pose suitable inquiry questions and also their understanding of the key disciplinary concepts of sources and continuity and change.

I have utilised the First Fleet database many times with Year 4 students (University of Wollongong 1999). By using the advanced search function, one class posed questions related to the nature of crimes committed, the balance of males and females, the number of convicts in particular age groups, the most common given names of the period and more specific questions, such as why only one male convict was on the *Prince of Wales*, which carried 49 female convicts.

From the questions developed, students used the database to locate, record, sort, represent and interpret relevant information and data in order to identify patterns. They also used the database to sequence information on the lives of individual convicts and events related to the First Fleet. The questions developed using the First Fleet database were used to refine further searches of the database, which demonstrated students' skills of analysis. A refined search by one student revealed that of the 49 female convicts on the *Prince of Wales*, there was one named Elizabeth Youngson who shared her surname with the only male convict onboard, George Youngson. In turn, this information suggested additional lines of inquiry. A range of primary and secondary sources was used to explore the lives of these siblings tried in Lancaster in 1787, which in turn provided further evidence for formative and summative assessment in the researching and analysing dimensions of inquiry. They also provided potential evidence of students' understanding of the key disciplinary concepts of sources, continuity and change, cause and effect, significance, perspectives and empathy.

Not only should opportunities be made for students to demonstrate understanding throughout the inquiry process, but students must also be aware of what is being assessed. Research undertaken by Harvard's Project Zero led to the development of the Teaching for Understanding Framework, which stressed the importance of setting goals for coherent understanding that are shared with students (Blythe and Associates 1998). The teacher must clarify and share with students at the outset of an inquiry what the learning intentions are and also outline the criteria by which success will be determined (Wiliam 2011: 51). A student who knows that they will be given credit for their observations and development of questions will be more likely to engage in the process of inquiry from the outset.

When evidence for formative and summative assessment of the inquiry skills of questioning, researching and analysing is gathered during the entire inquiry process, it sheds much greater light on a student's capacity to evaluate and reflect in order to present ideas, findings and conclusions than a final product by the student can do in isolation. A final product does not always reveal the questions asked, all sources that were used, why particular information was selected and which information was located but not used. It is also only through the assessment of process and product that disciplinary conceptual understanding can be assessed fully.

It is in this area that the practice of Australian primary teachers has a great deal to contribute, given that the latest international research on assessment in history relates primarily to secondary history and continues to focus largely on the structure of examination and testing methods isolated in many ways from ongoing inquiry in the classroom. Bruce VanSledright (2015: 28) talks of the ecological validity of assessment tasks in that they 'must be linked to what students have had an opportunity to learn in the history classroom'. This is a view of assessment that sees it as an end-point of teaching, removed from a holistic inquiry context, rather than learning experiences being valued as ongoing opportunities for assessment. While VanSledright (2015: 130–2) makes the point that assessment should be connected to the key concepts of history, such as sources, perspectives and significance (as referred to above), and not just 'topic understanding', he then looks at the quantitative means by which these two important elements can be addressed, such as through multiple-choice and document-based testing. Approaches that produce quantitative data on students are equated with assessment, rather than being seen as elements of a broader conception of assessment that also includes qualitative analysis of students' ongoing inquiry skills, knowledge and understanding.

Much of the debate by those who view assessment as an end-point of inquiry has tended to revolve around whether assessments measure historical thinking and understandings or general literacy levels of students (Ercikan & Seixas 2015: 36). A student experiencing areas of difficulty in literacy may struggle with complex source material in formal assessment tasks, just as a student with high-level literacy skills may have lower level understanding of key history concepts. Ongoing assessment throughout an inquiry that takes account of literacy demands and differentiation will shed far greater light on students' understanding. Such an approach will enable students to access the history curriculum and demonstrate historical thinking and understanding far more effectively than assessment tasks that are separated from teaching and learning.

THE AUSTRALIAN CURRICULUM GENERAL CAPABILITIES

The Australian Curriculum general capabilities, which consider the individual learning needs of all students, provide additional support for structuring learning and assessment opportunities. History should not be seen as a stand-alone experience occurring once a week for a period of around an hour. The notion of indicative times for areas of the curriculum restricts opportunities to make genuine links between curriculum areas. In order to enhance inquiry in history, it is important that links are made between history and related areas of the curriculum, including English and mathematics. One of the driving features of Project Zero's Teaching for Understanding Framework is that understanding is more powerfully developed when the focus of inquiry in one area of the curriculum is connected with other curriculum areas (Blythe and Associates 1998).

History provides meaningful inquiry contexts for the development of both the literacy and numeracy capabilities. While we want all students to develop the knowledge and understandings within their year-level of the Australian Curriculum, the literacy and numeracy capabilities should underpin approaches to the Inquiry and Skills strand, which in turn should guide decisions about differentiating the curriculum.

Returning to the example of a Year 3 inquiry into change over time in the local area, students were provided with images of the area from the mid-nineteenth century and film of the same area in the mid-twentieth century from which to develop dot-point observations. These dot points were used to develop sentences, and the sentences were then colour-coded to help students to structure paragraphs around common ideas. This writing was used to holistically address the literacy capability through incorporating history into a morning literacy learning block, linking it to a focus on the structure of sentences and paragraphs in the Australian Curriculum for Year 3 English. Differentiation occurred through expectations for the complexity of sentences developed and the organising ideas for paragraphs. For a student experiencing difficulty with independently writing sentences, the dot points provided a framework from which to develop simple sentences, while for a student needing to be extended, the dot points provided the basis for conceptual connections in history to be made in order to construct compound and complex sentences. In turn, the students used highlighters to select like ideas and used this colour coding as the basis for constructing paragraphs.

In Year 4, I have used a focus on the structure of text types in English to help students organise and structure their paragraphs in written work in history. Through highlighting key words and phrases in print and online texts about the First Fleet, students developed an understanding of the structure within and across paragraphs of a history text. This was used to inform the structure of their own written work around the First Fleet; the focus on this aspect in English thus enhanced students' capacity to present ideas, findings and conclusions in history.

Students also need to learn to look at different perspectives of the past in order to create persuasive texts that use devices to convince the reader of the validity of the perspectives they present. It is important that students analyse their own ways of thinking and interpretation in this process (Vasquez 2017: 22). By looking at different perspectives, students develop empathy and have the opportunity to further develop the general capability of critical and creative thinking. Teachers must consider how to connect knowledge, real-world inquiry problems and critical thinking (Ercikan & Seixas 2015: 15).

Approaches to critical literacy enable students to be more aware of considering perspectives. According to Vasquez (2017: 22), the world is a socially constructed text where no text is neutral—students must be aware of how the author's perspectives have shaped a text. They also need to be aware that others viewing the text at the time may have had different perspectives and ways of understanding. In investigating something such as Governor Arthur's proclamation board in the study of the colonial period in Year 5 history, I have focused on students' understanding of the artistic and cultural traditions of the creator of the board as well as those of the intended Aboriginal audience. An understanding of the intended message requires a notion that two-dimensional objects represent real three-dimensional objects, and that the message proceeds from the top left of the board and concludes at the bottom right. These Western traditions are not part of traditional Aboriginal ways of knowing and being. In this way, the study of history plays a central role in the development of the intercultural understanding general capability.

Students need to be supported in asking critical questions of art, as with other sources, such as:

- Who created the work?
- What was their purpose in creating it?
- Who was their intended audience?
- What are people in the image doing, and how does that contribute to the message?
- In what ways does it represent the reality of the time for the creator and the audience?
- How is the image framed, and what might be beyond the frame?
- What is in the foreground and background?
- What might have been omitted or added? Why?

While we want students to think critically, we also want them to think creatively to open up the range of possible perspectives through 'possibility thinking' (Cooper 2017: 32). Historical imaginative texts open up possible perspectives on the past. For young students, imaginative texts provide a grounding in skills that will eventually be transferred to historical inquiry. Through stories, they learn how the actions, motives and perspectives of people influence events, that events have causes and effects, and that the past displays aspects of continuity and change. Through looking at the actions of characters, they begin to develop empathy for other points of view (Cooper 2017: 14). Equally, fiction texts provide primary students with an engaging way to approach what is analogous to an overview in the secondary history curriculum. I have used the novel *Tom Appleby: Convict Boy* (French 2004) to build a broad understanding of people, events, society and daily life at the time of the First Fleet. Reading the text before beginning an inquiry provided all students with a way to develop some level of shared prior understanding.

The writing of historical fiction is a useful tool for assessing student understanding and misunderstanding in history. While an informative text can show how a student has gathered, analysed, evaluated, reflected upon and communicated information, it is possible that the student may have misunderstandings that are simply not shown in an informative text. A student in Year 1 exploring how family life has remained the same or changed over time through an informative text will do so through focusing on all those aspects of daily life encountered during the inquiry, and they will demonstrate their understanding and coverage of those aspects. No one inquiry will ever cover all aspects of daily life. An imaginative text is likely to bring in aspects of daily life needed to develop an effective and coherent storyline. These may include aspects not covererd during the inquiry, such as the Year 1 student who wrote in his imaginative text about me walking to school without shoes when I was a child. The idea of children not always having shoes a 'long time ago' was based on an earlier period of Australian history than my childhood. This misunderstanding of the past provided formative opportunities to direct further inquiry, which would never have eventuated from a text built only on planned inquiry activities aimed at informative writing.

Just as with literacy, the development of numeracy skills is most effective when connections are made for student learning between history and other areas of the curriculum. The Year 3 focus on the local area described earlier provided a meaningful connection to the mathematics curriculum through the creation of timelines, which also required a focus on working with four-digit numbers, an understanding of the use of the base ten number system, and consideration of the measurement of time. Each of these is important in the Year 3 mathematics curriculum. For a student struggling with place-value, timelines provided a real-world example of how place-value is applied. By looking at the images produced in the 1800s, and films and images from the 1900s, he realised that those beginning with 18 came before those with 19, and that the final two digits further organised the dates. It was possible for him, with an understanding of numbers to just beyond 100, to construct a timeline based on these observations and, through this process, to begin to understand the nature of larger numbers. Rather than his numeracy capabilities limiting inquiry, the contextual understandings developed through historical inquiry supported his development of numeracy capabilities.

As students progress through the years of schooling, their understanding of timelines becomes more sophisticated. They begin to develop a greater understanding of aspects such as scale in the mathematics curriculum, and the teacher can utilise this to apply mathematical understanding in the context of historical inquiry. Application of prior learning is a key component in assessment of student skills, knowledge and understanding. In this way, the creation of a timeline at a Year 5 or 6 level might be used to assess application of scale in mathematics and the capacity to apply ideas in history using a range of texts.

Similarly, the focus on the First Fleet in Year 4 is an ideal way for students to collect, interpret, analyse and present data, both through the First Fleet database and by collecting their own data. The numeracy capability is developed through meaningfully linking this to the Year 4 focus in mathematics on selecting and trialling methods for data collection, constructing data displays and evaluating their effectiveness.

Another of the capabilities that links closely to the Inquiry and Skills strand is Information and Communication Technology (ICT). In a Year 6 class I taught, I used an online mind-mapping app to visually organise and structure students' thinking in order to develop questions and plan an inquiry around the groups of people who had migrated to Australia since Federation. They used online data and information from the Australian Bureau of Statistics (ABS) website to investigate and analyse the changing origins of migrants over that period, and then examined digitised immigration records and images from the National Archives of Australia (NAA) to investigate the experiences of those migrants. Finally, they used Google Earth to present their findings spatially, with Quick Response (QR) Codes used as location markers on the map linked to files presenting information and conclusions related to each of the marked locations.

PEDAGOGICAL APPROACHES TO INQUIRY

One of the key approaches that has influenced pedagogy in both history and the visual arts internationally is that of *visible thinking*. Having been developed by Harvard's Project Zero, it is closely aligned to the Teaching for Understanding Framework already mentioned in this chapter. Together, these approaches provide practical ways to align conceptual development of the key history concepts, development of the general capabilities and assessment of all stages of inquiry.

Visible thinking incorporates a number of routines for developing deeper analysis of sources. For younger students, the 'What makes you say that?' routine requires students to not only say what they notice in a source but what it is that makes them 'say that' (Project Zero n.d.). If a Year 2 student says in an inquiry into the history of their school that one building is older than another, the teacher would ask, 'What makes you say that?' A student replying that the bricks look older and the 'stuff' between the bricks is wearing away is using evidence to backup a claim.

The 'see, think, wonder' routine encourages deeper analysis of sources, including images and artefacts (Project Zero n.d.). In the Year 3 example of looking at change and continuity in the local area, a student might first record everything they 'see' in an image to gather all possible evidence. They then move on to possible interpretations of the evidence in the 'think' phase and use this to develop potential questions for inquiry in the 'wonder' phase. Through the use of this process with a range of sources, students are using information from different sources, including observations, to pose questions, as outlined in the Australian Curriculum.

In analysing information to establish points of view in Year 4, students might engage in the 'circle of viewpoints' visible thinking routine around perspectives on the arrival of the First Fleet in Australia (Project Zero n.d.). Through this routine, students brainstorm a range of possible perspectives, make statements about what they believe people would think from those perspectives, ask questions from those perspectives and record new ideas they have as a result of considering those perspectives.

In the analysing, reflecting and communicating understanding phases of an inquiry, it is important to know not only what a student understands at the end of the process of inquiry but also how that connects to their prior understanding at the beginning of an inquiry. A routine such as 'I used to think . . . Now I think . . .' is useful for students to reflect on their initial thinking on the topic, which might be done by revisiting information gathered through the earlier thinking routines and the other ways in which they listed prior understanding, such as concept-mapping (Project Zero n.d.). Reflecting on how their thinking has changed provides useful information for assessment that cannot be gained from looking at the final piece of work in isolation.

CONCLUSION

While the Australian Curriculum has demonstrated the potential to impact on the teaching of history in Australian primary classrooms in terms of the development of conceptual understanding, formative and summative assessment of process as well as product, the development of general capabilities such as literacy and numeracy, and the development of inquiry skills, more research needs to be done to fully capture the degree and extent of these impacts. This chapter has sought to explore the potential benefits to the teaching of history in Australian primary schools when teaching, learning and assessment opportunities are fully realised.

REFERENCES

Australian Curriculum, Assessment and Reporting Authority (ACARA) 2008, *National History Curriculum Framing Paper*, <http://docs.acara.edu.au/resources/National_History_Curriculum_-_Framing_Paper.pdf>, accessed 13 December 2017.

—— 2015, *F–6/7 Humanities and Social Sciences: Concepts for Developing Historical Thinking*, <https://acaraweb.blob.core.windows.net/resources/F-6_7_HASS_Concepts_for_developing_historical_thinking.pdf>, accessed 10 July 2017.

—— 2017, *Australian Curriculum: HaSS*, <www.australiancurriculum.edu.au/f-10-curriculum/humanities-and-social-sciences>, accessed 1 August 2017.

Blythe, T. and Associates 1998, *The Teaching for Understanding Guide*, New York: John Wiley and Sons.

Coalition of Essential Schools 1990, *Performance and Exhibitions: The Demonstration of Mastery*, <http://essentialschools.org/horace-issues/performance-and-exhibitions-the-demonstration-of-mastery>, accessed 13 December 2017.

Cooper, H. 2017, *Teaching History Creatively*, London: Routledge.

Ercikan, K. & Seixas, P. (eds) 2015, *New Directions in Assessing Historical Thinking*, New York: Routledge.

French, J. 2004, *Tom Appleby: Convict Boy*, Sydney: HarperCollins.

Project Zero n.d., *Visible Thinking—Core Routines*, www.visiblethinkingpz.org/VisibleThinking_html_files/03_ThinkingRoutines/03c_CoreRoutines.html>, accessed 2 August 2017.

Seixas, P. 2006, *Benchmarks of Historical Thinking: A Framework for Assessment in Canada*, Vancouver: Centre for the Study of Historical Consciousness, University of British Columbia.

University of Wollongong 1999, *First Fleet Online*, <http://firstfleet.uow.edu.au/search.html>, accessed 13 July 2017.

VanSledright, B. 2015, 'Assessing for learning in the history classroom', in K. Ercikan & P. Seixas (eds), *New Directions in Assessing Historical Thinking*, New York: Routledge, pp. 123–43.

Vasquez, V.M. 2017, *Critical Literacy Across the K–6 Curriculum*, Oxford: Routledge.

Wiliam, D. 2011, *Embedded Formative Assessment*, Bloomington, IN: Solution Tree Press.

PART 2
TEACHING HISTORICAL SKILLS AND EFFECTIVE ASSESSMENT

CHAPTER 4
Scholarly historical practice and disciplinary method

Anna Clark

INTRODUCTION

This chapter explores public anxiety over historical knowledge, advancing a pedagogical discussion of the discipline in its place. In particular, it challenges those calling for a stronger national narrative in schools and suggests that an approach of 'historical thinking'—a term that incorporates the skills of scholarly historical practice and disciplinary method—not only better reflects the discipline, but is also more likely to promote historical engagement in the classroom.

THE HISTORY ANXIETY

The turn of the twenty-first century seems to have been a catalyst for major collective anxiety. As the year 2000 approached, analysts warned that everyone's computers would crash. Automated teller machines (ATMs) would spew out bank notes at midnight on New Year's Eve. Public transport would grind to a halt. Utilities such as power, water and sewerage might simply turn off. As the new millennium got closer, the 'millennium bug' took on even more sinister proportions.

In Australia, it wasn't just the future that was under attack. The past was also a palpable threat to social cohesion, apparently—but in this case, the problem with the 'history bug' was its *lack* of contagiousness. As the nation inched towards the celebratory milestone of its Centenary of Federation on 1 January 2001, alarm bells began ringing that most citizens didn't even know what Federation was.

A major survey in 1994 had already revealed that many young Australians had little or no understanding of their nation's political history and democratic institutions (Civics Expert Group 1994: 3, 10, 50, 143). That was just the beginning. Three years later, in 1997, research by the National Council for the Centenary of Federation showed that only 18 per cent of those interviewed knew the name of Australia's first Prime Minister (Edmund Barton) and 43 per cent of interviewees didn't even know what the term 'federation' meant (Taylor 2001). More Australians knew the presidents of the United States than Australia's own leaders (*The Courier-Mail* 2000: 5).

Politicians and commentators across the political spectrum responded forcefully to this apparent historical illiteracy. Anxious letters and editorials were written in major daily newspapers. Both Labor Prime Minister Paul Keating and his Liberal–National Coalition successor, John Howard, pledged millions of dollars to history education. And on the eve of the centenary, beaming into living rooms around the country at regular intervals, a national ad campaign asked, somewhat nervously, 'What kind of country would forget the name of its first Prime Minister?' (YouTube 2000).

Such is the troubled relationship over Federation that it was labelled the 'Edmund Barton Syndrome' by history educationist Tony Taylor (Taylor & Young 2003: 15). He maintained that the disinterest in Australia's Federation, especially among history students, was in inverse proportion to the insistence by politicians, historians and the general public on its centrality to Australian history.

This preoccupation with students' lack of national knowledge is hardly isolated. Every year it seems there is yet another survey highlighting their historical deficiencies. A 2006 report prepared for the Ministerial Council on Education, Employment, Training and Youth Affairs (MCEETYA) by the Australian Council for Education Research (ACER) revealed that the vast majority of Australian teenagers did not know that Australia Day commemorated the arrival of the First Fleet, and most were also ignorant of the reason for Anzac Day (MCEETYA 2004). But 2001 heralded a significant national anniversary: commemorative coins would be issued to all schoolchildren, national days of celebration and re-enactment were planned, local Federation arches were being built, and a wealth of resource materials was developed for teachers and classrooms. (There was little excuse for ignorance about *any* Prime Minister, let alone Australia's first.)

It is a paradox repeated around the world: a 1987 report by Chester E. Finn and Diane Ravitch in the United States argued that their test results of almost 8000 students revealed a generation 'gravely handicapped' by their own ignorance; in Canada, the youth cohort (18–24-year-olds) reportedly 'failed' a national history quiz convened by the Dominion Institute in 1997; and in 2001, the British *Daily Telegraph* reported significant public concern over the results of a survey in which some schoolchildren astonishingly thought Adolf Hitler was Britain's Prime Minister in World War II (Ravitch & Finn 1987: 201; *Edmonton Journal* 1997: A16; Lightfoot 2001).

In other words, outrage over the state of historical knowledge appears with predictable regularity. 'The whole world has turned upside down in the past eighty years, but one thing has seemingly remained the same,' American history educationist Sam Wineburg (2001: 306–7) wryly noted. 'Kids don't know history.'

'NATIONAL LITERACY' OR 'HISTORICAL LITERACY'?

This chapter critically contextualises public anxiety over historical knowledge, with pedagogical discussion of the discipline. In particular, it challenges those calling for a stronger national narrative in schools to consider what historical thinking actually entails, and how it works in a classroom context. As Canadian history educationist Peter Seixas (1993) acknowledges, poor survey results give weight to popular appeals to 'get back to the facts' when it comes to teaching national history. The question is whether this reflects historical practice in all its complexity.

I am not disputing that students' grasp of history, revealed by repeated surveys, is problematic. The historical knowledge of many young people in Australia is demonstrably patchy, which has implications for civic comprehension and engagement (Barton & Levstik 2004; Civics Expert Group 2004; Saha 2000). Knowing the nation's past puts its present into a context that is meaningful and comprehensible: understanding the origins of Australia's political institutions and civic life gives us critical insights into contemporary society and culture. Many Australians are rightly worried that students' exposure to their national history has been ad hoc and incoherent.

Yet focusing solely on this knowledge as a form of national literacy reduces 'history' to a sanctioned tally of critical facts and dates, which is a very *uncritical* view of history teaching. Such an approach prioritises a simplistic and jingoistic form of national literacy over what we might term 'historical literacy' or 'historical thinking'. As historians such as

Keith Barton, Linda Levstik and John Tosh insist, the study of history is vital, not because it makes more patriotic citizens, but because it develops the sort of 'critical citizenship' that is essential to participative, pluralist democracies (Barton & Levstik 2008; Tosh 2008). While history educators and historians have generally been supportive of a stronger and more coordinated history presence in schools, they are qualified in one fundamental aspect: any national history push must not be at the expense of historical complexity or student engagement.

Seixas (2002b) argues that 'the promise of critical historical discourse' is precisely its capacity to engage with multiplicity and contradiction: 'it provides a rational way, on the basis of evidence and argument, to discuss the differing accounts that jostle with or contradict each other'. As Peter Lee (2001), who heads the History Education Unit at the University of London, insists, 'Students need to know about the past or the whole exercise becomes pointless.' At the same time, he adds, 'understanding the discipline allows more serious engagement with the substantive history that students study, and enables them to do things with their historical knowledge'.

Certainly, educationists doubt whether history-as-fact can constitute a learning experience of any great depth. In an article in the *Journal of Curriculum Studies*, Canadian historian Desmond Morton (2006: 26) wondered whether the public and political obsession with national 'facts' could encompass history's complexity: 'Is knowing that Confederation happened in 1867 or the Winnipeg General Strike in 1919 "history" or simply an almost meaningless fragment of an event, a "factoid" as easily forgotten as memorized?' Such questions have important implications for the Australian context, where public calls for students to name Australia's first Prime Minister contrasted with professional discourses of historical thinking that consciously reach beyond factual recall.

Until now, arguments for a broader and complete disciplinary comprehension of history have been understood using a range of increasingly synonymous terms, such as 'historical literacy', 'historical understanding' and 'historical thinking'. As Chapter 1 of this book explores in greater detail, this 'inquiry' approach to history teaching has its origins in the UK Schools History Project led by Denis Shemilt in the 1970s, and was further developed by history educationists such as Peter Lee and Roslyn Ashby (Shemilt 1980, 2002). The inquiry approach they pioneered emphasised historical practice in the classroom, and outlined the pedagogical progression of historical skills such as source analysis and empathy. Its methodology was not simply a way of learning *about* the past, but was concerned with the discipline of history as an approach *to* the past.

Getting students to 'do' history didn't mean they were going to be historians, though. As Penney Clark and Stéphane Lévesque (2018: 121) explain, 'researchers explicitly acknowledged that most students would not become academic historians as adults'. But this was precisely their point: 'As few will ever learn history after high school, it was crucial that they learn how historical knowledge is created and used when they were still in high school.'

Internationally, others continued refining the skills of historical practice and their progression in an educational context. As part of the collaborative HiTCH (Historical Thinking—Competencies in History) project, German historical philosopher Andreas Körber defined a set of 'competencies' that students should acquire over time, which contained three levels of ability (basic, intermediate and advanced) (Körber 2015; Körber & Meyer-Hamme 2015). These included:

- competence in questioning, or inquiry
- methodological competence
- orientational competence (in relation to time), and
- disciplinary competence (in using the concepts of historical practice).

In Canada, Seixas established the Historical Thinking Project in 2006 (called the Benchmarks of Historical Thinking until 2011), which was to become the major focus of his Centre for the Study of Historical Consciousness, based at the University of British Columbia. Project reports, lesson plans and background papers are available on the Project's website (Historical Thinking Project 2018). The project produced six concepts, which defined the skills of historical thinking as complex, recursive and intersecting; these have become an important resource for teachers and curriculum designers alike (Seixas & Morton 2013):

- How do we decide what is important to learn about the past? The problem of *historical significance*.
- How do we know what we know about the past? The problem of *evidence*.
- How can we make sense of the complex flows of history? The problem of *continuity and change*.

- Why do events happen, and what are their impacts? The problems of *cause and consequence*.
- How can we understand the people of the past? The problem of historical *perspective-taking*?
- How can history help us live in the present? The *ethical dimension* of history.

In the United States, under the direction of leading history educationist Sam Wineburg, the Stanford History Education Group (SHEG 2017) has further developed the 'Reading Like a Historian' curriculum, which engages students in historical thinking and inquiry skills. Keith Barton and Linda Levstik (2004: 10) have also produced a list of 'cultural tools' necessary for students to engage in the act of 'doing history': *the narrative structure of history, inquiry as reflective thought, historical empathy as perspective recognition* and *empathy as caring* (which means the emotional connections and interests necessary to care *about* and *for* history) (Lévesque 2012; Wineburg et al. 2007; Zanazanian 2012).

Meanwhile, other recent work suggests that the concept of 'historical thinking' is as complex as the histories it seeks to reify. For example, research into historical consciousness has increasingly forced educators to (re)consider how theories of history education must take into account the epistemological beliefs of learners and teachers themselves (Lévesque 2012; Wineburg et al. 2007; Zanazanian 2012). Others demonstrate that assumptions of historical competence are based on Western-centric notions of both 'history' and 'pedagogy', and rub uneasily against other forms of knowledge and expertise, as Indigenous Canadian scholar Michael Marker (2004: 107) articulates: 'Aboriginal ways of knowing elude more universal theorizing because they are usually conveyed through oral tradition, which frames reality around the storied features of the landscape.' Thinking about the historical content *and* contexts of postcolonial, subaltern and Indigenous pasts and learners raises important questions about the function of historical thinking in cross-cultural contexts. (This concept is explored further in Chapters 20 and 21 of this book.)

Despite (or perhaps because of) these important challenges, the concept of 'historical thinking' continues to expand and develop in pedagogical circles. As Clark and Lévesque (2018) contend in their extensive survey, 'despite researchers' varied perspectives, backgrounds, and possible disagreements over questions of historical thinking, there is nonetheless significant convergence in the literature thanks in large part to the productive exchange network connecting scholars in the Western world'. Furthermore, such professional discourse increasingly represents an understanding of history education *beyond* popular and politicised demands for a stronger national story in schools. It provides a taxonomy of disciplinary understanding that emphasises the importance of teaching historical skills in school and challenges the notion that proficiency in history begins and ends with core national knowledge (Osborne 2003: 607).

This does not mean that the national narrative should not be taught, as Australian history teacher Nick Ewbank (2007) suggests, or that 'the facts' are not important. These history educators advocate learning content in the classroom because knowing historical context is critical to understanding the past. But they also insist on the importance of encouraging students to engage with history's complexity, such as negotiating contrasting perspectives, analysing different historical sources and understanding the tension between judging the past from our own present values and those of another age.

As Wineburg (2001) insists, historical thinking is an 'unnatural act'—and developing the skills of historical thinking requires time, effort and practice (see also Lee 2001; Rüsen 1989, 2002; Seixas 2002a, 2006). Historical practice, such as interrogating historical sources, negotiating different perspectives and reconciling historical values with contemporary judgements, is not intuitive but learned. 'Historical literacy can be seen as a systematic process with particular sets of skills, attitudes and conceptual understandings, that mediates and develops historical consciousness,' state Australian history educationists Tony Taylor and Carmel Young (2003: 5). The challenges of teaching, learning and assessing historical thinking, beyond the simple testing of facts, demand new methods of assessment, pedagogy and course design (Ercikan & Seixas 2015; Reisman 2012). In terms of classroom teaching, this means a lot more than a quiz on Federation, or recalling the name of Australia's first Prime Minister—despite the entreaties of government ad campaigns.

HISTORICAL THINKING IN THE CLASSROOM

The problematic narrowness of 'history by numbers' is not lost on students. During 2005 and 2006, I travelled around the country, speaking with nearly two hundred high-school students, history teachers and curriculum officials about their attitudes to Australian history. I visited schools in every state and territory: from the most urban, multicultural and cosmopolitan institutions to schools in remote corners of the continent; from low socio-economic cohorts to privileged independent schools; from Christian, Muslim and Quaker schools to those with a high proportion of Aboriginal and Torres Strait Islander students (for a full exploration of this research, see Clark 2008).

For these students, the Centenary of Federation promotions had the desired effect at one level: if students didn't know about Australia's first Prime Minister before 2001, they certainly did afterwards. Yet their responses provide a clear articulation of the limitations of an approach to history education with which many Australian readers will no doubt be familiar. When I asked a group of students at a public school in Hobart whether they could remember anything they had learned about Federation, Emma piped up, laughing: 'Edmund Barton! . . . It was on TV!'

She wasn't the only one. Morgan, a Year 10 student at an independent girls' school in Canberra, scoffed that someone might have actually missed him in class: 'It's like, to be politically correct today you've got to have a basic outline, and everyone knows who Edmund Barton is!' A group of Year 12 students in Perth were similarly dismissive. Garry explained that he had 'looked at it extensively in primary school during the Centenary of Federation'. 'In 2001, yeah,' added his classmate, Maddison. 'But I never fully understood what it was. I just thought, "*Ugh*, federation"—it wasn't explained to me.'

It was the narrowness of this approach that attracted the ire of the students with whom I spoke. Not only was memorising the name of Australia's first Prime Minister boring but, critically, students also picked up the disciplinary simplicity of its historical approach. If anything, this form of teaching didn't represent historical thinking but rather a *lack* of it. At a public school in suburban Brisbane, Miranda observed how she knew that Federation was in 1901, and that Barton was Australia's first Prime Minister. But then she added: 'We never did anything after that . . . Like I know the name of the first Prime Minister, but that's the only Prime Minister I really know, Edmund Barton, and I don't know anything about him, I just know his name. And I don't know anything about any of the other Prime Ministers.'

A striking outcome of this research was the number of participating students who advocated learning a more complex national story in their classes. They were surprisingly articulate about how exposure to multiple historical narratives, approaches and readings makes the subject more interesting and relevant. Responding to the question, 'How do you learn history best?', students from a Year 12 public-school class in suburban Melbourne said:

> *Tony:* Debate in class helps a lot. Because some people might actually bring something up that might not have come up before.
>
> *Michelle:* I guess class discussion, where our teacher will put up a question on the board that everyone has to answer in a paragraph, and then she'll say 'Who wants to say something?', and you'll get a lot of people put something in so you get a lot of different perspectives.
>
> *Mal:* Anything that shows two perspectives.

These students are more than capable of dealing with multiple perspectives. In fact, they suggest it is how they learn history best.

Far from simply being taught core facts, these Year 12 students from a public school in Darwin also wanted to learn through discussion and debate:

> *Gabby:* I think on the whole, I don't want to speak for everyone in our history class, but I get the feeling that we all *learn* better through the discussions . . . Through being able to ask those questions and that sort of thing, rather than just reading dates out of a textbook. Although that is helpful in some instances, I think as a whole a lot of our learning has been through discussion.
>
> *Mel:* Because it's engaging your mind, and through talking about it you learn more and it sticks in your brain more because you've actually tried to think about it, and actively.

That doesn't mean that knowing Edmund Barton's place in Australian history isn't important: those interviewed (students *and* teachers) overwhelmingly agreed that Australian history was essential knowledge. Yet they were adamant that their history education needed to reach beyond the facts to include critical interpretation. Knowing the name of the first Prime Minister should not be the historical end-game here—and students concur.

So facts aren't the problem; rather, they're a key element of historical understanding. They provide context and coverage, and they give students and teachers a way to construct narratives and make meaning from the past. But they must not be confused with 'history' itself. Any discussion of national literacy should encompass those complex and substantial elements of historical thinking, over and above any narrow fixation on core national knowledge. The desire for a greater emphasis on historical content and a more nationally affirming narrative in schools seems to be fundamentally challenged by the opinions of teachers and students, who do not doubt the critical importance of teaching Australian history, but ask that it be debated with the classroom in mind.

CONCLUSION

After growing international research into history education, it seems that these concerns are being accommodated—at least at the curricular level. In its latest national history curriculum, the Australian Curriculum, Assessment and Reporting Authority (ACARA 2017) describes history in these terms precisely:

> The Australian Curriculum: History aims to ensure that students develop:
> - interest in, and enjoyment of, historical study for lifelong learning and work, including their capacity and willingness to be informed and active citizens
> - knowledge, understanding and appreciation of the past and the forces that shape societies, including Australian society
> - understanding and use of historical concepts, such as evidence, continuity and change, cause and effect, perspectives, empathy, significance and contestability
> - capacity to undertake historical inquiry, including skills in the analysis and use of sources, and in explanation and communication.

The question is whether that will be backed up with ongoing training, professional development and resources. Will public discourses of Australian history accommodate those concepts of historical thinking when the next survey results inevitably appear and anxieties about national knowledge re-emerge? Surely the strength of historical thinking lies in its practice by teachers and students in the classroom, who can realise the abstract theorising of historians and educationists.

REFERENCES

Australian Curriculum, Assessment and Reporting Authority (ACARA) 2017, Australian Curriculum: History, www.australiancurriculum.edu.au/senior-secondary-curriculum/humanities-and-social-sciences, <http://v7-5.australiancurriculum.edu.au/humanities-and-social-sciences/history/aims>, accessed 19 August 2017.

Barton, K.C. & Levstik, L.S. 2004, *Teaching History for the Common Good*, London: Routledge.

Civics Expert Group 1994, *'Whereas the People . . .' Civics and Citizenship Education*, Canberra: Commonwealth of Australia.

—— 2004, *'Whereas the People . . .'*, Canberra: Commonwealth of Australia.

Clark, A. 2008, *History's Children: History Wars in the Classroom*, Sydney: UNSW Press.

Clark, P. & Lévesque, S. 2018, 'Historical thinking: Definitions and educational applications', in S. Metzger & L. Harris, *The Wiley International Handbook of History Teaching and Learning*, New York: Wiley Blackwell, pp. 119–148.

The Courier-Mail 2000, 'Students ignorant of history', 16 October.

Edmonton Journal 1997, Editorial, 'Canada's history is being lost', 2 July, p. A16.

Ercikan, K. & Seixas, P. (eds) 2015, *New Directions in Assessing Historical Thinking*, New York: Routledge.

Ewbank, N. 2007, 'Reviewing history: Whose interpretation do we go by?' *Crikey*, 27 June, <www.crikey.com.au/Politics/20070627-Reviewing-history-whose-interpretation-do-we-go-by.html>, accessed 14 February 2008.

Historical Thinking Project 2018, Website, <www.historicalthinking.ca>.

Körber, A. 2015, 'Historical consciousness, historical competencies—and beyond? Some conceptual development within German history didactics', Deutsches Institut für Internationale Pädagogische Forschung, <www.pedocs.de/volltexte/2015/10811/pdf/Koerber_2015_Development_German_History_Didactics.pdf>, accessed 20 June 2016.

Körber, A. & Meyer-Hamme, J. 2015, 'Historical thinking, competencies, and their measurement', in K. Ercikan & P. Seixas (eds), *New Directions in Assessing Historical Thinking*, New York: Routledge, pp. 89–101.

Lee, P. 2001, 'Understanding history', paper presented at the Canadian Historical Consciousness in an International Context: Theoretical Frameworks conference, University of British Columbia, Vancouver, <www.cshc.ubc.ca/pwias/viewabstract.php?10>, accessed 29 November 2007.

Lévesque, S. 2012, 'Between memory recall and historical consciousness: Implications for education', *Public History Weekly*, 12 October, <http://public-history-weekly.oldenbourg-verlag.de/2-2014-33/memory-recall-historical-consciousness-implications-education>, accessed 2 June 2016.

Lightfoot, L. 2001, 'Children who think Hitler was British', *Daily Telegraph*, 10 January.

Marker, M. 2004, 'Theories and disciplines as sites of struggle: The reproduction of colonial dominance through the controlling of knowledge in the academy', *Canadian Journal of Native Education*, vol. 28, nos 1/2, pp. 102–10.

Ministerial Council on Education, Employment, Training and Youth Affairs, 'Civics and citizenship Years 6 and 10 report 2004', Melbourne: Curriculum Corporation, 2006.

Morton, D. 2006, 'Canadian history teaching in Canada: What's the big deal?' in R. Sandwell (ed.), *To the past: History education, public memory, and citizenship in Canada*, Toronto: University of Toronto Press, p. 26.

Osborne, K. 2003, 'Teaching history in schools: A Canadian debate', *Journal of Curriculum Studies*, vol. 35, no. 5, pp. 585–626.

Ravitch, D. & Finn, C.E. Jnr 1987, *What Do Our 17-Year-Olds Know? A Report on the First National Assessment of History and Literature*, New York: Harper & Row.

Reisman, A. 2012, 'Reading like a historian: A document-based history curriculum intervention in urban high schools', *Cognition and Instruction*, vol. 31, no. 1, pp. 86–112.

Rüsen, J. 1989, 'The didactics of history in West Germany: Towards a new self-awareness of historical studies', *History and Theory*, vol. 26, no. 3, pp. 275–86.

—— 2002, 'Introduction: Historical thinking as intercultural discourse', in *Western Historical Thinking: An Intercultural Debate*, New York: Berghahn Books.

Saha, L.J. 2000, 'Political activism and civic education among Australian secondary school students', *Australian Journal of Education*, vol. 44, no. 2, pp. 155–74.

Seixas, P. 1993, 'Parallel crises: History and the social studies curriculum in the USA', *Journal of Curriculum Studies*, vol. 25, no. 3, pp. 235–50.

—— 2002a, 'CHR Forum: Heavy Baggage *En Route* to Winnipeg', *Canadian Historical Review*, vol. 83, no. 3, pp. 390–414.

—— 2002b, 'The Purposes of Teaching Canadian History', *Canadian Social Studies* 36(2), <www.quasar.ualberta.ca/css/Css_36_2/Arpurposes_teaching_canadian_history.htm>, accessed 15 July 2002.

—— 2006, 'What is historical consciousness?', in R. Sandwell (ed.), *To the Past: History Education, Public Memory, and Citizenship in Canada*, Toronto: University of Toronto Press, pp. 11–12.

Seixas, P. & Morton, T. 2013, 'Guideposts to historical thinking', in *The Big Six Historical Thinking Concepts*, Toronto: Nelson, pp. 10–11, <http://historicalthinking.ca/sites/default/files/files/docs/Guideposts.pdf>, accessed 20 August 2017.

Shemilt, D. 1980, *History 13–16: Evaluation Study. School Council (GB) History 13–16 Project*, Edinburgh: Holmes McDougall.

—— 2002, 'The Caliph's coin: The currency of narrative frameworks in history teaching', in P.N. Stearns, P. Seixas & S. Wineburg (eds), *Knowing, Teaching and Learning History: National and International Perspectives*, New York: New York University Press, pp. 83–101.

Stanford History Education Group 2017, 'Reading Like a Historian', <https://sheg.stanford.edu/rlh>, accessed 19 August 2017.

Taylor, T. 2001, 'Disputed territory: Some political contexts for the development of Australian historical consciousness', paper presented at the Canadian Historical Consciousness in an International Context: Theoretical Frameworks conference, University of British Columbia, Vancouver, <www.cshc.ubc.ca/viewabstract.php?id=17>, accessed 14 February 2008.

Taylor, T. & Young, C. 2003, *Making History: A Guide for the Teaching and Learning of History in Australian Schools*. Melbourne: Curriculum Corporation, for the Department of Education, Science and Training, <www.hyperhistory.org/images/assets/pdf/complete.pdf>.

Tosh, J. 2008, *Why History Matters*, Basingstoke: Palgrave Macmillan.

Wineburg, S. 2001, *Historical Thinking and Other Unnatural Acts: Charting the Future of Teaching the Past*, Philadelphia, PA: Temple University Press.

Wineburg, S., Mosburg, S., Porat, S. & Duncan, A. 2007, 'Common belief and the cultural curriculum: An intergenerational study of historical consciousness', *American Educational Research Journal*, vol. 44, no. 1, pp. 40–76.

YouTube 2000, 'What kind of country would forget the name of its first Prime Minister?' (2000), <www.youtube.com/watch?v=6niKTWMx4_c>, accessed 17 August 2017.

Zanazanian, P. 2012, 'Historical consciousness and the structuring of group boundaries: A look at two Francophone school history teachers regarding Quebec's Anglophone minority', *Curriculum Inquiry*, vol. 42, no. 2, pp. 215–39.

CHAPTER 5
The role of questions and sources in promoting historical thinking

John A. Whitehouse

This chapter explores the role of questions and sources in promoting historical thinking. It provides an example (the landing at Anzac Cove on 25 April 1915) and concludes by offering a range of pedagogical strategies. Research on the learning and teaching of history has become increasingly concerned with issues of method. A curriculum that is confined to dates and events does not equip students to engage in critical thinking. Furthermore, an approach to the teaching of history as a single national story fails to address different interpretations of the past and provides no means of evaluating these views (Lévesque 2008). Instead, our students need to engage in historical inquiry and to build arguments about the past. This requires different forms of historical knowledge.

Peter Lee and Rosalyn Ashby (2000) identify two kinds of knowledge in the study of the past. *Substantive knowledge* refers to events, periods, people, practices, ideas, institutions and developments; it is knowledge about the past. *Procedural knowledge* enables students to explore the past and construct interpretations; it is knowledge about how to engage in historical inquiry. To use terms coined by Elliot Eisner (2002), substantive knowledge has traditionally dominated the *explicit curriculum* (overt and unambiguous), while procedural knowledge has largely remained in the background as the *implicit curriculum* (covert and ambiguous) or has formed part of the *null curriculum* (not addressed). The Historical Thinking Project (2017) identifies six key procedural concepts that facilitate historical inquiry: *establish historical significance, use primary source evidence, identify continuity and change, analyse cause and consequence, take historical perspectives* and *understand the ethical dimension of historical interpretations*. For a recent discussion of this work, see Seixas (2017). VanSledright (2009) describes these concepts as 'knowledge-in-use' because they are learned most effectively through application.

ASKING QUESTIONS ABOUT THE PAST

Historical inquiry is driven by questions about the past. In the Netherlands, Jannet van Drie and Carla van Boxtel (2008) offer a model of historical reasoning that highlights the centrality of questions to historical reasoning. For these researchers, historical reasoning *is* the capacity to create an argument in response to such questions. Van Drie and van Boxtel identify four types of questions. Descriptive questions seek a basic account of the past—for example, *What was the Industrial Revolution?* Causal questions invite an explanation of why change occurred as it did—for example, *What caused the Wall Street Crash?* Comparative questions necessitate identification of the similarities and differences between sources, events, individuals, groups, practices and/or ideas—for example, *What were the similarities and differences between the Great War and World War II?* Evaluative questions are a subset of the first three types; such questions invite an assessment of an aspect of the past—for example, *To what extent was Julius Caesar responsible for the demise of the Roman Republic?*

Evaluative questions may be more effective at fostering historical reasoning than the other types (van Drie, van Boxtel & van der Linden 2006). A key contribution of these researchers to history education is their insistence on the need for students to ask questions and construct arguments about the past; these features of their work can be combined productively with procedural concepts identified by the Historical Thinking Project (Whitehouse 2015a).

As teachers, it is important for us to foster the questioning skills of our students. Philip Cam (2006) offers a helpful strategy for refining students' questioning skills. Working in the context of philosophy, Cam invites students to classify their questions according to two distinctions. The first is between open and closed questions. Closed questions invite a response that consists of 'yes', 'no' or a piece of information. Open questions lack these kinds of settled answers. The second distinction is between textual and intellectual questions. This reflects the origins of the approach in philosophy. One teaching strategy in philosophy is to offer students a short narrative as a springboard for the discussion of key concepts. Textual questions focus upon the narrative. Intellectual questions address ideas that are presented by the narrative. These concepts are the subject of philosophical inquiry. This Question Quadrant strategy is a helpful way to support the classification of questions in the humanities (Whitehouse 2008a). In history, it is useful to retain the distinction between open and closed questions. The second distinction is problematic, however, because historical inquiry is reliant on sources. Instead, it is valuable to distinguish between questions that focus on a selected source and those that point to broader historical inquiry (Whitehouse 2015b).

USING SOURCES AS EVIDENCE

Questions and sources are fundamental to historical inquiry, and teachers can plan learning and teaching sequences around selected sources. Frederick Drake and Sarah Drake Brown (2003) suggest that it is useful to distinguish between three kinds of sources. The first-order source provides the foundation of the learning and teaching sequence. The inclusion of second-order sources enables comparisons with the first-order source. They afford opportunities for corroboration of statements about the past. Such sources also enable exploration of aspects of the past that might not be addressed by the first-order source. Third-order sources are located by students when engaged in historical inquiry. Three orders of questions may be combined with this approach (Whitehouse 2015c). A first-order question is indispensable to the learning and teaching sequence—for instance, *What is the historical significance of the Great War?* Second-order questions facilitate comparisons between sources; furthermore, they enable teachers to focus on aspects of the past that are not directly addressed by the first-order question. Third-order questions are posed by students. Such questions may result from a teaching strategy such as the adaptation of the Question Quadrant outlined above. First- and second-order questions provide exemplars to students. Furthermore, it is helpful to review questions against historical thinking concepts (Counsell 2000).

Bruce VanSledright (2004) regards source work as essential to historical thinking and offers a useful four-stage model of source analysis. The first step is *identification*. It is necessary to establish the nature of a source before one can use it to make inferences about the past. The second step is *attribution*. The source was produced by someone at a certain time and place. The first two stages facilitate the third step: *judging perspective*. Any source offers a viewpoint on the past. Research by Sam Wineburg (2001) demonstrates that students who lack a strong understanding of the discipline tend to read sources as neutral repositories of information. From such a viewpoint, the perspective of the author might seem to be immaterial. This is not the case, however: the beliefs, values and attitudes of the author shape the inferences that might be drawn from the source. This means that the source must be placed in context. In order to do this, students require a base of historical knowledge structured around key concepts and landmarks in time (van Boxtel & van Drie 2012). *Reliability assessment* is the fourth step of this approach to reading sources. Having examined the perspective on the past afforded by the source, the student must assess its value. To what extent can and does the source further our understanding of the past? What are its strengths? What are its weaknesses?

AN EXAMPLE: THE LANDING AT ANZAC COVE

The pedagogical challenge is for the teacher to assist students to understand the source. This involves exploring key events and concepts. Take, for example, the landing at Anzac Cove, which took place on 25 April 1915. To contextualise this event, teaching would combine description, explanation and narration. The learning and teaching sequence would sketch the prevailing conditions in Europe with reference to concepts of imperialism, nationalism, alliances and militarism. These concepts are necessary, but not sufficient. It is important to explore the assassination of Archduke Franz Ferdinand as the immediate cause of the crisis. It is vital to examine the decisions of individuals and groups, including German leaders and the Russian Tsar. Having discussed the short- and long-term causes of the war, it is vital to explain the relationship between Australia and Britain (and the way news of the war was received in Australia). Turning to the Gallipoli campaign, it is important to identify the role of the Ottoman Empire, British imperatives in the region and attempts to force a passage through the Dardanelles. Having laid these foundations, the class could examine the first source: a dispatch by journalist Ellis Ashmead-Bartlett providing an account of the landing.

The source is a dispatch that was written for publication in the press (*identification*). Ellis Ashmead-Bartlett was an official British war correspondent. He accompanied the contingent to the Dardanelles, but came ashore on the peninsula *after* the landing occurred (*attribution*). These details are important because they influence what might be said about the past on the basis of the source (*judging perspective*). The first account of the landing to appear in Australian newspapers, the article was intended to appeal to the public:

> The Australians who were about to go into action for the first time under trying circumstances, were cheerful, quiet, and confident, showing no sign of nerves or excitement. As the moon waned the boats were swung out, the Australians received their last instructions, and men who six months ago were living peaceful civilian lives began to disembark on a strange, unknown shore in a strange land to attack an enemy of different race . . .
>
> The boats had almost reached the beach when a party of Turks entrenched ashore opened a terrible fusillade with rifles and a Maxim. Fortunately most of the bullets went high. The Australians rose to the occasion. They did not wait for orders or for the boats to reach the beach, but sprang into the sea, formed a sort of rough line, and rushed the enemy's trenches. Their magazines were uncharged, so they just went in with cold steel.
>
> It was over in a minute. The Turks in the first trench either were bayoneted or ran away, and the Maxim was captured.
>
> Then the Australians found themselves facing an almost perpendicular cliff of loose sandstones, covered with thick shrubbery. Somewhere about halfway up the enemy had a second trench, strongly held, from which poured a terrible fire on the troops below and the boats pulling back to the destroyers for a second landing party.
>
> Here was a tough proposition to tackle in the darkness, but those colonials were practical above all else and went about it in a practical way. They stopped a few minutes to pull themselves together, get rid of their packs, and charge their rifle magazines. Then this race of athletes proceeded to scale the cliff without responding to the enemy's fire. They lost some men, but didn't worry, and in less than a quarter of an hour the Turks were out of their second position, and either bayoneted or fleeing . . .
>
> But then the Australians, whose blood was up, instead of entrenching, rushed northwards and eastwards, searching for fresh enemies to bayonet. It was difficult country in which to entrench. They therefore preferred to advance. (Ashmead-Bartlett 1915).

This is not some unbiased, objective account from which the student can compose a factual summary; instead, the perspective of the author infuses every word of the dispatch. This means that the source must be subject to a process of evaluation before it can be used as evidence to support a statement about the past (*reliability assessment*). The account rests on the beliefs, values and attitudes of British society during the period: the Australian troops are presented as members of the British imperial family. Ashmead-Bartlett writes that they confront an enemy of another race. The land itself is menacing and alien. Nevertheless, when the Turkish guns open fire, the Australians meet the challenge. There is no reference to confusion: the Anzacs demonstrate initiative and resolve. Nor is there any mention of fear, pain or suffering in the extract; instead, the author prefers to laud the Australians. The men overcome the challenge before them. Undaunted by their losses, the heroic 'colonials' demonstrate a pragmatism that enables them to succeed. Thus, Ashmead-Bartlett crafts an account that appeals to the patriotism of his readers. Harvey Broadbent (2005: 145) observes that the dispatch marks the beginning of the first strand of the Anzac legend: *the digger who overcomes*. The second strand originates in the writing of Charles Bean: *the digger who endures*.

BUILDING UNDERSTANDING: A SECOND SOURCE

To acquire a nuanced understanding of the past, it is necessary to consider the perspectives of different people and groups. Teachers facilitate this by presenting students with sources that enable them to explore more than one perspective. This enables students to corroborate or question inferences about the past drawn from a previous source. In the case of the Gallipoli landing, the Ashmead-Bartlett dispatch is one of many accounts of events. Take, for example, the representation of the same event in *A Fortunate Life*, an iconic piece of Australian literature by Albert Facey (1981: 256):

> Suddenly all hell broke loose; heavy shelling and shrapnel fire commenced. The ships that were protecting our troops returned fire. Bullets were thumping into us in the rowing-boat. Men were being hit and killed all around me.
>
> When we were cut loose to make our way to the shore was the worst period. I was terribly frightened. The boat touched bottom some thirty yards from shore so we had to jump out and wade into the beach. The

water in some places was up to my shoulders. The Turks had machine-guns sweeping the strip of beach where we landed—there were many dead already when we got there. Bodies of men who had reached the beach ahead of us were lying all along the beach and wounded men were screaming for help. We couldn't stop for them—the Turkish fire was terrible and mowing into us. The order to line up on the beach was forgotten. We all ran for our lives over the strip of the beach and got into the scrub and bush. Men were falling all around me. We were stumbling over bodies—running blind.

The sight of the bodies on the beach was shocking. It worried me for days that I couldn't stop to help the men calling out. (This was one of the hardest things of the war for me and I'm sure for many of the others. There were to be other times under fire when we couldn't help those that were hit. I would think for days, 'I should've helped that poor beggar'.)

We used our trenching tools to dig mounds of earth and sheltered from the firing until daylight—the Turks never let up. Their machine-guns were sweeping the scrub. The slaughter was terrible.

I am sure that there wouldn't have been one of us left if we had obeyed that damn fool order to line up on the beach.

The perspective offered by Facey differs sharply from the account by Ashmead-Bartlett. Written in the first person, there is nothing of the romanticism of the dispatch. Facey paints a nightmarish scene of fear and slaughter. Wading ashore, Facey is confronted by the bodies of the dead and the screams of the wounded. The Anzacs must run for cover in disorder and confusion. Injured men are left behind. This provokes feelings of guilt in Facey as a survivor. A plan to assemble on the beach is both mentioned and dismissed with disdain.

It is important to note that this source is far from unproblematic. Writing for the Australian War Memorial, Brigadier Chris Roberts (2010; see also Roberts 2015) observes that Facey's record states that he came ashore at Gallipoli on 7 May—well after the landing. Roberts points out that machine guns may not have been used at Anzac Cove: official war historian Charles Bean and battalion diaries note heavy fire, not mass slaughter. This does not mean that the narrative is without value. It raises issues around the reliability of sources, memory and the prominence of Gallipoli in the historical consciousness of many Australians. Facey served in the Great War and experienced the horror of battle, but it seems that

A Fortunate Life is not a firsthand account of the landing. It is necessary to turn to further sources. Take, for example, the diary entry of infantryman Eric Rapkins for 26 April, as a contemporaneous account from a soldier's perspective (Rapkins with Coghill 2015):

> Landed last night . . . There plenty wounded. I have carried some dead uns past too. The shrapnel from the Turks is flying over as I write. The Turks bombarded us all day. We lost a few men. One of our sergeants got shot through the brain. Shrapnel has done a lot of damage to us. There are a hell of a lot of killed and wounded.

FURTHER POSSIBILITIES FOR HISTORICAL THINKING

The potential scope of historical inquiry is immense. To engage in research, historians select some aspect of the past to explore. Teachers and students also make choices that shape historical inquiry. Determination of historical significance is a judgement about the past. To make such an evaluation, it is necessary to identify and describe the aspect of the past. For example, the Gallipoli landing occurred on 25 April 1915. Troops from Australia and New Zealand came ashore on what would become known as Anzac Cove (in modern Turkey) and engaged Ottoman forces. This action formed part of a campaign to take the Gallipoli Peninsula. This is historical fact. Having said that, the establishment of elementary meaning is not necessarily straightforward. Furthermore, it is impossible to escape the influence of language: the words that we use to describe the past reflect the beliefs, values and attitudes of the present. With foundational understanding established, discussion can turn to the causes and consequences of the event. Beginners often employ limited criteria to support judgements about the relative importance of aspects of the past (Lévesque 2005; Seixas 1994, 1997). This means it is important for teachers to expand the frame of reference available to students. Possible criteria include how the event was understood at the time, the degree and extent of its impact, its duration and its contemporary relevance (Lévesque 2008; Partington 1980; Phillips 2002). Christine Counsell (2004) observes that an event might be *remarkable, remembered, resonant, resulting in change* or *revealing*.

From an Australian perspective, the landing at Anzac Cove dominated the public imagination It marks the origin of the Anzac myth/legend. This view of Australian soldiers has been invoked by countless commentators. The landing represents an important change: this was the first major engagement of Australian troops in the Great War. Conservative commentators hailed the event as a baptism of fire for the new nation. The landing and subsequent campaign resulted in death and injury for many servicemen on both sides of the conflict. From the British perspective, the campaign was a failure, as Turkey retained the peninsula. The event and its depiction reveal much about the beliefs, values and attitudes of the period, and different Australian historians have ascribed significance to the event for a range of reasons (Whitehouse 2008b). Teachers should offer students opportunities to do likewise.

As the above discussion indicates, historical thinking concepts are interrelated: evaluation of the historical significance of an event might involve an assessment of key changes that arose from it. The key pedagogical imperative is for teachers to offer students opportunities to *use* these concepts. A teaching and learning sequence that includes questions and source material is an important foundation. A range of cooperative learning activities will provide students with opportunities to use historical thinking concepts. Team Jigsaw is one such strategy intended to promote discussion. Following the desegregation of schools in the United States, this technique was introduced to promote interracial cooperation in classrooms (Aronson et al. 1978). Students form small groups of equal numbers. Each group is then allocated a different task. After completing the task, students form new groups, which include a representative of each of the base groups, and undertake a cooperative task. In the case of history, each base group might be allocated a different source on a topic such as the Western Front, recruiting or the conscription campaigns. The whole class could explore the same question, but different base groups could explore different sources. Students would then form new groups and report their findings. Following this, students might consider similarities and differences between the sources. This could provide the springboard for a discussion of historical perspectives or other historical thinking concepts. For more on the Team Jigsaw strategy and other useful cooperative learning activities, see Kagan (2007).

CONCLUSION

Questions drive inquiry. For students to pursue questions about the past in a rigorous and meaningful way, they need to draw on procedural concepts such as those identified by the Historical Thinking Project. Historians use material that has survived from earlier times to make inferences about the past. Importantly, a source must be evaluated before it can be used as evidence in support of an argument. This means that understanding the distinction between a source and evidence is fundamental to the discipline. Furthermore, the choices the teacher makes about the use of questions and the selection of sources exert a profound influence on what students learn. One of the most exciting aspects of current research on learning and teaching history is that it underscores the interpretative nature of the discipline and invites our students to investigate and argue about the past. It is one thing to tell students the significance of a historical event; it is quite another to ask students to evaluate its historical significance. Such an open-ended challenge necessitates addressing substantive and procedural knowledge.

REFERENCES

Aronson, E., Blaney, N., Stephan, C., Sikes, J. & Snapp, M. 1978, *The Jigsaw Classroom*, Beverly Hills, CA: Sage.

Ashmead-Bartlett, E. 1915, *The Sydney Morning Herald*, 8 May.

Broadbent, H. 2005, *Gallipoli: The Fatal Shore*, Ringwood: Penguin.

Cam, P. 2006, *Twenty Thinking Tools*, Camberwell: ACER Press.

Counsell, C. 2000, 'Historical knowledge and historical skills: A distracting dichotomy', in J. Arthur & R. Phillips (eds), *Issues in History Teaching*, London: Routledge, pp. 54–71.

—— 2004, 'Looking through a Josephine-Butler-shaped window: Focusing pupils' thinking on historical significance', *Teaching History*, no. 114, pp. 30–6.

Drake, F.D. & Drake Brown, S. 2003, 'A systematic approach to improve students' historical thinking', *The History Teacher*, vol. 36, no. 4, pp. 465–89.

Eisner, E.W. 2002, *The Educational Imagination: On the Design and Evaluation of School Programs*, 3rd ed., Upper Saddle River, NJ: Prentice Hall.

Facey, A.B. 1981, *A Fortunate Life*, Ringwood: Penguin.

Historical Thinking Project 2017, 'Historical thinking concepts', <http://historicalthinking.ca/historical-thinking-concepts>, accessed 10 December 2017.

Kagan, S. 2007, *Cooperative Learning*, Heatherton: Hawker Brownlow.

Lee, P. & Ashby, R. 2000, 'Progression in historical understanding among students ages 7–14', in P. Stearns, P. Seixas & S. Wineburg (eds), *Knowing, Teaching, and Learning History: National and International Perspectives*, New York: New York University Press, pp. 199–222.

Lévesque, S. 2005, 'Teaching second-order concepts in Canadian history: The importance of "historical significance"', *Canadian Social Studies*, vol. 39, no. 2, <https://sites.educ.ualberta.ca/css/Css_39_2/ARLevesque_second-order_concepts.htm>, accessed 10 December 2017.

—— 2008, *Thinking Historically: Educating Students for the Twenty-First Century*, Toronto: University of Toronto Press.

Partington, G. 1980, *The Idea of an Historical Education*, London: NFER Publishing.

Phillips, R. 2002, 'Historical significance—the forgotten key element?', *Teaching History*, no. 106, pp. 14–19.

Rapkins, J. with Coghill, J. 2015, 'Gallipoli 2015: Fragile WWI diary records five days of horror at Gallipoli', <http://www.abc.net.au/news/2015-04-18/fragile-ww1-diary-records-five-days-of-horror-at-gallipoli/6375816>, accessed 10 December 2017.

Roberts, C. 2010, 'Turkish machine-guns at the landing', *Wartime*, no. 50, pp. 14–19.

—— 2015, *The Landing at Anzac: 1915*, 2nd ed., Sydney: Big Sky Publishing.

Seixas, P. 1994, 'Students' understanding of historical significance', *Theory and Research in Social Education*, vol. 22, no. 3, pp. 281–304.

—— 1997, 'Mapping the terrain of historical significance', *Social Education*, vol. 61, no. 1, pp. 22–7.

—— 2017, 'A model of historical thinking', *Educational Philosophy and Theory*, vol. 49, no. 6, pp. 593–605.

van Boxtel, C. & van Drie, J. 2012, '"That's in the time of the Romans!" Knowledge and strategies students use to contextualize historical images and documents', *Cognition and Instruction*, vol. 30, no. 2, pp. 113–45.

van Drie, J. & van Boxtel, C. 2008, 'Historical reasoning: Towards a framework for analyzing students' reasoning about the past', *Educational Psychology Review*, vol. 20, no. 2, pp. 87–110.

van Drie, J., van Boxtel, C. & van der Linden, J. 2006, 'Historical reasoning in a computer-supported collaborative learning environment', in A.M. O'Donnell, C.E. Hmelo-Silver & G. Erkens (eds), *Collaborative Learning, Reasoning and Technology*, Mahwah, NJ: Lawrence Erlbaum, pp. 265–96.

VanSledright, B. 2004, 'What does it mean to think historically . . . and how do you teach it?', *Social Education*, vol. 68, no. 3, pp. 230–3.

—— 2009, 'Thinking historically', *Journal of Curriculum Studies*, vol. 41, no. 3, pp. 433–8.

Whitehouse, J.A. 2008a, 'Talking humanities: Questions and co-operative learning', *The Social Educator*, vol. 26, no. 1, pp. 32–6.

—— 2008b, 'Teaching the historians', *Agora*, vol. 43, no. 2, pp. 4–8.

—— 2015a, 'Historical thinking: A framework for learning and teaching history', *Educational Practice and Theory*, vol. 37, no. 2, pp. 51–8.
—— 2015b, 'Blue-water cruising on the high seas of time: What does the review of the Australian Curriculum mean for senior ancient history?', *Curriculum Perspectives*, vol. 35, no. 1, pp. 61–3.
—— 2015c, 'Historical thinking and narrative in a global culture', in J. Zajda (ed.), *Nation-Building and History Education in a Global Culture*, Dordrecht: Springer, pp. 15–27.
Wineburg, S. 2001, *Historical Thinking and Other Unnatural Acts: Charting the Future of Teaching the Past*, Philadelphia, PA: Temple University Press.

CHAPTER 6

Developing your approach to teaching history

Robert Parkes

For some of my students—many of whom were recent arrivals to Australia—it must have been a little perplexing when they walked into their Year 10 history classroom for the first time and read on the board the bold statement 'I don't teach history', which their new teacher had inscribed in chalk only moments before. It was my first-ever history class, and I was inevitably revealing the legacy of many years of martial arts teaching (my profession before I became a history teacher) by referencing good old Mr Miyaga (the Karate Kid's mentor in the films of the same name). You might remember (if you are old enough) that Mr Miyaga had two rules that he had framed in his home *dojo*. They were not the same as my rules, of course, but I was subtly connecting my own personal history with my new role as a history teacher when I wrote on the blackboard the following declarations:

> Rule number 1: I don't teach history—I develop historians.
> Rule number 2: There is no right and wrong in my classroom—only opinion backed by evidence.

In the moment of revelation, as I added the qualifications to each of my rules, I disclosed something important for both my students and myself. I was attempting to make explicit the particular pedagogical approach I would be adopting to the teaching and learning of history by sharing the two principles that would guide our journey together over the coming year.

At the time, my approach was very source-analysis focused, influenced strongly by the principles of cognitive apprenticeship (Parkes & Muldoon 2010), and self-consciously resisting what I considered to be the lure of teaching the seductive narrative—a position I would later reconsider.

This chapter discusses various approaches to history teaching. I outline some of the enduring debates over what, and how, history should be taught. Knowing where you stand on these debates, and why, will help you to develop and be able to justify your own approach to history teaching. After outlining these recurring debates, I will outline the three approaches to history teaching articulated by Peter Seixas (2000) in response to what was a growing concern with the postmodern challenge to history. The postmodern challenge might best be defined as a crisis of confidence in knowledge produced by our scientific organisations (such as universities) and a general distrust of authorities (civil, political, intellectual, religious, etc.). To understand the postmodern challenge further, see Lyotard (1979); for how this applies to the discipline of history, see Jenkins (1991); and for its application to history education, see Parkes (2014). I will then present a framework that I believe addresses a missing possibility in the model put forward by Seixas. I hope this alternative framework will provide a way for you to navigate between different approaches to history in the classroom, and allow you to reflect upon your own practice as it develops.

THE BIG DEBATES IN AUSTRALIAN HISTORY EDUCATION

A good place to start to understand the different approaches one might take to history teaching is to consider the recurring debates in the field. I focus on the debates I think are particularly relevant for someone about to enter the profession of history teaching in Australia. Where you stand in relation to each of these debates will undoubtedly have a profound impact on what, and how, you teach in the history classroom. Typically, with each of these debates, an overcommitment to one side of the argument may actually be pedagogically problematic, leading students to walk away with limitations in their historical knowledge or understanding of history as a way of knowing.

Skills versus content

Walk into any history staffroom across the country (and probably anywhere in the world), and you will hear the dilemma of how much content there is to cover. All history teachers are faced with the problem of the relative emphasis they place on the teaching of historical skills versus their coverage of curriculum 'content' (or historical knowledge). In Australia, this dilemma has its roots in what might be described as the Commonwealth curriculum reforms of the 1970s and 1980s. During the 1970s, we began to see a movement towards the critical appraisal and interpretation of sources in the classroom, and the development of 'historical empathy' (see Chapter 7 in this book for a keen exploration of this concept). During the decade that followed, the influence of the British Schools Council became more wide reaching, and systematic attention to historical reasoning processes (van Drie & van Boxtel 2008), student inquiry, interpretation of evidence, historical empathy and historical perspective shaped the curricula of the 1980s (Parkes & Donnelly 2014).

Van Drie and van Boxtel (2008: 89) define historical reasoning 'in the context of history education as an activity in which a person organizes information about the past in order to describe, compare, and/or explain historical phenomena', and note that students are engaged in historical reasoning whenever they ask 'historical questions, contextualize, make use of substantive and metaconcepts of history, and support proposed claims with arguments based on evidence from sources that give information about the past'. The Historical Thinking Project (2017) argues that historical perspective-taking 'means understanding the social, cultural, intellectual, and emotional settings that shaped people's lives and actions in the past'.

The well-rehearsed dichotomy of skills versus content that arose during these reforms has its legacy in debates over approaches to history teaching today. Paul Kiem's appeal for the place of direct teaching of historical knowledge in this volume (see Chapter 9) can be understood as a contribution to this ongoing debate. Here, Kiem draws upon the work of Counsell (2000) and Seixas and Morton (2012). Rightly I think, he draws attention to research arguing that without historical knowledge, historical skills make no sense. Of course, the reverse could also be true. At the turn of the millennium, Denis Shemilt (2000) proposed an approach that addressed history as 'a form of knowledge' that offers students the skills they need to evaluate knowledge claims, while simultaneously teaching a summary of 'the whole of human history' that should be revisited frequently throughout the student's history education in order to provide a context for what he believed they should otherwise learn thematically. Arguably, a version of these ideas is present in the Australian Curriculum: History, through its articulation of the historical skills and concepts students must learn and utilise, and the requirement to address specific topics against a larger historical overview of the period in question. While resolved to some extent in curriculum policy, the emphasis on skills versus content remains a problem for each teacher to sort out in their own practice.

Black armband versus white blindfold history

It would be hard to imagine a history teacher today who was not aware of the black armband versus white blindfold history debate—or what Stuart Macintyre and Anna Clark (2003) have called the History Wars. This debate has been largely a conflict between historians and politicians, rather than history teachers. It was initially triggered by Geoffrey Blainey (1993), a well-known Australian historian, during his delivery of the John Latham Memorial Lecture in 1993, in which he argued that Australian history had become too focused on past wrongs rather than the celebration of our achievements as a nation, and that this was creating a mournful view of the past. Blainey's 'black armband history' phrase was then picked up by Prime Minister John Howard, and political attention was increasingly directed towards the history curriculum, particularly in Queensland (Land 1994) and New South Wales (Clark 2003), where the term 'invasion' had entered the curriculum at the same time as Blainey's original address. In curricular terms, the initial debate centred on representations of Australia's colonial past (Clark 2004; Parkes 2007), and arguably was one of the key motivators of the movement towards a national curriculum, along with the apparent need for a singular national narrative to build civic cohesion as an antidote to the perceived growing 'terrorism' threat (Howard 2006). It was followed more recently by concerns over the place and representation of Gallipoli in the Australian curriculum (Parkes & Sharp 2014). In research I have conducted with colleagues at the University of Newcastle, as part of our Remembering Australia's Past (RAP) project, we found pre-service history teachers holding both 'black armband' views of the colonial past and 'three cheers' views of Gallipoli (Parkes 2016), which arguably reflects contemporary public discourse, and perhaps a politically acceptable view of both topics. Knowing your own position in this debate, interrogating your own assumptions and casting a critical eye on any histories you consume will remain important for history teachers. Certainly, this debate has raised public consciousness of the conflicting accounts that exist about our national past, and this has introduced controversy into Australian history in a way that can be mobilised in the history classroom, allowing teachers to emphasise the importance of carefully interrogating secondary accounts, just as they have done previously with primary sources.

As I have argued elsewhere, this debate over black armband versus white blindfold history has resonances in a problem articulated by Friedrich Nietzsche (1983). Nietzsche identified three forms of historical discourse: the *monumental*, which focuses upon the veneration of great events and deeds as models for the present; the *antiquarian*, which attempts to preserve the past as cultural heritage and a source of identity; and the *critical*, in which aspects of the past are interrogated and challenged from the standpoint of present wisdom. From Nietzsche's perspective, balance is necessary. If one ignores the monumental and antiquarian, then the individual is effectively denied resources from which to build a moral compass, and a sense of identity and orientation as a historical being. If one ignores the critical, then the individual may become trapped in the rules and traditions of the past, and be denied the right to seek change and transformation. For an understanding of how this plays out in the context of Australian history textbooks, see Parkes and Sharp (2014).

Integrated social studies versus disciplinary history

The debate over whether history should be taught as a discrete subject or as part of an integrated social studies curriculum has been a recurring question for curriculum designers, and history and social science educators. In the 1990s, most states in Australia moved to an integrated/interdisciplinary social studies curriculum called Studies of Society and Environment (SOSE). New South Wales was the only state at the time to maintain a discrete Years 7–10 History curriculum, adopting the integrated approach it called Human Society & Its Environment (HSIE) in primary schools only, largely as the result of the efforts and advocacy of the NSW History Teachers' Association (HTA). In the early 2000s, with the move to a national curriculum with a disciplinary focus, the debate resurfaced (Harris-Hart 2008; Henderson 2005). Typically, this debate swings between the focus on discrete disciplines versus the call for interdisciplinary teaching (Harris & Marsh 2007). Some scholars, such as Peter Seixas (1994) in Canada, have questioned whether one can really learn history in an interdisciplinary context. I would argue that missing from this debate is an important third alternative in the form of a metadisciplinary approach—much like one sees in the International Baccalaureate's mandatory Theory of Knowledge (TOK) course. In the TOK course, students must reflect on the nature of knowledge in each of the disciplines they are studying; how we know what we claim to know; what counts as evidence in different disciplines; and how we judge which models offer the best representation of a phenomenon. Such an approach would ideally involve students coming to a deep understanding of the epistemologies of the disciplines they study, and addressing transdisciplinary problems using a variety of disciplinary approaches, recognising that each approach has its own theories, values, rules, methodologies and so on, and that applying these produces different forms of knowledge. One example of such a curricular approach in history education in Australia is probably the NSW Extension History course, which asks students to consider, in the context of studying different historians and schools of historiography, questions about the aims and purposes of history, and the different ways in which history has been constructed and recorded over time. There is a growing body of literature that supports this approach—especially in the education of pre-service history teachers; it is especially important in the context of postmodern culture, where multiple narratives thrive, and sometimes it is difficult to figure out what information to trust. Historiography generally is understood to refer to the study of the writings of historians, including the different traditions of historical scholarship, such as empiricist, feminist, Marxist and postmodern.

THE POSTMODERN CHALLENGE

As Anna Clark notes in Chapter 4 of this book, the millennium appeared to be a catalyst for all sorts of collective anxiety, whether in relation to the Y2K 'millennium bug' or what she describes as the 'history bug' (a concern for the public's lack of historical knowledge of important Australian people and events). This political and media-driven concern over historical knowledge mirrored an academic anxiety in the second half of the twentieth century that Jean-François Lyotard (1984: 27) described as an 'incredulity towards metanarratives', and that would become widely known as the postmodern 'crisis of representation'. Metanarratives are sometimes also known as grand narratives or master narratives. They refer to any theory (or storyline) that tries to give a total or comprehensive account of the nature of the world, human history, human experience, or social and cultural conditions. Metanarratives tend to be presented as all-encompassing accounts, and thus are inherently ahistorical, as they fail to recognise their own historical origins. 'Metanarratives' was a term originally employed to explain the nature of knowledge in the late twentieth century.

Lyotard and other writers who followed (e.g. Fallace 2012; Mathis 2015; Parkes 2009; Yilmaz 2007) understood the postmodern moment as ushering in a legitimation crisis, where all knowledge claims in the social sciences and humanities were now being contested. This was at least partly a legacy of colonialism and its collapse, as the narratives of the coloniser were interrupted by the rival narratives of those they had colonised, and there was an increasing political tension to recognise such narratives as equally legitimate representations of the past (Young 1990). This meant that history (together with historical narrative) was not immune from this crisis. The early 1970s had seen Hayden White (1973) argue that history was a literary artefact following Roland Barthes's (1967: 120–3) declaration that history produced its 'reality effect' (its claim to represent the real world) through a series of rhetorical manoeuvres (rather than being a simple mirror of the world). Together with Louis Mink, these authors would argue for a position that has become known as 'narrative impositionalism'—that is, an argument that the past only becomes 'history' through its narrativisation, and that the act of constructing a narrative imposes an order on the past (Holton 1994). Perhaps the most useful work in this area is that of historical theorist Frank Ankersmit (2001), who argues that a historical narrative is an explanatory account that always exceeds the sum of its referential statements. In the words of my introductory paragraph, and at the risk of over-simplifying Ankersmit, this means that a historical narrative is an opinion that always exceeds the evidence upon which it draws.

Understandably, many historians were unhappy with this representation of the narrative products of the history discipline as a form of fictive discourse. Unsurprisingly, postmodern theory was quickly accused of proliferating revisionist histories, fostering relativism and generating a fertile ground for historical denial (Lipstadt 1994). Revisionist histories are typically new interpretations of the past that present a revised picture from the account that is commonly given. For a critique of revisionist histories, as provided in the context of the rejection of postmodernism, see Windschuttle (1996); see Evans (1997) for a critique of relativism in history. Critics of relativism see it as the idea that all knowledge (including moral values) is socially or historically constructed, and thus leaves no grounds for deciding what to believe. A more positive view of relativism suggests that we should respect all knowledge as constructed, and thus as open to debate.

Historians argued that it represents an attack on historical reason (Appleby, Hunt & Jacob 1994), and a direct assault on the epistemological foundations of history as a discipline (MacRaild & Taylor 2004) that is wilfully obscurant and politically paralysing (Roth 1995) and has little to do with what professional historians actually *do* when they are writing histories (McCullagh 2004). They were greatly concerned that if postmodernism were taken seriously, then people would be left in the position of being unable to determine the truth or trustworthiness of the historical narratives they encountered. It was in the context of this concern over the problem of postmodernism and its threat to history that Peter Seixas (2000) considered the question of postmodernism in the context of history education in what would become one of his most influential essays, 'Schweigen! Die kinder! Or does postmodern history have a place in the schools?' (see Elmersjö, Clark & Vinterek 2017).

A FRAMEWORK FOR THINKING ABOUT APPROACHES TO TEACHING HISTORY

In 'Schweigen! Die kinder!', Seixas (2000) outlines three approaches to history education: *collective memory, disciplinary* and *postmodern*. This section explores these three approaches as a prelude to reworking this framework to add a fourth approach.

Seixas's three approaches to history teaching

Seixas (2000: 21–3) describes the *collective memory* approach as one in which the teacher seeks to teach the best story about the past that we have available. This is not surprising, because whenever teachers go to professional development with historians, what they tend to get taught is precisely the best story the historian has available. The same historian attending a history conference will tend to explain all the pitfalls of the available evidence, or the specific problems of interpretation they have faced, but when they offer professional development for teachers, Seixas notes that they omit discussing these problems in favour of presenting teachers with 'historical knowledge' (Seixas 1999). Seixas's collective memory approach to history teaching can be related to what Keith Jenkins and Alan Munslow (2004) term the 'reconstructionist' approach, or the belief that the historian's job is to relate the past as it was. Those very few historians who still adopt such an approach would undoubtedly believe they were using an objective methodology that results in a truthful interpretation of the sources that can be written up in the form of an impartial or unbiased thesis. Seixas suggests that, at its best, the collective memory approach promises social cohesion, common social purpose and shared identity. At its worst, this approach becomes doctrinaire and nostalgic, and focuses on the rote memorisation of names and dates.

For Seixas (2000: 24–6), there is a second approach to history teaching, which he describes as the *disciplinary* approach (or history as a way of knowing). This approach involves students in historical investigation using historical method, and learning the discipline-specific criteria for what constitutes a plausible account. Students are encouraged to actively engage in building historical knowledge. It aims to encourage the adoption of historical distance, so that historical claims and the accounts of others may be evaluated carefully. According to Phillips (2015), 'historical distance' is essential to historical thought. It is generally understood as a metaphor for taking a critical perspective on the past that recognises that human beings have understood their worlds differently in different times and places (see also Den Hollander, Paul & Peters 2011).

In this approach, the goal is to reach warranted conclusions about which interpretations best fit the evidence, extracted from an interrogation of available sources that should include the assessments of other historians. This approach reflects what Jenkins and Munslow (2004: 81) call the 'constructionist' epistemology. Constructionist historians—those who perceive the work of the historian to be an interpreter of the past—tend to study the actions of people as members of social groups, and may use a range of concepts and theories such as race, class, gender, ethnicity, imperialism, colonialism and nationalism to make sense of 'the past'. They recognise the positioned nature of historical accounts, but seek to determine the most plausible account given the weighing up of the evidence.

The final orientation outlined by Seixas (2000: 26–31) is described as the *postmodern* approach. This approach recognises the narrativity and textuality of sources, the positionality of historians, and is suspicious of narratives of progress. It resists adjudicating between rival historical accounts, and aims instead to reveal to students how power is always implicated in the construction of differing historical accounts. This approach corresponds with what Jenkins and Munslow (2004: 12) call the 'deconstructionist' epistemology. Deconstruction is used by Jenkins and Munslow as a general term for the postmodernist viewpoint that all knowledge is constructed and that there is a separation between language and reality; or, metaphorically speaking, between the menu and the meal, or in the context of historical work, between history (the historical account, text, or narrative) and the past (what actually happened). Deconstructionists reject that the past can easily be represented, and argue that there can be no clear distinction between fact and fiction in historical writing.

Developing a framework for understanding history teaching

While I found Seixas's (2000) framework useful for thinking about history teaching, his description of the collective memory and disciplinary approaches cast them both as seeking a single best story, and I felt that his depiction of the postmodern-equated acceptance of multiple accounts of the same event as uncritical relativism. It seemed to me that this denied the possibility of a critical pluralism (see option 4 below) that would simultaneously allow for the existence of multiple conflicting accounts—each of which may be reasonable given the methodology used to produce it—and allow for assessment of the plausibility of any specific account. This brought me to an alternative way of understanding the various approaches one might take to history teaching that I outline in Figure 6.1.

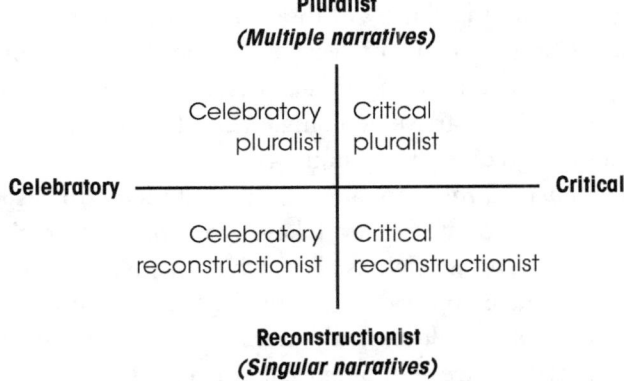

Figure 6.1 Alternative approaches to teaching history

I will start by suggesting we divide approaches to history teaching based on their relative emphasis, or aim to achieve singular versus multiple accounts of the same past. This produces the vertical axis on the diagram on p. 81, and can be understood as a split between a reconstructionist desire for arriving at a single accurate representation of the past, and a pluralist desire for the recognition of multiple competing accounts of the past. The horizontal axis on the diagram is formed by considering whether the pedagogue approaches the narrative/s they present from a celebratory stance or critical perspective. This leads logically to four possibilities for history pedagogy that are described below.

1   The *celebratory reconstructionist* shares with their students the story of the past as it is depicted in dominant discourses, either of the society in which they are teaching or their own social group. Their approach blurs the line between history and public memory, and is what Seixas describes as the collective memory approach to history teaching. The story of the past they offer reflects dominant narrative templates of the mnemonic community of which they are a member (Wertsch 2008), and their approach to the study of the past constructs history teaching and learning as an act of remembrance and commemoration. Wertsch's notion of a 'mnemonic community' means a group that has a shared memory of the past, based on a shared culture and experience.
2   The *critical reconstructionist* assists their students in coming to a defensible account of the past, based on the weighing up of evidence. This is the disciplinary approach in Seixas's model, where the emphasis is on promoting historical inquiry and the explicit teaching and learning of historical thinking skills. On the contemporary scene, the historical investigations students undertake may be situated within a larger chronological narrative frame that assists them to make sense of them. The desire is still to arrive at a single best story of the past, but it is achieved through disciplined inquiry.
3   The *celebratory pluralist* encourages their students to respect every account they encounter. They take a position that might best be described as 'cultural relativism', in which a politically correct and culturally sensitive approach is adopted when examining the historical narratives of non-dominant cultural groups. While this approach encourages acceptance of difference, it also leads to the kind of relativism that potentially leaves students unable to adjudicate between rival

accounts. This closely resembles the postmodern approach described by Seixas (2000).
4 The *critical pluralist* recognises that multiple accounts of the past are inevitable, given that every historian is themselves a historical being and the product of a specific historical culture (Gadamer 1994; Koselleck 2004). It is what might be described as a historicist position (Berger 2001), which historically has been associated with the German history and hermeneutic traditions, and locates individuals in their historical context in order to understand their views and actions. By definition, a historicist position is one in which significance is attributed to the historical period as a shaping force on human thought and action.

There are different forms of historicism. Some are deterministic, such as Marxism, where all of human history is thought to work according to particular universal laws. Others are more relativistic, rejecting any idea of an unchanging human nature or universal perspective that exists outside of a particular time and space. Berger (2001) argues that historism should be distinguished from historicism, most obviously in Marxist philosophy, where it is the tendency to interpret history as being guided by universal laws, and embracing a particular teleology (optimum end-point). Historicists such as Droysen and Dilthey categorically reject the teleology of historicism in favour of understanding every historical situation as unique (Berger 2001); the critical pluralist realises that each account of the past was produced using specific methodologies that enshrine specific values, rules of evidence and so on, and that can be examined as more or less plausible based on an evaluation of the (formal or naïve) methodologies that produced them and, in the case of academic histories, how well these methodologies were used. This requires a metadisciplinary approach, in which understanding historiography is just as important as historical knowledge and historical skills. It is the approach that is missing from Seixas's model.

Of course, the above is a logical typology, rather than an empirical model. It is offered here as a framework for reflecting on your own practice. Differentiating pluralism into celebratory and critical varieties overcomes a limitation in the model articulated by Seixas (2000), which depicts the acceptance of multiple narratives as inherently relativist—that is, as leaving a student unable to adjudicate between rival histories, and thus open to the influence of fake news or historical denial. In the model depicted above, recognition that multiple narratives are inevitable and an empirical fact does not prevent the student historian or the history teacher from critically interrogating rival narratives of the same event. There are important questions that this model might also raise. As my Swiss colleague Christian Mathis suggested to me during a recent Australian sabbatical, a good teacher should be able to tell a historical narrative in all four modes depicted in this model. This makes obvious to students the core of each stance and its limits. This may, of course, be an inherently critical pluralist position (or what we might call a 'philosophical hermeneutic' position), in which historical knowledge is itself historicised (Koselleck 2004; Mathis 2015, 2016; Parkes 2014). It does raise, as Mathis has suggested, the question of whether it is possible to depict an event such as the Holocaust in some modes rather than others—a question that was also levelled at Hayden White (1997), who raises the question of whether it is possible to depict an event such as the Holocaust in anything other than a tragic mode. See also my discussion of the same issue, with reference to White's argument, in Parkes (2013).

CONCLUSION

As a newly qualified history teacher, you will have to determine where you stand on a range of issues associated with the teaching and learning of history. Will you emphasise historical skills or historical knowledge in your teaching about the past? Will the historical narratives you introduce to your students reflect a rigorous examination of 'black armband' and 'white blindfold' histories, or will they reflect dominant narrative templates? What sorts of curriculum structures will you want to teach within: disciplinary, interdisciplinary or transdisciplinary, or metadisciplinary? Will your approach to history teaching reflect an emphasis on a single best story of the past, or embrace narrative diversity? Will the stories you share in the history classroom reflect a celebratory or critical position? One thing is certain: your answers to these questions are likely to reflect the historical time in which you are teaching and, like all historical phenomena, are likely to change over time. Hopefully, on your journey as a history teacher, the frameworks presented in this chapter can be carried along as a welcome navigational guide.

REFERENCES

Ankersmit, F.R. 2001, *Historical Representation*, Stanford, CA: Stanford University Press.

Appleby, J., Hunt, L. & Jacob, M. 1994, *Telling the Truth About History*, New York: W.W. Norton.

Barthes, R. 1997 [1967], 'The discourse of history', In K. Jenkins (ed.), *The Postmodern History Reader*, London: Routledge, pp. 120–3.

Berger, S. 2001, 'Stefan Berger responds to Ulrich Muhlack', *Bulletin of the German Historical Institute London*, vol. 23, no. 1, pp. 21–33.

Blainey, G. 1993, 'There is a rival view, which I call the "black armband" view: The John Latham Memorial Lecture', in S. Warhaft (ed.), *Well May We Say . . . The Speeches That Made Australia*, Melbourne: Schwartz, pp. 267–78.

Clark, A. 2003, 'What do they teach our children?', in S. Macintyre & A. Clark (eds), *The History Wars*, Melbourne: Melbourne University Press, pp. 171–90.

—— 2004, *Teaching the Nation: Politics and Pedagogy in Australian History*, Melbourne: Melbourne University Press.

Counsell, C. 2000, 'Historical knowledge and historical skills: A distracting dichotomy', in J. Arthur & R. Phillips (eds), *Issues in History Teaching*, London: Routledge, pp. 52–71.

Den Hollander, J., Paul, H. & Peters, R. 2011, 'Introduction: The metaphor of historical distance', *History and Theory*, vol. 50, pp. 1–10.

Elmersjö, H.Å., Clark, A. & Vinterek, M. (eds) 2017, *International Perspectives on Teaching Rival Histories: Pedagogical Responses to Contested Narratives and the History Wars*, London: Palgrave Macmillan.

Evans, R.J. 1997, *In Defence of History*, London: Granta Books.

Fallace, T.D. 2012, 'Once more unto the breach: Trying to get pre-service teachers to link historiographical knowledge to pedagogy', *Theory & Research in Social Education*, vol. 35, no. 3, pp. 427–46.

Gadamer, H.-G. 1994 [1975], *Truth and Method*, 2nd ed., J. Weinsheimer & D.G. Marshall trans., New York: Continuum.

Harris, C. & Marsh, C. 2007, 'SOSE curriculum structures: Where to now?', paper presented at the Biennial Conference of the Australian Curriculum Studies Association (ACSA), Melbourne.

Harris-Hart, C. 2008, 'History versus SOSE: Is that the question?' *Curriculum Perspectives*, vol. 28, no. 1, pp. 55–6.

Henderson, D. 2005, 'What is education for? Situating history, cultural understandings and studies of society and environment against neo-conservative critiques of curriculum reform', *Australian Journal of Education*, vol. 49, no. 3, pp. 306–19.

Historical Thinking Project 2017, 'Historical perspectives', <http://historicalthinking.ca/historical-perspectives>, accessed 20 August 2018.

Holton, R. 1994, *Jarring Witnesses: Modern Fiction and the Representation of History*, Hemel Hempstead: Harvester Wheatsheaf.

Howard, J. 2006, 'Unity vital in battle against terrorism', *The Sydney Morning Herald*, 26 January.

Jenkins, K. 1991, *Re-thinking History*, London: Routledge.

Jenkins, K. & Munslow, A. (eds) 2004, *The Nature of History Reader*, London: Routledge.

Koselleck, R. 2004 [1979], *Futures Past: On the Semantics of Historical Time*, K. Tribe trans., New York: Columbia University Press.

Land, R. 1994, *Invasion and After: A Case Study in Curriculum Politics*, Brisbane: Griffith University.

Lipstadt, D.E. 1994, *Denying the Holocaust: The Growing Assault on Memory and Truth*, New York: Plume.

Lyotard, J.-F. 1979, *The Postmodern Condition: A Report on Knowledge*, G. Bennington & B. Massumi trans., Minneapolis, MN: University of Minnesota Press.

—— 1984, *The Postmodern Condition: A Report on Knowledge*, Manchester: Manchester University Press.

Macintyre, S. & Clark, A. 2003, *The History Wars*, Melbourne: Melbourne University Press.

MacRaild, D.M. & Taylor, A. 2004, *Social Theory and Social History*, London: Palgrave Macmillan.

Mathis, C. 2015, *'Irgendwie ist doch da mal jemand geköpft worden'—Didaktische Rekonstruktion der Französischen Revolution und der historischen Kategorie Wandel*, Baltmannsweiler: Schneider-Verlag Hohengehren.

—— 2016, '"The revolution is not over yet". German-speaking ninth graders' conceptions of the French Revolution', *International Journal of Historical Learning, Teaching and Research*, vol. 14, no. 1, pp. 81–92.

McCullagh, C.B. 2004, *The Logic of History: Putting Postmodernism in Perspective*, London: Routledge.

Nietzsche, F. 1983 [1874], 'On the uses and disadvantages of history for life', R.J. Hollingdale trans., in D. Breazeale (ed.), *Untimely Meditations*, Cambridge: Cambridge University Press, pp. 57–123.

Parkes, R.J. 2007, 'Reading history curriculum as postcolonial text: Towards a curricular response to the history wars in Australia and beyond', *Curriculum Inquiry*, vol. 37, no. 4, pp. 383–400.

—— 2009, 'Teaching history as historiography: Engaging narrative diversity in the curriculum', *International Journal of Historical Learning, Teaching and Research*, vol. 8, no. 2, pp. 118–32.

—— 2013, 'Postmodernism, historical denial, and history education: What Frank Ankersmit can offer to history didactics', *Nordidactica: Journal of Humanities and Social Science Education*, no. 2, pp. 20–37.

—— 2014, 'No outside history: Reconsidering postmodernism', *Agora*, vol. 49, no. 3, pp. 4–10.

—— 2016, 'Black or white? Reconciliation on Australia's colonial past', *Public History Weekly*, vol. 4, no. 16, n.p.

Parkes, R.J. & Donnelly, D. 2014, 'Changing conceptions of historical thinking in history education: An Australian case study', *Revista Tempo e Argumento, Florianópolis*, vol. 6, no. 11, pp. 113–36.

Parkes, R.J. & Muldoon, N. 2010, 'The tutorial as cognitive apprenticeship: Developing discipline-based thinking', In R.H. Cantwell & J. Scevak (eds), *An Academic Life: A Handbook for New Academics*, Melbourne: ACER Press, pp. 55–64.

Parkes, R.J. & Sharp, H. 2014, 'Nietzschean perspectives on representations of national history in Australian school textbooks: What should we do with Gallipoli?' *ENSAYOS: Revisita de la Facultad de Educación de Albacete*, vol. 29, no. 1, pp. 159–81.

Phillips, M.S. 2015, *On Historical Distance*, London: Yale University Press.

Roth, M.S. 1995, *The Ironist's Cage: Memory, Trauma, and the Construction of History*, New York: Columbia University Press.

Seixas, P. 1994, 'A discipline adrift in an "integrated" curriculum: History in British Columbia schools', *Canadian Journal of Education*, vol. 19, no. 1, pp. 99–107.

—— 1999, 'Beyond "content" and "pedagogy": In search of a way to talk about history education', *Journal of Curriculum Studies*, vol. 31, no. 3, pp. 317–37.

—— 2000, 'Schweigen! Die kinder! Or does postmodern history have a place in the schools?', in P.N. Stearns, P. Seixas & S. Wineburg (eds), *Knowing, Teaching, and Learning History: National and International Perspectives*, New York: New York University Press, pp. 19–37.

Seixas, P. & Morton, T. 2012, *The Big Six Historical Thinking Concepts*. Toronto: Nelson.

Shemilt, D. 2000, 'The caliph's coin: The currency of narrative frameworks in history teaching', in P.N. Stearns, P. Seixas & S. Wineburg (eds), *Knowing, Teaching and Learning History: National and International Perspectives*, New York: New York University Press, pp. 83–101.

Taylor, T. 2008, 'National curriculum, History and SOSE—an evidence-based perspective', *Teaching History*, June, pp. 52–4.

van Drie, J. & van Boxtel, C. 2008, 'Historical reasoning: Towards a framework for analyzing students' reasoning about the past', *Educational Psychology Review*, vol. 20, no. 2, pp. 87–110.

Wertsch, J.V. 2008, 'Collective memory and narrative templates', *Social Research: An International Quarterly*, vol. 75, no. 1, pp. 133–56.

White, H. 1973, *Metahistory*, Baltimore, MD: Johns Hopkins University Press.

—— 1997, 'Historical emplotment and the problem of truth', in K. Jenkins (ed.), *The Postmodern History Reader*, London: Routledge, pp. 392–6.

Windschuttle, K. 1996, *The Killing of History: How Literary Critics and Social Theorists are Murdering Our Past*, New York: The Free Press.

Yilmaz, K. 2007, 'Introducing the "linguistic turn" to history education', *International Education Journal*, vol. 8, no. 1, pp. 270–8.

Young, R.J.C. 1990, *White Mythologies: Writing History and the West*, London: Routledge.

CHAPTER 7
Teaching empathy and the critical examination of historical evidence

Tyson Retz

We are used to hearing about empathy. Barack Obama declared before and during his presidency that America's federal deficit was less of a problem than its 'empathy deficit'. His message to graduating students in commencement speeches across the country (2006): 'Cultivate empathy—the world doesn't just revolve around you.' He may well have told them: 'Study history—the world doesn't just revolve around you.' An education in history has long been seen to broaden one's horizons; for the past several decades, empathy has been the method for entering into a past world of human meaning and experience different from one's own.

Empathy entered history teaching phraseology in the early 1970s on the basis of the belief that students must avoid what a seminal social historian had called 'the enormous condescension of posterity'. It had an ethical purpose. Students were not to assume that their station in the present day afforded them a loftier vantage point from which to judge the beliefs that people held in the past and the actions they took. By 'putting themselves in the shoes' of the people who lived in the past, students could see that, just as in their own lives, the beliefs that people held in the past and the actions they took were grounded in the specific context of their time and place. Judged from our modern-day standpoint, these beliefs and actions could appear to be the work of simpletons; judged from the past context of an earlier generation's experience, history could present itself less as a catalogue of foolish behaviour and more as a humanly study of past peoples who acted within a context of possibilities and limitations specific to their time and place.

From the very beginning, this humanistic endeavour to have students avoid holding the past in contempt was paired alongside a most fundamental principle of historical method: the critical examination of historical evidence. Peter Lee (1983) announced that empathy was a 'cognitive act' without which historians had no hope of using historical evidence in a way that explained why people acted the ways they did. It rose in the esteem of history educators who believed that empathy defined or even constituted historical method. Empathy penetrated to the distinct context of the actions that historians, in their study of historical sources, could understand in the light of that context.

When we speak of empathy in the everyday sense, we are generally referring to an *emotional* capacity to engage directly with another person's experience while suspending our own thoughts and feelings momentarily. Thus it is no small wonder, given its basis in feeling and emotion, that empathy has met resistance when taken as a central component of historical teaching and learning. Historians have long acknowledged that history's disciplinary boundaries are blurry, but they are largely united in their belief that it has a stout methodological identity rooted in the critical examination of historical evidence. What place could empathy have in raising the young to this disciplinary standard?

The view held among history educators was largely removed from what academic historians were saying about the historical craft. Important books written at a time when university history departments were undergoing substantial expansion barely raised the topic. E.H. Carr (1961) recognised that historical facts appear differently depending on the angle from which they are approached, but this in no way entails that the historian is obliged to establish a kind of contact to the persons attached to the facts. G.R. Elton (1967) saw no point in merely 'hearing' what people said in the past; historians must ask questions that reveal the hidden meanings contained in historical texts. George Kitson Clark (1967) warned against the temptation to explain the past through general categories and suggested that nominalism—the doctrine that no universal or abstract categories exist, only individuals—provided a healthy dissolvent that assisted historians to break up the past into its constituent parts.

Empathy's educational architects knew that they were importing into the classroom a term that carried a wider variety of meanings than the one they were trying to give it. They considered such alternatives as 'rational understanding', 'perspective-taking' and plain 'understanding', but proceeded with 'empathy', confident that, with work, history teachers would appreciate that they were being asked to cultivate an enriched understanding of historical context, in order to more effectively bring past and present into dialogue instead of the present serving as a soapbox to talk down on the past. Such were the good intentions behind empathy's introduction to historical teaching and learning. Given how rooted they were in an understanding of historical context, the surprise is that the precise nature of this historical context has remained unspecified.

What is a historical context? Does explaining why people acted the ways they did involve grasping the beliefs, values and goals that they held? Or do these beliefs, values and goals themselves belong to a specific historical context? Do they arise from particular historical conditions that history students would do better to identify and describe as the basis for their explanations of past behaviour? The purpose of this chapter is to show how a far richer pasture for historical explanation unfolds when the context to be understood is regarded as that in which it was *possible* for past agents to hold their beliefs as true and to act upon them accordingly.

THE NEED FOR EMPATHY

It is a curious fact that so much research in history education is conducted with little concern for the history of the concepts it uses. There have been few cases of scholars applying philosophical argument in the history of ideas to problems in historical teaching and learning. Our efforts to specify the precise nature of the historical context that empathetic inquiry should attempt to identify and describe is one instance where a historical approach is particularly beneficial, for the history of the concept is full of the tensions and debates that provide the material for a workable solution.

The first point is that empathy's emergence in school history came about as the result of a large-scale shift in the structure of the English educational landscape. The so-called comprehensive revolution had by the late 1960s brought students of mixed academic ability under the one roof, and a subject that a predominantly Piagetian research agenda had characterised as best suited to the more academically gifted faced the challenge of reforming itself in this new, more egalitarian environment.

Piaget's 'ages and stages' model gave way to an educational psychology and philosophy that claimed any school subject could be taught in a manner true to its principles, so long as that subject was broken down into its most fundamental elements—particularly influential were Bruner (1960) and Hirst (1965). The epistemology or forms of knowledge of the discipline from which a school subject derived were translated into its pedagogy. Educationists embarked on a process of *disciplinary distillation* to isolate the concepts through which learning in its corresponding school subject could be publicly registered and tested. This is the historical origin of present-day concept-based approaches to teaching and learning—in history, the second-order, procedural or historical thinking concepts that fill teacher-training programs, curricular documents and textbooks.

This need to specify the conceptual structure of the school history subject leads to the second historical point: texts in the philosophy of history offered themselves to educationists as resources for articulating the concepts that affirmed history's status as a distinct form of knowledge. Empathy was founded on R.G. Collingwood's re-enactment doctrine that 'all history is the history of thought'. Collingwood (1889–1943) was an Oxford historian, philosopher and archaeologist who liked his intellectual influences to come from a different time and place. By placing thought at the centre of history, he was rebelling against his realist 'scissors-and-paste' colleagues who produced histories by assembling sources in a manner that told stories of past ages, but made no attempt to penetrate the mindsets of those ages. In re-enactment, Collingwood proposed that by following in one's own mind the chains of reasoning behind past people's actions, those mindsets were brought into the present day as objects for self-knowledge, and potentially for dealing with present-day problems. For reasons coeval with a methodological turf war between the human and natural sciences, this idea was refurbished by analytical philosophers of history seeking to establish the discipline as a humanistic enterprise. Movements in the philosophy of history affected directions taken in school history (Retz 2016).

To the new generation of history educationists working to establish history's conceptual structure, these texts by analytical philosophers of history served to highlight that historians did something that history students traditionally had not done: they penetrated behind appearances and achieved insight into historical situations; they revived, re-enacted, rethought and re-experienced the hopes, fears, plans, desires, views and intentions of those they sought to understand. Collingwood's seemingly empathetic theory of re-enactment was laid as the cornerstone of a structure of historical inquiry designed to have students achieve this task.

The educational writings on empathy give us little further direction on where this battery of metaphors is supposed to take us. They have stated all along that empathy enriches our understandings of historical context, and from that basis we are in a position to explain why people acted the ways they did. We shall have to delve further into the historical methodology known as *contextualism*. A prior task is to allay fears that this focus on historical context removes the present from the picture and reduces history's capacity to be a force for social good. It will then be possible to explain how it is only by allowing ourselves to be conducted by the past and its meanings that we are able to genuinely learn from the past while using it as a mirror for self-knowledge and present-day understanding.

BETWEEN PAST AND PRESENT

The disciplinary conception of empathy has been regarded by some as limiting the concept's potential to contribute to a fuller historical experience in history classrooms. Keith Barton and Linda Levstik (2004) contend that simply understanding people who lived in the past is insufficient, and maintain that if studying history is to improve the health of our pluralist democracies, empathy must inspire us to care about them and their perspectives. Jason Endacott (2010) argues that we must first experience 'affective empathetic arousal' of the past people under investigation. The question for him is less about how empathy can help us to understand the past than about how it can engage students with the past. Christopher Blake (1998) takes issue with history claiming a false distinctiveness of inquiry by attaching its name to a concept (historical empathy), the fluid and cross-functional nature of which surpasses the limits that any one academic tribe can circumscribe.

Such criticisms have in common the view that empathy's disciplinary formulation as a way of investigating the past cheats the concept of a role in advancing the social and political aims of contemporary educational programs. They are well intentioned but rest on a false assumption that concentrating our attention on the past and its forms of meaning must come at the expense of illuminating aspects of the present. The question that empathy raises is not whether past or present should receive more or less attention, but rather how our present-day questions, concerns and frames of reference blend with the past in historical investigation. Empathy calls on history students to perform a balancing act. The problem they navigate is hermeneutical, concerned with where we identify the *location of human meaning* and the purposes for which we convey it into the present.

Hermes was the mythological Greek deity who was the 'messenger of the Gods'. Hermeneutics arose as a theory of interpretation concerned with the methods that exegetes apply to religious texts to fathom these divine messages. Nowadays it is an umbrella term encompassing the interpretation of written and non-written communication in the humanities, law, history and theology particularly. Three categories applied to its use in education can help us to measure where we sit on the empathetic spectrum: conservative, moderate and radical (Gallagher 1992).

A *conservative* hermeneutics considers meaning to belong unchangingly to historical texts. It is rather the texts' significance that varies as historians attribute to them different values. To understand the past in this sense is to reproduce its original meaning. To consider this meaning in relation to present-day forms of meaning is a matter of evaluation rather than understanding.

At the opposite end, a *radical* hermeneutics treats the past with suspicion and, from the outset, mistrusts the notion that its meaning could be conveyed to us here in the present. Whatever a past text meant in the past is irrelevant because that meaning has changed in its passage through time and different interpretive traditions. The past is looked upon as a repository of mostly false beliefs that provides us with material for conducting social critique. The task is not to understand the past but rather to juxtapose it against the present-day inequalities and injustices that we seek to remedy.

A *moderate* hermeneutics, as I have suggested elsewhere (Retz 2015), offers us the best framework for conceiving a variety of historical thinking able to negotiate the territory separating past and present. As with the conservative approach, there remains the ideal of reproducing the meaning attached to historical texts, but unlike the conservative approach, this reproductive endeavour takes place in full knowledge that the meaning derived from the past is determined by the questions and concerns that historians apply to their study of the past. The past is the source of the meaning, but our habits of mind dress the past in modern-day clothing. This refashioning in no way diminishes the integrity of historical knowledge; it is the fact that sustains and renews history, for every new generation breathes new life into the past by bringing to it the questions it deems important. We continue to produce new histories because we continue to ask different questions.

Sam Wineburg (2001) was alluding to this moderate hermeneutics when he characterised historical thinking as an 'unnatural act'. On the one hand, capturing the distinct meaning of the past seems to require a temporary suspension of our own conceptions. We must put aside the very conceptual *forestructure* that makes sense of our perceptions as we experience the world. On the other hand, capturing from the past its own distinct meaning would prove futile were we unable to both incorporate that content into what we already know, and express it through publicly inscribed language and concepts. As Wineburg (2001: 10) puts it, 'Trying to shed what we know in order to glimpse the "real" past is like trying to examine microbes with the naked eye: The instruments we abandon are the ones that enable us to see.'

A moderate hermeneutical approach does not dichotomise the problem—it does not ask whether we should study the past for its own sake or study it for the sake of changing the present; instead, it operates at the productive interface of past and present. It is with good reason that Wineburg (2001) points to the philosophy of Hans-Georg Gadamer as the best equipped to deal with this back-and-forth. A student of Heidegger and without doubt the most renowned hermeneutist of the twentieth century, Gadamer's intellectual inheritance presented him with two alternatives: he could work to uphold the tradition from which empathy emerged in the mid-nineteenth century as a psychological reconstruction of past thought, or he could borrow from Hegel the dialectical approach that looked upon understanding as a critical integration of past thought into one's own thought (Gadamer 1981: 40).

Through the concept of 'effective history', Gadamer pursued the latter course by arguing that there is no understanding of the past in the real sense, only understanding *through* the past. History has an effect or hold on us of which we remain mostly unaware. Its value is *contrastive* in the way that it stirs up and brings to the surface our tacitly held prejudices and assumptions when we approach it not with an air of mistrust, but rather with a readiness to learn from it. Only through a principle of charity that the past has something to teach us can history help us to understand ourselves.

This readiness to learn from the past is more than a moral disposition: it is a methodological commitment. In elaborating it further, Collingwood's philosophy that supplied empathy with its theoretical foundation in history education can be brought within the framework of Gadamer's integration of past and present.

THE PROBLEM WITH EMPATHY

Human beings have, of course, always empathised, but the noun itself only emerged in Germany in the 1870s (*Einfühlung*), and appeared in English nearly four decades later. The leaders of an 'empathy school' in German psychological aesthetics—thinkers concerned with theories of beauty—defined the term as a projection of human emotions onto an object of artistic appreciation, whereby the distinction between the self and the object breaks down, allowing the self to be 'in' the object (Guyer 2014). Wilhelm Dilthey, the first theorist of the human sciences (*Geisteswissenschaften*), worked broadly within this framework in elucidating his conception of historical understanding as reached through a 'vital connectedness' of what has been passed down to us in the historical world and the 'acquired psychic nexus' of our own reality within that world (2002: 234). The widely used concept of 'historical consciousness' in history education also has this at its foundation.

A new generation of phenomenologists found this conception unsatisfactory. Phenomenology is the study of the structure of consciousness as experienced from the first-person perspective. They argued that this state of being 'in' the object removed the possibility of the object standing up against the self as something in need of comprehension. Edmund Husserl (quoted in Makkreel 1996: 200) was unsure how empathy could extend knowledge, for in projecting the 'other' as a subject analogous to my own self, 'it does not produce something novel over against the self'. Gadamer (2004: 354–64) took a similar line in rejecting Dilthey's psychologistic conception of humane understanding. What could breaking down the distinction between past and present selves hold up against ourselves as something striking us as alien and in need of our comprehension? We sometimes hear that we are too deep *in* a situation to observe it for what it is and so act upon it critically with a view to making change. On the question of how humane understanding could expunge its psychologistic lineage, Gadamer found Collingwood the most instructive.

Both thinkers inveighed against their forebears for conceiving historical thinking as a kind of *retrieval* from the past, and for concluding that the challenge for historical thinking therefore consists in preventing present-day modes of thinking from intruding into this 'pure' act recovery. They agreed that historical understanding occurs by the past asserting its difference against the present. Collingwood did not propose in re-enactment a way of entering into a past frame of mind merely to understand it. The critical step comes afterwards when historians reconstitute that frame of mind in their own minds and at the same time objectify that very reconstitution—that is, they affirm its belonging to its past context while drawing it into the present-day context in rethinking it (Collingwood 1994: 441–2). The act of historians seeing this *contrast* between past and present is what allows the past to be held up to analysis and criticism; it involves an *untangling* of past and present ways of thinking, which is what gives us a fuller conception of mind and its possibilities for deliberate and purposive action in the present. This is the political and educational philosophy at the heart of the empathetic and re-enactment conceptions of historical understanding, although it is the re-enactment version that articulates it more clearly (Retz 2017).

THE CONTEXT OF HISTORICAL UNDERSTANDING

We have yet to specify the precise nature of the historical context that empathetic inquiry should attempt to identify and describe. Collingwood's logic of question and answer illuminated to Gadamer the highest principle of hermeneutics: the statements that historians study in a historical text should be understood as *answers to questions* that arose from a *problem-context* specific to the time and place in which that text was produced (Gadamer 1976: 11). The locution appears byzantine, but in fact invokes a principle we all recognise without difficulty: everything we think, believe and do has a background that is the source for explaining those thoughts, beliefs and actions. In history, it is not what people held in mind that in itself explains their actions, but rather the broader intellectual, social, economic and political conditions that allowed those beliefs to be held as true and acted upon accordingly.

Help with elucidating this contextualist approach, rooted in Collingwood's logic of question and answer, is available from the English intellectual historian Quentin Skinner (2001). Skinner's thesis is that the words historians study in a historical text must be treated as *actions* that contributed to or intervened in the preceding context in which that text was produced. For example, the student endeavouring to understand Machiavelli's political philosophy must do more than simply affirm that he believed force and fraud were indispensable to political success (Skinner 2014). Empathy's function in historical understanding has been conceived largely along these lines of affirming beliefs, and it is methodologically inadequate. Rather, the student must investigate the conditions that gave rise to this belief. Students must be given the contextual resources enabling them to know that Machiavelli launched his contention into a moral and political context that still held to Cicero's humanist account of the *virtus* that brings princely glory. Machiavelli reminded his readers of Cicero's claim, questioned its authority, satirised it, and thereby opposed and redefined a standard tenet of humanist political thought. His words are historically significant and worthy of our attention today because they redefined a political paradigm that gave rise to subsequent political ways of thinking.

An exercise in a common alternative to empathy, 'perspective-taking', brings this example home to classroom practice. It must be emphasised that in both concepts we are referring to the same activity. The Canadian Peter Seixas worked with empathy in laying the groundwork for his well-known historical thinking concepts until, on the sidelines of a conference in 1993, Peter Lee implored him to cease using the term, worried that his cross-Atlantic colleague might add a new chapter to its already scandalous biography (Retz 2018: 173–212).

Perspective-taking in Seixas's (1998: 312–13) formulation preserves the notion that students need to place themselves in the situations of historical agents if they are to have any hope of explaining why these agents acted the ways they did. More so than in the British research, this past situation is rightly conceived as a social context in which the texts produced are 'speech acts' that do things with words. This is the indispensable principle stretching back to Collingwood and Skinner's Cambridge school: historians should consider words as actions that aimed to redefine the context in which they were pronounced.

In practice, however, perspective-taking does not have students extend this far back. A textbook exercise asks students to explain why Canadian Prime Minister Lester B. Pearson was 'so rude so publicly' to Charles de Gaulle when he rebuked him on public radio during a state visit to Canada in 1967 (Seixas & Morton 2013: 145). The 'immediate context' for reconstructing Pearson's perspective is given as consisting of a speech that de Gaulle concluded the previous day in Montreal with the exclamation, *'Vivre le Québec libre!',* the rallying cry of Quebec separatists during a period of intense Quebec nationalism, which is offered as the 'context' for understanding Pearson's outrage.

The chain of reasoning by which students are to evaluate Pearson's admonishment of the French president is thus set as follows: there was a Quebec separatist movement; Pearson believed that Canada should remain united; de Gaulle threw fuel onto the separatist flame; therefore Pearson publicly rebuked him and de Gaulle cut short his visit.

In fact, the conditions that made possible this series of events never enter the inference. De Gaulle's speech should not be understood as the 'immediate context', but rather as the action that preceded and led Pearson to condemn de Gaulle on radio. De Gaulle's action was a breach of diplomatic protocol, but this in itself does not explain Pearson's response to it. To speak of contexts as actions that lead to other actions says nothing of the conditions underlying their relations. If the question driving the inquiry is to understand how Pearson could be impudent to de Gaulle, the context to be identified consists of the system of presuppositions upholding the belief that Canada should remain united. Without doubt, his action showed little regard for diplomatic politesse, but it is to be understood as the action that led to the subsequent action of de Gaulle leaving, not the context explaining his departure. The context that explains the chain of events lies further back in the presupposition held by twentieth-century statesman that they had a duty to safeguard the sovereignty of the territory over which they governed.

In undertaking this investigation of historical context—a phrase more accurately aimed at the objective empathy has tried to achieve—students might rightly ask why statesmen upheld this principle, and whether it has always been so. Should every people not have the right to national self-determination? And suddenly this study of a historical episode turns to questions relevant to the present-day world in which we live.

REFERENCES

Barton, K.C. & Levstik, L.S. 2004, *Teaching History for the Common Good*, Mahwah, NJ: Lawrence Erlbaum.
Blake, C. 1998, 'Historical empathy: A response to Foster and Yeager', *International Journal of Social Education*, vol. 13, no. 1, pp. 25–31.
Bruner, J.S. 1960, *The Process of Education*, Cambridge, MA: Harvard University Press.
Carr, E.H. 1961, *What is History?* London: Macmillan.
Clark, G.K. 1967, *The Critical Historian*, London: Heinemann.
Collingwood, R.G. 1994 [1946], *The Idea of History,* Jan van der Dussen ed., Oxford: Oxford University Press.

Dilthey, W. 2002 [1910], 'The understanding of other persons and their manifestations of life', R.A. Makkreel and W.H. Oman trans., in R.A. Makkreel & F. Rodi (eds), *Selected Works, Volume III: The Formation of the Historical World in the Human Sciences*, Princeton, NJ: Princeton University Press, pp. 205–35.

Elton, G.R. 1967, *The Practice of History*, Sydney: Sydney University Press.

Endacott, J.L. 2010, 'Reconsidering affective engagement in historical empathy', *Theory and Research in Social Education*, vol. 38, no. 1, pp. 6–47.

Gadamer, H.-G. 1976 [1966], 'The universality of the hermeneutical problem', in *Philosophical Hermeneutics*, D.E. Linge trans., Berkeley, CA: University of California Press, pp. 3–17.

—— 1981, 'The heritage of Hegel', in *Reason in the Age of Science*, F.D. Lawrence trans., Cambridge, MA: MIT Press, pp. 36–68.

—— 2004 [1960], *Truth and Method*, 2nd ed., J. Weinsheimer & D.G. Marshall trans., New York: Continuum, pp. 354–64.

Gallagher, S. 1992, *Hermeneutics and Education*, Albany, NY: State University of New York Press.

Guyer, P. 2014, *A History of Modern Aesthetics: Volume 2: The Nineteenth Century*, Cambridge: Cambridge University Press.

Hirst, P.H. 1965 'Liberal education and the nature of knowledge', in R.D. Archambault (ed.), *Philosophical Analysis and Education*, London: Routledge and Kegan Paul, pp. 113–38.

Lee, P. 1983, 'History teaching and philosophy of history', *History and Theory*, vol. 22, no. 4, pp. 19–49.

Makkreel, R.A. 1996, 'How is empathy related to understanding?' in T. Nenon & L. Embree (eds), *Issues in Husserl's Ideas II*, Dordrecht: Kluwer Academic, pp. 199–212.

Obama, B. 2006, 'Obama to graduates: Cultivate empathy: "The world doesn't just revolve around you"', Northwestern University Commencement Speech, 19 June, <http://www.northwestern.edu/newscenter/stories/2006/06/barack.html>, accessed 22 June 2018.

Retz, T. 2015, 'A moderate hermeneutical approach to empathy in history education', *Educational Philosophy and Theory*, vol. 47, no. 3, pp. 214–26.

—— 2016, 'At the interface: Academic history, school history and the philosophy of history', *Journal of Curriculum Studies*, vol. 48, no. 4, pp. 503–17.

—— 2017, 'Why re-enactment is not empathy, once and for all', *Journal of the Philosophy of History*, vol. 11, no. 4, pp. 606–23.

—— 2018, *Empathy and History: Historical Understanding in Re-enactment, Hermeneutics and Education*, New York and Oxford: Berghahn Books, pp. 173–212.

Seixas, P. 1998, 'Student teachers thinking historically', *Theory and Research in Social Education*, vol. 26, no. 3, pp. 310–41.

Seixas, P. & Morton, T. 2013, *The Big Six Historical Thinking Concepts*, Toronto: Nelson.

Skinner, Q. 2001, 'The rise of, challenge to and prospects for a Collingwoodian approach to the history of political thought', in D. Castiglione and I. Hampsher-Monk (eds), *The History of Political Thought in National Context*, Cambridge: Cambridge University Press, pp. 175–88.

—— 2014, 'Belief, truth and interpretation', Keynote Address, Intellectual History: Traditions and Perspectives conference, Ruhr Universität Bochum, 18 November.

Wineburg, S. 2001, *Historical Thinking and Other Unnatural Acts: Charting the Future of Teaching the Past*, Philadelphia, PA: Temple University Press.

CHAPTER 8
The nature of values and why they matter in the teaching and learning of history

Deborah Henderson

INTRODUCTION

Values were rarely discussed in Australian classrooms when I started teaching history in the late 1970s. I soon realised, however, that values were not only implicit in the textbooks my students used but that they also shaped the particular versions of the nation's past I was expected to teach. Indeed, my principal was adamant that students studying history at 'his' school should learn about the achievements of Empire and the benefits of colonisation. As an inexperienced teacher, I struggled to reconcile the history I had studied at university with the conservative assumptions in my school about the sort of history to teach, and how it should be taught.

The realisation that history education was 'drenched in politics' (Seixas 2012: xxi)—that particular values shaped curriculum documents, the views of those who interpreted them and the assumptions about the past my students brought to the classroom—was daunting. Fortunately, this sentiment was tempered by my postgraduate studies. It was reassuring to learn that history education was contested in many nations; it was also exciting to discover that history educators were advocating for a focus on disciplinary concepts and processes to disrupt transmissive, celebratory approaches to teaching the nation's past. An emphasis on exploring the ways in which young people understand history, and how they make sense of the disciplinary processes associated with it, was evident in much of the emerging scholarship on history education.

This chapter explores the nature of values and looks at why they matter in the teaching and learning of history in Australian classrooms. It argues that values are embedded in those primary sources that survive the past, and are implicit in the narratives historians construct about the past. Values also permeate the decisions history teachers make about how history is encountered in classrooms. It suggests that students can engage with different values in historical studies by investigating their origins and studying their impact on human affairs. My argument is that when teachers' practice focuses on developing their students' progression in historical thinking, students will acquire a vocabulary to analytically engage with those values embedded in conflicting accounts of the past. Addressing values in this way assists students to decide which values might guide them to act in ethical and morally just ways, as in their everyday lives young people need to understand situations, identify causes of change and continuity and place them in a long-term perspective. Young people also need to acknowledge the value perspectives of others, develop personal values, make judgements and reflect on their decisions.

WHAT ARE VALUES?

Values are fundamental to all forms of human activity, and can be defined in a number of ways. Rokeach (1973) suggests that values comprise enduring beliefs about what is important and desirable in our personal and social lives. Drawing from research in values education, Halstead and Taylor (2012: 169) define values as 'principles and fundamental convictions which act as general guides to behaviour, the standards by which particular actions are judged to be good or desirable'. Although values and attitudes relate to the affective domain, or the feeling component of human behaviour, they are not separate from the cognitive domain—or thinking. Some values are linked to deeply held beliefs about what is right or wrong, so if an individual values justice, they might consider it morally wrong when an injustice occurs. In this case, justice is a *moral value*. When an individual makes a value judgement, they evaluate something in terms of criteria associated with a particular value—for example, the criteria of protecting human rights might influence an individual's value judgement about whether a particular event can be considered historically significant if human rights are placed at risk.

An *ethic* is a principle that guides an individual's values, attitudes and practices. Ethics can be described as the link between the values an individual holds and the things an individual does; if an individual values justice, their guiding ethic might include a commitment to treating others in 'fair' ways. In their proposal for values clarification, Raths, Harmin and Simon (1996) claim that an individual can only be said to hold a value about something if that person is prepared to act on it and carry it out.

HOW ARE VALUES CONCEPTUALISED IN AUSTRALIAN EDUCATION?

The idea that young people will experience character development if they are inculcated with society's values through schooling is a longstanding assumption in educational thinking and practice (Henderson 2011). This view, together with a contrasting perspective, was noted in the international literature on values education in an Australian government-commissioned report, the *Values Education Study: Final Report* (Curriculum Corporation 2003). The report (2003: 175) distinguishes the two approaches:

> The first approach, commonly called character education, concentrates on the development of particular attributes or 'virtues'; and the second places emphasis on reasoning, problem-solving, and critical thinking ... the former values transmission and placed emphasis on shared or approved values, whereas the descriptive approach, by contrast, emphasises the ways of thinking and reasoning children need to acquire if they are to be morally educated.

Fortunately, much has changed since my first year of teaching history, as history education today is concerned with the second approach, whereby students identify values at work in past actions, events and situations and make value judgements about the fairness of past practices. In history classrooms, students can investigate the development of certain value positions and critically examine what happens when some values are challenged and new values emerge, and students can discuss and refine their own value positions. Values are also specifically identified in the *National Declaration on Educational Goals for Young Australians*, which underscores schools playing a vital role in 'promoting the intellectual, physical, social, emotional, moral, spiritual and aesthetic development and well-being of young Australians' (MCEETYA 2008: 4).

HOW ARE VALUES POSITIONED IN THE AUSTRALIAN CURRICULUM: HISTORY YEARS 7-10?

Values were identified as integral to thinking and reasoning about the past in the *National History Curriculum Framing Paper* (NCB 2008) and in a revised document, *The Shape of the Australian Curriculum* (NCB 2009), which informed the writing of the history curriculum. *The Shape of the Australian Curriculum* foregrounded historical understandings in terms of a set of concepts that are 'core components of historical understanding' (NCB 2009: 6). It drew on the work of history education theorists based in the United States, Canada and the United Kingdom, including Sam Wineburg (2001), Peter Seixas (2006) and Peter Lee (2006), who described the 'understandings' as organising ideas that 'give meaning and structure to our ideas of the discipline of history' (NCB 2009: 131).

Importantly, encountering values in terms of *ways of thinking and reasoning about past events* was encompassed in the concepts of contestation and contestability, identified as one of the eight components of historical understanding in the *National History Curriculum Framing Paper* (NCB 2008) and *The Shape of the Australian Curriculum* (NCB 2009). In the latter's elaboration of why dealing with alternative accounts of the past is significant, the draft states that, 'History is a form of knowledge that shapes popular sentiment and frequently enters into public debate. [Contestation and contestability] requires the ability to connect the past with the self and the present and appreciation of the rules that apply to professional and public debate over history' (NCB 2009: 5). In addition to contestation and contestability, the other understandings included concepts of evidence; continuity and change; cause and consequence; significance; historical perspectives; historical empathy and moral judgement—concepts that highlight the debatable nature of historical interpretation and explanation, and shape the nature of historical thinking. The eighth concept, problem-solving, was deleted from later versions of the history curriculum document. The historical concepts, together with 'historical knowledge' (NCB 2009: 6) and 'historical skills' (NCB 2009: 7), constitute the formulation of historical education in the Australian Curriculum.

In the most recent Version 8.3 of *The Australian Curriculum: History 7–10* (ACARA 2017), emphases on inquiry, interpretation, and engaging with and thinking about different values and perspectives are explicit:

> The study of history is based on evidence derived from remains of the past. It is interpretative by nature, promotes debate and encourages

thinking about human values, including present and future challenges. The process of historical inquiry develops transferable skills such as the ability to ask relevant questions; critically analyse and interpret sources; consider context; respect and explain different perspectives; develop and substantiate interpretations; and communicate effectively.

This wording suggests that the curriculum encourages teachers to go beyond the limitations of basic inquiry and to offer opportunities for students to probe the more challenging, often problematic, yet rewarding values-based characteristics of historical inquiry and of historical knowledge itself.

WHAT ARE THE CHALLENGES AND POSSIBILITIES OF TEACHING VALUES IN THE HISTORY CLASSROOM?

In history education, discourse is critical to any consideration of values as historical sources are imbued with the moral vocabulary of the period under investigation. Furthermore, when students work with primary and secondary sources, they draw from those current values and assumptions embedded in discourse to decide whether such sources can be considered as items of evidence in their investigation of the past; and they employ this vocabulary to express their conclusions. However, some history teachers are challenged by and uncomfortable about handling values issues and associated attitudes and beliefs in the history classroom, while others raise questions about whether students can be expected to arrive at judgements about the actions and practices of people who lived in the past. In the recent past, this might be less problematic. For example, the Soweto Student Uprising of 16 June 1976 in South Africa can be investigated, explained and judged according to moral criteria used today that are also relevant to those human rights concerns raised during the period of Apartheid. However, it could be argued that applying modern-day values may be invalid when an event or process under investigation is remote in time, place and culture.

Some history educators raise concerns that a focus on those values dilemmas, moral issues and lessons about the past whose legacies continue to influence us today could mitigate against informed decision-making about what occurred. Kinloch (2001) argues that a study of the Holocaust should be located within a *historical* rather than a moral framework. His view is that some history teachers in the United Kingdom have been so concerned with teaching the lessons of the Holocaust that they have neglected important historical questions about why and how the Holocaust occurred, warning that their students' outcomes might only be 'the most banal of moral conclusions' (Kinloch 2001: 104).

Nonetheless, such concerns about the place of values in history education assume that students will engage with values and arrive at a moral judgement in *uncritical ways*. This chapter contends that placing the focus on *analysing values* through the development of historical thinking provides a vocabulary for students to *critically engage* with values embedded in conflicting accounts of the past. According to Canadian-based history educator Peter Seixas (2009: 29):

> If the story is meaningful, then there is usually an ethical judgement involved; it would be hard to imagine a good history of aboriginal-white contact in the North, of the Holocaust, of slavery in the southern United States, or of Spanish conquistadors slaughtering the native people of the Americas, that did not take an ethical stand. We expect to learn something from the past that helps us in facing the ethical issues of today.

Furthermore, as interpretation lies at the heart of any decision-making concerning the value of historical endeavour, E.H. Carr's (1961) classic observation is worth noting. Carr (1961: 79) reminds us that 'historical facts... presuppose some measure of interpretation; and historical interpretations always involve moral judgements'. In a recent review of the literature, Gibson (2014) contends that it is now generally acknowledged that judgements about the past are unavoidable, and that they shape the questions that drive historical inquiry, the choice of language used by historians and the structure of historical narratives. As discussed, Version 8.3 of *The Australian Curriculum: History 7–10* (ACARA 2017) focuses on young people's interpretative engagement with the past via seven key concepts. This emphasis not only fosters students' capacities to *think about* conflicting accounts about the past by understanding the *value-laden nature of historical interpretation*; it also serves as a generative process through which young people can *actively engage with* those 'fundamental epistemological and ontological problems of history' (Seixas 2015: 559).

In examining some of the possibilities of including values in history education, I explore how teachers can engage students in historical thinking about historiography and conflicting accounts about the past. I then draw from three approaches to values education identified by the Australian Education Council (AEC 1994: 5). The AEC notes that values can influence what is selected for study; values can be the object of study; and certain values result from a study. These approaches can be adapted as useful guidelines for devising discipline-specific approaches to teaching values in the history classroom, and are explored with reference to questions about memorial obligation and cultural memory, decisions about what specific values should be taught, and the selection of pedagogical strategies to foster students' historical thinking. For clarity, each approach is discussed separately; in practice, however, these approaches are often interconnected.

Thinking about 'troubling questions' that rise 'to the fore' in historiography

While debates about what should be valued about a nation's past prompt 'troubling historical questions' to rise 'to the fore' (Curthoys & Docker 2006: 220), they present rich opportunities to foster students' historical thinking in the classroom as they engage with the value-laden nature of historical interpretation. In Australia, one such debate centres on different interpretations of the degree of violence on the frontiers of European settlement in Tasmania during the early nineteenth century, referred to as the History Wars. These disputes concern historical theory in terms of the nature of evidence, how historians engage with primary and secondary sources, how this is manifested in historical narratives about Australia's past and the ways in which it is valued and memorialised.

Historians such as Henry Reynolds (1982), among others, argue that the process of colonisation transformed the Australian landscape into a site of 'conflict', not 'settlement', and that conflict over possession of Aboriginal lands resulted in both 'war' and 'resistance'. It was also argued that 'frontier' conflict established the general pattern of relationships between Aboriginal and non-Aboriginal Australians, and that this history continued to impact on Aboriginal and Torres Strait Islander peoples (Attwood 2005). By contrast, Keith Windschuttle (2002) claimed such interpretations of the treatment of Aboriginal people on the frontier of white settlement amounted to fabrication, contending that academic historians writing about the frontier were politically inspired. Windschuttle (2002) also asserted that the work of 'frontier' historians was poorly researched and was not supported by evidence. Conservative commentators praised Windschuttle, while many historians contested his claims and methodology (Attwood 2005; Macintyre & Clark 2003; Manne 2003; see also Chapters 1, 2 and 6 in this book).

Students can investigate the History Wars and debates about representations of frontier encounters, and consider broader notions of history's role in recording the collective memory of Australia's past. They can critically interrogate assumptions that the history of settler nations such as Australia is about progress and success, and reflect on the manner in which national historical narratives serve a role in harnessing national pride. In sum, students can consider whether history should play its part in nation-building by *valuing* and telling a particular story that purports to encapsulate its heritage.

Values and the selection of topics for study: memorial obligation and cultural memory

Teachers need to be mindful of the role played by their own values in selecting particular topics and how they frame questions to guide historical inquiry in the classroom that relates to significant events linked to national identity. For example, questions about what is most valued in the nation's past arise in relation to contested views about memorial obligation and cultural memory. Cultural memory is a term that encapsulates the variety of memorial forms and the transformations of experience that all forms of remembrance entail (Nora 1996). Cultural memory focuses attention on the multiple ways in which images and stories of the past are constructed, communicated, shared and valued among members of a community, or a nation. Despite attempts to 'fix' the past by recounting a 'collective story' of nationhood during and after a significant event, cultural memory is dynamic in that it is a composite of texts and technologies from literature, commemorative rituals, historiography and other memorial media, through which images of the past are actively produced, circulated, received and transformed.

As discussed, troubling questions come to the fore in matters to do with valuing, memorialising and teaching about the past. Students can consider how major events from the past, such as those related to war and military intervention, are commemorated and selected to represent the nation's values and identity. Students can investigate the representation of the Anzac landings on the Gallipoli Peninsula in 1915 as an event that has entered the cultural memory of many Australians and as one bound to issues of collective identity and nationhood (Bean 1941; see also Chapter 5 in this book). The transmission of memory of this event to future generations of Australians is regarded by some as an issue of great national importance, as demonstrated by John Howard's concerns about the manner in which the Gallipoli campaign was remembered and represented in historical narratives and how it was taught in history classrooms when he was Prime Minister (Howard 1996, 2006).

Students can critique how the Gallipoli campaign has been presented to generations who possess no direct memory of the Anzac landing, together with an analysis of whose voices have been included or excluded in sources about this event. Furthermore, students can examine the claims of those historians who suggest that the narratives and traditions surrounding the memory work of Anzac are more mythic than historically representative in nature (Andrews 1993; Stanley 2008). In investigating how historians engage with primary and secondary sources about the Gallipoli campaign, students can also reflect on the ways in which historiographical accounts of Gallipoli can be critiqued as narratives that position cultural memory as both referential and imagined.

As politicians of different political persuasions continue to commemorate the nation's values and heritage through its involvement in military campaigns, students can apply the investigative strategies noted above to study debates about whether there should be a shift in emphasis on what is valued in Australian history and identity from World War I to World War II. Advocates for this change in focus do not downplay the value of World War I, the Gallipoli campaign and what occurred on the Western Front, but they contend that it is time to reassess the significance of the Pacific War. The Kokoda campaign in Papua New Guinea during World War II is one of the best-known Australian battles of that time, and some would argue that it is more representative of modern Australian values (Lindsay 2002; Nelson 2007). When Prime Minister Paul Keating (1992) chose New Guinea as the site of his first Anzac Day speech in 1992, he claimed that

> the Australians who served here in Papua New Guinea fought and died, not in defence of the old world, but the new world. They died in defence of Australia and the civilization and values which had grown up here. That is why it might be said that for Australians, the battles in Papua New Guinea were the most important ever.

A detailed explanation and classroom-based inquiry of these issues in relation to the significance of Gallipoli and Kokoda, with accompanying primary and secondary sources, can be seen in Hennessey's (2009) work for senior students.

Deciding what specific values should be studied in the history classroom

The Melbourne Declaration (MCEETYA 2008: 5) emphasised that 'national values of democracy, equity and justice' should be addressed in the curriculum. Such attendance to values is especially significant for history education, as students can investigate the origins and development of core values upon which there may be different definitions and ranging levels of commitment. A historical investigation and analysis of the development of a particular value, such as democratic process, has the merit of focusing on the substantive knowledge base for the idea that everyone should have equal rights and be allowed to participate in making important decisions in their society. Establishing a knowledge base for learning about specific values is critical, for as Soley (1996: 10) observes, 'it is useless ... to learn how to think unless there is something important to think about'.

Barton and Levstik's (2004: 107) reflection that 'some aspects of morality will vary among groups', while 'others are rooted in the nature of ... democracy' suggests that a focus on selected core values is acceptable; however, in immigrant, multicultural societies such as Australia where classrooms are increasingly culturally and linguistically diverse (ABS 2016), teachers need to be mindful of the communities in which their students live and the range of family and peer group value positions young people encounter in their daily lives. With reference to the examination of the commemoration of the significance of Gallipoli, as noted above, in classrooms where some students are of Turkish family origins, students can investigate how one of the Turkish commanders on the ground, Mustafa Kemal Atatürk, emerged as the heroic founding father of the Republic of Turkey and why, for many Turks, Gallipoli is now viewed as the birthplace of modern Turkey.

Fostering students' historical thinking about those values that result from historical inquiry

In history classrooms, the skill of contextualisation is a critical first step for thinking and reasoning about values. History teachers can design specific questions to guide student investigations into the social and political circumstances surrounding a source in order to gain greater insight into the historical period in which it was produced (Seixas & Morton 2013). It is also important that history teachers devise questions to prompt student interpretation and analysis of individual sources, together with questions about origin and authorship. Students can inquire into why a particular text was written, who wrote it, who the intended audience was, whether any biases were inherent in the information, whether the source has been translated and, if so, by whom and for what purpose. Students may decipher whether any gaps occur in the discussion, whether or not omissions in certain passages were inadvertent, and how the information has been used to interpret various events. Students should also access a range of different primary and secondary sources that deal with the same event or process, so they can investigate the gamut of value positions and standpoints embedded in each source and corroborate their findings across the selected sources collectively to determine their representativeness and reliability as items of evidence about the past.

An increased awareness of the need to value and protect human rights often emerges from historical investigations of the past. Nickel (1987: 561) describes human rights as those 'basic moral guarantees' to which people in all countries and contexts have access, given their very existence as human beings. When students analyse human rights as an outcome of a particular historical investigation, it can provide them with opportunities to develop their historical consciousness (Rüsen 2004), or informed awareness of how the past can be known and how the discipline of history can be understood, by viewing history beyond national terms. Students are able to appreciate that history operates at many levels—local, regional, national, transnational—as well as public and private. Students are able to critically examine historical periods when human rights are at risk or denied, such as when the national values of governments or regimes warrant resistance. The Germans who opposed the Nazi regime are a case in point of people whose individual values differed from those of the nation; similarly, with Civil Rights activists, the Abolitionists and Suffragettes (see Henderson 1996 for a senior classroom-based critical inquiry of the pursuit of equal rights in gender relations in the United Kingdom and Australia). In this context, a values clarification approach (Raths, Harmin & Simon 1966) enables students to reflect on what they have learned about the significance of human rights, consider their own personal stance and apply this to their own lives and actions.

Kohlberg (1975) suggests that appropriate moral positions based on universal concepts such as human rights and social justice, expressed in official statements such as the United Nations Universal Declaration of Human Rights, can be taught to students through the skills of moral reasoning. The view that moral reasoning enables young people to reflect on their decision-making about their value positions draws from psychological theories that humans can and do grow morally, and that this growth can be stimulated by teachers. Clarification of what pedagogies are appropriate to thinking about values emerging from a historical inquiry can be informed though various strategies. These include discussion of why different value positions on a particular issue are held, and why some individuals hold one value position and others a different one. A helpful technique for engaging students in a discussion of value-laden events when human rights were denied, such as the Holocaust, is to structure an activity towards the end of their inquiry, whereby students adopt the role of particular actors in this event in terms of one of four categories: victims, perpetrators, rescuers or bystanders. Students can examine the actions, motives and decisions of each group and portray all individuals, including victims and perpetrators, as human beings who are capable of moral judgement and independent decision-making.

Another useful pedagogical approach to fostering historical thinking and moral reasoning about those values that result from historical inquiry is to ask students to develop a plan for taking action on their knowledge. Lemin, Potts and Welsford (1975) suggest that asking students to consider a plan of action based on reasonable autonomous decisions is an important outcome from an increased awareness of a particular value. Recognition of some of the challenges of, and possible approaches to, including values in history education should prompt important reflection on the part of history teachers concerning the practical methods and strategies they might adopt within their classrooms.

CONCLUSION

Much has changed since I ventured into the history classroom as a beginning teacher. Four decades on, history education has moved away from a focus on students passively accumulating particular accounts of the past. Instead, emphasis is placed on disciplinary-focused approaches that draw from empirical research on how young people understand history and the disciplinary processes associated with it. A considerable body of this scholarship acknowledges that values play an important role in the development of students' historical thinking. When teachers' practice focuses on developing students' progression in historical thinking, young people have opportunities to acquire a vocabulary to analytically engage with those values embedded in conflicting accounts of the past. Fostering students' capacities to think about the past by engaging with and understanding the value-laden nature of historical interpretation serves as a generative process through which they can actively engage with those fundamental epistemological and ontological problems of history. This approach to teaching values in the history classroom provides students with a means to not only respond to the values and perspectives of others from the past and the present, but also to value the application of the historical method in their studies and in their own lives, both now and in the future.

REFERENCES

Andrews, E.M. 1993, *The Anzac Illusion: Anglo Australian Relations During World War I*, Cambridge: Cambridge University Press.

Attwood, B. 2005, *Telling the Truth About Aboriginal History*, Sydney: Allen & Unwin.

Australian Bureau of Statistics (ABS) 2016, *2016 Census, Australia Today*, Canberra: ABS.

Australian Curriculum, Assessment and Reporting Authority (ACARA) 2017, *The Australian Curriculum: History 7–10*, Version 8.3, Canberra: ACARA.

Australian Education Council (AEC) 1994, *A Statement on Studies of Society and Environment for Australian Schools*, Melbourne: Curriculum Corporation.

Barton, K. & Levstik, L. 2004, *Teaching History for the Common Good*, Mahwah, NJ: Lawrence Erlbaum.

Bean, C.E.W. 1941 [1929], *Official History of Australia in the War of 1914–1918, Volume III: The Australian Imperial Force in France, 1916*, 12th ed., Sydney: Angus & Robertson.

Carr, E.H. 1961, *What is History?* Harmondsworth: Penguin.

Curriculum Corporation 2003, *Values Education Study: Final Report*, Melbourne: Curriculum Corporation.

Curthoys, A. & Docker, J. 2006, *Is History Fiction?*, Sydney: UNSW Press.

Gibson, L. 2014, 'Understanding ethical judgements in secondary school history classes', PhD thesis, University of British Columbia.

Halstead, J. & Taylor, M. 2012, 'Learning and teaching about values: A review of recent research', *Cambridge Journal of Education*, vol. 30, no. 2, pp. 169–202.

Henderson, D. 1996, 'Changing Gender Relations—A History', in B. Hoepper, D. Henderson, J. Hennessey, D. Hutton, & S. Mitchell, *Inquiry 2—A Source-Based Approach to Modern History*, Brisbane: Jacaranda Wiley, pp. 333–93.

—— 2011, 'Values, controversial issues and interfaith understanding', in C. Marsh & C. Hart (eds), *Teaching the Social Sciences and Humanities in an Australian Curriculum*, 6th ed., Sydney: Pearson, pp. 155–89.

Hennessey, J. 2009, 'Shaping a legend: Gallipoli and Kokoda', in B. Hoepper, J. Hennessey, K. Cortessis, D. Henderson & M. Quanchi, *Global Voices 2: Historical Inquiries for the 21st Century*, Brisbane: Jacaranda Wiley, pp. 25–72.

Howard, J. 1996, 'The liberal tradition: The beliefs and values which guide the federal government', Sir Robert Menzies Lecture, Canberra: National Library of Australia (NLA).

—— 2006, 'A sense of balance: The Australian achievement', transcript of address, National Press Club, Canberra, 25 January.

Keating, P. 1992, 'Anzac Day—25 April 1992', speech, Ela Beach, Port Moresby.

Kinloch, N. 2001, 'Parallel catastrophes? Uniqueness, redemption and the Shoah', *Teaching History*, no. 104, pp. 8–14.

Kohlberg, J. (ed.) 1975, 'The cognitive–developmental approach to moral education', *Phi Delta Kappan*, vol. 56, no. 10, pp. 670–7.

Lee, P. 2006, 'Understanding history', in P. Seixas (ed.), *Theorizing Historical Consciousness*, Toronto: University of Toronto Press, pp. 129–64.

Lemin, M., Potts, H. & Welsford, P. (eds) 1975, *Values Strategies for Classroom Teachers*, Melbourne: ACER Press.

Lindsay, P. 2002, *The Spirit of Kokoda: Then and Now*, Melbourne: Hardie Grant Books.

Macintyre, S. & Clark, A. 2003, *The History Wars*, Melbourne: Melbourne University Press.

Manne, R. 2003, *Whitewash: On Keith Windschuttle's Fabrication of Aboriginal History*, Melbourne: Black Inc.

Ministerial Council on Education, Employment, Training and Youth Affairs (MCEETYA) 2008, *The Melbourne Declaration on Agreed Goals for Schooling*, Melbourne: MCEETYA.

National Curriculum Board (NCB) 2008, *National History Curriculum Framing Paper*, Melbourne: NCB.

—— 2009, *The Shape of the Australian Curriculum*, Melbourne: NCB.

Nelson, H. 2007, 'Pacific Currents—Kokoda and Two National Histories', *Journal of Pacific History*, vol. 42, no. 1, pp. 73–88.

Nickel, J. 1987, *Making Sense of Human Rights: Philosophical Reflections on the Universal Declaration of Human Rights*, Berkeley, CA: University of California Press.

Nora, P. 1996, *Realms of Memory: Rethinking the French Past*, A. Goldhammer trans., New York: Teachers College Press.

Raths, L., Harmin, M. & Simon, S. 1966, *Values and Teaching*, Columbus, OH: Merrill.

Reynolds, H. 1982, *The Other Side of the Frontier: Aboriginal Resistance to the European Invasion of Australia*, Ringwood: Penguin.

Rokeach, M. 1973, *The Nature of Human Values*, New York: The Free Press.

Rüsen, J. 2004, 'Historical consciousness: Narrative, structure, moral function, and ontogenetic development', in P. Seixas (ed.), *Theorizing Historical Consciousness*, Toronto: University of Toronto Press, pp. 63–85.

Seixas, P. (ed.) 2006, *Theorizing Historical Consciousness*, Toronto: University of Toronto Press.

—— 2009, 'A modest proposal for change in Canadian history education', *Teaching History*, vol. 137, pp. 26–30.

—— 2012, 'Preface', in T. Taylor & R. Guyver (eds), *History Wars and the Classroom: Global Perspectives*, Charlotte, NC: Information Age, p. xxi.

—— 2015, 'A model of historical thinking', *Educational Philosophy and Theory*, vol. 49, pp. 593–605.

Seixas, P. & Morton, T. 2013, *The Big Six Historical Thinking Concepts*, Toronto: Nelson.

Soley, M. 1996, 'If it's controversial, why teach it?', *Social Education*, vol. 60, no. 1, pp. 9–14.

Stanley, P. 2008, 'The Gallipoli campaign: History and memory, myth and legend', in D. Gare & D. Ritter (eds), *Making Australian History: Perspectives on the Past Since 1788*, Melbourne: Cengage Learning, pp. 311–16.

Windschuttle, K. 2002, *The Fabrication of Aboriginal History, Volume 1: Van Diemen's Land 1803–1847*, Sydney: Macleay Press.

Wineburg, S. 2001, *Historical Thinking and Other Unnatural Acts: Charting the Future of Teaching the Past*, Philadelphia, PA: Temple University Press.

CHAPTER 9
The value of direct teaching and historical knowledge

Paul Kiem

It is generally accepted that approaches to the teaching of history in Australian secondary schools changed during the 1980s, with the focus shifting from acquisition of knowledge to the development of skills and a move towards more student-centred inquiry-style learning. How comprehensive this transformation actually was at the classroom level has always been very difficult to assess. However, at the level of curriculum rhetoric, the changes of the 1980s have given rise to a dominant orthodoxy that celebrates inquiry-based and skills-focused learning and, either explicitly or implicitly, downgrades teacher-centred learning and the acquisition of knowledge. A crude polarisation between 'progressive' and 'traditional' that too often characterises curriculum discussion is particularly unhelpful for beginning teachers. This chapter briefly surveys the impact of the 1980s changes, takes a critical look at some of the outcomes and suggests the need for more balanced and constructive discussion around pedagogy and the place of knowledge in history education.

While there was some movement towards a greater emphasis on skills and variety in teaching methods prior to 1980, it was the work of the British Schools Council History Project (SCHP) that gave impetus to the 'new' history from the 1980s onwards. Established in 1972, the SCHP highlighted the role of evidence in history and promoted an inquiry approach whereby students conducted their own investigations using sources. The goal was to show students how history was constructed rather than simply transmitting information. It was thought that working with sources and developing skills in the analysis of evidence would be more relevant and engaging, especially for students who appeared to struggle with traditional content-driven history.

One of the ways in which the new approach was popularised was through distribution of a *What is History?* teaching kit. It contained source material for a number of mysteries, including 'The Mystery of Mark Pullen'—students were able to investigate, detective-like, the mystery of the fictitious Mark's death using the contents of his wallet and a police report. *What is History?* was influential and, even though a curriculum artefact of the 1970s, still remains popular. It has been digitally updated and was recently the subject of enthusiastic discussion on the History Teachers in NSW Facebook page (Mootz 2017). We are still not sure what happened to Mark Pullen. That was the point: the emphasis had moved from the answer to the process.

The influence of the SCHP was evident in New South Wales by the early 1980s. A number of key figures associated with the project visited Australia, and major articles appeared in the History Teachers' Association (HTA) journal, *Teaching History*, documenting the impact of their new ideas. In one of these articles, Gary Johnston (1982: 72) suggested that the work of the SCHP was 'probably the most important of all factors affecting the development' of a new NSW junior secondary syllabus in 1980. He highlighted the SCHP's influence in the new syllabus's focus on 'the nature and the use of evidence' and 'emphasis on History as enquiry'. While Johnston noted with approval some transition towards these elements in the syllabus used between 1972 and 1980, he was clear in his disdain for the syllabus and history pedagogy that had operated prior to 1972. Under this syllabus, according to Johnston (1982: 65, 72), 'History was a passively learnt, textbook ridden subject', the texts were 'for the most part crammed with factual material and were fairly dull and uninteresting to read' and to many students, history was 'a list of dates and events to be memorised and regurgitated'. Oddly, this same syllabus encouraged my own love of history when I was at school (Kiem 2013: 123).

Notwithstanding my own happy recollections, use of the word 'regurgitation' appears to be almost mandatory in accounts of the development of history education and, along with other jaundiced descriptors, helps to set up a simple story of progress out of an educational dark age, when direct teaching and rote learning supposedly ensured universal boredom. In a more recent version of this progress narrative, Robert Parkes and

Debra Donnelly (2014: 116) outline the emergence of 'historical thinking' as a 'term used by History educators to reject History education as simply a function of memorization and regurgitation'. From the solid foundation put in place in the 1980s, and marred only by the 'more constrained, conservative and content-driven syllabus' (2014: 121) introduced for a short period in 1998, Parkes and Donnelly (2014: 123, 126) discern a regular advance, with NSW syllabuses exhibiting a 'growing sophistication in the articulation of historical thinking'.

As Parkes and Donnelly (2014: 116–18) explain, 'historical thinking' is one of a number of similar terms associated with the approach to history education that has evolved from the SCHP's original groundbreaking work. Historical thinking, as defined by Canadian history educators Peter Seixas and Tom Morton (2013: 2), 'is the creative process that historians go through to interpret evidence of the past and generate the stories of history'. Different terms may be used for 'historical thinking', and it may be unpacked with varying emphases in different settings, but it essentially involves using a range of skills and concepts to describe the historical process in some detail. In Australia, the Teaching History unit on the AC History Units website (AC History Units 2013) provides a concise outline and explanation of the skills and concepts used in the Australian Curriculum: History. In summary, under the influence of historical thinking principles, we have developed elaborately constructed syllabuses that anticipate, among many other things, quite sophisticated learning across knowledge, skills and concepts.

However, while the comprehensiveness of recent history syllabuses certainly suggests progress and impressive learning on paper, in Australia there has been very little widely disseminated evaluation of, or reflection about, what actually happens in practice. What goes unremarked is that syllabuses inspired by historical thinking, in their anticipation that school students will get behind the stories of history to grapple in a meaningful way with how those stories have been constructed, are extremely ambitious—especially if we are expecting this to happen in an environment that offers limited classroom time to history, may not guarantee a history-trained teacher, purports to assess student achievement in an improbably precise way and promises significant 'transferable' benefits. Without genuine scrutiny of this ambition, there is the danger that we allow some form of curriculum concoction, from busy-work classroom skills activities through to self-serving data-gathering assessment tasks, to masquerade as the study of history. Mischievous, profound and informed by actual historical practice, the thoughts of the great French historian Marc Bloch (1954: 53) should at the very least give some pause to those who trumpet the ability of source-based tasks to allow students to 'work like historians':

> Many people and, it appears, even some authors of manuals entertain an extraordinarily simplified notion of our working procedure. First, as they are only too eager to tell you, there are the documents. The historian collects them, reads them, attempts to weigh their authenticity and truthfulness. Then, and only then, he makes use of them. There is only one trouble with this idea: no historian has ever worked in such a way, even when, by some caprice, he fancied that he was doing so.

The tendency in Australia to enshrine elements of the 'new' history is nowhere better illustrated than with the source-based question in the NSW Modern History HSC exam. Largely unchanged since the late 1980s, it retains a dated obsession with identifying the usefulness and reliability of sources and encourages formulaic responses that either reveal little insight into source analysis or betray basic misunderstandings, as in the perennial 'the source is reliable because it is primary'. While the release of a new NSW Modern History syllabus during 2017 has offered the opportunity for updating this approach, at the time of writing the details of any new HSC exam remain a mystery. Extraordinarily, four decades on from the SCHP revolution, there has been no transparent and broadly informed evaluation of source-based assessment to accompany the syllabus-development process.

Outside Australia, there appears to have been a more robust examination of the SCHP's legacy. In Britain, history educators have long recognised and discussed the shortcomings of source-based work in practice. Among the concerns expressed in articles in the Historical Association's journal was Tony McAleavy's (1998: 13) observation that the source-based domination of textbooks had 'created a wholly new type of boredom and difficulty for lower attainers'. Michael Fordham (2016) has commented on not only the tedium of source work but also its potential to be counterproductive: '"death by sources A–F" became so detached from what historians do that it lost its very *raison d'être*'. Most recently, British teacher Paula Worth (2016) has published a thoughtful examination of 'Evidential Thinking' in *Masterclass in History Education*. The common concerns are the tedium of much source work, its reliance on students learning routines that fail to develop independent insight and the contradictions between school-based source work and the historical process. Boredom, difficulty for 'lower attainers', routines being learned by rote and uncritically applied—the irony should be obvious.

In the United States, Keith Barton (2005) is another researcher who has brought a critical perspective to the source work that is at the core of 'new' history. His exposure of seven myths about source work (from misunderstandings about primary sources to the notion that students will automatically be engaged when sources are on the table), and the extent to which they resonate among thoughtful teachers around the world, raises some important questions about what is being taught and how successfully it is being taught. As Barton explains (2005: 753), each and the myths 'derives from the assumption that analyzing sources constitutes an end in itself—as though meaning inheres in the sources rather than in the uses to which they are put'. This highlights the danger of the agenda being set by curriculum imperatives with only weak links to the discipline of history:

> scholars who have little experience with historical methods appear to be passing on mistaken ideas about what historians do. In other cases, the use of primary sources seems to be driven less by a concern with historical authenticity than by demands for standards and accountability. (2005: 746)

Published more than a decade ago, but with its observations still very current, I would recommend Barton's (2005) 'Primary sources in history: Breaking through the myths' as mandatory reading in all Australian pre-service programs for history teachers. It challenges us to examine uncritical assumptions about the virtues of source-based inquiry and the supposed limitations of more traditional approaches. The truth, long evident to experienced practitioners, is that working with sources is complex and hard to do well, for both teachers and students. While source work in some form clearly belongs in a history classroom, the focus should be on quality work that serves a purpose within well-thought-out learning sequences. These learning sequences need to be developed from a rich array of pedagogical approaches, including direct instruction (teacher-centred learning), and a holistic understanding of the discipline of history that values historical knowledge (subject content).

In his book *Visible Learning*, John Hattie (2009: 204) observed that 'every year I present lectures to teacher education students and find that they are already indoctrinated with the mantra "constructivism good, direct instruction bad"'. While Hattie was referring to education in general, and 'constructivism' relates to broader notions of inquiry learning rather than specifically to historical inquiry, the point is made that, amid the enthusiasm for inquiry, direct instruction has somehow got a bad name. Hattie's observation certainly reflects my own experience in encounters with pre-service history teachers who feel that they have been given 'an agreed set of truths and commandments against direct instruction'.

Even though practising teachers may rely on direct instruction more than the rhetoric suggests, they are inclined to be cautious about admitting this, perhaps conceding that a little bit of direct teaching might be appropriate to introduce a topic or frame a student inquiry. History educator Tony Taylor (2012: 127) captured the constraint, but maybe not the nationwide classroom reality, when he suggested that 'a sensible classroom compromise that uses restrained and knowledgeable teacher guidance while encouraging individual student initiatives is now the mainstream position among the majority of Australian educators'.

Direct instruction gets a bad press for a number of reasons. First, who wants to be associated with 'rote-learning and regurgitation'? This frequently used caricature shows very little understanding of the complex nature of direct instruction as outlined, for example, by Hattie (2009: 204-6) or as demonstrated by one of the historical thinking gurus, Sam Wineburg. In his influential book, *Historical Thinking and Other Unnatural Acts*, Wineburg (2001) presents two case studies depicting both an 'invisible' and a 'visible' teacher, the former a 'guide on the side' who skilfully choreographed her students' activity and the latter a dynamic 'sage on the stage'. The point is that they were both highly effective history teachers, not because they adhered to a particular pedagogical doctrine but because they were enthusiastic, prepared and, most significantly, 'masters of their subject matter'.

A second reason why direct instruction is perceived as a poor second-best is the widespread acceptance that the best learning only takes place when students are 'active'. Again, the alternative is not presented as an attractive option—who wants to be the sponsor of 'passive' learning? Uncritical acceptance of the efficacy of all forms of active/inquiry/participatory learning is widespread, despite the fact that there is limited evidence to support the assumption. Even when introducing the concept of inquiry in *Place and Time: Explorations in Teaching Geography and History*, Tony Taylor (2012: 126) concedes that 'while it seems that inquiry-based learning ought to be an improvement on the old-fashioned didactic approach, there is no hard and fast proof that it, of itself, works quite as well as its more enthusiastic proponents argue'. Indeed, as British history educator Terry Haydn (2017) points out, generalisations along the lines that retention rates for learning rise from only 5 per cent for 'lectures' to 75 per cent for 'practice by doing' (these improbably precise figures drawn from a widely disseminated Learning Pyramid) are not simply unhelpful but have no research basis. Haydn (2017: 23) goes on to argue that 'Learning in history can be achieved by teacher exposition, dialogue between teacher and pupils, interaction between pupils . . . The "success rate" depends on many variables, not least how well the teaching intervention is planned, scaffolded and executed.'

A third reason why there is anxiety about direct instruction in history classrooms is that knowledge transmission—one element in direct instruction—is sometimes equated with a conservative political agenda, or it is assumed that it must strip history of the many nuanced understandings associated with 'historical thinking'. In reality, there is no good reason to link either outcome to a particular teaching approach. On the other hand, there are some very good reasons to address the need for knowledge transmission.

John Cleese, the English comedian and actor, was briefly a history teacher. In his memoir (Cleese 2014: 95), he recalls needing to learn the kings and queens of England so that one of his primary pupils, a 'little white-haired bastard' who was an authority on England's monarchs, could not catch him out in class. The happy outcome, according to Cleese, was that *he* now began to enjoy history because he had a framework on which he could 'hang odd bits of information'. He wondered 'why the skill of memorising ("learning by rote" as its detractors always refer to it) has got itself such a bad name'. Cleese has sound but similarly unfashionable views on classroom management: 'if you catch a whiff of impending insurrection, use sarcasm' (2014: 92). Cleese is famous as a performer whose craft required him to learn lines, rather than an educator. Nevertheless, his point about knowledge frameworks that assist in creating overall understanding and perspective is clearly supported by the observations of British history educator Christine Counsell (2016). As a teacher in post-SCHP Britain, she became 'increasingly convinced that "lower-attaining" students stayed "lower-attaining" chiefly for want of sufficient content security to move about freely within narratives and to recognise recurring abstract references when introduced into historical accounts'. Counsell (2016: 247) goes on to suggest that contrary to the 'then-emerging orthodoxies', it was knowledge rather than skills that was an 'enabler', offering students a transferable benefit.

Counsell has written extensively on the place of knowledge in history education. In an important book chapter entitled 'Historical knowledge and historical skills: A distracting dichotomy' (Counsell 2000: 54–5), she notes that while the 'new' history had introduced new priorities around 'skills', 'concepts' and 'attitudes', knowledge was left sitting 'rather uneasily alongside other objectives' and that, while it 'never goes away', it 'moves awkwardly in the professional language of many history teachers'.

In my own experience, I have heard teachers blithely announce that 'we don't teach knowledge anymore, just skills'. Such statements flow not just from acceptance of the false dichotomy that Counsell (2000) identifies, but also from an interpretation of Bloom's taxonomy that, contrary to the experience of anyone who has practised history, insists upon anything to do with knowledge being regarded as 'lower order' while anything designated a skill must be 'higher order'. Unfortunately, the digital revolution has given us a new reason to devalue knowledge. Conflating information with knowledge and understanding, we are now routinely told that adolescents 'have all the knowledge they need in their back pocket'.

Ironically, most of the proponents of source-based inquiry and historical thinking never intended to downgrade knowledge. As Seixas and Morton (2013: 4) stress in *The Big Six Historical Thinking Concepts*, the 'concepts make no sense at all without the material, the topics, the substance, or what is often referred to as the "content" of history'. For some time now, Christine Counsell has been exploring the ramifications of ignoring this advice. She argues persuasively for the cumulative nature of knowledge acquisition (Counsell 2000: 62): 'The more pupils know the more they are in a position to learn. To say that learning content is unimportant is to ignore its subtle role in future learning.' This is especially important for weaker students—the very ones 'the skills and concepts revolution was designed to serve' (Counsell 2000: 65). For all students, Counsell sees one of the key transferable takeaways from a study of history as the 'residue' knowledge that builds literacy, historical and general, and broad understanding. This will not come from disparate skills activities:

it requires well-thought-out learning sequences, incorporating sustained reading and writing and designed to allow students to build knowledge and understanding throughout one unit of work and into the next. Counsell (2017) acknowledges the challenges this may involve when it comes to topic selection, developing a coherent sequence that reinforces learning and avoiding the dreaded boredom that a focus on knowledge was alleged to have engendered back in the pre-SCHP dark days.

The boredom issue will always be a challenge. We are never going to get anywhere until we engage students in any area of learning. As Counsell (2000: 63) argues, the critical question for teachers is how to ensure that 'the virtuous circle of cumulative knowledge acquisition replaces the vicious circle of boredom and difficulty'. One advantage history does offer is the ability to deliver knowledge as engaging narrative, with this sustained narrative also doubling as a convenient vehicle for literacy. The historical thinkers Seixas and Morton (2013: 3) would not be satisfied with this as a final goal. They argue, using an over-simplification, that to 'tell stories about the past and to have students tell them back to us in essays' is not aiming high. But it is a great starting point that may be too easily overlooked when there is a need to tick off compliance with a daunting range of skills and concepts.

Seixas and Morton (2013: 3) use an interesting analogy to explain their approach to historical thinking, suggesting that historians are like directors of plays and that they would like students to be able to 'peer backstage, to understand how the ropes and pulleys work that make the play possible'. My response is that I would very happily encourage this approach in a senior historiography class, but that I would prefer junior students to have the opportunity to be simply entranced by the play and gain a basic comprehension of the plot without getting lost and confused among the complex of props and struts that support the construct. They may be in a slightly different situation from students, but I expect most play-goers would feel the same.

It should not come down to a mutually exclusive choice between watching the play and examining what goes on behind the scenes. Just as none of the proponents of the 'new' history advocate an abandonment of historical knowledge or teacher-directed learning, none of the advocates of the latter are calling for a return to a fabled time of a narrow canon of knowledge transfer, rote learning and regurgitation. Keith Barton (2005: 753) acknowledges the central role of sources:

Original sources should certainly be a centerpiece of the history classroom, because they are the foundation of historical knowledge. However, their use should be informed by a more complete and reflective understanding of their utility, rather than by popular but misguided myths.

Christine Counsell (2000: 55) endorses the need for an understanding of skills and concepts: 'I do not dispute the idea that mastery of . . . skills and concepts ought to inform our goals; I want to suggest, rather, that we have built up a package of uncritical and questionable assumptions about how pupils might reach them.'

Nevertheless, the qualifications upon which Barton and Counsell insist are important. They remind us of the need for evaluation and reflection rather than unthinking compliance. They challenge us to go beyond a polarised view that, at its extreme, presents a simple story of good and evil whereby the SCHP and its various legacies have rescued history from the terrible practices of the past. A moment's reflection would suggest that at one level such a view is poor history. It is only sustainable if we accept that pre-1980s history teaching was always done badly while source-based, student-centred inquiry is always done well. And it effectively excuses 'new' history from the sort of scrutiny that Barton and Counsell have called for. Most importantly, if some version of the good/evil fiction is pedalled to beginning teachers, it risks limiting the strategies they will be able to consider in assessing and responding to their students' needs and may severely constrain the experience of history they are able to offer.

Just as many experienced history teachers undoubtedly do, beginning teachers should feel entitled to use a full array of pedagogical approaches, old and new, the main criteria for selection being what best supports student learning and, secondarily, what contributes to variety. Within that context, the status of direct instruction, and its many elements, needs to be restored. Especially in a classroom where students do experience a variety of approaches throughout the year, there is no good reason why entire units or significant parts of them should not be delivered predominantly via direct instruction. It can be efficient in covering a large area in a short time; it can help to ensure that all students have a common foundation or starting point (rather than this being determined, for example, by an individual's research skills); and there is no reason why it should not be engaging and eagerly anticipated by students. Above all, if we consider knowledge important, then we need to accept knowledge transmission as a valid teaching activity.

CONCLUSION

As Christine Counsell has said, historical skills and concepts 'ought to inform our goals'. In other words, they should certainly be inherent in every teacher's understanding of history. But the skills and concepts that have been identified by history education theorists do not constitute a category that is separate from and superior to historical knowledge. For some of us, Counsell's views on knowledge are a welcome endorsement of its essential place in history teaching; for others—perhaps concerned about selectivity and the constructed nature of all historical knowledge—they may be disturbing. Nevertheless, Counsell's arguments regarding the need to emancipate 'lower-attaining' students by equipping them with better historical knowledge demand attention. What she envisages is certainly easier said than done, assuming that the goal would be knowledge acquisition, consolidation and genuine understanding. It may also require a fundamental rethink if current priorities favour disparate skills activities. It would also be reliant upon teachers being masters of their subject matter and confident in the inherent fascination of history.

REFERENCES

AC History Units 2013, Teaching History, <www.achistoryunits.edu.au>, accessed 5 August 2018.

Barton, K. 2005, 'Primary sources in history: Breaking through the myths', *The Phi Delta Kappan*, vol. 86, no. 10, pp. 745–53.

Bloch, M. 1954, *The Historian's Craft*, P. Putnam trans., Manchester: Manchester University Press.

Cleese, J. 2014, *So, Anyway . . .*, London: Random House.

Counsell, C. 2000, 'Historical knowledge and historical skills: A distracting dichotomy', in J. Arthur & R. Phillips (eds), *Issues in History Teaching*, London: Routledge, pp. 54–71.

—— 2016, 'History teacher publication and the curricular what? Mobilising subject-specific professional knowledge in a culture of genericism', in C. Counsell, K. Burn & A. Chapman (eds), *Masterclass in History Education*, London: Bloomsbury, pp. 243–51.

—— 2017, 'The fertility of substantive knowledge: In search of its hidden generative power', in I. Davies (ed.), *Debates in History Teaching*, London: Routledge, pp. 80–99.

Fordham, M. 2016, 'Against the generic use of sources in history lessons', *Clio et cetera*, 25 November, <www.clioetcetera.com>, accessed 2 August 2017.

Hattie, J. 2009, *Visible Learning: A Synthesis of Meta-analyses Relating to Achievement*, London: Routledge.

Haydn, T. 2017, 'Secondary history: Current themes', in I. Davies (ed.), *Debates in History Teaching*, London: Routledge, pp. 30–45.

Johnston, G. 1982, 'An historical perspective of the 1980 syllabus in history for Years 7–10', *Teaching History (NSW)*, vol. 15, no. 4, pp. 65–81.

Kiem, P. 2013, 'History goes to school', in A. Clark & P. Ashton (eds), *Australian History Now*, Sydney: NewSouth Publishing, Ch. 7, pp. 122–35.

McAleavy, T. 1998, 'The use of sources in school history 1910–1998: A critical perspective', *Teaching History (NSW)* (UK), May, pp. 10–16.

Mootz, D. 2017, 'Looking for mysteries?', History Teachers in NSW Facebook group, 19 July, <www.facebook.com/groups/1429707913949675>, accessed 3 July 2017.

Parkes, R. & Donnelly, D. 2014, 'Changing conceptions of historical thinking in history education: An Australian case study', *Revista Tempo e Argumento*, vol. 6, no. 11, pp. 113–36.

Seixas, P. & Morton, T. 2013, *The Big Six Historical Thinking Concepts*, Toronto: Nelson.

Taylor, T. 2012, 'Introduction to inquiry based learning', in T. Taylor, C. Fahey, J. Kriewaldt & D. Boon (eds), *Place and Time: Explorations in Teaching Geography and History*, Sydney: Pearson, pp. 123–28.

Wineburg, S. 2001, *Historical Thinking and Other Unnatural Acts: Charting the Future of Teaching the Past*, Philadelphia, PA: Temple University Press.

Worth, P. 2016, 'Evidential thinking: Language as liberator and gaoler', in C. Counsell, K. Burn & A. Chapman (eds), *Masterclass in History Education*, London: Bloomsbury, pp. 77–104.

CHAPTER 10
Inquiry approaches to assessment in the history classroom

Heather Sharp

CURRENT TRENDS IN ASSESSMENT: AN OVERVIEW

This chapter covers the topic of assessment in the history classroom from the perspective of an inquiry approach. There is a focus on the school classroom context, with practical examples embedded in established theories of history education and assessment provided for teachers to use. Topics covered include providing a clear overview of the purposes of assessment; the importance of developing historical thinking in students over privileging only historical facts and figures; and a variety of modes of assessment, linked to ideas of assessment *for* learning and assessment *of* learning to help teachers better understand the various reasons and intentions for implementing assessment tasks. In focusing on inquiry approaches, the work of respected educators such as Bruner and Dewey is used to frame a discussion on theoretical underpinnings of constructivism in assessment. More relevant to contemporary contexts, the work of Hoepper, Gilbert, Taylor, Young, Marsh, Cooper, Chapman and others is applied to inquiry assessment approaches. The importance of providing quality feedback to students is also highlighted. In addition, the chapter touches on issues to do with external-based assessment—for example, the Higher School Certificate (HSC) and NAPLAN testing. Ways to provide quality feedback, beginning with a well-structured assessment task, are broached, including suggestions for a variety of modes that will engage students to listen to and implement the teacher feedback that has been provided. The following statement made by David Boud (1995: 35), an expert in assessment, resonates with the information included in this chapter: 'every act of assessment gives a message to students about what they should be learning and how they should go about it'. It is therefore important for teachers and administrators to ensure that any assessment practices carried out are of high quality and are equitable for all stakeholders.

Over recent decades, there has been an increasing international trend towards externally mandated, high-stakes testing of school students across all year levels, jurisdictions and school systems. This is ostensibly an attempt to gain evidence of student achievement for the purposes of transparency and accountability in schools. However, as Klenowski and Wyatt-Smith (2012: 67) argue, 'it is fair to say that Australia has not achieved high quality and high equity in the national testing initiatives'. In highlighting many of the negative and other unintended consequences of external testing in Australia, Klenowski and Wyatt-Smith (2012: 75) also draw on research questioning the validity of data produced by such a testing regime. They highlight the importance of diagnostic testing, which can inform content (or topic) selection, pedagogy and teaching practices for student achievement, rather than 'snapshot, point-in-time evidence of performance achievement'. They recommend that in an environment where there is a focus on a single test as an indicator of student ability, there is a need to consider the multifaceted nature of teaching and learning, as well as achievement. The rise in external-based assessment tasks has arguably led to students (and their parents) feeling increasingly stressed and anxious about their scholastic achievements. Media reports proliferate, especially around the time of high-stakes external assessment tasks such as the NSW HSC and the nationwide NAPLAN test.

Despite significant scholarship outlining the fundamental skills of learning to think historically, international assessment practices frequently are more concerned with the object of knowledge, rather than learning the discipline. As a result, current forms of assessment, influenced by international tests, are more concerned with the collection of data, aiming to classify student achievement. Gómez Carrasco and Miralles Martínez (2016) present a comprehensive analysis of research about assessing historical thinking, arguing that a definition of a cognitive learning model for history needs to be established before historical knowledge can be assessed correctly. Darling-Hammond and McClosky (2008) compared the systems of assessment in many countries of the world with that of the United States, which at the time was based largely on external and standardised national tests to rank student and school performances. Overall, they found 'the integration of curriculum, assessment, and instruction in a well-developed teaching and learning system creates the foundation for much more equitable and productive outcomes' (2008: 271). In the Canadian context, Volante and Beckett (2011) found that, for the most part, teachers of primary and secondary students had a good understanding of formative assessment and were increasingly focusing on the process of learning rather than the overall grade. However, they found that many teachers struggled with synthesising the results of formal, summative assessments with other forms of student data. Consequently, they recommended a greater focus on the *practical aspects* associated with particular assessment techniques. For teachers, this means scaffolding learning prior to the assessment task due date by modelling the expected text type and skills through classroom activities. For example, if students are expected to write an essay critically analysing sources, then they should have the opportunity in class to participate in activities where they are provided with sources to analyse, including a scaffold. Feedback should be provided so that students can adjust their writing in order to be able to meet assessment criteria.

INTRODUCTION TO AND THE PURPOSE OF ASSESSMENT IN HISTORY CLASSROOMS

Teachers regularly use a variety of assessment forms, including diagnostic, formal, informal, summative and formative. Informal and diagnostic assessment is carried out continuously by teachers in the classroom. Whether it is checking for understanding by asking students questions, via student-initiated questions, observations of students working and staying on task, or checking homework or other class written work, teachers are frequently observing students and making judgements about students' level of understanding of topics, skills and concepts. Formative tasks are often used as a practice run, leading into summative assessment. More formal than diagnostic testing, teachers use these tasks to monitor learning progress during a unit of work. Formative assessment is useful, as it provides ongoing feedback to teachers and students and can be seen as assessment *for* learning (AfL). This approach enables both teachers and students to reflect on the teaching and learning processes that were undertaken prior to the assessment task. Strategies can then be put in place to improve or sustain learning outcomes, and to use the assessment task as a meaningful reflective tool to learn the skills and/or content that students did *not* demonstrate, going some way to ensure all learning outcomes of the syllabus or other curriculum documents are met.

There are many reasons to assess students, and what follows is just a sample. As well as providing a point-in-time record of student achievement, teachers can use assessment to chart student progress, and students are able to receive feedback on what they are doing well and areas for improvement. Assessment is commonly used as the basis of reporting and, for reflective practitioners, assessment can be used as a tool to set the direction for further teaching and learning and to improve practice, both in terms of pedagogical and content decision-making. Assessment is most commonly used to check whether students are achieving the formal learning outcomes of the history curriculum, which usually means assigning a grade mark against the outcome using an A–E scale or similar—for example, very high achievement to very limited achievement (VHA–VLA) in the Queensland context.

The focus of this chapter is on the more formal summative assessment. This is the assessment that is planned, structured and typically used in order to rank or provide marks, with the aim of showing students and their parents or other adult caregivers how the student is going, academically. This assessment is usually, although not always, completed at the end of a unit of work, term or semester to provide official documentation of the level of student achievement. Results are commonly communicated via an end-of-year or end-of-semester report card. Summative assessment is therefore seen as assessment *of* learning (AoL).

ASSESSMENT IN HISTORY CLASSROOMS

Sheehan (2013) argues that the development of historical thinking is necessary for students to make sense of the past and participate as critical citizens in society. However, he argues (2013: 69) that to think historically, incorporating the operations of the discipline, is not a natural process and requires 'systematic instruction in the methodologies and vocabulary of the discipline'. Sheehan conducted a study in New Zealand secondary schools, aiming to explore how internal assessments through coursework could contribute to student motivation and capacity to think historically. Students were asked questions exploring understandings of the historical concept *significance*, as well as being asked a number of questions relating to Gallipoli and Anzac Day, aiming to indicate their historical thinking. Findings of this research indicated that both intrinsic and extrinsic motivations influenced the students, who were found to develop more advanced understandings of historical thinking while completing internal, or school-based, assessment tasks (2013: 69–83).

Gómez Carrasco and Miralles Martínez (2016: 132), exploring the uses of inquiry approaches to history teaching, explained that, 'History teaching based exclusively on memorizing facts and concepts is not only inefficient in terms of obtaining a solid base for understanding social phenomena, but also obsolete in today's instant information internet world.' While the use of inquiry-based methods requires intensive planning by the teacher to ensure that sufficient attention is paid to students' understanding of content, as well as disciplinary skills, the authors (2016: 133) argue that 'qualitative assessment tools are indispensable as a means of measuring what is a tremendously subjective situation'. In this way, students also need to be aware of their own metacognitive judgements, and how using self- and peer-assessment can assist in such reflection. Similarly, Ormond (2011) explored the unintended consequences of standards-based assessment on history education, highlighting the ways that teaching is modified as a result of the lack of attention paid to the place of knowledge in relation to assessment. Standards in New Zealand were developed for the assessment of students' historical skills, while teachers were assured by policy-makers that there was no need for existing teaching programs to be significantly altered:

> In the first few years after the NCEA's [the National Certificate of Educational Achievement] introduction, teachers did not respond by targeting the learning so precisely or narrowly to the requirements of the various standards but over time the selection of content has become tuned to what is needed to succeed in assessments, at the expense of broader, more comprehensive approaches. (2011: 10)

Alternatively, external testing carried out periodically in Finland is utilised as a means of moderation, as the majority of assessment is classroom- or school-based. Rather than results being made public (as is the case with Australia's NAPLAN), the results are provided only to teachers, so that they may decide how best to utilise the data to improve teaching and learning (Rantala 2012). Rantala found that, despite a move to a less substantive approach to history teaching following a traditional nationalistic teaching of history in the 1990s, students displayed evidence of greater emphasis on substantive knowledge, and struggled when asked to draw on disciplinary knowledge. Rantala (2012) maintains this is evidence that many Finnish teachers were designing history programs based mainly on historical content, despite the emphasis on disciplinary knowledge. While teachers have a high level of autonomy in Finland, particularly in designing their curriculum, Rantala (2012: 204) argues that:

> A choice of teaching emphasis must be made. In content-based teaching, historical events fill the lessons while procedural knowledge remains peripheral. In turn, the content to be studied in skill-based teaching must be restricted because skill-based studying is usually thematic and the learning is based on in-depth studies.
>
> A skilful history teacher can involve substantive knowledge so that students will also develop their procedural knowledge.

ASSESSMENT IN PRACTICE

Applying assessment tasks in the real-world classroom setting can be difficult and time-consuming. Teachers must be aware of the potential for unintended bias to occur in particular assessment types. Wiliam, Klenowski and Rueda (2010: 261) argue that a solution to potential biases is to focus on the construction of the assessment. It is also beneficial to provide a variety of assessment modes so students get used to communicating their historical thinking and understanding in a variety of ways—see the assessment mode suggestions outlined in Table 10.1.

In AfL, while assessing student learning, there are a number of options teachers can consider based on the outcomes met and not met by students. Some examples are reporting on students' progress and moving on to the next topic; re-teaching a skill or content area in which many students seem not to have demonstrated proficiency; providing targeted support for some students in identified and specific areas; revising the teaching and learning activities for the next time the topic is taught; and/or engaging in additional professional learning, whether pedagogical or content development.

Table 10.1 Modes of assessment

Mode	Examples
Written	Essays Exams Multiple-choice questions Short-answer questions
Non-written	Speech
Hybrid	Speech with a written research component Multi-modal presentation (for example PowerPoint with a speech that has an embedded YouTube clip)
Less traditional	Work samples (writing, drawing, concept map, model) Interviews and conferences (taped, verbal, peer assessment, group discussion) Portfolios (diaries, sketches, journals, digital files) Performance (role-play, structured discussions, debates) Major work (exhibition, invention, investigative project, recital) Response to stimulus

INQUIRY LEARNING APPROACHES TO ASSESSMENT

Inquiry learning has been the dominant approach to history teaching and learning in Australian secondary schools across a number of decades. Influenced by the UK Schools History Project (see Chapter 1 of this book) and positioned within a progressivist approach to education, inquiry learning encompasses constructivist beliefs of how knowledge is attained—particularly that students learn best 'by doing'. Bruner, and Dewey before him, are both commonly accredited with developing this approach for schooling contexts. Of the foundations of such an approach, Bruner (2006: 63) writes:

> There appear to be . . . a series of activities and attitudes, some directly related to a particular subject and some of them fairly generalized, that go with inquiry and research. These have to do with the *process* of trying to find out something and while they provide no guarantee that the *product* will be any *great* discovery, their absence is likely to lead to awkwardness or aridity or confusion.

Using the term 'constructing' or 'construction' when discussing the content of history curriculum is in keeping with the inquiry approach.

In a practical (classroom context) sense, inquiry processes incorporate or involve

> commitment of the learner to continuous reflection and re-evaluation of the direction and purposes of the inquiry ... Productive inquiry cannot be conducted in a strictly linear fashion with the questions that guide the inquiry remaining the same throughout. Students and teachers need to adopt flexible approaches so that in the light of information gathered, knowledge being constructed, and skills and processes being enhanced, additional or different questions and/or hypotheses can be adopted. (Naylor 2000: 8)

History is viewed as an active process of 'doing' research, a position shared by Chapman (2009: 3), who states that 'the discipline of history *is* a process of enquiry and an effort to ask and answer questions about the past through critical engagement with the traces of the past that remain in the present in the form of relics and reports'. Furthermore, 'constructing interpretations of the past through selecting, interpreting and combining sources is central to history' (Cooper & Chapman 2009: 15). The Australian Curriculum: History (Board of Studies NSW 2012: 13) also highlights the importance of using an inquiry approach:

> History is a disciplined process of inquiry into the past that develops students' curiosity and imagination. Awareness of history is an essential characteristic of any society, and historical knowledge is fundamental to understanding ourselves and others ... The process of historical inquiry develops transferable skills, such as the ability to ask relevant questions; critically analyse and interpret sources; consider context; respect and explain different perspectives; develop and substantiate interpretations, and communicate effectively.

If inquiry is used in the classroom to teach content and historical thinking skills, it makes sense to also meaningfully incorporate it into assessment tasks. Inquiry starts with an authentic focus on student-centredness as the basis of effective learning. Just as it poses learning as a question or a problem to be solved through open-ended questioning, the same principle can be applied to assessment. Gilbert and Hoepper (2011: 201) write that, 'Through inquiry, students try to mirror the work of historians in posing questions, probing sources and constructing explanations, albeit in a much less sophisticated way.' Extending this to an assessment context not only gives students ownership of their work and research, but also aims to replicate the work of historians. Not entirely relinquishing the responsibilities of an educator, Gilbert and Hoepper (2011: 205) go on to state that 'An inquiry approach certainly gives students more scope to be active and independent learners, but the teacher remains an instructor, a model and a guide.'

Inquiry requires careful teacher planning, and needs to be modelled in the classroom so that students then know how to successfully apply this approach in their own work. Teachers can use a variety of resources and scaffolds to support students in their investigative work. Regarding supporting students, an inquiry approach question for an essay can be seen in the following example. A question such as *What happened at Gallipoli?* requires a statement or factual response only. A better question would be: *Why did the Australian and New Zealand Army Corps (Anzacs) land at Gallipoli in 1915 and what did they achieve and fail at, both immediately and in the long-term?* This question requires students to engage in a process of inquiry: it meets 'the Wikipedia test'—that is, if the assessment question can't be answered by reading a Wikipedia entry or making a simple Google (or other search engine) query, it probably incorporates a sophisticated inquiry approach.

Supporting students to engage in successful research using an inquiry approach can be achieved via structured research guides; regular checkpoints that can assist with accountability; a variety and abundance of resources; strong student support; and sufficient background knowledge so that students can extend on what they already know. A guiding question where students work towards an answer is also important as a scaffold in the junior years of high school; as they become more experienced, students are then able to be supported to develop their own guiding questions.

The use of sources in history teaching in Australian schools is well established as a vital component of teaching the subject. For example, the external exit exam for Year 12 students in New South Wales—the HSC—emphasises this importance through the inclusion of primary sources in its history exams. It is important that teachers equip students with the skills to be able to describe, comprehend and analyse sources so that, during this high-stakes external assessment, students can apply those skills to answering questions. Markers' notes, collated and published online by the Board of Studies NSW (2015), indicate the areas where students excel and areas for improvement. It is noted that students

> showed strength [in] using the sources and/or the text to identify ... using [two] sources and own knowledge to outline attitudes ... using own knowledge to either add value to the information contained in the sources or clearly differentiating from that contained in the sources ... making a judgement about the usefulness of sources ...

Also according to the markers' notes—and this is an area that should be of particular interest to teachers and curriculum developers and writers—students

> need to improve in these areas ... making a clear interpretive link between the text and photo ... referring to both sources ... avoiding simplistic generalisations [about source reliability] ... ensuring that both sources are given thoughtful consideration ... providing a judgement rather than a description of the sources. (Board of Studies NSW 2015)

From this information, it can be suggested that when provided with only one source, students used it to outline, identify and make judgements; however, when provided with more than one source, students struggled to answer the exam questions comprehensively, providing simplistic generalisations about the sources and not making interpretive links. Higher-order thinking skills of analysis and using information to transform, as an emancipatory knowledge type, are not widely demonstrated by students; this is a potential area on which curriculum writers and teachers need to focus so students' skills are developed. This is important not only for high-stakes assessment, but also so students are demonstrating the skills of the historian that can assist them in further studies and in interpreting and understanding the world around them.

Assessment tasks can be an avenue that teachers use to build students' skills for proficient use of primary sources. Providing students with opportunities to use primary sources for formative assessment tasks, including class activities, is important. This allows the teacher to see what the students are doing during in-class activities and to redirect as appropriate. Explicitly including primary sources in assessment-task descriptions, and providing an opportunity for students to select or use provided primary sources in the context of their assessment item, will scaffold students' use of primary sources in their assessment task. Likewise, primary sources need to be included in the grading criteria. This can help to ensure there is a clear alignment between what occurs in class, what occurs in the criteria and what occurs in the assessment-task description. When comparing assessment practices across countries, Darling-Hammond and McClosky (2008: 271) found 'the integration of curriculum, assessment, and instruction in a well-developed teaching and learning system creates the foundation for much more equitable and productive outcomes'.

Writing of humanities education, Gilbert and Hoepper (2011) and Marsh and Hart (2011) examine a variety of assessment approaches that may be used in the classroom. They discuss the importance of formative assessment, focusing on providing meaningful feedback for student improvement. Gilbert (2011: 106) writes that 'we need to assess deep understanding of subjects rather than superficial and isolated pieces of information'. Similarly, Marsh and Hart (2011) explain that assessment should focus on declarative and procedural knowledge, including the skills required to undertake an inquiry approach to learning. History education should focus on students' understanding and emulating the work of the historian (Gilbert 2011). To undertake an inquiry approach, students should be encouraged to work independently or in small groups, with the teacher present to provide support and/or scaffold the processes of inquiry. In particular, students should gain an understanding of the contestable nature of historical knowledge (Hoepper 2011: 209). In terms of assessing inquiry, teachers should provide feedback throughout the inquiry process to encourage student improvement. Focusing on historical inquiry, Taylor and Kriewaldt (2012) espouse the use of assessment for learning throughout the process. They highlight the importance of modelling and scaffolding in inquiry teaching as well as frequent and useful feedback, recommending that students should be told what they have achieved and their level of achievement, and provided with suggestions for improvement. At the same time, there is a need to ensure that assessments are *authentic*, or related to real-world problems, in order to encourage critical thinking in history (Gilbert & Hoepper 2011).

In their influential work, *Making History: A Guide for the Teaching and Learning of History in Australian Schools,* Taylor and Young (2003: 104) argue that assessment in history should be part of the regular classroom routine, as students often 'show their capabilities in the daily routine of classroom activity'. While Taylor and Young recommend that formative assessment should allow students to show their capabilities through varied task types, they acknowledge that international trends are placing increased emphasis on summative assessment types for reporting and accountability purposes. Moreover, when judging progress in history teaching and learning, they state that teachers need to consider the complex nature of historical thinking:

> History is about problem-posing and solving, about asking questions and forging explanations from evidence and imagination. As such, assessment approaches that focus predominantly on skills or recall of content fail to represent history authentically (that is, as a distinctive form of knowledge and way of understanding the world) and offer thin evidence on which to judge progress. (2003: 102)

They also make the case (2003: 101–4) that students should be involved in the assessment process through self- and peer-assessment, as well as being exposed to a diversity of teaching strategies and resources, as different learners will develop historical understanding at different rates, depending on the learner and the classroom environment.

FEEDBACK AND EFFECTIVE, EQUITABLE MARKING

Aligned with the notion that assessment can be an emotional experience for students, feedback that students receive can similarly evoke feelings of panic, even if the mark is known beforehand. Teachers can prepare to mark effectively and equitably by developing their own principles, influenced by the suggested practice options detailed here. Preparing a model answer, especially when there is more than one marker or it is a large cohort, can not only assist with the speed of marking, but also ensure that students are marked consistently. For assessment such as research essays, it can also be useful to provide students with a sample of a model essay, usually on a different topic. This then provides students with a clear guide on structure and/or referencing, the expected use of meta-language, and the level of analysis and depth of knowledge required. Providing students with a sound or satisfactory (typically C level) sample and a very high achievement (typically A level) sample can also show students the differences between the standards. A model assessment task in the classroom can also be used as a pedagogical tool to teach students disciplinary thinking and to demystify assessment expectations. Students can frequently be unsure of what a completed assignment should *look like*, and this uncertainty can lead to further anxiety about starting, much less completing, the assessment task.

Clear marking criteria assist both students and markers. If teachers, prior to providing students with the assessment task, have considered what outcomes students need to achieve and to what level, confusion and uncertainty may be avoided—for both teacher and student. Clear marking criteria, which extend beyond simple statements with an allocated mark out of, say, 10, is of benefit to students in guiding their work and in demystifying history-disciplinary thinking. Then, when it comes time to mark, equitable and effective marking can take place, as there are clear criteria to guide marking, and the language of the criteria can be used to provide meaningful feedback to students. Just as assessment criteria should follow learning outcomes, feedback is most useful for student learning when it is specific and comments on students' work in relation to those outcomes. In an outcomes-based curriculum, it is important that students know how they have achieved against those outcomes, even when they are presented as criteria.

Just as it is important to have clear practice principles on the marking of assessment tasks, it is also important to consider what kind of feedback will be provided, as well as a predetermined timeframe to return the assessment results and feedback to students. A wide array of feedback options are available, and different types will suit different cohorts and can be dependent on geographical location, size of cohort, year level, the purpose of the assessment tasks and type of assessment task, as well as other factors. For example, in teaching students who attend Schools of Distance Education (formerly School of the Air), due to limited contact with their teachers, receiving recorded feedback—whether audiovisual or just audio—can provide a real boost to their motivation to achieve success. The decisions that teachers can make about timing and type of feedback include whether they will give feedback on drafts or pre-mark an assessment task; the length of feedback to give when marking; and whether this is written throughout the assessment task or as one comment at the end. In addition to individual feedback, it may also be valuable to provide whole-of-class or year-level feedback that encompasses the major points identified in student submissions—both constructive criticism and praise—as well as offering students the opportunity of a one-on-one conference and discussion about their marks and feedback in order to learn for the next assessment task. A decision also needs to be made about whether to provide only written feedback or additional recorded feedback. In order to support students in understanding that assessment is not just the end-point, it can be useful to provide a structured worksheet to enable critical reflection on their assessment task and how they plan to improve next time.

CONCLUSION

As an important component of student learning, assessment cannot be understated. David Boud (1995: 35) reminds teachers of the importance and priority of assessment: 'Students can, with difficulty, escape from the effects of poor teaching, they cannot (by definition if they want to graduate) escape the effects of poor assessment.' This chapter has outlined some of the major considerations for teachers when planning and implementing assessment in their classroom. Assessment can be an emotional experience for teachers, parents and caregivers, and of course students, with some seeing results as a personal reflection on themselves (this does not preclude parents!). Students need to be provided with opportunities to demonstrate learning outcomes; assessment tasks, criteria and feedback need to be aligned; feedback needs to be meaningful; and for quality, effective and equitable learning to be achieved, assessment needs to be both *for* and *of* learning. The chapter also considered focusing on assessment as part of an inquiry approach to learning, and effective assessment practices.

REFERENCES

Board of Studies NSW 2012, *NSW Syllabus for the Australian Curriculum: History Years 7–10*, vol. 2, Sydney: Board of Studies NSW.

—— 2015, *Notes from the Marking Centre Modern History*, Department of Education HSC Exams, <www.boardofstudies.nsw.edu.au/hsc_exams/2015/notes/modern-history.html>, accessed 16 August 2016.

Boud, D. 1995, 'Assessment and learning: Contradictory or complementary?', in P. Knight (ed.), *Assessment for Learning in Higher Education*, London: Kogan, pp. 35–48.

Bruner, J. 2006, *In Search of Pedagogy Volume 1: The Selected Works of Jerome S. Bruner*. London: Routledge.

Chapman, A. 2009, 'Introduction: Constructing history 11–19', in H. Cooper & A. Chapman (eds), *Constructing History 11–19*, London: Sage, pp. 1–8.

Cooper, H. & Chapman, A. (eds) 2009, *Constructing History 11–19*, London: Sage.

Darling-Hammond, L. & McClosky, L. 2008, 'Assessment for learning around the world: What would it mean to be internationally competitive?', *The Phi Delta Kappan*, vol. 90, no. 4, pp. 263–72.

Gilbert, R. 2011, 'Assessment for student learning', in R. Gilbert & B. Hoepper (eds), *Teaching Society and Environment*, 4th ed., Melbourne: Cengage Learning, pp. 96–114.

Gilbert, R. & Hoepper, B. (eds) 2011, *Teaching Society and Environment*, 4th ed., Melbourne: Cengage Learning.

Gómez Carrasco, C.J. & Miralles Martínez, P. 2016, 'Historical skills in compulsory education: Assessment, inquiry based strategies and students' argumentation', *New Approaches in Educational Research*, vol. 5, no. 2, pp. 130–6.

Hoepper, B. 2011, 'Teaching history: Inquiry principles', in R. Gilbert & B. Hoepper (eds), *Teaching Society and Environment*, 4th ed., Melbourne: Cengage Learning, pp. 203–10.

Klenowski, V. & Wyatt-Smith, C. 2012, 'The impact of high stakes testing: The Australian story', *Assessment in Education: Principles, Policy & Practice*, vol. 19, no. 1, pp. 65–79.

Marsh, C. & Hart, C. 2011, *Teaching the Social Sciences and Humanities in an Australian Curriculum*, 6th ed., Sydney: Pearson.

Naylor, J. 2000, *Inquiry Approaches in Secondary Studies of Society and Environment Key Learning Area: Occasional Paper Prepared for the Queensland School Curriculum Council*, Brisbane: Queensland School Curriculum Council.

Ormond, B. 2011, 'Shifts in knowledge teaching: The unexpected consequences of assessment practices on secondary history', *Pacific-Asian Education*, vol. 23, no. 1, pp. 5–22.

Rantala, J. 2012, 'How Finnish adolescents understand history: Disciplinary thinking in history and its assessment among 16-year-old Finns', *Education Sciences*, vol. 2, pp. 193–207.

Sheehan, M. 2013, '"History as something to do, not just something to learn": Historical thinking, internal assessment and critical citizenship', *New Zealand Journal of Educational Studies*, vol. 48, no. 2, pp. 69–83.

Taylor, T. & Kriewaldt, J. 2012, 'Assessment in geography and history', in T. Taylor, C. Fahey, J. Kriewaldt & D. Boon (eds), *Place and Time: Explorations in Teaching Geography and History*, Sydney: Pearson, pp. 216–41.

Taylor, T. & Young, C. 2003, *Making History: A Guide for the Teaching and Learning of History in Australian Schools*, Melbourne: Curriculum Corporation.

Volante, L. & Beckett, D. 2011, 'Formative assessment and the contemporary classroom: Synergies and tensions between research and practice', *Canadian Journal of Education/Revue Canadienne de l'éducation*, vol. 34, no. 2, pp. 239–55.

Wiliam, D., Klenowski, V. & Rueda, R. 2010, 'What counts as evidence of educational achievement? The role of constructs in the pursuit of equity in assessment', *Review of Research in Education*, vol. 34, pp. 254–84.

CHAPTER 11
Social history in the classroom

Claire Golledge

> It behoves us therefore to cast aside all easy and misleading catchphrases and to press on to *real* analyses by uncovering the *real* forces at work—structures, classes, hierarchies, ethical codes, ideologies, sacred and profane beliefs. There we shall find solid ground for explanations, far from conventional views and superficial clichés. (Bédarida 1991: xiv)

An ongoing challenge of history teaching is how to provide all our students with learning experiences that foster deep historical understanding but are also highly engaging. This chapter explores the possibility of meeting these dual aims by including social history in the classroom and thus reframing for our students what is considered 'official' history, providing an accessible and relatable entry point to historical issues and eras.

In our efforts to give students a sense of the grand sweep of both world and national history, the role of social history can easily be forgotten. As we help our students to comprehend the rise and fall of societies, nations and leaders, the course of wars and the origins of ideologies, it is easy to relegate the role of social history in the classroom to that of mere trivia—knowledge that satisfies a certain curiosity our students might have about everyday life in the past, but less important than political or military history. But to think that would be to underestimate both the importance and the power of teaching social history to our students. Social history allows us to better contextualise and imagine major historical moments for our students. It goes some way towards explaining why particular narratives and themes have ended up dominating the historical landscape while others have been forgotten, opening up opportunities to broach more complex metahistorical ideas in the classroom. Social history is also a way of capturing the imagination and intrigue of a wider range of students, providing them with a more accessible way of thinking about what life was like in the past and simultaneously opening up the complex task of historical thinking.

At its most basic, social history refers to an approach to history that is focused on exploring the lives and social worlds of ordinary people. Interest in and attention to the 'new' social history emerged in the 1960s and 1970s as a growing interest in 'history from below', combined with more multidisciplinary approaches to researching history. Waterhouse (2009) characterises social history as being influenced by the Annales School and the Cambridge Group for the History of Population and Social Structure, as well as economic and labour history and historical archaeology. These new methodologies opened up historical periods to new interpretations and created new themes in historical research, such as women's history and the history of the family unit. These approaches to history stood in stark contrast to more traditional approaches, which concerned themselves with the lives of economic and political elites, warfare, and national and religious movements—often referred to as the 'great man' approach to history. As Susan Treggiari (2002: 6) notes in her social history of Roman society, a social history approach might be concerned with the structure of a society, or how people in that society interacted with one another or, on a more micro level, individual families, households or a group of children playing in the street. Social history challenges old-fashioned definitions of what history is about and requires us as teachers to think critically when we engage with curriculum documents that might direct our teaching choices. It is an approach that expands our students' understanding of 'the historical' to include more than just nations, warfare and 'great' figures in history; it encompasses 'the hearth, the hospital, the family and the community' (Bair & Ackerman 2014: 227).

WHY USE SOCIAL HISTORY IN THE CLASSROOM?

Social history as 'solid ground'

At its best, learning history can be a profound, perspective-changing and even exhilarating experience. History teachers are often drawn to the profession through either a love of learning history or because of their own positive experiences of learning history at school. But despite the positivity and passion of teachers, and the potential of our subject to deeply enrich the lives of our students, the reality is that many students find learning history dull, irrelevant and abstract. Anna Clark (2008), in her conversations with both students and teachers of history, has captured with devastating clarity just how bored and uninspired many students feel about learning the 'facts' of Australian history. We would do well as educators to bear this feedback in mind when thinking about how we approach history with our students, and to think carefully about ways in which we can aim for both rich and deep learning that our students will also find engaging and enjoyable.

Social history is, as Tom Griffiths (2016: 287) describes it, 'history in the active sense, an ethnographic portrait of people doing things, where the fragrance of baking bread mixes with the stench of offal, and the sounds of raucous street life intrude upon quiet moments of domestic intimacy'. Pedagogical approaches that include a social history approach have the ability to engage students by drawing on this sense of life and vibrancy in the classroom, and can be a good counterpoint to more broad or theoretical approaches to historical study. Bédarida (1991) commends this ability of social history to illuminate this 'realness' of history that can often be glossed over when we try to summarise or generalise about historical periods or movements—in his case, he argues for a more complex appreciation of the nature of British national history and British national 'character' by looking at the richness and diversity of British society over time. Similarly in Australia, the work of Grace Karskens (1999, 2009) on Australia's early colonial history has added depth, richness and complexity to a well-worn trope in Australian history—that of the 'convict experience'. Karskens' work is an excellent way of securing students' understanding of historical ideas in ways that defy clichés and stereotypes, and is an interesting way to expose students to the methodologies of social historians. Karskens uses artefacts uncovered in the archaeological exploration of Sydney's historic The Rocks, as well as government and personal records, to vividly and compellingly re-create everyday life in convict Sydney. For students who traditionally consider archaeology to be a tool of the ancient historian, it can be surprising and compelling for them to consider it as a technique that helps us to piece together everyday life in the more recent past. As Waterhouse (2009: 8) notes, it is an approach that shows us that The Rocks 'was not simply a slum inhabited by oppressed convicts and working-class people. Rather, it consisted of women and men making money, accumulating material possessions, creating families and communities.' In this way, approaching the study of an event or era through the lens of social history can provide a more solid, engaging and meaningful footing for students' historical understandings.

A mirror to our classrooms

Engaging with social history is a powerful way in which we as teachers can recognise the capacity of school-based history to speak to broader themes of identity, nationalism and belonging. It is worth remembering that until the very recent past, students would learn nothing of Aboriginal and Torres Strait Islander history or the history of British invasion at school, as Aboriginal perspectives remained unacknowledged in the official 'grand narrative' of Australia. Today, we can readily critique approaches to history education in the past that excluded the voices and experiences of cultural and ethnic minorities as being not only inaccurate representations of Australia's past but also woefully inadequate if we are seeking to engage the imagination and interest of our diverse community of students. While the history curriculum today is much more sensitive to including the experiences and perspectives of groups and individuals who were once ignored in the teaching of history, as teachers we need to remain vigilant about the choices we make in representing the narratives and evidence of the past to our students.

In contrast to a broad-brush 'grand narrative' approach to history that seeks to generalise or universalise the experiences of the elite throughout history, social history seeks to illuminate the experiences of the majority of people who lived in the past. Such an approach considers the voices that are often left out of official historical narratives and creates greater opportunity for students to see people like themselves reflected in the historical record (Bair & Ackerman 2014: 223). Students bring their own sense of history to the classroom—developed through understandings of history in popular culture and the media but also very powerful and personal notions of history developed from family stories and connections to places (Seixas 1996: 766). One of the ways in which the teaching of history at a school level can be most powerful is in helping students to make sense of these personal understandings of history and the ways they sit beside, within or apart from other 'official' historical narratives—and to account for these in relation to bigger historical movements and ideologies.

Social history can be a powerful bridge for our students to help them make the cognitive leap of understanding their own personal history as part of a much broader narrative. This means that although official historical records are often silent on the contributions and significance of women, we must look for and highlight these contributions in places other than mainstream historical source material. For Aboriginal and Torres Strait Islander students, it is through social history and its strong relationship to local histories, oral history and notions of ancestry that we can more directly address the imbalance in official historical records that excluded the voices and experiences of the first Australians, and devalued Aboriginal and Torres Strait Islander ways of knowing and understanding history (Harrison 2012: 7). Ahonen (2001: 192) notes that 'society is a mosaic rather than a monolith'; by incorporating social history into our classrooms, we can ensure that the historical narratives we explore with our students are more sensitive to and reflective of this mosaic.

HISTORICAL THINKING THROUGH SOCIAL HISTORY

Teaching for historical thinking means inducting students into particular ways of thinking about the past, about the meaning and handling of evidence and the coming to conclusions based on that evidence (Seixas & Morton 2013: 2). By including social history in our teaching—particularly in the context of teaching about political, economic and military history—we are providing many more avenues for this rich historical thinking to occur. In particular, including social history in your classroom engages students in considering different historical perspectives on events and the selecting, interpreting and contextualising of historical evidence. It is also through a social history perspective that students can engage in the kind of thinking that leads to meaningful empathetic understandings of the past.

Historical perspectives

Social history is a powerful way of demonstrating to students, in a practical sense, the importance of evidence and perspectives in thinking about the past because it is a direct challenge to 'the fallacy in believing that groups marginalized in the historical record played no active role in shaping the course of history' (Bair & Ackerman 2014: 223). The flourishing of social history over the last several decades also has a lot to teach our students about the process of researching and writing history and the role of the historian's stance in mediating how we encounter historical ideas. Take, for example, the Eureka Stockade, which has long been a feature of history curricula around Australia—most often taught as a distinctly masculine story of mateship, anti-authoritarianism and collectivism, which in turn was a reflection of the prevailing historiography of the goldfields until recently. Historian Clare Wright (2013) provides an interesting case study to discuss with students—not least because of the way she brings the Victorian goldfields to life so vividly through a new reading of the source material. Wright's revisiting of the sources relating to Eureka revealed to her what had remained unseen by those many historians who had gone before her: the presence and activism of women in the Ballarat goldfields, and their active participation in the Eureka Stockade. Wright's work is a stark and powerful reminder to our students of the way in which the prevailing orthodoxy on a particular historical issue is often a reflection of the perspective of individual historians (or, in this case, the collective maleness of all the historians of Eureka who had gone before Wright), and that even well-traversed historical ground can still contain treasures and voices yet to be unearthed, and that different source material can illuminate the perspectives of a more diverse range of historical actors (Barton & Levstik 2004: 257).

Indeed, in the context of teaching Australian history, Eureka sits with a number of other significant national historical 'legends' (Anzac among them), which remain key features of the teaching of history in our schools and where the dominant narratives persist in presenting a particularly one-dimensional view of history. Marilyn Lake (in Lake et al. 2010: 140) argues that the centrality of the Anzac story to the teaching of Australian history has had the effect of marginalising other accounts and explanations for the formation of our national values through other social and political traditions. The teaching of social history in this climate is not only important to balance the dominance of militaristic narratives, but also to impress upon our students that these narratives represent only *one* perspective on our national history. Social history, with its focus on looking at micro-level historical detail, can also work to disrupt neat or simplistic historical explanations by highlighting the particular and thus create a more nuanced context for 'big picture' history (Cohen 2014: 80). Moving away from grand narratives towards a more complex understanding of our history that can accommodate social historical perspectives is also a way of more explicitly engaging our students in historical thinking by considering the multiple, often competing, interpretations of our national history that are in an ongoing jostle for academic supremacy and that resist the idea of history as a logical narrative of progression.

Evidence

Social history also conveys important lessons for our students about the nature of historical evidence. A key aim of developing historical thinking in our students is to take them beyond developing just content knowledge to understand the procedures and tools that are used in developing historical understandings (Lévesque 2008: 27). By using a social history approach, we can distinguish for our students the difference between *reading about* ordinary people from a historical period and *encountering* social history through other artefacts. Historical court records, newspaper reports, wills and the papers of government and charitable organisations are all commonly used by social historians to provide insight into the daily life and world of the general citizenry, but they remain sources primarily written by those who were literate and possessed a degree of social and political power (Shedd 2007: 26). The voices and experiences of everyday people—the working class, women, children, migrants, Aboriginal and Torres Strait Islander people—remain silent or at best mediated. That is not to say we shouldn't make use of such sources with our students—indeed, quite the contrary. It is through the consideration of such source material and through encouraging our students to consider both their uses and limitations that we engage them in the deeper work of historical thinking: looking at whose version of the past is preserved in the artefacts that we collect and pass on over time, and whose voices are left out. Alongside such official records, we could expand our students' understanding of what constitutes historical evidence by using oral history and family stories, the reading of cultural artefacts and everyday objects such as clothing, as well as popular press, magazines and advertisements. Considering such material as historical evidence is a key step in helping our students to develop a more complex understanding of history, as we challenge their prevailing assumptions about what constitutes a source, and what we can learn from the artefacts of the past (Bair & Ackerman 2014: 223).

BRINGING SOCIAL HISTORY INTO THE CLASSROOM

It is clear to see that social history has much to offer our students, and can enrich our teaching of history in a number of ways; however, including social history requires the commitment of teachers to find meaningful space and opportunities in the existing curriculum to explore these ideas. It also involves confronting the challenge presented by the imbalance in the historical records that traditionally leave out the voices of ordinary citizens—an imbalance that we can also see reflected in school history textbooks and other teaching resources (Shedd 2007: 26).

Nevertheless, the opportunities provided by social history to both enrich the learning of historical thinking and engage our students in history in ways that they enjoy mean these challenges are worth confronting. There is a natural synergy between social history approaches to researching and learning history, and pedagogical strategies that embrace project- and topic-based learning, as well as non-linear approaches to historical ideas. Social history can therefore be viewed as a flexible and creative option that might find a place in your classroom in a number of different ways. With this in mind, I now make four practical suggestions as to how to use social history in the classroom.

Do empathy well

Empathy is one of the most sophisticated skills for our students to develop in history, because it involves reconciling our common humanity with those things that separate us humans across time periods (von Heyking 2004). Often, many of the teaching and learning strategies used in history classrooms presuppose that students have a good grasp of social history and can forget that the exercise of historical empathy requires students to have sufficient contextual historical knowledge to understand the actions and decisions of people in the past (von Heyking 2004). When we ask our students to undertake a creative writing task that imagines a day in the life of an English peasant, or to write a diary entry pretending they are a soldier in the trenches of World War I, or we ask them to role-play a particular character in history, we need to be mindful that students need to have the necessary knowledge and understanding of social history to do these things well. In order for students to properly engage in these tasks, which require the exercise of historical empathy, we must first provide them with an understanding of the social structures and relationships of these people, their home life, their background, the community to which they belong, their work, their level of wealth and the reasons that underlie their particular social role in the historical period being studied. Developing students' understanding in these areas is no straightforward task, and often involves looking outside traditional historical source material to think about the artefacts and evidence of people's social lives; it raises wider questions to discuss with students about the nature of history from 'above' or 'below'.

Engaging with sources that reveal everyday life in the past allows students to more readily mentally 'time travel' to those times and places. This more secure understanding of the nature of everyday life in the past is an important step towards supporting them in developing a deep empathetic understanding of the past that allows them to set aside their own personal, moral perspectives and better evaluate historical events and ideas in context (Lee & Shemilt 2011: 40).

Use social history as an entry point

While we may need to work within the confines of the topics required by history syllabuses, most historical topics can be approached, or at least introduced, from a social history perspective, which can provide students with important context and understanding, and create a solid foundation to begin a historical inquiry. This may also be a good opportunity to connect political or national history with more personal and local histories that may resonate with your particular students. Before you start drawing maps of the trench system in World War I, perhaps you could look at family connections that your students might have to the Great War. Local newspaper reports might give some insight into life in your students' local community at the time of the war, and will help establish for your students the important contextual understanding that 'societies, not just armies, fight wars' (Bair & Ackerman 2014: 222).

Help students make sense of historiography

There is often little time and space in the history classroom to teach our students about historiography. In the drive to teach them about different historical events or people, we often lose the opportunity to discuss the wider questions of selection, interpretation and representation of those events and people in historical works (and even the choices that have resulted in their inclusion in the syllabus). Social history, in the way it offers alternatives to official sources and dominant narratives, works to demonstrate to our students what we mean by history as an interpretive discipline marked by ongoing 'epistemological turmoil' (Fallace & Neem 2012: 331), in which different groups and historians have understood issues and events differently over time (Parkes 2007: 126).

In *The Art of Time Travel*, Tom Griffiths (2016: 119) describes a writing technique used by historian Greg Dening, in which he asked his first-year undergraduate history students to write about their own social worlds as a way of fostering an understanding of history as 'a form of consciousness, a definition of humanity, a way of seeing—and changing—the world'. Asking our students to describe their own worlds—their school or their friendship groups—or to nominate the artefacts and evidence of their lives in which a social historian of the future might be interested (for example, their mobile phones, their instant-messaging histories, their photo streams, their clothing or food preferences) is a powerful way of helping them to conceptualise history as a research discipline that is reliant on interpretation and evidence. An activity such as this can then provide an entry point to discussing with students how historians draw conclusions and make arguments based on the evidence they have, and can be an accessible way for students to understand how different historians reach different conclusions about historical events.

Let your students experience the history

Perhaps one of the most engaging ways of harnessing social history in your classroom is to let students explore it themselves. Some ideas of how to do this include:

- asking students to conduct an oral history interview with someone they know who lived through an interesting era or event
- teaching students how to request records at a local archive or use an online resource such as Trove to find records relating to military history or migration, then reading these together to find out what they can learn from these records
- exploring a physical or online museum space that represents some aspect of social history
- encouraging students to ask about their own family and community histories and share examples of their family's own social history, either through photographs, films or objects of significance
- considering the history of food—through recipes published in old magazines and newspapers or from their own family history. What do recipes from the past tell us about how people farmed, shopped, cooked, lived, ate and celebrated in the past?
- using the commonality of the school environment as a shared social history experience for your students. Explore old school photos, newsletters and yearbooks with students—discuss changes that they observe over time. Perhaps they notice the raising of hemlines and the

appearance and disappearance of subjects such as 'home economics', and you could use this as a way of discussing the history of gender and education? Or perhaps reflect on changes in the size and ethnic diversity in the school and what these tell us about changes in your local community.
- reading local newspapers to identify local stories and sites of controversy and conflict that may have been long forgotten, but at the time were passionately fought.

CONCLUSION

Social history presents an opportunity to allow your students to experience history firsthand. It provides an avenue through which you can engage them in the process of researching, interpreting evidence and developing their own conclusions about historical eras and events. It provides an entry point to cultivating discussion and debate in your classroom, as you require students to justify their interpretations and engage with new perspectives. It is a chance to make the learning of history lively, vivid and, most importantly, enjoyable. Not only will such an approach see your students expand their understanding of history in a disciplinary sense, but they will also develop a more sophisticated and multidimensional understanding of the past as they consider history from this new point of view. Let the 'ordinary people' of the past come to life in your classroom!

REFERENCES

Ahonen, S. 2001, 'Politics of identity through history curriculum: Narratives of the past for social exclusion—or inclusion?', *Journal of Curriculum Studies*, vol. 33, no. 2, pp. 179–94.

Bair, S.D. & Ackerman, K. 2014, 'Not your father's civil war: Engaging students through social history', *Social Studies*, vol. 105, no. 5, pp. 222–9.

Barton, K.C. & Levstik, L.S. 2004, *Teaching History for the Common Good*, Mahwah, NJ: Lawrence Erlbaum.

Bédarida, F. 1991, *A Social History of England, 1851–1990*, 2nd ed., London: Routledge.

Clark, A. 2008, *History's Children: History Wars in the Classroom*, Sydney: UNSW Press.

Cohen, M. 2014, 'Population, politics and unemployment policy in the Great Depression', *Social Science History*, vol. 38, nos 1–2, pp. 79–87.

Fallace, T. & Neem, J.N. 2012, 'Historiographical thinking: Towards a new approach to preparing history teachers', *Theory & Research in Social Education*, vol. 33, no. 3, pp. 329–46.

Griffiths, T. 2016, *The Art of Time Travel: Historians and Their Craft*, Melbourne: Black Inc.

Harrison, N. 2012, 'Putting history in its place: Grounding the Australian Curriculum: History in local community', paper presented at the Joint AARE APERA International Conference, Sydney.

Karskens, G. 1999, *Inside The Rocks: The archaeology of a neighbourhood*, Sydney: Hale & Iremonger.

—— 2009, *The Colony: A History of Early Sydney*, Sydney: Allen & Unwin.

Lake, M., Reynolds, H., McKenna, M. & Damousi, J. (eds) 2010, *What's Wrong with Anzac? The Militarisation of Australian History*, Sydney: NewSouth Publishing.

Lee, P. & Shemilt, D. 2011, 'The concept that dares not speak its name: Should empathy come out of the closet?', *Teaching History*, no. 143, pp. 39–49.

Lévesque, S. 2008, *Thinking Historically: Educating Students for the Twenty-first Century*, Toronto: University of Toronto Press.

Parkes, R.J. 2007, 'Teaching history as historiography: Engaging narrative diversity in the curriculum', *International Journal of Historical Learning, Teaching and Research*, vol. 8, no. 2, pp. 118–32.

Seixas, P. 1996, 'Conceptualizing the growth of historical understanding', in D.R. Olsen & N. Torrance (eds), *The Handbook of Education and Human Development: New Models of Learning, Teaching and Schooling*, Cambridge, MA: Blackwell, pp. 765–83.

Seixas, P. & Morton, T. 2013, *The Big Six Historical Thinking Concepts*, Toronto: Nelson.

Shedd, J.A. 2007, 'Bringing ordinary people into the picture', *The History Teacher*, vol. 41, no. 1, pp. 25–37.

Treggiari, S. 2002, *Roman Social History*, New York: Routledge.

von Heyking, A. 2004, 'Historical thinking in the elementary years: A review of current research', *Canadian Social Studies*, vol. 39, no. 1, <https://files.eric.ed.gov/fulltext/EJ1073974.pdf>, accessed 20 June 2018.

Waterhouse, R. 2009, 'Locating the new social history: Transnational historiography and Australian local history', *Journal of the Royal Australian Historical Society*, vol. 95, no. 1, pp. 1–17.

Wright, C. 2013, *The Forgotten Rebels of Eureka*, Melbourne: Text Publishing.

PART 3
TEACHING APPROACHES

CHAPTER 12
Teacher talk within the history classroom

Tim Allender

That really worked. How did such great history teaching really happen? I wonder how many of us have asked ourselves that question on a good day—or, better still, asked an experienced teacher the same question after seeing a particularly inspiring history lesson. Chances are the reply is steeped in strong disciplinary language: an intuitive response that offers good description of the orchestration of skills, key competencies and key concepts as they come together to interrogate subject content. Reassuringly, we also know that there is much more to our craft than just deciding what content is to be included. This is unlike the political debate in the general community around history teaching, mostly run by non-experts who only have a superficial narrative about content choice to offer as we are told what to teach the young.

There are other forces at work, too, which tend to obscure deeper understanding of best-practice history teaching as it actually occurs in the classroom. For teachers, the busy teaching day renders only brief resting points to reflect on teaching success. But these are moved on quickly as other, more mundane, imperatives press themselves to the fore. The only witnesses to such praxis are usually students, without perspective or professional expertise, yet the chief beneficiaries of such teaching expertise.

THE SETTING

To attempt to recover some of the deeper script, this chapter explores in more explicit terms the disciplinarity of history teaching (its distinctive features) by briefly examining some of the interactive structures within the classroom that usually go undocumented. The chapter is based on research that was part of a four-year Australian Research Council funded project, comparing the teaching of novice and best-practice history teachers, as well as teachers teaching other disciplines. The teaching level researched was the last two years of senior school, taught by experienced and creative teachers.

The research examined mostly contiguous lessons within six-week units of work, and its emphasis was on scrutinising the phenomenology of day-to-day teaching. This was without holding any teacher up to a putative standard of 'excellence' in the classroom, or seeing any transferable recipe of success, given the many variables typically impacting history classroom teaching. Interviews with teachers before and after each lesson were also conducted to discover intended teacher classroom directions before the lesson, and to hear teacher accounts of variance to these directions after each lesson. For clarity concerning content discussion, in this chapter the analysis is confined to two experienced history teachers (each with over 30 years' experience in the classroom) teaching just one topic each: the Cuban Missile Crisis and Ancient Republican Rome.

While some academics see modern and ancient history as two separate disciplines, this chapter sees them more as two parts of one disciplinary whole. The teachers studied saw the practice of their craft in these terms as well. They also identified their classes as mixed-ability, and their students belonged to the same age group and were of the same gender. However, to talk to these teachers about their history teaching, their language was always discipline specific, highly self-reflective on practice, and accretive in terms of what might be done better next time.

Their honing of teaching practice according to 'what works' in the history classroom over many years is seen as significant. This chapter references research that more formally elaborates some of their approaches. Yet the chapter seeks to recover the voice of experienced history teachers in school whose practice has sometimes been neglected as university-driven historical thinking models have been developed around the world.

What of the students? Before looking at these teacher actions in more detail, it is important to say something of what their students brought to the classroom. A distinguishing feature of this secondary school-based history teaching was the student part of the conversation as adolescent learners. Part of this conversation concerned them as unconscious conduits for imperfect community understandings of what the craft of the historian actually is. This was worth thinking about. The most alluring aspect of popular history was that these students projected an enthusiasm and curiosity promoted by things such as feature films and family ancestral lore—fertile territory for the canny teacher. Yet community interest in history also established stereotypes and notions of history's 'lessons' that were liable to be inserted back by these students into contemporary political debates where they did not belong. Much more could be said here, except to mention the work of Amy von Heyking (2011) and Ruth Sandwell (2014), who also trace in detail the different deficits in understanding historical processes that primary school children and undergraduate students (quite apart from secondary school level) typically display as they learn the discipline.

Now to the experienced history teachers. This interest in, and sometimes misappropriation of, history was already part of the cultural capital that most of these secondary school students brought to school. And rendering it, in terms of the authentic academic discipline, was about how these expert teachers destabilised student assumptions and untangled student understandings in relation to what the discipline might yield in terms of deeper and contestable interpretation. In this sense, these teachers stood astride the complex relationship that John Tosh (2008) identifies between academic and popular history: a dichotomy that Hsu-Ming Teo (2011) concludes is also prevalent where Asian student settings and popular culture are taught. This is also where professional practice in history stands for furthering historical knowledge and where popular history is mobilised for many other purposes, including policy justifications, celebrity identity projects and money-making entertainment. There are also other choices for the teacher to make. As new research by Henrik Elmersjö, Anna Clark and Monika Vinterek (2017), among others, demonstrates, single narratives about whose history to include and whose to leave out require revision with finely honed skills in teaching rival histories within one teaching setting.

The relationship between popular and academic history also provided more immediate dilemmas for these classroom teachers. For example, how did they move students away from the false binaries and characterisations that have been inherited from the protagonists of the 'black armband' polemic about Australia's nineteenth-century contact history (Macintyre & Clark 2003)? Or popular and over-romanticised commemoration of war history (Lake et al. 2010)? Or earlier, often repeated, student exposure to graphic film footage on television of the horrors of the Holocaust that somehow detach students emotionally from its reality (Elder, Gassert & Steinweiss 2017)?

Facilitation in moving students beyond these mentalities to frame their observations and interpretations in more formal academic ways was an important part of the history classroom learning that was observed.

TEACHER VOICE

The impact of witnessing these large history classes being taught complex topics was immediate. The research quickly identified the agency of teacher voice as central to the craft of history teaching, particularly in the way it orchestrated the disciplinary intersections between epistemology and pedagogy, teacher procedure and student cognition. This voice was also built using a repertoire of intuitive adaptations to classroom realities in terms of student interest and knowledge deficits, although these adaptions remained largely unscripted—even to the teachers themselves.

Compared with less experienced teachers, these experienced teachers were conscious that the greatest variance and distinctiveness in their teaching style was likely to be in the category of classroom verbal exchanges. This was because they viewed their professional discretion at its strongest and most negotiable here, mostly dependent on their formative assessment of student progress as their respective units of work developed over several weeks. For them, the prompts for changes in classroom exchanges could be on several levels concerning student cognition. For example, student deficits in historical literacy, such as understanding the contextual meaning of words such as 'patron', 'client' or 'sacerdotal' in Ancient Rome, or flaws in their grasp of social change in the 1960s at the time of the Cuban Missile Crisis, were likely to redirect how these teachers orchestrated classroom exchanges in subsequent lessons. However, these changes in direction were not an entirely spontaneous phenomenon. They were still directed by teacher-favoured forms of teacher–student interaction and a wish by these teachers to remain motivated over a long career span by deliberately changing parts of their dominant strategies on a year-by-year basis.

> *Experienced History Teacher 1 (EHT1):* Look, to be honest I get bored incredibly easily ... I do it differently each year ... [although] storytelling is a key part of my teaching.

THE INTERACTIVE FEATURES OF QUESTIONING IN CLASSROOM EXCHANGES

A critical feature of the discipline for these experienced teachers was the use of questioning in classroom exchanges: a multidimensional activity in history teaching. Questioning was conducted by these teachers as a central part of learning about the discipline, and was also linked by them to formal assessment questions at the end of the unit. This latter linkage was used to indicate to students ahead of time what mastery of the subject looked like, at least as far as the syllabus was concerned. And successful teacher prosecution of this learning required strong disciplinary expertise.

> EHT2: If you can't design good test questions, how can you design good questions for your classroom? I don't think the two skills are that different, but I guess it does depend on the experience of the teacher... it doesn't necessarily mean teacher experience in terms of years, just: 'Do they [the teachers] know what they are doing?'

Broadly speaking, classroom exchanges that involved questioning fell into three categories: two that were teacher sponsored and one that was initiated by students.

Category 1 exchanges

The first category was the most powerful in orchestrating disciplinary procedure. This category involved questioning used to initiate students into historiography, revisionism and new interpretation as a central part of the discipline. In this category, carefully devised questions were used to posit new lines of inquiry and to test earlier assumptions that were first deliberately established by the teacher as a pretext for deeper research.

For example, EHT1, when teaching the Cuban Missile Crisis, first established the late 1960s Western stereotype of Kennedy's 'victory' over the Soviets using Arthur Schlesinger's pro-Kennedy assessment of an unconditional Soviet 'backdown' that supposedly ended the crisis. The teacher portrayed this myth as established knowledge by posing several broad questions. Only then, as a second step in later lessons, were new questions asked to reveal the 1990 revisionist view, which focuses on US missiles in Turkey and the Cold War situation in Berlin, and a less sympathetic understanding of the Kennedy administration in 1962.

This questioning also suggested what might be significant when using these newly revealed sources as students embarked on their independent research.

> *EHT1:* Bearing in mind ... how Kennedy handled the crisis ... about measured steps ... but really laying down the line about retaliative action ... and Kennedy's ability to leave the door open ... would you say Schlesinger has got it pretty right?

then ...

> *EHT1:* If new evidence became available that was about the Soviet perspective on the Cuban Missile Crisis, how might this change our view that Kennedy had won and no deals were done in secret regarding Berlin and Turkey?

The multifunctionality of such questions was often the centrepiece of classroom interchange, building student understanding about how myths are built and how dominant they can become in the popular imagination.

Astute teacher prompting, and the introduction of new documents drawn from authentic online government archives (and carefully introduced by the teacher so not to swamp students with too much information at once), then allowed students to move from this interpretative site to their own account of events.

The new interpretation was still relatively unsteady as students began reassessing the evidence to make sense of it. But the teacher questions themselves offered a source of academic stability in this interim stage of student academic speculation. Student source analysis then became a more manageable exercise in verification and interpretation, leading to varied student-led theorisations of events that were solid enough to allow for cross-contestation by fellow class members.

Category 2 exchanges

A second category of teacher questioning was used more frequently. These were questions that concentrated on historical thinking key concepts such as 'contestability' and 'perspectives' (see the examples that follow) to explore one aspect of the discipline.

Additionally, mapping of questioning in this category showed important differences in teacher approach, with one teacher concentrating on contextual and inference-style questioning, while the other focused more on grouping affective/empathy and evidence category questions.

EHT2: Might the patron–client relationship established during the Pre-Republican period provide a foundation for a stable, conservative society? Or undermine it?

EHT1: Is it possible that the Soviet Union felt threatened by the United States? Provide evidence for your answer.

Both teachers strategically positioned their questioning. Their questions were expressed in simple language, but they sought responses in higher-order categories of analysis, synthesis and evaluation. These questions were mostly inserted in the middle to concluding lessons of the unit. They also had new propositions embedded in them, involving subtle and complex deductions, particularly about social attitudes, customs or political intrigue. Shifting the frame in this way also indicated to the teacher how deeply students understood the topic.

Category 3 exchanges

The third category concerned student-initiated questions, and these were quite different. In both classes, students were encouraged by their teacher to ask simpler questions as these questions occurred to them, to give meaning to the past events about which they were learning from primary evidence, secondary reading, handouts or teacher talk. The variety in genre of student questioning included simple comprehension, establishing context, cause and effect, attempting judgements, relational and comparative, and chronology/ordering-style questions. A key feature in both classes, though, was that once students were acquainted with the central themes of the unit, and were reassured by the boundaries around the inquiry, both teachers judged the success of their teaching by the emergence of simple, affective, empathetic questions initiated by their students.

Did Romans value their wives?
I wonder what the Russians thought of Kennedy?

These questions were then used as teacher talking points, as part of agreed and seemingly spontaneous student-created agendas, to foster deeper analysis for further classroom work.

Although reliant on some content foundation, students were also encouraged (usually in group settings) to ask questions of significance that naturally arose to them and to share these as part of cross-mentoring exercises. Teacher intervention was deliberately constrained here as teacher-directed learning gave way to the complementarity of allowing students to find out more spontaneously what interested them and to articulate its significance as a means of building their own learning pathways (for more on this phenomenon, see Coomeyras 1995). The orchestration of the teacher, as part of classroom talk, was then to bring disciplinary order to these discussions, through follow-up questions that had as their subtext the application of skills, concepts and competencies apposite to the key content of the unit of study.

TELLING THE STORY: WHAT WERE THE PROCEDURES?

Another generative for students to understand interpretation in history was teacher use of narrative (Husbands 1998: Ch. 4; Kennedy 1998). The procedure was used to configure learning well beyond the lesson in which it was used, and it provided reference to the entire unit under study. In this way, the teacher maintained control of the central lines of inquiry and the order in which key content was brought into play.

What made this procedure compelling for students was how the history teacher inserted their personal experience about an earlier life setting. This virtuosity was strongly idiosyncratic in terms of the standpoint of the teacher, but it verifies Salber Phillips' (2013: 91–2) assertion that orientation of the self and the past can be regarded as a crucial axis for the intellectual progression of students of history as they grasp the nature of change.

The telling of personal teacher stories was also the site where these teachers chose to illustrate how the use of different categories of evidence could yield different interpretations. For example, how might a sympathetic biography offer different interpretative opportunities compared with an archive that contains an array of previously unworked primary sources? When taught in the abstract, this latter pursuit concerning archival evidence is often too dry to sustain school student interest. But learning became instinctive and more easily calibrated and applicable when it was built out from personal narrative.

For example, when teaching the Cuban Missile Crisis of 1962, EHT1's organisation of the topic was around his personal story, where additional stimulus material was deliberately absent. His personal experience was in the social and political context of Ireland in 1962:

> On the morning of Tuesday, 23 October ... I had just stepped out of bed and was heading to the kitchen to get breakfast ... my parents were listening very intently to the radio, and I heard Kennedy's speech about the discovery of Soviet missiles in Cuba. Something had clearly occurred because Cuba had not been in the news and missiles in Cuba did not make any sense. The President was saying there could be a full-blown retaliative response upon the Soviet Union. And it was quite clear that ... something very dangerous was happening ... I remember all day at school there was a real concern that we could be plunged into a nuclear war.
>
> That afternoon after school, sitting with my friend Clare on the wall outside her house, we talked about it. We were quite worried about it ... and then something really uncanny happened, we heard some rolling thunder in the distance and it just kept going ... it was just a thunderstorm ... but there was some real palpable sense of ... that maybe it has really started ... there was a full-blown crisis much greater than any events I had ever known.
>
> Finally, on Sunday, 28 October we heard the crisis was over ... There was no doubt in ... our minds that Kennedy had won ... that the Russians had caused it ... and that Kennedy, the young handsome President of that time who we all loved, had basically stood firm and the Russians had backed down.

EHT1 then used his story to reveal international circumstances, framing in the process a site for possible student contestation and inquiry:

> Something else occurred after that I suppose. I don't think I ever looked at the world again in exactly the same way. In the weeks after the Cuban Missile Crisis, I found I took much more interest in what was going on in the world, became much more conscious of the Cold War situation ... I also found my musical taste was changing because I stopped listening to songs like ... 'Happy Birthday Sweet Sixteen': didn't seem to make a lot of sense anymore ... in the following May, Bob Dylan released *Freewheelin'* and that was the path I chose ... I was very interested that he didn't condemn Kennedy, he didn't condemn Kruschev ... but he wrote a song called 'Masters of War' that attacked the makers of weapons ... who then live off the profits of them ...

EHT1 was using a story to begin the unit based on a strong account of lived experience. Aware that his students could not effectively interpret further until they had sufficient content knowledge, he was able to pursue the topic because he was in control of 'his' story and the realities apparent to him in 1962. The story—'personal, romance, me as a boy'—built in perceptions of what it was like to experience the crisis firsthand. The frame was then shifted to identify the assumptions established by US propaganda, but with an inkling that EHT1's subsequent more radical political outlook would develop as his growing political awareness intersected with the radical socio-political change of the later 1960s.

Substantial content was almost absent from these early lessons of the unit. However, the hidden teacher agenda was to give students the sense that a problem-solving exercise awaited in broad frame as to who were the 'victors' of the Cuban Missile Crisis and some suggestion of the interpretive role of the historian in determining this.

This kind of classroom speculation took students quickly into the realm of history's deeper disciplinary procedure. Although the new topic, and their developing understanding of it, remained anchored by the teacher story at its centre, the advantages of the approach were in maintaining student interest and offering well-defined lines for subsequent inquiry, interpretation and problem-solving. The teacher was aware, however, that this procedure meant other student academic deficits about key content and context were likely to be greater to begin with than if plainer, more directional classroom activities were employed, such as traditional essay writing or short-answer responses. These deficits necessitated a regrouping in other ways to consolidate student learning.

EHT1 then moved to a primary source about a Kennedy–Lyndon Johnson exchange during the Cuban Missile Crisis, where new levels of interpretation were admitted by teacher talk. The teacher informed the class that Kennedy knew the exchange was being recorded and asked how this might influence what was being said. The class was also asked what the source revealed about the broader international scene at the time. Group work then began with these two key points as themes, but with each group assigned basic research questions into different aspects relating to them. Cross-mentoring was encouraged and student learning was facilitated by the obligation of each group to explain their findings to the class and to question their peers in other groups about their responses to the question posed for their group. The teacher also heavily narrated the student-centred learning approach in the reporting-back phase to the class. The safety and accessibility of his easily understood personal story was returned to as a kind of academic refuge, to regroup when students became lost in later lessons when ambitious primary source inquiry to test higher-order skills had moved too quickly.

This procedure needed to consider less able students as well. As Wineburg (1991), among others, has shown, students are least likely to be able to see alternative and many meanings in textual analysis of sources. Less able students in particular were more likely to find the second step of rich source analysis very difficult because this involved a rapid disciplinary shift into higher-order skills that the storytelling approach had foregrounded. And here, group work was seen as the key.

> EHT1: Some of the 'weaker students' are then able to present to the rest of the class reasonably effectively . . . they turn themselves into experts . . . they have to make an effort . . . and they are also picking up on the advice and the ideas they are getting from the stronger students in the group.

Personal storytelling used in this way as an effective procedure was reliant on one key student skill: students' capacity to use empathy. Though there is insufficient space here to elaborate, it is interesting that by way of contrast, EHT2 used empathy and personal narrative more in terms of role-play to reinforce student understanding of the interactive legal, social and economic elements of early Ancient Rome. This gave her students a stronger and more adaptive knowledge so they were able to anticipate the effects of change on Roman society and also to make stronger links to the contemporary world.

However, despite these differences in approach, empathic understanding was regularly embedded in both EHT1's and EHT2's teaching procedures, even though they did not identify the use of this skill as the primary focus in any one lesson. Part of the reason for this may have been that the applicability of the use of empathy over a wide range of individual student perceptions and emotional responses makes it difficult to codify and formally assess, and therefore problematic to teach in explicit terms.

Finally, it is important to note that the storytelling approach using teacher talk that has just been illustrated could just as easily be adapted to the lived experiences of others experiencing different events in history.

They might be invited guests to the classroom or their story could be conveyed as a recorded digital story—many of which are available online. Their attendant subjectivities could then be explored in the classroom using the historian's craft of verification or problematisation, by examining many different categories of evidence in the documentary record relating to the relevant historical topic.

HOW DO THE ACTIVITY STRUCTURES PREVALENT IN THE CLASSROOM WORK?

As already mentioned, teacher talk was usually at the meta level where stronger thematic overlays were imposed to order content. Both teachers also used interpretations of their central script to regulate the pace at which they moved through key phases of the topic. Student concerns were usually about content knowledge, which for them was also the main barometer of their mastery of the discipline. However, teacher perception and focus on the issue of student learning were more about the deliberate pacing of lessons, an explanation of the discursive elements around key concepts and making themselves, as teachers, sufficiently accessible to monitor predictable student insecurities when higher-order speculation and contestation became part of their teacher talk.

> *EHT2*: Students need to feel comfortable with me to be able to say what they are feeling . . . And so at one point they had a meltdown and they came in and they said, 'we're not getting this, this is so hard' and then we had to basically take that whole lesson out as a revision . . . [and] consolidate. It wasn't that they weren't getting it but that it was hard, that they felt the pace was a bit fast and that they were telling me that they needed to stop and just check their understanding.

Testing higher-order skills through the sequencing of activities and teacher talk intervention was also a strong part of teacher reflection on practice. For example, when responding to student confusion about how key content fitted in with the themes associated with early Rome, EHT2 speculated that had role-play activities been introduced earlier in the unit, this problem might have been addressed better. This was even though this kind of alterative activity still needed to be delayed until students had sufficient content knowledge and perspective.

Of course, these carefully orchestrated strategies could only hold student interest for so long. Part of learning content was also to have fun. The quirky and even the slightly prurient were used by both teachers, and here the play was seemingly just as much about entertaining teacher reactions as it was about a semblance of new knowledge. In fact, both teachers resisted a sense that content might be censored for their senior students, and they were conscious that brief diversions into the anecdotal were useful catalysts in history learning. These diversions included anecdotes about what counted as masculinity in Ancient Rome, including a close reading of Herodotus and the practice of necrophilia. Or the case of Alexander the Great: hero or tyrant, depending on who was writing about him and his social context, which identified different sexual mores compared with today.

Or, at the height of the confrontation with the Soviets during the Cuban Missile Crisis in 1962, it could be four-year-old Caroline Kennedy interrupting a meeting and asking her father why her friends were not allowed into his office and then a conversation about eating candy as they left the room with her father's arm around her shoulder.

> EHT1: 'then he [Kennedy] came back in again and continued his meeting about the missiles in Cuba . . . so I said to the class that was probably the most important moment of the Cuban Missile Crisis— why do you think I would say that? . . . then one girl put up her hand and said, 'Well probably because he saw what he had to lose' and I thought, that's the moment [of final decision-making], just there, that was the moment.

Stéphane Lévesque (2008: 60) rightly argues that to be meaningful, the past must be organised coherently, and part of this coherence is to teach students what is significant and what is trivial. However, the trivial was an important motivator for both teachers as they emerged from deeper scholastic endeavours that could only hold student attention for so long.

FOREIGN INTERVENTION: ASSESSMENT

The nexus between activity structures and the learning of content was also responsible for teacher sensitivity to the intervention of external examinations. These examinations disrupted their professional discretion because these methods of assessment were necessarily blind to the dynamics and the individual learning needs of their classrooms. This was particularly so when syllabuses over-prescribed mandated content and thereby telescoped unmanageably high volumes of disciplinary practice needed to work this content into a discourse worthy of senior school history. Traditional written external examination as a means of surveillance of student content knowledge, rather than other forms of school-based examination, was also seen as complicit in this extra-disciplinary assessment imposition.

> *EHT1:* [If the] curriculum is overcrowded, you cut back and cut back but then you've got stuff you just don't want to compromise.
>
> *Tim Allender:* So the danger is the pedagogy sort of fades away and becomes more a function of fused, almost transferable prescribed content?
>
> *EHT1:* That happens when we're doing that kind of exam work as opposed to, say, next term when we do a research piece where they do orals in the exam block.

For both teachers, content organised around key teacher-sponsored learning activities, independent of external examination procedures, was seen as a more desirable educational practice. This was provided that teachers were experts in history disciplinary practice, and the use of skills and concepts was taught deliberately to progressively enhance student competencies for the study of subsequent history topics.

HOW DO TEACHERS DESCRIBE THE KNOWLEDGE BASE AND THE DISTINCTIVE BENEFIT FOR THEIR STUDENTS?

Before addressing this question directly, it is perhaps apt to make the following general observations. Of course, history's place in any schooling curriculum is never an assured thing. A good example of this lack of surety was in the mid-1970s in England, when the Schools Council History Project (1976) began designing a new history curriculum for students aged thirteen to sixteen years. It rightly predicated its work on history being a unique discipline in terms of its procedural 'symbols' and conceptualisations. However, this externalisation of history's disciplinarity in the classroom to education bureaucrats and other powerbrokers yielded uncomfortable surmises. Earlier work, such as that of Hallam (1967, later revised) and McNally (1970), had already concluded that much of this discipline, in this high academic sense, was only available to students with a Piagetian cognitive level typical of 16.5 years or older. If this was the case, should not the study of history be limited only to the latter years of senior school because, so the argument went, students were not old enough in the junior years to authentically study its true academic depth?

Fortunately, this largely non-expert logic was headed off partly because of the separate projects of scholars Dennis Shemilt (1987) and Martin Booth (1994). Their work demonstrated history's capacity in the junior schooling years to generate complex thought that was recognisable as part of the discipline, independently of Piaget's cognitive stages. The proviso was that it needed to be taught by expert teachers well versed in the subject and in its discipline-specific pedagogy. History syllabuses in Australia, though rather palely reflecting other history academic revisionisms, incorporated these developments by entrenching their new skills-based approaches in the 1990s.

A generation later, in contemporary Australia, it would seem even more probable that history should slip from the curriculum scene in an age more interested in cultural studies, neoliberalism, globalisation and transnational critiques. Yet, if anything, history is becoming more embedded—admittedly imperfectly—as a first-order academic subject in schools as the Australian Curriculum is implemented.

For the experienced teachers studied, their case for teaching history did not carry this theoretical perspective. However, their case was heavily dependent on what they saw as happening in their classrooms, which was of much broader application.

> EHT2: I've always thought that kids need to be taught how to think because only some of them do it as a natural part of their daily lives ... they don't develop themselves as critical thinkers anymore ... they don't know how to think logically, they don't know how to analyse and plan strategically so they have to be taught how ... the skills that they are bringing are in terms of being able to think globally, think socially and think empathetically, they're valuable but the world still needs analytical, evaluative, logical thinking as well, and that needs to be taught.

The contribution here was to in fact work against what Sam Wineburg (1991) has long cautioned is a default shortcoming of even the most talented history students in seeing history as mostly only a set of settled facts to be merely recounted. Ruth Sandwell (2003: 171), citing the work of many others, has characterised this well-identified academic challenge for the history teacher in another way. This is the need for the teacher to contest flawed student approaches that are usually deeply attached to the notion that history is only about absolute knowledge rather than about the art of processes and interpretation. At this level, as part of this taught academic proficiency, EHT2 saw a strong student need to be able to take on criticism and draw from it as part of their academic development rather than being overly dependent on unqualified praise by parents and friends when responding to their developing thought processes.

Yet, distinguishable from this issue, both experienced teachers also viewed the benefits of history in terms of the linkages students were able to make between the past and the present. This was not so much in terms of the problematic learning from history's 'lessons'; rather, it was learning about the human condition and behaviour in the past. This was by direct reference to the development of their students' values and attitudes in the modern world, where they have a script that they can more confidently articulate.

Both teachers were comfortable in allowing this development to occur independently of their own values, and were even proactive in identifying the different formative social context in which they had grown up some three decades earlier compared with today. But what these teachers were mostly concerned with was exercising the student mind to engage and contest the values of other eras, and to understand the historicity that is attached to all value formation, including that of the present student generation.

> *EHT2:* I have a social agenda that I want my students to be critical and questioning [of] ... and to be able to articulate what values they think are important, even if they're different values to mine ... one thing that is very different is the view of my generation on feminism ... most of the girls that I teach think feminism is an outmoded, outdated concept ... whereas to people of my generation, it's still a pretty powerful concept.

With these formative procedures in mind, reference to the contemporary world, and life experience contained within it, was a vital part of both teachers' praxis. This had a twofold purpose: first, to provide tentative comparisons with past societies and their values; and second, to offer a deeper understanding of the assumptions and inheritance of the modern world insofar as it impacts upon their students in the classroom.

CITIZENSHIP AND EMPATHY

So what of the teaching of citizenship and the related issue of empathy? Research into the use of differentiated empathy in the study of history at senior school levels strongly suggests that it is not possible until students have a well-developed sense of who they are and the values and attitudes that drive them (Yeager & Foster 2001: 15). Yet these teachers tended to turn this equation on its head: a significant part of their teaching was driven by end-points where historical study was used to deliberately encourage students to think about their own values and to speculate what forces were driving these values.

In teaching Ancient History, EHT2 focused strongly on the issue of 'citizenship' where Australia's foundational story was compared with Livy's narratives concerning Ancient Rome. The picture was presented in parallel with Australia's experience, but principally to accentuate key differences in citizenship values. For example, having posed a tentative scenario of likeness with student understandings of Australia's citizenship values, the teacher deliberately imposed the 'critical idea' that if the gods planned Rome then did this not justify the abduction of the Sabine women? Or, regarding personalities, comparing Barack Obama's missive that 'if we are going to defend democracy, we have to be seen to be acting in a moral way' with how this might be different from the ethical underpinnings of the rule of Augustus. This comparison was then used by students to speculate about their own understandings of how citizenship values were formed 2000 years ago and how Livy's writings might have reflected these different values.

> EHT2: I think history is good in that it teaches students to take both perspectives—to be able to empathise but also to be able to step back and be detached and look at, well, okay, to *me* this is an unusual practice. To *me* this is a horrific practice. Why then did they do this, there must have been a different value set that made this less horrific to them ... I need to look at the power relationships that made this possible.

At this stage, in the final wrapping up of the unit, the learning broadened to include universal questions requiring good student general knowledge and sophisticated but fluid classroom conversation. How does any society accommodate change to make it stronger? EHT2 saw the classroom response as a 'highly conceptualised discussion now', where Roman expansion embraced multiculturalism but in a different configuration compared with contemporary Australia. Even at this last stage, the students' immediate experience was used by the teacher to build a more complex picture of the past by looking at its differences and similarities, as well as challenging students' ethical norms. Carthage was destroyed in a way utterly unlike what happened to Germany following World War II. The question was also posed of whether individual rights—including the notion of 'indemnity'—strengthen or destabilise society. When considering slavery, Hadrian says yes, while others such as Augustus and Gracis can see both the case for yes or no, and sometimes both. While it is clear that Ancient Rome is a very different society than Australia in the twenty-first century, EHT2 assessed students' understanding of the nearly completed unit by their capacity and fluency to range over much territory: to think in more than one perspective and to see, for example, the interconnection of morality/government/economics, where if one aspect changes, everything else does, too.

EHT1 offered similar views when identifying the principal benefits of the mastery of the subject, including embedded notions around citizenship and empathy. This teacher premeditated what might be a useful conceptual framework to work with regarding values. The example below is EHT1's strategy as a student considers embarking on a case study concerning black deaths in custody and the links with contact history.

> I want [her] to be able to conceptualise things . . . to have a sort of concept in her head about the world as she understands it, say in terms of justice [regarding black deaths in custody] . . . Did she feel that there was something not working in terms of a just society and how a just society operates, and then having her apply that [judgement] to the case study that she wanted to look at . . . So she began to formulate something around respect so I think the mastery is about, for those senior students, it's about coming to terms with the world they live in, who they are as human beings and their understanding of their world and the better place they'd like it to be and then applying it to

history. I want my students really to do history ... [to understand] the subject, its relevance for their life. What is it saying to them about human beings and how human beings should behave.

CONCLUSION

Broadly speaking, comparisons made by this research of both classroom history teachers found that expertise sometimes looked different and was developed in distinctive ways over time by these experienced teachers. These surface differences were strongly underpinned by common aims in the way history's disciplinarity was played out in their respective classrooms in terms of the orchestration of skills, key concepts and key competencies.

However, teacher talk and the way it was interwoven within this rich classroom pedagogic tapestry was a much more defining and organising feature in what these experienced history teachers brought to their respective classrooms. A syllabus and even a formal historical thinking framework are invaluable guides for the inexperienced teacher to use to build and expedite their expertise. Yet this research found the habitus of the experienced teacher in their respective classrooms—fidgety yet assertive in the way they used teacher talk to build historical understanding—was a much more spontaneous and demanding phenomenon.

ACKNOWLEDGEMENT

This chapter is based on research that was part of a four-year Australian Research Council-funded project, ARC DP0663300 P. Freebody, T. Allender, N. Bahr, C. Christenson, A. Wright, 'Disciplinarity and Classroom Practice' (2006–09). Excavating the disciplinary nature of history teaching was assisted by comparing history teaching with that in other subjects, namely physics, biology and music.

REFERENCES

Booth, M. 1994, 'Cognition in history: A British perspective', *Educational Psychologist*, vol. 29, no. 2, pp. 61–9.
Commeyras, M. 1995, 'What can we learn from student questions?', *Theory and Practice*, vol. 34, no. 2, pp. 101–6.

Elder, J.S., Gassert, P. & Steinweiss, A.E. 2017, *Holocaust Memory in a Globalizing World*, Göttingen: Wallstein Verlag.

Elmersjö, H., Clark, A. & Vinterek, M. (eds) 2017, *International Perspectives on Teaching Rival Histories: Pedagogical Responses to Contested Narratives and the History Wars*, London: Palgrave Macmillan.

Hallam, R.N. 1967, 'Logical thinking in history', *Educational Review*, vol. 19, pp. 183–202.

Hansen-Glucklich, J. 2014, *Holocaust Memory Reframed: Museums and the Challenges of Representation*, New Brunswick, NJ: Rutgers University Press.

Husbands, C. 1998, *What is History Teaching? Language, Ideas and Meaning in Learning About the Past*, Buckingham: Open University Press.

Kennedy, D. 1998, 'The art of the tale: Storytelling and history teaching', *The History Teacher*, vol. 31, no. 3, pp. 319–30.

Lake, M., Reynolds, H., McKenna, M. & Damousi, J. (eds) 2010, *What's Wrong with Anzac? The Militarisation of Australian History*, Sydney: NewSouth Publishing.

Lévesque, S. 2008, *Thinking Historically: Educating Students for the Twenty-First Century*, Toronto: University of Toronto Press.

Macintyre, S. & Clark, A. 2003, *The History Wars*, Melbourne: Melbourne University Press.

McNally, D.W. 1970, 'The incidence of Piaget's stages of thinking as assessed by tests of verbal reasoning in several Sydney schools', *Forum of Education*, vol. 29, pp. 124–34.

Salber Phillips, M. 2013, *On Historical Distance*, New Haven, CT: Yale University Press.

Sandwell, R. 2003, 'Reading beyond bias', *McGill Journal of Education*, vol. 38, no. 1, pp. 168–86.

—— 2014, 'On historians and their hearings: An argument for teaching (and not just writing) history', in R. Sandwell & A. von Heyking (eds), *Becoming a History Teacher: Sustaining Practices in Historical Thinking and Knowing*, Toronto: University of Toronto Press, pp. 77–90.

Schools Council History Project 13–16 1976, *A New Look at History*. Edinburgh: Holmes McDougall.

Shemilt, D. 1987, 'Adolescent ideas about evidence and methodology in history', in C. Portal (ed.), *The History Curriculum for Teachers*, London: Falmer Press, pp. 39–61.

Teo, H.-M. 2011, 'Popular history and the Chinese martial arts biopic', *History Australia*, vol. 8, no. 1, pp. 42–66.

Tosh, J. 2008, *Why History Matters*, London: Palgrave.

von Heyking, A. 2011, 'Historical thinking in elementary education: A review of research', in P. Clarke (ed.), *New Possibilities for the Past Shaping History*

Education in Canada, Vancouver: University of British Columbia Press, pp. 175–94.

Wineburg, S. 1991, 'On the reading of historical texts: Notes on the breach between school and the academy', *American Educational Historical Journal*, vol. 28, no. 3, pp. 495–519.

Yeager, E.A. & Foster, S.J. 2001, 'The role of empathy in the development of historical understanding', in O.L. Davis, E.A. Yeager & S.J. Foster (eds), *Historical Empathy and Perspective Taking in the Social Studies,* Lanham, MD: Rowman & Littlefield, pp. 13–20.

CHAPTER 13
Personalised narratives of war and teaching engaging history

Jacqueline Z. Wilson and Keir Reeves

INTRODUCTION

Drawing on its authors' experience teaching history in a regional university, this chapter recounts the key theoretical and practical elements in a project designed to stimulate student engagement in individual research, sample the potential of online archival resources and enhance their appreciation of the subject overall. The approach is premised on a need for discipline-specific topics and activities that cater to a relatively broad range of academic abilities and degrees of historical understanding among the student cohort. As some of the authors' teaching has been in pre-service teacher education, the project is designed to be readily adaptable to the secondary-level history curriculum, and thus serves as a model project for student teachers to take into their own future classrooms.

Sam Wineburg (2001: 5) speaks of 'a tension that underlies every encounter with the past: the tension between the familiar and the strange, between feelings of proximity and feelings of distance in relation to the people we seek to understand'. He identifies conceptual benefits and traps in both sides of this dichotomy if either becomes the dominant mode of historical perception: as he says, 'the pole of familiarity pulls most strongly,' with its potential for us to 'locate our own place in the stream of time ... [b]y tying our own stories to those who have come before us'. The pitfall here is that 'in viewing the past as usable, something that speaks to us with intermediary or translation, we end up turning it into yet another commodity for instant consumption' and in a sense move to a position where the past is deployed primarily as a tool for understanding in the present day—in effect becoming heritage rather than history (2001: 6). Although they are intimately related in their concern for remembering the past, history and heritage are odd companions. By definition, history remembers facts of the past and as a discipline has a commitment to an analytical establishment of what transpired, whereas heritage is the depiction of the past in the present day and not necessarily, or always, interested in factual remembrance.

For Wineburg (2001: 6), 'The other pole in this tension, the strangeness of the past, offers the possibility of surprise and amazement . . . [of opportunities] to reconsider how we conceptualize ourselves.' Approached and perceived in this way, history 'can be mind-expanding in the best sense of the term' (2001: 6). But Wineburg (2001: 6) warns that such an approach, if followed too assiduously, 'detached from the circumstances, concerns, and needs of the present, too often results in a kind of esoteric exoticism'— it is of interest, ultimately, only to a few beyond the relatively narrow circle of professional historians and typified by a connoisseurly approach that can tend towards obscurantist, rather than revelatory as intended.

It follows, then, that the history teacher, whether teaching in a school or university environment, must seek a balance between the two 'poles' of which Wineburg (2001) speaks. This is especially true when faced with students of disparate learning styles and capabilities, unfamiliarity with (or even hostility towards) history as an academic discipline and a generalised dearth of cultural capital owing to personal backgrounds of low socio-economic circumstances and/or geographical isolation. Wineburg (2001: 6) argues 'that historical thinking, in its deepest forms . . . goes against the grain of how we ordinarily think'—a precept all the more apposite when one is attempting to impart the principles of historical thinking to those acculturated to avoid, or even to distrust, history—a detailed intellectual pursuit that by its very nature is nuanced and inherently indeterminate.

A further related aspect to which the history teacher must be vigilant and prepared to counter in the student is what Wineburg (2001: 19) terms '"presentism"—the act of viewing the past through the lens of the present', which is 'our psychological condition at rest, a way of thinking that requires little effort and comes quite naturally'. It is just such 'natural' world-view responses and conceptualisations that most readily characterise many of our students, and that can require the most innovative bespoke teaching. Asking questions of the past through the present is understandable and an obvious way to get students to engage with history. The underlying issue with presentism, though, is that it is ahistorical (non-historical; lacking historical qualities or attributes) because the past is not understood on its own terms as history, but instead is applied to the present day, and is invariably framed by historical sympathies and political persuasions.

HISTORY IN A REGIONAL CONTEXT

We have taught history and history curriculum in the School of Education and Arts at a regional university in Victoria, Australia. Between us, we have over 30 years' teaching experience. The majority of our students are of remote, rural or peri-urban origin; many are the first in their family to undertake tertiary education; and for a variety of reasons, a significant proportion of them arrive with relatively low tertiary-entry scores and many come from low socio-economic backgrounds (Australian Education Union 2008; Australian Government 2008; Hall 2012). They therefore come to us with a wide range of learning needs and capabilities that necessitate an equally diverse range of teaching approaches. For many, the traditional university lecture as the core pedagogical mode is unlikely to be effective, and may well prompt not merely disengagement but unacceptably high dropout rates. Instead, a flexible delivery mode of teaching is deployed that emphasises place-based learning as well as more personalised (and time-consuming) approaches to teaching.

With such imperatives in mind, and mindful of the need to model such eclecticism for those of our students who, as future school teachers, will have to accommodate similarly diverse needs in their own students, we have devised a series of 'hands-on' projects designed to provide context for specific curriculum areas, to 'personalise' the survey-histories that form the basis of much curriculum and to provide opportunities for an interactive experience of primary-source research. A survey-history is a broad historical account of a period, topic or society that identifies the major events and personages deemed to have played key roles in shaping the times. It is more likely to focus on rulers, prominent figures and major conflicts such as wars than on the lives and activities of ordinary people.

These projects are designed to be adaptable for both tertiary- and secondary-level learning. In this chapter, we provide an outline of one example, focusing on World War I, which we have utilised within our own courses and which has also been adapted successfully with minimal alteration to feature in secondary-school settings as a depth study component of the standard Year 9 curriculum.

The project is part of our broader aim to encourage students to employ and explore varieties of media as research tools and educational resources, ultimately including overseas field-based learning. Of particular value, we have found, are sources of a visual nature of the kind that may be readily accessed via the internet. Education theorist bell hooks (2005) argues for the value of visual media that is novel and resonates emotionally with students, in its capacity to promote critical thinking and the personally 'transformative' benefits of constructive questioning and critiquing of students' own assumptions. As we will demonstrate, although much of the material examined by students is nominally verbal text, in the form of its presentation—as scanned digital representations of original, primary-source records—it provides the viewer-researcher with a far more vivid, real-world visual experience than is afforded by the mere reading of words.

THE PROJECT

The project is one we call 'Adopt a Soldier'. The broad Area of Study is World War I, within which our students specifically address the key inquiry question 'What was the significance of the war?' Students are guided to examine three primary sources, accessed via the internet: a pre-World War I political map of Europe (1914); a postwar map of the same region published *c.* 1920, showing the national boundaries resulting from the Versailles Peace Conference; and the 'personnel dossier' of an Australian soldier who fought in the war—that is, his military record (US Army Medical Department n.d.). The following discussion outlines the nature and relevance of, and the conceptual relationship between, those three sources. In the process, we touch upon at least some of the hoped-for intellectual gains envisaged for the students undertaking the project.

Sources 1 and 2: the maps

As Wineburg (2005) states, 'History comes alive when viewed as a patterned story open to ongoing debate.' And unless it *does* somehow come alive, he maintains, those compelled to study it will find it irrelevant and boring beyond endurance—a view that all too often prevails for the rest of their lives. This, then, is a core exercise in problem-solving for the history teacher: how to locate and evoke the 'patterned stories' that reside, perhaps well hidden, within the sources towards which students are guided—hidden, as often as not, because although readily recognised as repositories of *information*, those sources are not so easily perceived as vehicles of 'storytelling'.

It is characteristic of the outlook of many of our students—and this arguably reflects a broad sensibility of our era—that maps, most often in the form of GPS-generated digital 'apps', are utilised and viewed almost entirely as ad hoc aids to personal navigation. For those sharing this technology-driven and radically utilitarian conception of maps, the notion that a map might be viewed as an embodiment of *historical narrative* is at the very least novel, and may well prove palpably alien. There are good reasons for encouraging such a reaction in the educational setting.

The work of the cartographer reflects a momentary, contemporaneous world view, in that it is a synthesis of the available technology/methodology by which location—of topographical features, structures, borders and so on—may be determined, and the prevailing conception and interpretation of those elements depicted. Although familiarity through usage today can encourage us to forget their nature, all maps are inherently symbolic, both in their overall purport and in their diagrammatic particulars; the degree to which those symbols reflect the empirical realities found on the ground may be no more than slight. Thus, to take two obvious examples, an international border that appears precisely defined on a map may effectively be lost among the maze of impossibly rugged terrain of a mountain range, and hence be highly 'porous'; and the neatly drawn arrows and lines on a wartime military map depicting the array of forces at the front inevitably bear no useful resemblance to the shell-churned sea of mud in which soldiers played out their role.

The first map to which our students are guided, via a specific URL, is a scanned high-resolution image of a political map of Europe as it was in 1914 (Wordpress.com n.d.). Given the geo-political disruption about to occur, this map exemplifies the conceptual symbolism of national boundaries and the ephemeral nature of such representations. To underscore this notion, students are then directed to the second map, which provides a stark visual comparison. As the *c.* 1920 map shows, in the half-decade immediately after the 1914 map was current, the territory of many of the European nation-states altered greatly (Hammond & Co. *c.* 1920). The borders of a number of Germany's immediate neighbours shifted, all to Germany's detriment. France became significantly larger in area, Poland resumed its interrupted existence as an independent state, and both the Austro-Hungarian and Ottoman Empires were dissolved completely, leaving the various nationalities in their respective territories to form a number of new or revived independent states.

From a geo-political perspective, and to relate this source to the key inquiry question, World War I is of obvious 'significance', in that it literally transformed the map of Europe. But lines and colours on a map are no less symbolic in 1920 than they were in 1914. It is a key attribute of any map that, although it may represent the artefacts, structures and habitations of people, it does not represent the people themselves. In this way, the political map, when viewed as a historical source (and especially if viewed in juxtaposition with a later map of the same region), stands as a moment in the depersonalised 'grand narrative' typical of the traditional survey history (Wordpress.com, n.d.).

VanSledright (2004: 231) speaks of the historical novice's understanding of the inherent 'bias' in a source as embodying a naïve 'good–bad dichotomy (telling the truth or lying)'. It is arguable; however, that such a 'moralistic' judgement of the work of reputable professional cartographers might be relatively unlikely today, even from the tyro; in company with our day-to-day familiarity with and reliance on maps, we confer upon them a significant degree of authority—that is, we assume they are reliable. Thus we suggest that a first viewing of the pre-World War I map (assuming some familiarity with Europe's post-World War I geography, or at least in conjunction with the marked changes visible in the 1920 map) might be more likely to give rise to a mild case of what psychologists refer to as 'cognitive dissonance'—the sensation of disorientation, confusion and/or defensiveness experienced when *expected* perception does not match experience. From a pedagogical standpoint, such a sensation, if managed constructively within the learning environment, may well give rise to the curiosity needed for optimum student engagement, and facilitate the sense of strangeness, of 'culture shock', that promotes the beginnings of deep historical understanding (Wineburg 2001: 10–11).

Source 3: the soldier

The third source discussed is the military record of Private Joseph Mauldon, a resident of the Melbourne suburb of Collingwood (National Archives of Australia n.d.). Private Mauldon was chosen for convenience, as he happens to have been a distant relative of one of the authors. Mauldon enlisted on 2 February 1917, embarked on the troop transport ship *Ballarat* on 19 February and, after a voyage of some nine weeks, arrived in England on 26 April. The record as it stands tells us nothing about why the voyage took so long; without considerable further research into the activities of the *Ballarat*, we are confined to speculation.

What it does tell us is that at some point during the voyage, Private Mauldon committed a minor infraction of discipline that attracted a penalty of extra duty; this becomes something of a recurring theme in his military career, and suggests a personality unsympathetic to the constraints of authority and orders. Subsequent entries show him going absent without leave, refusing lawful orders, neglecting to wear his uniform correctly when ordered to do so, and ultimately, on 26 December 1917, being subject to a full court-martial for disobeying an order 'in such a manner as to show wilful defiance of authority'. Although found not guilty of the appended charge regarding his attitude, he was found guilty of disobeying the order, and received a suspended sentence of one year's imprisonment.

Further details that one may glean from the record are occasions on which Private Mauldon reports sick, including admissions to hospital, most seriously in October 1918 with influenza—a victim, presumably, of the global influenza pandemic of that year, which killed between 50 million and 100 million people (Harvard University Library n.d.). He survived the flu and, given that he fell sick so close to the end of hostilities in November 1918, saw no further active service. Prior to his hospitalisation, the record tells us that on 25 August he was 'wounded in action'—a bullet wound in the arm—and it appears that it was while he was on leave convalescing from this mishap that he contracted the illness that saw him hospitalised for the duration of the war.

Interpretation

What, then, are we to make of the three sources presented here, and what—if any—is their relationship to one another? In the first place, all may be viewed as 'institutionally' authored, and their chief characteristic in this respect is their tendency to *depersonalise*. This is obvious and uncontroversial in the case of the maps; as we have seen, the maps, in company with *all* maps, by their nature depict no individuals. The military personnel record, however, appears at first glance to be entirely concerned with an individual. But this is illusory. Joseph Mauldon's record is typical, in form, style and content, of the service record of the day, and in a number of aspects may be seen as epitomising the institutional source in that it, too, depersonalises its subject. We learn virtually nothing of Private Mauldon's personal *experiences*. Although he saw action on the Western Front, the only entries directly pertaining to his time in the field are those reporting that he has been wounded.

Further to this depersonalising process is the letter sent from the Melbourne Base Records Office to his wife, Mary. A strikingly impersonal document, given the highly personal import of its message, it takes the form of a 'cloze' exercise in which key words such as (in this case) 'regret' may be inserted where appropriate, along with the nature of the loved one's situation ('suffering from gunshot wound, right arm') (Boyle 1996; Baum & Johnson, n.d.). Cloze exercises are a teaching/testing device in which a passage of text relevant to the subject or topic is provided to the student with key words left blank. The student must fill in the gaps with the correct words. With striking indifference to the recipient's sensibility, the explication concludes simply 'actual condition not known'. A printed section below makes a distant gesture towards reassurance by stating, notably in the inherently depersonalising passive voice, that, 'In the absence of further reports it is to be assumed that satisfactory progress is being made' (National Archives of Australia, n.d.).

Perhaps one of the most potent influences generating and promoting 'presentism' in the minds of today's students is popular culture—particularly Hollywood. Decades of action movies, Westerns and crime thrillers have taught modern generations that certain categories of bullet wound are not only eminently survivable, but relatively trivial, as physical insults to the body go (Boyle 1996). Hence the myth of the 'flesh wound' that leaves the victim minimally incapacitated and able to airily dismiss the injury while continuing to function at a high level. The reality of bullet wounds—to any part of the body—tends to be far more egregious, owing to the devastating manner in which a high-velocity projectile inflicts damage upon and within an object it is able to penetrate (Di Maio 1999). It is often necessary, therefore, to point out to students that the succinct phrase 'gunshot wound, right arm', which seems to imply a wound of no great consequence, could in fact refer to an event of very significant and possibly life-changing impact on the young Joseph Mauldon, including a degree of permanent disability or ill-health.

As VanSledright (2004: 231) says, 'Making sense of the author's perspective or positionality often takes the form of reading between the lines or below the surface of the text.' As a historical source, it is apparent that the war-service record is replete with *implied* narratives. The 'natural' tendency might be to respond to the lacunae in the record by attempting to personalise the narrative through inference or further research with a view to 'fleshing out' the person, but it is equally profitable to interpret the record as it stands. It may then be seen as an expression of the institutional purpose: to embed the micro-narrative within the grand narrative, to render the individual purely as a functionary of the institutional process—in this case, to win World War I.

It is the paradoxical bureaucratic tendency to omit from the micro-narrative almost all of those deeds and experiences of the common soldier that contribute most materially to the grand narrative—for instance, the periods of his life spent on the field of battle—because his contribution can only be effective when he is acting as an anonymous microcosm of a vast, radically depersonalised mass (an army). By viewing the record in this way, we can make a connection between the individual soldier's story, as told in the hyper-functional precis form of the bureaucracy and, ultimately, the reshaping of Europe.

As a coda to this, one may extend the idea beyond the individual soldier who is the subject of the record. It would be a mistake to infer that any of the individual authors of specific entries in Private Mauldon's dossier were in any meaningful way conscious of their, or his, role in such a schema; rather, they, too, were, at their various levels of authority and agency, also functionaries in the process. In this way, even when a specific entry is signed by an identifiable officer—as they mostly are—the anonymous 'institutional' authorship of the source applies.

Effectiveness

The argument mounted above would, we suggest, be unlikely to engage Year 9 students if presented in the form of 'instruction', and could well fail to excite our undergraduates; the concept of the depersonalisation of vast masses of warriors, while arguably central to questions regarding the nature and significance of World War I, could be received as rather too abstract to be interesting. As Canadian education researcher Peter Seixas (1994: 285) says, 'Students structure their own historical understandings according to the schemata of their historical knowledge.' Therefore an approach that is more likely to succeed is one utilising the same resources, but that enables students to identify with, and thus in effect personalise, that which has been depersonalised.

Seixas (1994: 291–3) found that a number of the students he had interviewed responded strongly to the specifically Canadian topics surveyed. Assuming his data is, within reasonable bounds, transferable to non-Canadian students (and assuming, too, that his Grade 10 students' responses are approximately equivalent to those of an Australian Year 9 class), it is reasonable to expect that the use of an Australian soldier's record will be of some interest to students on the lines of national identity. This applicability to an Australian context in an educational setting is also evident in Vance's (2000: 234–8) discussion of teaching war history to Canadian schoolchildren. Further, the attraction of both narrative and analogy as avenues to historical understanding may be brought into play, as students both make connections between the individual Australian soldier and world events then and subsequently, and view the effects of the war as 'lessons' for today (2000: 294).

With these factors in mind, our aim is to facilitate students' engagement with and development of historical awareness through a project of 'adopting a soldier'. Students are provided with the information technology facilities needed to access, in the first instance, the 1914 map of Europe, and the archival record of Private Mauldon's dossier (National Archives of Australia n.d.). Their first task is to track Private Mauldon's movements in Britain and France using the map and the entries regarding his various postings, voyages and hospitalisation. They are encouraged to notice the gaps in his narrative as depicted in the official record, and to imagine (within rigorously defined boundaries of what is historically possible) what *might* have been occurring during those periods not itemised. His numerous infractions of military discipline are discussed and considered in light of other sources that characterise the typical Australian soldier of that time as notoriously contemptuous of authority. One such source, which students view, is a 2008 episode of the ABC TV program *Four Corners* that serves both to personalise the stories emerging from the war and to illustrate the complexities of contested narratives (Australian Broadcasting Commission 2008).

The Base Records Keeper's perfunctory letter to Mary Mauldon, Joseph Mauldon's wife, is also examined closely, both as a textual insight into the bureaucratic approach and as an avenue into discussion and investigation of the experiences of those whom the soldiers left at home—wives, parents, children, siblings. Students are encouraged especially to consider the role of women in the war, and to examine social developments following World

War I that began to contribute to changes in women's place in society over subsequent decades (National Archives of Australia n.d.).

A further area of investigation for students arising from Private Mauldon's record is the 1918 influenza pandemic. This, too, provides a conceptual link between the man on the European front and the domestic environment he has left behind, as the disease affected people in literally every corner of the globe. It also potentially provides a point of engagement for students, given the highly personal (and for some students peculiarly fascinating) nature of deadly diseases.

Having dealt with Private Mauldon's record, students are then encouraged to further explore the National Archives website to locate and 'adopt' a soldier of their choice. The records held in the National Archive provide invaluable opportunities for students to access and utilise primary sources that by nature are partial or implied narratives. The incomplete narrative is the stock-in-trade of the social historian, and requires a blend of rigorous, fact-based research, creative imagination and 'historical empathy'—the ability to put oneself in the mind of the typical person of that time, taking into account social and economic status, gender, occupation and so on. Some students find an ancestor to follow; others select at random. In either case, the task is to an extent open-ended: students are to use the map to track their soldier wherever he went, note the events the official record keepers deemed worthy of inclusion in the dossier and, by inference, those they omitted. These events at the individual level may then be correlated to large-scale events such as major battles or campaigns, or their absence. In the course of their investigations, students are given opportunities to come together as a class and compare notes, observing the features the records have in common and where they diverge.

The personalised account as a way of exploring and considering the broader historical themes of World War I is an integral part of a broader engagement strategy to get secondary and tertiary students to study history. Anecdotally, 'Adopt a Soldier' and other biographical approaches to studying Australians at war have proven successful. One student examined their own local history through a biographical exploration of East Ballarat-born Leslie 'Bull' Allen, orphan, who was a recipient of the Military Medal and later, while serving with the US Army, the Silver Star in a subsequent conflict (one of only thirteen Australians to receive this honour). These offerings and approaches are part of a suite of learning opportunities. They also include an Anzac podcast created in collaboration with UK-based Audiopi (2017), an online learning company that produces subject-specific material developed by academics, teachers and practitioners to provide content aimed at schools. These are also complemented by a second- and third-year field-based learning experience in which students walk the battlefields of the Western Front and, via an app produced by In Flanders Fields Museum, retrace the experiences of the Anzacs in and around Ypres, Belgium.

CONCLUSION

Whether teaching students of history or students who will themselves go on to teach history, the task remains essentially the same: one must find ways of bringing the past to life for the individual learner that strike the essential balance (Wineburg 2001: 5–6) between over-familiarity with those they encounter in the past, and excessive alienation or distance from them. In this chapter, we have recounted an attempt to achieve this by setting students off on an archival journey that they can take individually, focused on a ground-level participant in events of enormous historical moment. This journey, juxtaposed with the contextual resources provided in the form of maps embodying the geo-political narrative from pre-war to postwar, locates the individual within the broadest possible landscape in a way that effectively facilitates a perceptual synthesis between the 'macro' and 'micro' histories involved.

We have found that 'Adopt a Soldier' and other allied activities enhance students' understanding of the historical significance of World War I, both on the global, 'grand narrative' scale, and on the way it impacted on the ordinary person. In this respect, a ground-up approach enables understandings of the way that the ordinary person, in company with a multitude of other individuals, experienced the Great War. In the process, students can better understand the lived experiences, as well as the underlying broader historical themes, of the Great War and, indeed, conflict more broadly during the twentieth century.

REFERENCES

Audiopi 2017, 'Inspirational GCSE and A level audio tutorials for teachers and students', <www.audiopi.co.uk>, accessed 2 September 2017.

Australian Broadcasting Commission 2008, 'The Great History War', *Four Corners*, ABC TV, presented by Chris Masters, 10 November, <www.abc.net.au/4corners/special_eds/20081110/war>, accessed 20 June 2018.

Australian Education Union 2008, *Victorian Parliament's Education and Training Committee's Inquiry into Geographical Differences in the Rate in which Victorian Students Participate in Higher Education: Australian Education Union (Vic) Response*. Melbourne: Australian Education Union, Victorian Branch.

Australian Government 2008. *Review of Australian Higher Education: Final Report*, Canberra: Commonwealth of Australia, <www.innovation.gov.au/HigherEducation/Documents/Review/PDF/Higher%20Education%20Review_one%20document_02.pdf>, accessed 2 November 2012.

Baum, G. & Johnson, S. n.d. 'Locked & loaded: The gun industry's lucrative relationship with Hollywood', *The Hollywood Reporter*, <http://features.hollywoodreporter.com/the-gun-industrys-lucrative-relationship-with-hollywood>, accessed 2 February 2018.

Boyle, I. 1996, 'The sounds of violence: Don't shoot me—I'm only the Foley artist', *Arena Magazine*, no. 25 (October–November) pp. 45–50.

Di Maio, V. 1999. *Gunshot Wounds: Practical Aspects of Firearms, Ballistics, and Forensic Techniques*, 2nd ed., Boca Raton, FL: CRC Press.

Hall, B. 2012, 'Door open for a new band of students', *The Age*, 1 May, <www.theage.com.au/national/education/door-open-for-a-new-band-of-students-20120430-1xuqu.html>, accessed 29 October 2012.

Hammond & Co. c. 1920, *Hammond's Enlarged Map of Europe of Today Showing Boundaries of the New States as Determined by the Peace Conference*, <www.digitalcommonwealth.org/search/commonwealth:4m90fn82z>, accessed 1 May 2017.

Harvard University Library n.d., 'Contagion: Historical views of diseases and epidemics: Spanish influenza in North America, 1918–1919', Harvard University Library Open Collections Program, <http://ocp.hul.harvard.edu/contagion/influenza.html>, accessed 1 May 2017.

hooks, b. 2005, *Cultural Criticism and Transformation*, Media Education Foundation, <www.mediaed.org/assets/products/402/transcript_402.pdf>, accessed 20 February 2017.

National Archives of Australia n.d., Service record of Pte James Mauldon, AIF3101,. NAA: B2455, bar code 8039662, <http://recordsearch.naa.gov.au/scripts/Imagine.asp>, accessed 20 February 2017.

Seixas, P. 1994, 'Students' understanding of historical significance', *Theory and Research in Social Education*, vol. 22, no. 3, pp. 281–304.

US Army Medical Department n.d., *Map of Europe 1914*, <http://history.amedd.army.mil/booksdocs/HistoryofUSArmyMSC/page36.jpg>, accessed 20 February 2017.

Vance, J.F. 2000, *Death So Noble: Memory, Meaning and the First World War*, Vancouver: UBC Press.

VanSledright, B. 2004. 'What does it mean to think historically . . . and how do you teach it?', *Social Education*, vol. 68, no. 3, pp. 230–3.

Wineburg, S. 2001, *Historical Thinking and Other Unnatural Acts: Charting the Future of Teaching the Past*, Philadelphia, PA: Temple University Press.

—— 2005, 'A history of flawed teaching', *Los Angeles Times*, 24 February.

Wordpress.com n.d., *Map of Europe 1871–1914*, <https://highpointresearch foreign.files.wordpress.com/2011/05/map-europe-1871-1914.jpg>, accessed 20 February 2017.

CHAPTER 14
Using fiction to develop higher-order historical understanding

Grant Rodwell

INTRODUCTION

This chapter is about developing students' higher-order historical understanding, student motivation to study classroom history, students' appreciation of historiography and how the history lesson might be linked with English literature—particularly through the time-slip novel and the power of the narrative it represents. Although teachers have found many strategies to incorporate this genre into the history lesson, seldom is the genre used as a core part of a history lesson or unit of work. Rachel Edwards's experiences, discussed in this chapter, well exemplify how this highly motivational experience can lead to students' higher-order historical understanding.

Among other things, students' higher-order historical understanding embodies an understanding of the way in which, in the past, history—and particularly school history—has been skewed by colonialist attitudes, gendered and racist points of view, and history 'written from above' from bureaucratic and official perspectives. The incorporation of historical novels, in their various genres, can do much to develop students' higher-order historical understanding.

RACHEL EDWARDS'S AND CLAIRE BROCK'S EXPERIENCES

Hobart-based Rachel Edwards is a literary aficionado, editor and publisher who attended a Hobart primary school in the early 1980s. She vividly remembers the school librarian introducing her and some of her Year 5 friends to Ruth Park's *Playing Beatie Bow* (1980), a young adult (YA) time-slip historical novel. This was at a time when the teaching of history as a stand-alone subject was optional in Tasmanian primary schools; consequently, for Rachel and her young friends, this was a relatively rare moment to engage in some historical content, and develop some higher-order historical understanding.

And Ruth Park did not disappoint. For Rachel, this was the first opportunity she had to understand history told from a young, working-class female's point of view. For her, time-slip historical fiction affords a unique and engaging opportunity to engage in history. Moreover, use of the time-slip provides a 'magical' and captivating means to engage with the reader, and to elevate higher-order historical thinking, along with the understanding that history has a voice. Moreover, the novel provided an especially enlightening opportunity to have young women or girls as characters, providing her (female) peers with the opportunity to connect with history in a manner mostly avoided by the formal curriculum.

Thirty-three years later, Rachel vividly recalls the literary/history experience of how, immediately after beginning the novel, she and her friends rushed off and formed a Beatie Bow club, which would meet regularly in a most fascinating structure in the school's adventure playground—a most appropriate venue—discussing Abigail's adventures as she slipped back a century in time in *Playing Beatie Bow*, from Sydney's The Rocks district in the late 1970s to a very different place in that same district (Edwards 2017).

At a 2014 History Teachers' Association gathering in Adelaide, Claire Brock argued for the value of Felicity Pulman's *A Ring Through Time* (2013), a time-slip historical novel, in her Year 5 history class. Brock contended that she found the time-slip novel valuable as a pedagogical device because of the subtle and thought-provoking questions it posed, which she could use in her search to develop her students' higher-order understanding of history (Brock 2014). Brock's arguments are certainly supported by Rachel Edwards's and her friends' Year 5 experience, suggesting appropriate historical novels are a very legitimate history-learning experience in schools, particularly in respect to student engagement, and a pedagogical tool for higher-order historical thinking.

We need to be sure, however, about where time-slip historical fiction sits in the general genre of historical fiction and its relationship to the various other sub-genres of historical fiction.

HISTORICAL FICTION AND ITS SUB-GENRES

The list below is adapted from *A Guide for Historical Fiction Lovers* (Providence Public Library 2014). Readers should note that the list is not set in concrete, but forever evolving as authors develop new approaches to the historical novel genre.

Traditional historical novels

Traditional historical novels emphasise a straightforward and historically accurate plot, with characters close to the historical figures—for example, Australia's Colleen McCullough's *The First Man in Rome* (1990), a novel about an alliance empowering two men during the twilight of the Roman Republic. Another novel in this sub-genre might be Kate Grenville's *The Secret River* (2005), which tells the story of European/First Nations Australian relations during the early years of the European invasion of the traditional land of the Darug people.

Multi-period epics

The sub-genre of multi-period epics arguably is best represented by James Michener's work, prolific in the post-World War II decades. These novels show how a specific place changes over centuries—for example, *Hawaii* (1959), *Chesapeake* (1978) and *Poland* (1983), showing how countries, regions or peoples evolved. Usually, there is no principal character driving the plot, rather it is the region, country or people pushing the narrative.

Historical sagas

Historical sagas follow families or groups of friends over time, usually generations. Heseltine (1964: 200) demonstrates that during the second half of the nineteenth century, Australian fiction was dominated by 'the saga, the picaresque and the documentary'. These were novels conceived 'primarily in terms of time' (1964: 200). They were sagas in their 'purest form', but often approaching the documentary in type. According to Heseltine, 'the classic pioneering novel ... charters the course of an Australian family from its (usually humble) beginnings through a whole range of good and evil fortune, and against a background of assorted natural phenomena—the inevitable floods, fires and droughts' (1964: 200).

Australian authors of historical saga fiction have made a major contribution to Australian culture as well as to our understanding of the past through well-researched novels in this genre. For example, Nancy Cato (1917–2000), a fifth-generation Australian, is best known for her historical sagas. *All the Rivers Run* (1958) is a novel about Australian life along the Murray River. Especially popular in the United States, this book was made into a television series. The book became the first of a trilogy—with *Time, Flow Softly* (1959) and *But Still the Stream* (1962)—which, when published in a single volume, became internationally popular (Zinn 2000).

Western or Australian outback historical novels

Western or Australian outback historical novels, including traditional American Westerns, take place in either the American West or remote areas of Australia. For example, in Louis L'Amour's *Hondo* (1953), set in nineteenth-century Arizona, an ex-Cavalry scout protects a woman and her son from the Apaches and a brutal husband. For Australian outback historical fiction, I recommend Nicole Alexander's *Absolution Creek* (2012).

Historical mysteries

Historical mysteries are very popular among certain groups. In this sub-genre, there is a cross of historical fiction with the mystery genre—for example, Steven Saylor's *Roma Sub Rosa* series, set in Ancient Rome. I recommend *Roman Blood* (1991), with its meticulous research, characterisation and tight plot. Anecdotal evidence suggests this sub-genre has particular appeal for the growing number of Australian secondary and tertiary students undertaking courses in ancient civilisations and ancient history.

Romantic historical novels

Romantic historical novels, including historical romances, are love stories set in history—for example, popular over generations are Georgette Heyer's novels in this sub-genre (including *These Old Shades*, 1926). Also look to Ernestine Hill's *My Love Must Wait* (1941). These can provide much valuable classroom discussion concerning their historical integrity. For example, *My Love Must Wait*, a work depicting Matthew Flinders, is very Anglo-centric, portraying Flinders' imprisonment on Mauritius by the French (1803–10) in very ahistorical terms.

Historical adventure novels

Historical adventure novels feature heroes who travel widely, usually on the hostile frontier, surmounting astonishing obstacles. A multimillion bestselling author in this sub-genre is the South African Wilbur Smith (e.g. his *The Power of the Sword*, 1986). While certainly entertaining reading, most teachers and educators would consider this sub-genre to have limited pedagogical value in the history classroom.

Historical thrillers

Historical thrillers put their heroes in danger. The plot is action driven—for example, in Alan Furst's *The Foreign Correspondent* (2007), a journalist in Paris dodges fascist secret police. A well-researched, strongly plotted novel in this sub-genre with convincing characterisation can stimulate considerable valuable classroom enthusiasm for history.

Literary historical novels

Literary historical novels examine contemporary themes in lyrical or dense language. An example includes Peter Carey's *True History of the Kelly Gang* (2000), historiographic metafiction that, among other things, provides an opportunity to introduce the notion of commodified history, and challenge many aspects of it while at the same time looking for other examples, such as the Anzac legend. According to Toman (n.d.), in relation to commodified history, or 'popular marketing of the past':

> In a globalizing world, references to the past as a way of identity formation have become more and more important. Even though the 'production' of history is the major field of academic historiography, the past is addressed in many popular contexts that are consumed and appropriated by immense numbers of people. Though the forms in which history is brought to life differ widely, most of them have one feature in common: they promise the distribution of knowledge via entertainment, and this is what makes them so popular. Producing history outside academia is often reduced to discussing history as business, and forms of 'marketing the past' have been criticized in academic discourse. Fears of standardization and a loss of diversity are being voiced in this critical evaluation.

An Australian example may be the treatment of Ned Kelly as a historical subject. History teachers who choose to use such novels in their classrooms usually have a solid understanding of the need to develop an appreciation of historiography in their students (Parkes & Donnelly 2014).

Christian historical novels

Christian historical novels reflect Christian themes—for example, in Catherine Marshall's *Christy* (1967), set in the Appalachian fictional village of Cutter Gap in the early twentieth century, a nineteen-year-old teacher at a mission school improves her own life as well as that of others.

Historical fantasy novels

Historical fantasy novels mix history with fantasy. Typically, the sub-genre embraces historical events from the point of view of the mythical history prevalent at the time. At its best, the sub-genre looks at functioning societies through metaphor and allegory—for example, Traci Harding's *Chronicle of the Ages* (2008).

Steampunk

An emerging sub-genre of science fiction and fantasy novels is steampunk, with a special appeal for young adult (YA) readers—possibly because of its associated fashion (EBSCO 2015). With origins dating back to the science fiction of Jules Verne and H.G. Wells, this sub-genre features advanced machines and other technology based on nineteenth-century steam power, with the stories taking place in a recognisable historical period or a fantasy world. Popular early steampunk began with works such as Ronald W. Clark's *Queen Victoria's Bomb* (1967) (Rabe & Greenber 2010). There are many enthralling challenges here for teachers and students in using this sub-genre to advance students' higher-order historical thinking in the history curriculum.

Alternate histories

Alternate histories imagine history happening differently; this is sometimes referred to as counterfactual history—for example, Nick Hasluck's *Dismissal* (2011), in which on 11 November 1975, Australian history takes a very unexpected turn. There have been many such novels written on Nazi Germany and Hitler, so much so that a single academic monograph has been published on these (Rosenfeld 2002). The same author has also demonstrated the powerful contribution that alternate histories can make to students' historiographical understanding (Rosenfeld 2005).

Time-slip novels

Time-slip novels shuttle their characters between epochs—for example, an Oxford student slipping back to the Middle Ages accidentally lands in the time of the plague in Connie Willis's *Doomsday Book* (1992). Partly set in wartime Sydney, my (Grant Rodwell) *Saving Sydney* (2017) is a historical time-slip thriller in this same tradition.

TIME-SLIP AND TIME-TRAVEL HISTORICAL NOVELS

Time-slip novels should not be confused with time-travel historical fiction, although in many instances the nomenclature 'time-travel' is more suited than 'time-slip' because of the former's more apt description of the condition of a time-slip. Where the novel involves a deliberate attempt by the protagonist(s) to travel back or forward in time (e.g. H.G. Wells' *The Time Machine* [1895]), whether by mechanical devices or otherwise, surely that is best described as time-travel. Where the protagonist(s), however, slips back in time through an accidental or other means, this needs to be considered as a time-slip novel (e.g. Ruth Park's *Playing Beatie Bow* [1980]). The *Urban Dictionary* explains:

> Time-slip occurs in a novel or a film, when the action or hero is suddenly transported to another period in history, their past or their future; when two or more stories are told concurrently, but each one is set in a different period of time [e.g. Yvonne Harlech, *Mistress of the Temple* [2011]).
>
> Time-slips occur in novels such as *The Historian* [2005] and *The Swan Thieves* [2010] by Maria Kostova; *Holes* [1998] by Louis Sacher; *A Study in Scarlet* [1887] by Arthur Conan Doyle; but not *The Time Traveler's Wife* [Audrey Niffenegger, 2003] or *The Time Machine* [H.G. Wells, 1895], which are novels about time travel. (*Urban Dictionary* n.d.)

So what special high-order historical understanding can time-slip novels add to the history curriculum?

AUSTRALIAN TIME-SLIP HISTORICAL NOVELS

Ruth Park's (1980) *Playing Beatie Bow* received a mention of almost a page in length in Wilde, Hooton and Andrews's edition of *The Oxford Companion to Australian Literature* (Wilde, Hooton & Andrews 1994). There is, however, no mention of time-slip or time-travel literature in what is generally regarded as the most comprehensive survey of Australian literature.

While Australian time-slip historical fiction written for children and YA readers has an increasing number of titles in publication, I cannot find any such work written for adults, except for my *Saving Sydney* (2017), a novel concerning Axis attempts to invade Sydney during World War II, which would provide invaluable stimulus for high-order understanding in senior history classes.

EXPLAINING THE POPULARITY IN TIME-SLIP YA LITERATURE

Recently, an increasing number of peer-reviewed academic journal articles have been published dealing with the appeal of time-slip literature—particularly that written for young adults—as a teaching/learning strategy, usually in the English curriculum, but with very strong implications for history teachers. Others examine the appeal of this sub-genre in the wider school curriculum. Claudia Marquis's (2008) article takes four time-slip novels— Philippa Pearce's *Tom's Midnight Garden* (1958), Margaret Mahy's *The Tricksters* (1986), Beverly Dunlop's *Spirits of the Lake* (1957) and Ruth Park's *Playing Beatie Bow* (1980)—and through some very erudite comparisons explains the huge appeal these works have for children and young adults. With respect to this genre, Marquis (2008: 59) observes that it

> allows the child reader to track the time-slipping child character into a past that serves as a play-space, where the child is granted the privilege of independence from the constraints and complications of his or her ordinary experience. Insofar as the child is propelled back towards a moment where s/he comes to an understanding of self in part by realising where s/he comes from, the highly personal narrative opens up a further possibility: understanding of the continuities between generations that compose a larger narrative, the history of the community of family, or even the nation.

Marquis's (2008) central concern is one that has considerable symmetry with this chapter. She is interested in understanding the

> function by which the child is located in the cultural present by being relocated, for a time, in a past that is remarkable, paradoxically, by

its apparent insignificance. The line of such a narrative is not that of adventure or romance, nor that of fantasy. (2008: 59).

That line of narrative is surely about developing a historical curiosity. Moreover, it is the sheer marvellousness of the apparent experience for the young reader. Indeed, 'the effect of this excursion is to acquaint the child—character and reader—with history as a lived experience, lived as it logically cannot be, for sure, but also lived as closely as if it were deep in memory' (Marquis 2008: 59).

Marquis (2008: 60) writes of 'the fictive operation by which the re-created past is presented: time is re-conceived in spatial terms, which, of course, gives room to objects'. She concludes:

> Time-slip fiction typically delivers a past to its children, character and reader, a world that radically extends the world of quotidian reality, by peeling away the present, only to disclose it again in an equally valid form, that which we know in our rational lives as the past. The modern, children's fantastic works this way—not by having some variety of supernatural challenge the primacy of ordinary reality, but by setting past and present in tension, before looking to relax this condition by harmonising worlds and moments.

Valerie Krips (2000) describes a common preoccupation by authors of YA time-slip fiction with 'achieving an appropriate orientation to the present in terms of the past' with reference to the British loss of Empire, and the nascent heritage industry, in an argument ranging widely over many different types of YA literature. A study of Australian YA time-slip literature shows concerns about injustices done to First Nation Australians (e.g. Kate Constable's *Crow Country*, 2011), changes in childhood and society (e.g. Jackie French's *Somewhere Around the Corner*, 1994), and young lives and colonial heritage (e.g. Ruth Park's *Playing Beatie Bow*, 1980).

Indeed, issues associated with heritage are common in much Australian YA time-slip fiction. Cosslett's (2002: 2) thoughtful paper pinpoints 'the special features of the time-slip genre, and [relates] them very explicitly to ideas of heritage'. At the same time, she argues, 'this genre provides ways out of some of the dilemmas and negative features of "heritage" as a concept and a practice'. Moreover, with vivid pointers to the time-slip novels employed by teachers in the case-study classrooms visited later in this chapter, Cosslett (2002: 2) contends:

> in many of its variants, the time-slip narrative offers an openness to 'other' histories, rather than the potentially nationalistic search for roots; it problematizes the simple access to the past promised by the heritage site; it critiques empty reconstructions of the past; and because of the way it constructs childhood, it evades the dangers of nostalgia.

Witness the four time-slip novels written by Australian young people's authors Kate Constable, Ruth Parks, Jackie French and Felicity Pulman, and the way they feature heritage in their works.

YA time-slip literature has attracted the attention of some erudite teachers and academics. For example, the late Dr Margaret Locherbie-Cameron (1996) provides a pathway to the use of this genre in the classroom, especially in literature-based lessons. A renowned literature educator, Locherbie-Cameron was for many years a member of the English Department of Bangor University. In her footsteps, the enthusiastic history teacher will see obvious connections here with her subject-matter.

Aware of the vast potential of developing a readership among young Australian readers, Belinda Murrell embraced the time-slip historical novel genre. She is a bestselling author of books for young readers. Her publications include the *Lulu Bell* series, for six- to nine-year-olds, which is 'about a girl called Lulu growing up in a vet hospital so there are many adventures involving family, friends and lots of lovely animals' (Storrs 2013). In her interview with Storrs, Murrell explained her use of time-slip (Storrs 2013):

> I've always been fascinated by history and the idea of travelling back in time. I also love the idea of taking a modern-day character, with all their experiences and foibles, and putting them in a completely unfamiliar environment where they have to deal with the dangers and difficulties that were faced by our ancestors. Through this experience, each of my modern-day protagonists discovers something about their own life, strengths and inner courage.

Murrell has promised a literary feast for young readers who engage in this literary genre.

HISTORICAL FICTION AND STUDENTS' HIGHER-ORDER HISTORICAL UNDERSTANDING: PEDAGOGICAL ENGAGEMENT AND THE PROCESSES OF ENHANCEMENT

During the second half of the twentieth century, historical thinking and historical writing underwent massive changes, paralleling new developments in the pedagogy of the history curriculum. Increasingly, history-curriculum theorisers were calling for a vastly increased level of historiography in the pedagogy of history (Parkes 2011; Parkes & Donnelly 2014). The medium was obvious—time-slip novels were the ideal tools for this new pedagogy of the history curriculum. Teachers and educators began to realise that they could harness the manifest interest specifically in time-slip history, and in historical fiction generally, to enhance students' historical literacy and higher-order thinking through historiographical classroom discussions. Consequently, the teaching of history has undergone massive changes over the last several decades. Pertinent 'What if . . . ?' questions now have become the order of the day, as have discussions about voice and social class (Lévesque 2008; Rodwell 2013; Seixas 2004). As shown at the beginning of this chapter, this is a point endorsed by Rachel Edwards in her memories of first reading *Playing Beatie Bow*.

Thoughtfully chosen historical novels, however, have much more to offer history teachers. In particular, the time-slip sub-genre provides a fresh and enlivening means to look at prominent issues in various topics because the principal characters are brought into a new time/space—for example, in the case of *Playing Beatie Bow*, the emerging upmarket tourist hub of The Rocks district in the 1980s in parallel with the same district in the late Victorian period, when it was commonly spoken of as the 'sewer of the South Pacific'. This provides a teacher with the opportunity to compare the two historical eras through the engaging eyes of the principal characters—in this case, the young female protagonists.

SAMPLE QUESTIONS FOR THE CLASSROOM

The following questions are useful in relation to historical fiction:

- From your readings and understandings, how do the various sub-genres of historical fiction differ, particularly with respect to the way they might be used in the history classroom?

- What do you consider is the special appeal of the time-slip genre in historical fiction?
- How do you think historical fiction might enhance our higher-order historical thinking?
- What are your students' opinions on how historical fiction might best be incorporated into the history curriculum?
- How might historical fiction be used in the history classroom to dismantle the influence of commodified history on our historical understanding?
- What do you understand about the meaning of the term 'historiography'?
- How might the use of historical fiction enhance students' appreciation of historiography in elevating higher-order historical thinking?

CONCLUSION

Student engagement is the first step towards developing students' higher-order thinking in history, and most teachers who have chosen to do this through the use of historical novels will attest to their effectiveness as potent pedagogical tools. A well-chosen and relevant historical novel is highly engaging for students, an important first step in the development of higher-order historical thinking. Then the novel becomes a pedagogical strategy for the teacher to ask pertinent questions, also stimulating students' high-order thinking.

In the absence of formal history lessons, for some students—such as those gathered in the Beatie Bow club with Rachel Edwards and her young friends at the Hobart primary school in the early 1980s—higher-order thinking in history can be developed through the simple reading of a historical novel. This can be incidental, but mostly it is the product of planned pedagogy with strategic teacher-directed questions at appropriate times and/or critical moments. First, there is a demonstrated need to put a historical novel of an appropriate sub-genre in the student's hands. To achieve this, history teachers need to develop an appetite and comprehensive understanding of the historical novel and its varied sub-genres.

REFERENCES

Alexander, N. 2012, *Absolution Creek*, Sydney: Random House.

Brock, C. 2014, 'Higher-order historical thinking: Case study and interview: Year 5: Convict Life', Adelaide, 23 July.

Carey, P. 2000, *True History of the Kelly Gang*, Brisbane: University of Queensland Press.

Cato, N. 1958, *All the Rivers Run*, New York: St Martin's Press.

—— 1959, *Time, Flow Softly*, New York: St Martin's Press.

—— 1962, *But Still the Stream*, New York: St Martin's Press.

Clark, R.W. 1967, *Queen Victoria's Bomb*, London: Jonathan Cape.

Constable, K. 2011, *Crow Country*, Sydney: Allen & Unwin.

Cosslett, T. 2002, '"History from below": Time-slip narratives and national identity', <http://eprints.lancs.ac.uk/4471/1/HISTORY_2.pdf>, accessed 2 February 2018.

Dunlop, B. 1957, *Spirits of the Lake*, London: Hodder.

EBSCO 2015, 'The benefits of using Young Adult (YA) literature in classrooms', 10 September, <www.ebsco.com/blog/article/the-benefits-of-using-young-adult-ya-literature-in-classrooms>, accessed 19 September 2017.

Edwards, R. 2017, Interview, Salamanca Place, Hobart, 8 February.

French, J. 1994, *Somewhere Around the Corner*, Sydney: HarperCollins.

Furst, A. 2007, *The Foreign Correspondent*, Sydney: Hachette Australia.

Grenville, K. 2005, *The Secret River*, Melbourne: Text Publishing.

Harding, T. 2008, *Chronicle of the Ages*, Sydney: HarperCollins.

Hasluck, N. 2011, *Dismissal*, Sydney: Fourth Estate.

Heseltine, H.P. 1964, 'Australian fiction since 1920', in G. Dutton (ed.), *The Literature of Australia*, Ringwood: Penguin, pp. 196–202.

Heyer, G. 1926, *These Old Shades*, London: William Heinemann.

Hill, E. 1941, *My Love Must Wait*, Sydney: HarperCollins.

Krips, V. 2000, *The Presence of the Past: Memory, Heritage and Childhood in Postwar Britain*, London: Taylor & Francis.

L'Amour, L. 1953, *Hondo*, New York: Fawcett Gold Medal.

Lévesque, S. 2008, *Thinking Historically: Educating Students for the 21st Century*. Toronto: University of Toronto Press.

Locherbie-Cameron, M. 1996, 'Journeys through the amulet: Time-travel in children's fiction', *Signal*, no. 79, pp. 45–61.

Mahy, M. 1986, *The Tricksters*, London: Dent.

Marquis, C. 2008, 'Haunted histories: Time-slip narratives and Antipodes', *Explorations into Children's Literature*, vol. 18, no. 2, pp. 58–64.

Marshall, C. 1967, *Christy*, New York: McGraw Hill.

McCullough, C. 1990, *The First Man in Rome*, London: Arrow Books.

Michener, J. 1959, *Hawaii*, New York: Random House.

—— 1978, *Chesapeake*, New York: Random House.
—— 1983, *Poland*, New York: Random House.
Park, R. 1980, *Playing Beatie Bow*, Melbourne: Thomas Nelson.
Parkes, R.J. 2011, *Interrupting History: Rethinking History Curriculum After 'the End of History'*, New York: Peter Lang.
Parkes, R.J. & Donnelly, D. 2014, 'Changing conceptions of historical thinking in history education: An Australian case study', *Revista Tempo e Argumento*, Florianópolis, vol. 6, no. 11, pp. 113–36.
Pearce, P. 1958, *Tom's Midnight Garden*, London: Oxford University Press.
Providence Public Library 2014, *A Guide for Historical Fiction Lovers*, <www.provlib.org/guide-historical-fiction-lovers>, accessed 24 June 2014.
Pulman, F. 2013, *A Ring Through Time*, Sydney: HarperCollins.
Rabe, J. & Greenber, M.H. (eds) 2010, *Steampunk'd*, New York: DAW Books/Penguin.
Rodwell, G. 2013, *Whose History? Engaging History Through Historical Fiction*, Adelaide: University of Adelaide Press.
—— 2017, *Saving Sydney*, London: Austin Macauley.
Rosenfeld, G. 2002, 'Why do we ask "what if?" Reflections on the function of alternate "history"', *History and Theory*, no. 41, pp. 90–103.
—— 2005, *The World Hitler Never Made: Alternative History and the Memory of Nazism*, New York: Cambridge University Press.
Saylor, S. 1991, *Roman Blood*, New York: St Martin's Press.
Seixas, P. (ed.) 2004, *Theorizing Historical Consciousness*, Toronto: University of Toronto Press.
Smith, W. 1986, *The Power of the Sword*, New York: Pan Macmillan.
Storrs, E. 2013, 'Belinda Murrell—author interview', *The Australian Literature Review*, 24 March, <https://auslit.wordpress.com/tag/the-locket-of-dreams-by-belinda-murrell>, accessed 2 February 2018.
Toman, J. n.d., 'Commodification of history: The past as source of entertainment and commerce', <www.hsozkult.de/event/id/termine-36535>, accessed 26 June 2018.
Urban Dictionary n.d., <www.urbandictionary.com/define.php?term=Timeslip>, accessed 23 January 2017.
Wells, H.G. 1895, *The Time Machine*, New York: William Heinemann.
Wilde, W.H., Hooton, J. & Andrews, B. 1994, *The Oxford Companion to Australian Literature*, 2nd ed., Melbourne: Oxford University Press.
Willis, C. 1992, *Doomsday Book*, New York: Bantam Spectra.
Zinn, C. 2000, 'Nancy Cato: Novelist and poet capturing the spirit of the Australian outback', *eGuardian*, 12 July, <www.guardian.co.uk/news/2000/jul/12/guardianobituaries.books>, accessed 8 September 2009.

CHAPTER 15
Drama pedagogy in the teaching of history

Kelly Freebody and Alison Grove O'Grady

This chapter is about the use of drama pedagogy to teach history. It aims to provide interested students and teachers with an introductory perspective on what drama pedagogy is, why it might be useful for students of history and how it can be implemented in classrooms, schools and communities. We begin by outlining three disclaimers about the work contained in this chapter.

First, a lot of drama work that is done in Human Society & Its Environment (HSIE) areas builds on strong theoretical frameworks—feminist theory, social justice, critical pedagogy, creativity theories and so on. This chapter does not explicitly draw on one particular theoretical framework. Instead, it recruits a particular practice in drama education—drama pedagogy—sometimes known as educational drama, process drama or theatre in education. Here participants learn through experience and embodiment. It is a conceptualisation of 'drama as a practice and as a process for learning rather than as a body of texts for passive reception' (Winston 1998: 75).

Second, this chapter is based on the idea that drama does good—that there are affordances in drama work that allow students to engage in ideas, problems, relationships and institutions in different ways, and that this is a good thing. That does not mean there is not bad drama in the world, or bad drama teachers, or that it is unproblematic; rather, we argue that drama is a tool, like other pedagogical tools, which when used in the right circumstances can allow new possibilities of knowing content, understanding the world, questioning knowledge and thinking critically and empathically about people, time, contexts and events.

Finally, our intention is not to suggest that all history or historical learning should be done with or through drama. Our argument for the work here is based on its ability to be complementary to other learning in history. Research has suggested that drama is an excellent way to provide students with emotional and intellectual pathways into new units of work, or to extend understanding beyond static facts or perspectives within units of work.

WHAT DO WE MEAN BY 'DRAMA'?

Often when people think about drama or performance, they think about the school *subject* drama—studies in theatre, learning about plays, performing to audiences and so on. That is not what we are referring to in this chapter. Here we are discussing drama *pedagogy*. This means the use of drama as a tool for teaching a variety of content areas—in this case, history.

In order to discuss the potential and practice of drama pedagogy, we first need to outline the *elements of drama*, which are a core part of any understanding of the dramatic form. There is some minimal variation between the curriculum documents of different states in Australia. However, an accepted and accessible introduction to the elements of drama was offered by Haseman and O'Toole, two seminal Australian drama educators, in 1986; their work has since been revised and was republished in 2017:

- We start with *the human context*—the 'real-world' elements that are brought into the dramatic action, such as roles, relationships and situations.
- The human context becomes driven by *dramatic tension*—'the force that drives the drama' (Haseman & O'Toole 1986: 18).
- Dramatic tension is directed through *focus*.
- It is then made explicit in *place* and *time*, through *language* and *movement* to develop and use *symbols* to create *mood* (Haseman & O'Toole 1986).

Drama pedagogy employs the elements of drama through structured activities or strategies commonly referred to as drama conventions (discussed below) to create educational experiences (Wagner 1979). Often, there is no 'audience'; rather, the entire group is involved in the same enterprise (Bolton 1998), with all participants (teachers and students) simultaneously both spectators and actors, or 'spectactors' (Boal 1979).

Drama pedagogy uses story and role as distancing devices so participants can 'live through' (Heathcote 1984: 81) the dramatic play while having 'freedom from the consequences and arbitrary occurrences of real life' (Bolton 1998: 178). This aims to construct a safe space for students to engage with issues that explore personal weaknesses, prejudices and sociocultural understandings. Role protection aims to allow participants to enter into empathic identification with their characters while providing them with the distance to be able to critically reflect on the situation and actions of the characters within the drama so that 'there is both distance and presence' (O'Neill 1995: 90). Carroll, Anderson and Cameron (2006) explore the ways in which the 'performance frame' delineates the difference between real life and the representation of reality that is being created within a drama. Within this performance frame, dramatic conventions (Neelands 1990) are used to structure the drama work and present material in the fictional world. Conventions are 'tools' that participants and facilitators of drama utilise; they include things such as games, improvisation activities, play-making and writing/making exercises. There are literally hundreds of conventions that a drama educator could employ. In this chapter, we outline some of these we feel are particularly suited to a history classroom, exploring what they look like through examples of practice. A more comprehensive outline of dramatic conventions employed by practitioners when planning and implementing drama pedagogy is provided by Neelands (1990) and Neelands and Goode (2015).

WHY DRAMA IN HISTORY?

Practitioners and researchers discuss the opportunities presented in drama work for students to develop skills that exist beyond the curriculum, including developing empathy, confidence, collaboration and creative ways of using the imagination as a principal tool to think about the future (Sardar 2010). Recent research suggests that drama also provides students with a discrete skill set that precipitates new ways in which they can experience and mediate the world as democratic citizens (O'Grady 2016). This differentiates the subject of drama from other disciplines because students are inculcated with the freedom to express themselves and their views within a carefully facilitated mediated space where it is safe to disrupt the status quo.

History education is often conceptualised as a way to understand facts, and is therefore seen as a relatively straightforward matter. Drama, on the other hand, is often perceived as less factual, more aesthetic, and less bound and constrained by an adherence to factual accounts. Kempe (2013: 195) describes the relationship between drama and history as 'a dance between the real and the fictitious'. However, we argue that similarities and synergies between history and drama are more relevant than the differences.

How students understand history and the past is suggested by Lee (2006) as knowing that there is not just one view of the past, but a range of views that may be contradictory, complementary and/or clashing. The singular testing of an event in history, such as the study of the causes of World War I, cannot on its own provide a broad and valid education in history. Rather than a facilitation of disparate factual accounts, drama can provide the tools and space—both physical and pedagogical—to test validity by drawing on different kinds of understanding and explanation.

One of the notable characteristics of drama is the capacity for it to be planned and structured to interrogate subtext that might emerge from the reinvention of the past. Luff (2011) suggests that drama and history can provide teachers with the language that is important for this type of understanding and knowledge building. When drama is activated in a history lesson, students are capable of drilling down to the lived details of the facts that may surround a certain event by reimagining characters particularly through embodied ways of knowing, but also through effective use of writing strategies. Opportunities to articulate how a character might have arrived at a decision, gaining insight into motivations and critically analysing or reconstructing an event, coalesce to give form to fact and enable engagement in empathic understanding of past events.

WHAT DOES DRAMA DO? DISCUSSIONS OF PRACTICE

Critical empathy

There is a body of research work in drama pedagogy that explores the relationship between empathy and drama. Empathy is a multifaceted term in history education. Here we are referring to a theory of empathy, drawing on Hughes (2017: 110), which highlights relatedness. It is where students 'recognise another person's individuality ... that he or she can be related to in terms of the universal themes of humanity (desires, feelings, family, body, love, and so on)'. We argue here that good drama pedagogy, by encouraging students to understand historical events from the imagined perspective of those who were there, provides spaces for this kind of recognition to happen. Of course, we know that students in a drama classroom in Sydney can never really experience World War II or ancient Pompeii. But we also know that by asking students to react authentically (without a script, as they think is appropriate in the moment) to historical events as a soldier, or a father, or a king allows them to experience *something else* than they would if they were to read about the events from someone else's perspective. It is also an excellent way for teachers to gain new insights into how their students are thinking about the content and context of the work.

Critical empathy in practice: a case study

The example of practice that we discuss here was an event that took place in 2017 at the Sydney Theatre Company, called *Teaching the Truth about Refugees* (O'Connor et al. 2017). The facilitators presented Hughes's (2017) framework for reducing prejudice through education and then used the picture book *Home and Away* (2008) by John Marsden as a pretext for a two-hour drama pedagogy workshop for teachers. This conceptualisation of empathy differs slightly from examples on which we may have drawn in a classroom. It is concerned with the idea that experiential learning can develop deeper insights into events, circumstances and characters, but it is also more critical in its intention. This workshop was concerned with developing and displaying empathy as a political act.

In this section, we will not describe the drama in detail, as descriptions of drama practice are readily available elsewhere; rather, we will discuss a few conventions that were used in the program in order to outline *how* this kind of drama work gets done. *Freeze frames* were used often, particularly towards the beginning. Also known as tableaux, these involve asking a group of students to put together a frozen image. They are excellent ways of embodying and representing. They can be used to express both abstract or concrete concepts: moments, people, relationships, events. Their public nature allows the meaning to be viewed by others in the group, but the simplicity of the task allows them to be low risk and easy to implement. In this case, freeze frames were used to develop character: to show relationships between family members, and to set up the context. Each group devised three freeze frames and then performed them one after the other, with no sound, to demonstrate three moments in the movement from a happy family portrait to a family living in a war zone.

A core convention used in these dramas was *teacher in role*, understood as occurring when the teacher enters the drama as a character and acts alongside the other participants. Teacher in role can be used to move the narrative along, to add moments of tension by being the catalyst for some change or to provide information and content knowledge that the students may not already have. Teacher in role is also an excellent way of encouraging students to take charge of the direction of the drama—particularly if the teacher takes on a role that is subservient or of lower status to the students (such as an unemployed father going from employer to employer seeking work during the Great Depression).

In the refugee drama, teacher in role was used right at the end of the session. Tensions were running high as the young family with which we had journeyed for 90 minutes was in peril. The father had died on the boat, the mother had died in detention and the children were facing an unknown amount of time in a processing centre. The teacher became the Minister for Immigration—the only person able to sign their release to be resettled with a local family. After setting up the role, the teacher sat behind a desk and waited. Tentatively at first, but then with more confidence and passion, participants tried to get him to sign the papers—with no script or rehearsal, participants requested, yelled, rationalised, protested and pleaded, using a variety of tactics. Eventually they won, and the papers were signed.

This is a good opportunity to discuss one of the most important aspects of drama pedagogy: *debriefing*. This is absolutely vital for the drama work to be considered both safe and good, and will focus on different aspects of the drama experience, depending on the circumstances. At the end of the refugee drama, the debrief not only gave participants the opportunity to discuss their feelings after such an emotional lesson, but also to reflect on and problematise the catharsis they experienced when the minister finally signed the papers. Yes, the participants in this drama 'won' in this case, but the 'problem' of people in detention was not solved. It is in these discussions at the end of the drama lessons that participants have an opportunity to step back from their feelings and consider what those feelings and experiences have taught them. This is where teachers need to clearly make links between the lessons and their purpose.

Understanding historical events

The following case study is included to demonstrate how drama pedagogy used in the history curriculum enables students to explore different perspectives on historical events. As we have previously said, allowing students to reconstruct the past and to understand that historical accounts are not fixed, but can move and adapt according to new findings, is important in setting up the conditions or conventions of drama in this context. Students bring to this type of learning their tacit knowledge of what the event might have been like for those who were there; as Lee (2006) argues, it is also assumed that they will understand what history is by picking up metahistorical concepts or ideas that lie beyond the scope of historical narrative or inquiry as they learn and acquire more content knowledge. Drama allows the students to conjugate these knowledges by activating their imaginations (Lee 2006: 131).

Understanding historical events in practice: a case study

> In Flanders fields the poppies blow
> Between the crosses, row on row ... (*The Beaver* 2005)

Canadian students are familiar with the 1915 poem 'In Flanders Fields', written by John McCrae to commemorate and memorialise the events of World War I. The poem is widely taught in both elementary and senior schools in Canada, and is cited by some historians as an appropriate representation of Canada's coming of age during the war and beyond. The poem is not unproblematic historically and ideologically, but was used extensively as a pretext to precipitate thinking about commemoration as part of an international research project. The project involved drama and history academics from Australia, New Zealand, Canada and the United Kingdom. The drama workshop discussed here was written by Professor Peter O'Connor from the University of Auckland. It was then taught by the drama educators at several different sites. The project looked at the way drama and history curricula in some Commonwealth countries taught the commemoration and memorialisation of World War I in their classrooms.

This case study is illustrative of the way drama and poetry can be used to teach about the theatre of war and the context in which World War I was fought. Participants found that the pedagogy could be powerful, and it provided opportunity for scrutinising war narratives from a highly personal, familial or community perspective. The processes and the conventions that this process drama uses focus strongly on making personal connections to and about World War I in order to understand why memorials and commemorations are both revered and vexed in many towns and communities—a consequence of the deeply personal associations of the war and its consequences.

The processes and conventions that were utilised in this project focused strongly on what pre-service teachers might need to know when they are teaching about World War I. The participants were initially asked to share and tell stories about *any* war that might be told in their families or in the families of someone close to them. The stories are shared and retold by another group member where appropriate, and the teacher acknowledges that the subject can be closely guarded and emotional in some groups. This sets the tone for thinking about war from many different perspectives by acknowledging the lasting effects of war narratives through family and community storytelling.

The drama has a number of activities or steps to it, each with a relevant and carefully planned dramatic convention that allows participants to further immerse themselves in the reconstructed historical past. To ascertain prior knowledge and 'set the scene', the participants respond to a series of provocations that ask them to consider what they want their students to know about war, what worries them about teaching World War I and what they need to know before they start teaching about the war. Participants put their responses on butcher's paper and walked around the room to read quietly, taking note of responses that sparked interest or concern. This convention is known as a *gallery walk*. This allows a collective picture to emerge about where common concerns lie and where the grey areas are for teachers in building students' knowledge about war.

As the drama unfolds, various conventions are learned by the participants, including creating a memorial by using tableaux and freeze frames, reading the poem and asking questions about the differences between the language of the poem and the text's illustration, and then engaging in a *soundscape* activity. This powerful activity exemplifies the effectiveness of dramatic interaction through a confluence of elements that focus on the granular details of a simple line in the poem: '*Loved and were loved*'. The drama starts to build and re-create the scene at the train station through soundscape. With closed eyes, participants imagine the scene and add noises: soldiers in uniform by the hundred boarding the train bound for the other side of the world, steam shrouding the view of the departing and those left behind, mothers stoically waving handkerchiefs while driving their fingernails into the flesh of their hands to avoid public displays of grief, while the band plays a merry tune. What would the station sound like? What would the *external* sounds be like? What would the *internal* sounds be like? The drama builds as the groups create the soundscape, which gets louder as more participants join in. As the tension builds, the facilitator, acting as conductor, loudly declares, '*All aboard, stand clear, train leaving . . .*' The soundscape provides participants with an aesthetic experience of place and time, setting the scene of the drama, which encourages the group to think about the public and private dialogue of war.

Space, stories, sources

Drama influences participants' sense of place, space and time, and can connect history and place in powerful learning experiences for students. Place and time are not only elements of drama in the way they inform the context of drama work (in the fictional frame)—which allows, for example, Australian school students in 2017 to be factory workers in England during the Industrial Revolution; they are also central to the physical performance of drama work. At an everyday level, doing drama can transform classrooms into tropical islands, or whole schools into medieval villages. The embodied nature of drama work allows for space to be used, imagined, reimagined and disrupted for participants and audiences. History allows an extra layer here: spaces can be imagined across timelines, monuments can be constructed, generational stories can merge and physical contexts (land, space, props) can become characters in the drama and 'sources' of history.

Space, stories, sources in practice: a case study

The example of drama work on which we draw to illustrate and discuss this kind of work took place in Hong Kong in the early 2000s. More aligned with community theatre than 'drama pedagogy', this project nonetheless provides us with ample opportunity to discuss how sources, stories and spaces can intermingle in drama to engage people in learning experiences that draw on historical thinking, cultural geography and cultural identity. The theatre project in Hong Kong (Wang 2016) was 'based on local history and living stories of inhabitants in order to reclaim public space for the general public . . . and to negotiate and communicate their ever-evolving identities' (2016: 42). It was titled *A Dramatic Bus Journey Touring Hong Kong Heritage*, and was developed by The Theatre Space Company using actors, international artists and students. The theatre piece was performed on three bus lines that were travelling to three heritage sites. Three female actors were positioned on each bus and performed realistic monologues that intersected with one another. These monologues were based on interviews with local elderly female residents about the challenges of living in Hong Kong over their lifetime. The buses arrived at the heritage site and a large-scale performance, relevant to the specific site, was performed incorporating object theatre, physical theatre and multimedia workshops. There is not sufficient room here to detail all three sites or performances, so we will discuss only one; for more information on this project, and others like it, see Wang (2016).

Shek Kip Mei Estate, built in the 1950s, is one of Hong Kong's oldest public-housing estates, and has a history that includes the housing of mainland Chinese resettlers fleeing the Chinese Civil War. At the time of the performance, the government was planning to demolish the building to make way for new skyscrapers. The theatre practitioners and performers worked in the space for over two months, gathering sources about past and present life in that place. The final performances included snippets from interviews in the dialogue, photographs projected on screens and possessions of inhabitants as props. This presents an opportunity to rethink how sources are used to develop historical understanding, through embodiment, contexualisation and storytelling.

This case study is included here predominantly to demonstrate the ways that drama pedagogy and performance can be used to shape meaning and understanding around place, and specifically the powerful way place and time can mingle in a dramatic context to create new meaning and new understanding. Considering the *elements of drama* outlined earlier in this chapter, we can see how work such as this 'plays' with notions of place and time to create a particular kind of dramatic meaning. Similarly, the symbols of props and photographs act as historical sources to both build historical meaning in the event and explicate the human context, affecting the mood of the performance. The use of *interviews* alongside devised work contributing to the development of performances is not uncommon in drama projects concerned with representations of communities and/or events, and again allows us to consider and extend the definition of 'historical sources' as a way of developing an understanding of the past. There are various drama conventions that are, or could be, drawn upon in projects such as this. Although this was not a typical 'drama pedagogy' in that there was a clear audience and a performance, the interwoven monologues on the buses align with the convention of *overheard conversations*—effectively making the audience into participants in the place, space and context of the drama. It also adds to intimacy, by providing the audience with insight into a conversation into which they would not normally be invited. It recruits aspects of 'promenade theatre', where audience members follow the action and move with the actors, again using the place as a character in the drama. From a historical perspective, this opens up possibilities for students of history. Places *are* characters in history, and even further, places at *particular times* are characters. Sometimes cultures and communities draw upon ritual or ceremony (two more frequently used conventions) to acknowledge and make distinctive a particular time in the history of a place. At other times, the transition is less defined: the gentrification of suburbs, increasing urbanisation, building development, political movements and so on. Drama pedagogy allows teachers and students the opportunity to explore space, place and time in interwoven ways in order to develop nuanced understandings of the relationship between them. The embodied and performative nature of the work allows participants to see and feel a place in different contexts and times.

CONCLUSION

In consideration of the previous exploration and discussion of the synergies between drama and history, it is reasonable for us to conclude that drama pedagogy is useful and indeed complementary in developing and advancing young people's understanding of the past. The affordances that reside in the elements of drama also build confidence in teaching about history in a comprehensive way that allows participants to walk—albeit briefly—in the shoes of others. Zatzman (2005) suggests that drama and history potentially activate 'the boundaries of remembering' (2005: 95), allowing for a lived experience that invites new ways of thinking about the body and the self in space and time (Nicholson 2012). The value of drama in history teaching is therefore manifold. The learning experience encourages students and teachers to hold a mirror up to their views and, as a result of that insight, perhaps change views or gain further understanding of people and events in history. Equally, drama enables a reflective and critical approach to the acquisition of historical knowledge, thus fostering independent thinking, which is now considered a goal in the history classroom. Drama used for good can therefore provide students with a particular agency that promotes and generates new knowledge about the world they inhabit and the world that has gone before them—an empowering and humanising experience.

REFERENCES

The Beaver 2005, 'Dec. 8, 1915: "In Flanders Fields" published', *The Beaver: Exploring Canada's History*, vol. 8, no. 6, p. 11.

Boal, A. 1979, *Theatre of the Oppressed*, London: Pluto Press.

Bolton, G. 1998, *Acting in Classroom Drama*, Stoke on Trent: Trentham Books.

Carroll, J., Anderson, M. & Cameron, D. 2006, *Real Players? Drama, Technology and Education*, Stoke on Trent: Trentham Books.

Haseman, B. & O'Toole, J. 1986, *Dramawise: An Introduction to the Elements of Drama*, Melbourne: Heinemann.

Heathcote, D. 1984, 'Drama as challenge', in L. Johnson & C. O'Neill (eds), *Dorothy Heathcote: Collected Writings*. London: Hutchinson.

Hughes, C. 2017, *Understanding Prejudice and Education: The Challenge for Future Generations*, London: Routledge.

Kempe, A. 2013, 'Drama and history: A kind of integrity', in M. Anderson & J. Dunn (eds), *How Drama Activates Learning: Contemporary Research and Practice*, New York: Bloomsbury.

Lee, P. 2006, 'Understanding history', in P. Seixas (ed.), *Theorizing Historical Consciousness*, Toronto: University of Toronto Press, pp. 129–64.

Luff, I. 2011, 'Beyond "I speak, you listen, boy!" Exploring diversity of attitudes and experiences through speaking and listening', *Teaching History*, no. 105, pp. 10–18.

Marsden, J. 2008, *Home and Away*, Sydney: Hachette.

Neelands, J. 1990, *Structuring Drama Work*, Cambridge: Cambridge University Press.

Neelands, J. & Goode, T. 2015, *Structuring Drama Work: 100 Key Conventions for Theatre and Drama*, 3rd ed., Cambridge: Cambridge University Press.

Nicholson, H. 2012, 'The performance of memory: Drama, reminiscence and autobiography', *NJ*, vol. 36, no. 1, pp. 62–74.

O'Connor, P., Freebody, K., Jacobs, R. & Saunders, J. 2017, *Teaching the Truth about Refugees: A Professional Learning Event*, <www.sydneytheatre.com.au/community/education/teacher-learning/professional-learning>, accessed 5 October 2017.

O'Grady, A. 2016, 'Always in the process of becoming: How five early career drama teachers build their worlds through language and discourse', PhD thesis, University of Sydney.

O'Neill, C. 1995, *Dramaworlds*. Portsmouth, NH: Heinemann.
Sardar, Z. 2010, 'Welcome to postnormal times', *Futures,* vol. 42, no. 5, pp. 435–44.
Wagner, B.J. 1979, *Dorothy Heathcote: Drama as a Learning Medium*, London: Hutchinson.
Wang, W.J. 2016, 'Creating alternative public spaces and negotiating identities and differences through community theatre praxes in Hong Kong and Taiwan', *Applied Theatre Research,* vol. 4, no. 1, pp. 41–53.
Winston, J. 1998, *Drama, Narrative and Moral Education*, London: Falmer Press.
Zatzman, B. 2005, 'Staging history: Aesthetics and the performance of memory', *Journal of Aesthetic Education*, vol. 39, no. 4, pp. 95–110.

CHAPTER 16
Integrating filmic pedagogies into the teaching and learning cycle

Debra J. Donnelly

This chapter focuses on film as a teaching resource in the history classroom, and suggests ways in which film representations can be integrated into the teaching and learning cycle. It uses examples of teacher practice to highlight effective pedagogical approaches.

In this digital age, young people are immersed in visual representations of the past seen in movie theatres, on television, on computer screens and increasingly on portable entertainment and communication devices. Blockbuster feature films become major artefacts of popular and youth culture, and for a brief interlude they bestow global-scale historical significance on their filmic narratives of the past, with interest being intensified by media hype, social networking clamour, gaming adaptations and product merchandising. Historically based films have the potential to motivate and engage today's visually orientated students and to connect them both emotionally and intellectually to historical narratives, which can offer varying perspectives and points of view (Metzger 2007; Seixas 1994). Whether archival footage, feature films, documentaries or docudramas, film links school with the world of the students beyond school, and can give history lessons a vitality that is lacking in most other teaching resources. A recent Australian study found that 90 per cent of students strongly agreed that films helped them to remember and to learn in history classes, and the multisensory experience of film was cited by both teachers and students as supporting memory and engagement (Donnelly 2014).

ISSUES AND CHALLENGES OF USING FILM TO TEACH HISTORY

The very nature of commercial film production is an issue when using film for educational objectives in history. Most films are money-making enterprises, and as such need to attract an audience. It is often the case that following historical evidence and narrative is sacrificed in the name of entertainment, with distortions, compressions and fictional additions. Perhaps the worst problem is that of *presentism*—that is, imposing contemporary ideas on the past. This is a problem in the presentation of values, attitudes and societal roles of the past, which may jar with modern sensibilities (Weinstein 2001). For example, many contemporary audiences may not be comfortable with the rigid codes of behaviour and limited expectations about the independence of women in some past—and indeed contemporary—societies. It may be tempting for filmmaking to falsify the historical record, and so misrepresent the past and undervalue the dynamic shifts in sex-based roles in human history. As Australian educators Taylor and Young (2003) point out, these distortions need to be recognised and examined during history classroom encounters with film.

It is testament to the power of the film viewing experience that there appears to be a tendency for history and filmic representation to become muddled in the memory and historical consciousness. This phenomenon was observed by Sam Wineburg (2001) when he interviewed students and their families about their historical identities (see also Wineburg, Mosborg & Porat 2001). Wineburg reported that popular films, such as *Forrest Gump* (1994) and *Schindler's List* (1993), were cited as supporting evidence for evaluating historical events. In addition, research suggests that there is a contradiction in student utilisation of films as historical documents (Marcus 2003; Paxton & Meyerson 2002). Students readily acknowledged the limitations of films, and demonstrated a healthy scepticism about their reliability, citing issues of motive and profit. When films were used in class, however, these same students tended to believe the filmic presentations and relied on them for their understandings. Afflerbach and VanSledright (2001) coin the term 'Disney effect' to explain the power of film to establish ideas and attitudes about historical events, and warn that teachers need to guide their students to identify the mechanisms of filmic representations and relate this knowledge to a broader examination of the historical evidence. The 'Disney effect' refers to the use of historical events and people as a basis for fantasy—for example, in Walt

Disney films such as *Pocahontas* (1995) and *Anastasia* (1997) (Afflerbach & VanSledright 2001).

The effective use of film to teach history is not a simple matter, and requires clear learning objectives and explicit teaching. American scholars Wineburg and Martin (2004: 42–5) warn that without careful time allocation and explicit teaching, film can become another 'distraction' to the examination and analysis of historical sources. Many other researchers agree (e.g. Rosenstone 1995; Meyerson & Paxton 2007; Seixas 1994). They conclude that if students only passively engage with the film and are not required to deeply investigate and respond to it as a historical artefact, then the film runs the same risk as internet searches, computer slide shows and other technology: of being a distraction from historical literacy skills and blurring the lines between history and fiction. As American history professor Paul Weinstein (2001: 42) concludes, 'Film is an artificially created model of reality. It is our task to train the eye and mind to translate these entertaining images into data for comparative and critical analysis.'

INTEGRATING FILM INTO HISTORY TEACHING PRACTICE

A recent Australian research project investigated teaching practices using film in the history classroom using survey, interview and classroom case studies methodologies (Donnelly 2014). The data from the research project identified recommended strategies for effectively embedding historical film in the secondary history classroom and tapping into the potential of film as a history teaching resource. The project concluded that film is not only engaging and memorable for students, but can also be used to highlight historical concepts and explore the nature of history. Examples from the case studies are provided to further explain the recommendations.

Establishment and application of conceptual framework

One important key strategy for effectively integrating film was the development of a conceptual framework prior to the film being introduced. This framework is set up by a focus question or questions, encourages the treatment of the film as a source and so allows for the film to be compared with the other historical sources. The nature of history as contestable and changing, depending on perspective, is an important concept that needs to be explicitly explained and discussed.

Mrs Drew (pseudonym) began her unit on Ned Kelly by collecting images of heroes and villains, with labels that indicated the ambiguity of these terms. For example, Nelson Mandela's photo was entitled President of South Africa from 1994 to 1999 and militant anti-apartheid activist, and the leader and co-founder of the armed wing of the African National Congress (ANC). Mrs Drew called on students' prior knowledge, but deepened their understandings in a collaborative discussion. She used a 'think, pair, share' strategy to encourage collaborative thinking. Students were asked to individually develop a list of characteristics for a hero and a villain, then share it with a partner, then join together with another pair to form a group. The group then developed its list before Mrs Drew called for contributions from the five groups to make a class description of heroes and villains. The students were asked to come out and write one word or phrase that they knew about the bushranger. Then the focus question was posed to the class for a vote, 'Was Ned Kelly a hero or a villain?' The class watched clips from various Ned Kelly films and examined the questions, 'Presentation in this film—hero or villain? What makes you think this?' This was followed by a class discussion in the next lesson.

Exploring the nature of the film genre

As with any historical source, when using a film it is important to look at the nature of the film type being used and the devices used to create the filmic narrative. Mrs Drew had her students list the ways in which information was conveyed in the docudrama *Pompeii: The Last Day* (2003). The class discussed whether the dramatised scenes had more impact than a talking expert, and whether these helped them 'care about' the fate of the ancient city and its people. Similarly, Mr Green (pseudonym) used the interviews with the various production team members provided in the DVD to emphasise the point that *Kingdom of Heaven* (2005), like all feature films, was created by a team of specialists and that the historian was only one of many who contributed to its production. He posed the questions, 'Why was this film made?' and 'Is it claiming to be history?'

Graphic organisers and learning scaffolds for viewing and recording

The case study teachers often used graphic organisers, such as T-charts (columns), spider diagrams and mind-maps, as communication and summary devices to show the organisation and relationships of information, concepts and ideas, and to capture ideas and observations while viewing the films. By arranging information spatially, students were able to select the essential ideas, and these were often used as the basis for assessment tasks. Teachers frequently asked individual or pairs of students to create preliminary constructions and then led the class in a collaborative final draft. One of the other teachers, Ms Stacey (pseudonym), had her class redevelop a collaboratively designed mind-map using the Prezi software. This allowed for the inclusion of primary and secondary sources, relevant quotations and images.

Rather than give students worksheets with questions to answer while watching, it was found that graphic organisers were more effective, as they helped the students to become more strategic learners, and gave them opportunities to modify and adapt their original ideas to accommodate the thoughts of others. Some of these teachers understood the advantages of public display and had the class's collaborative work and individual efforts hung around the classroom. This allowed the graphic organisers to be integrated into later lessons, used as a teaching or reviewing tool, and modified to capture further insights.

Cognitive apprenticeship teaching and learning design

Most of the case study teachers used the *cognitive apprenticeship model* of instruction, although no one recognised the term when asked. The cognitive apprenticeship model is a framework for teaching and learning that is suited particularly to teaching source analysis and essay skills in history. It is composed of three stages: the expert models and explains the skills and/or understandings; the learner attempts the skill or understanding with scaffolded support and coaching from the teacher and in collaboration with other learners, while teacher support is faded as a function of learner mastery; and the learner independently develops and practises the newly acquired skill (Collins, Brown & Newman 1989; Parkes & Muldoon 2010). It appears that their adoption of this learning design had grown from years of experience in the classroom, rather than from training or outside instruction. This constructivist pedagogy has stages of development towards a complex task, from modelling and imitation to coaching and collaboration, then to fading support and independent exploration. For example, the teacher models analysis of one scene from the film as a historical source, then has students continue in pairs with the aid of class discussion for the next few; finally, individuals are allocated scenes to evaluate and present to class. Collective notions of historical representation in the film are developed.

A good example of this method of teaching history is Mrs Warner's (pseudonym) lesson sequence for using *V for Vendetta* (2005). First, the students were guided in the development of a conceptual framework of the issues and historical terms, then they applied the framework in the case of Guy Fawkes. The viewing of selected clips from the film *V for Vendetta* was then used to extend their intellectual investigation of the topic and intensify their affective response to the ethical dilemmas of governmental control, freedom and revolution. The cognitive demands are increased when the unit moves to the next stage: the debates focused on Nelson Mandela, Mahatma Gandhi and Yasser Arafat. Here, grouped students prepare a case for or against these historical figures being freedom fighters or terrorists, and argue—using evidence—their allocated point of view. Mrs Warner's role in these lessons was one of facilitator and coach. Although they are working with some independence at this stage, the students' responses were developed from their group work collaborations. The final stage of this progression was the independent researching and reporting stage. Each student examined a terrorist group, individual or event, and was tasked with answering the big questions raised by the topic with reference to their topic. Although she gave some advice to individual students regarding topic selection for their assignment, Mrs Warner tended to give general answers about the task and encouraged them to work independently. The quality of the presentations for the assignment demonstrated that a number of students had achieved deep understanding of the discipline through the cognitive apprenticeship learning design.

Close analysis of the film as a source

It was found that close analysis of film was important for effective integration. Several of the case study teachers spent some time examining elements of film-making, such as soundtrack, costuming and camera angles, in their analysis of the film as a source. Mrs Drew was explicit in her treatment of the film as a historical source. She used an analytical template that was headed with the focus question and was a T-chart with the two columns headed 'Notes' and 'My Ideas'. As they viewed the film, the students took notes in relation to the focus question and colour coded the observations to indicate whether research information corroborated or refuted the filmic representation and to show new pieces of evidence beyond the film. They used another colour to indicate emotional manipulation and persuasive techniques. Mrs Drew also focused attention on the value of film as history, with concluding questions such as, 'Can a feature film be a history?' and 'Does this film claim to be history?'

Mrs Walker's (pseudonym) approach to interrogating the film was different. She made little reference to the film as a historical source, but rather used sections of the film as stimuli for investigation of the further historical information and sources. For example, in a unit using a 20-minute clip from *Gallipoli* (1981), the class completed a T-chart, headed 'Reasons to Join Up' and 'Evidence from the film'. The class then studied recruitment and other patriot posters from World War I and added to the summary with annotations. This study then moved to textbook investigation with the question, 'Do other sources support the film narrative?' Notes were taken under teacher-supplied headings as information from the film and textbooks was compared and contrasted. These notes became the basis for a test essay. Although she did not carry out source profiling on the film, Mrs Walker did effectively embed the film into the study and contrasted it with other source material to test its reliability.

Addressing the values dimension

Another important consideration when using film is the opportunities they provide to include a values or ethics dimension. Some of the case study teachers explicitly identified and defined particular values, attitudes and beliefs, such as human rights and citizenship rights and responsibilities, examining them in relation to their historical investigation, connecting them to contemporary society and using film as a catalyst for class discussion. It was found that by removing a controversy in time and place, some films set in the past provided a 'safer venue' for exploration and discussion of debatable issues, such as racism and immigration.

Using feature films enabled the use of analogies and parallels to current controversial situations, and the filmic narrative provided a platform from which multiple perspectives could be considered and evaluated. For example, Mrs Warner led her students to consider a moral and ethical dilemma using sections of *Rabbit-Proof Fence* (2002). She posed for class discussion, 'Why did the government take the children away from their families? How could they think they were doing good?' The final task assignment of this unit was an individual research assignment in which students were encouraged to explore Aboriginal people's resistance to dispossession and their fight for self-determination and land rights.

The performative in filmic pedagogy

Another important filmic pedagogical practice to emerge from the project was the inclusion of the performative. In this instance, the term 'performative' suggests the need for students to create a work to provide clarity to their historical understandings, or at least including their learning from viewing and/or interrogating the film. Performative tasks can range from writing argumentative essays, constructing websites, building models or making historical 'artefacts' to role-plays, speeches and dramatic simulations. This task-orientated focus encourages further exploration and synthesis, relates the films to other historical material and deepens understanding.

The project observed a wide array of approaches to the performative, with effective teachers understanding the importance of tasking students to apply and recontextualise the knowledge they have learned. They guided their students in their historical writing, spending time on the essay as a form and the development of historical writing skills, such as embedding sources to support the argument. Often, quick quizzes, timelines and maps were used to establish the foundational knowledge of the period under study. Mr Howard (pseudonym) set his class the task of producing mini-documentaries as the final assessment item for his unit on World War I. Groups of three students were given a topic to explore, such as life in the trenches, the development of tanks or women at the front, and instructed that at least three primary sources had to be used, as well as a voiceover and soundtrack. Students made these films on their mobile phones and presented them to the class. Those that were deemed the most successful were then used in the school's Anzac Day ceremony.

A number of the teachers used empathy exercises based on writing in alternate perspectives, creating historical reproductions and model-making. Mr Green had his class use their historical reproduction and models as the basis of a week-long peer-teaching event. The students were responsible for teaching a section of the topic based around their reproduction or model, and produced teaching resources and summaries, as well as items for a class test at the end of the unit.

Mrs Drew took a more traditional approach, with tasks based on the writing of historical argument. She had her students extensively annotate primary and secondary sources and used post-it notes to highlight important themes and ideas. The classes were assigned carefully designed and instructionally aligned writing tasks, with particular attention given to historical literacy and conventions of historical writing. The work produced was of a sophisticated standard and demonstrated the benefits of the cognitive apprenticeship-style training regime. This example from the conclusion of a Year 10 essay demonstrates the intellectual quality of the work:

> All history is partial and the validity of the history is determined by the accuracy of its sources. Films and documentaries can be useful and should be used to teach history, as long as their credibility and utility and representativeness can be assessed. Good histories, such as *Pompeii: The Last Day*, can often be extremely engaging and educate a modern-day audience in a more effective way than standard lessons. However, bad representations of history, like *Pocahontas*, distort past events and teach children biased misconceptions about people and events in history.

CONCLUSION

Film can be used to teach rich lessons about the nature of historical inquiry and the subversion and redrafting of history in contemporary media. Its appeal to the cognitive and emotional endows film with an enduring impact that can be exploited by teachers in epistemological and ethical investigations, and that can lead to the development of metacognitive frameworks of historical understanding. The recommended strategies discussed above are drawn from the work of practising teachers, and are designed to encourage the interrogation of film as a historical source, with the aim of enhancing students' interest in history, historical literacy skills and understandings of historical representation and historiography. So, equipped with empowering critical multiliteracy skills, historical understanding can become a lens for interpreting the present as well as the past, and making the future.

REFERENCES

Afflerbach, P. & VanSledright, B. 2001, 'Hath! Doth! What? Middle graders reading innovative history text,' *Journal of Adolescent and Adult Literacy*, vol. 44, no. 8, pp. 696–707.

Collins, A., Brown, J.S., & Newman, S.E. 1989, 'Cognitive apprenticeship: Teaching the crafts of reading, writing and mathematics', in L.B. Resnick (ed), *Knowing, Learning and Instruction: Essays in Honor of Robert Glaser*, Hillsdale, NJ: Lawrence Erlbaum, pp. 453–94.

Donnelly, D.J. 2014, 'Using feature films in teaching historical understanding: Research and practice,' *Agora (Sungrapho)*, vol. 149, no. 1, pp. 4–12.

Marcus, A.S. 2003, 'Celluloid blackboard: Teacher practices with film and students' historical understanding', unpublished PhD thesis, Stanford University.

Metzger, S. 2007, 'Pedagogy and the historical feature film: Towards historical literacy,' *Film and History*, vol. 37, no. 2, pp. 69–76.

Meyerson, P. & Paxton, R. 2007, 'Stronger than the classroom: Movies, texts and conceptual change (or lack thereof) amidst sociocultural groups', in A.S. Marcus, *Celluloid Blackboard: Teaching History with Film*, Charlotte, NC: Information Age, pp. 167–86.

Parkes, R.J. & Muldoon, N. 2010, 'The tutorial as cognitive apprenticeship: Developing discipline-based thinking,' in R.H. Cantwell & J.J. Scevak (eds), *An Academic Life: A Handbook for New Academics*, Camberwell, Victoria: Acer Press, pp. 55–63.

Paxton, R. & Meyerson, P. 2002, 'From *Birth of a Nation* to *Pearl Harbor*: The influence of movies' perspective on students' historical understanding', paper presented to Annual Meeting of the American Educational Research Association, New Orleans.

Rosenstone, R.A. 1995, *Visions of the Past: The Challenge of Film to Our Idea of History*, Cambridge, MA: Harvard University Press.

Seixas, P. 1994, 'Confronting the moral frames of popular film: Young people respond to historical revisionism,' *American Journal of Education*, vol. 102, pp. 261–85.

Taylor, T. & Young, C. 2003, *Making History: A Guide for the Teaching and Learning of History in Australian Schools*, Melbourne: Curriculum Corporation.

Weinstein, P.B. 2001, 'Movies as a gateway to history: The History and Film Project', *The History Teacher*, vol. 35, no. 1, pp. 27–48.

Wineburg, S. 2001, *Historical Thinking and Other Unnatural Acts: Charting the Future of Teaching the Past*, Philadelphia, PA: Temple University Press.

Wineburg, S. & Martin, D. 2004, 'Reading and writing history', *Educational Leadership*, vol. 52, no. 1, pp. 42–5.

Wineburg, S., Mosborg, S. & Porat, D. 2001, 'What can *Forrest Gump* tell us about students' historical understanding?' *Social Education*, vol. 55, pp. 55–8.

Films

Anastasia (1997)
Forrest Gump (1994)
Gallipoli (1981)
Kingdom of Heaven (2005)
Pocahontas (1995)
Pompeii: The Last Day (2003)
Rabbit-Proof Fence (2002)
Schindler's List (1993)
V for Vendetta (2005)

CHAPTER 17
Using websites to develop historical thinking

James Goulding

INTRODUCTION

This chapter aims to provide a broad and principled approach to thinking about the use of digital resources in the history classroom that can be applied flexibly to any resources you might happen to find online, and to help you and your colleagues use them to their greatest potential. I first draw upon recent research to shed light on why students appear to be reluctant to critically engage with certain types of websites. This is followed by a discussion of the type of thinking we should be promoting in history classrooms, and a consideration of how historical thinking (and rich understandings of historical evidence) can productively be developed. The final section discusses strategies for improving students' critical digital literacy.

AN EPISTEMIC GAP BETWEEN THE CLASSROOM AND THE 'REAL WORLD'

I recently conducted research that involved asking students to evaluate historical websites, including open-source material from Wikipedia. The results surprised me. When I asked students whether a particular page from Wikipedia was believable, many replied that Wikipedia was incredibly useful for providing 'the basic facts' for an assignment (and that they used it regularly); however, it was not viewed as a reliable source of information, so they would never cite it in their research.

It struck me as odd that what is arguably the most important source in their research—the overview source—was also the one they left off the reference list. The treatment of the conventional pages was not much better, as many students seemed to focus almost entirely on the narrative content provided and paid little attention to the other elements of the page that could be used to build a picture of the perspective being put forward. (Some did examine the URL, but to be honest, how much light does .com or .org really shed on the complexities of a historical perspective?) What surprised me was not that the engagement with online sources was relatively superficial (my pre-reading of the literature in this area prepared me for that), but that I knew these particular students were capable of adopting a much more critical stance. It was almost as if, upon seeing certain types of online historical sources, they set aside the critical thinking skills that they would normally use with more conventional sources in the classroom.

I soon discovered that I am not alone in observing this, and that current research into student use of sites such as Wikipedia paints a similar picture (Hilligoss & Rieh 2008; Menchen-Trevino & Hargittai 2011). Brian Hilligoss and Soo Young Rieh (2008: 1480), who conducted research on how students determine website credibility, describe this phenomenon as *context-bounded credibility*, where online information is considered credible in some settings but not others. In their interviews with students, they found that even though students were confident about using the web to conduct research, they were worried about what their teachers would think if they saw websites in their list of citations. Interestingly, their view of print-based material was equally problematic—when the authors spoke to students about the credibility of the information given to them by their teachers or published in the class textbook, students replied that 'it's reliable in the context of the class; it may or may not be reliable in the real world', and 'even if it's false, it's true within the bounds of the classroom' (2008: 1480).

These findings are cause for concern, as having entire categories of online sources that are viewed as believable but not 'citable' is counterproductive to the enterprise of critical historical thinking. The issue is given particular weight by the fact that open-source sites such as Wikipedia are among the most widely used by students to conduct research online, and usually the first site they visit (Konieczny 2016). When a website is used but not cited, it is much more likely that the function of the site becomes purely about content; 'getting the basic facts' is a phrase that recurred again and again in my own research, but for historians there is no such thing as 'the basic facts': every source has an author, a purpose, an audience and a context, which shapes the way the 'facts' are presented.

I think existing approaches to teaching information literacy may be partly to blame: a website, like any other historical source, is not just something that is or is not credible, it is a thing of richness with many shades of grey. I think perhaps the concern over misinformation on the internet has prompted many to see online sources in a manner that is somewhat binary, and as a result we ride roughshod over the nuance that is the hallmark of disciplinary historical inquiry.

These findings also have implications for what many see as the core purpose of history education: preparing students for participation in democratic citizenship. An epistemic gap between the classroom and the 'real world' is quite problematic if we want students to apply critical historical understandings to issues outside the school gate. It also worries me that the research suggests this may be linked to the perceived expectations placed on them by their teachers (Hilligoss & Rieh 2008: 1479). Despite the great gains we have seen in the last three decades in terms of the use of print-based material in classrooms, it appears that when it comes to using certain types of online sources, we may be back where we started.

WHAT TYPE OF THINKING SHOULD WE BE TEACHING IN HISTORY CLASSROOMS?

If one had to summarise the research into the teaching and learning of history over the last three decades in one sentence, it would be that the ultimate aim of every history class is not teaching content, but teaching *thinking*. When faced with the question of what type of thinking we should be teaching in the classroom, the answer might seem obvious: surely *critical thinking* should be our end goal? Of course, general critical thinking is important; however, in the history classroom a general capacity for critical thinking is not actually the primary aim. What we must seek to develop are discipline-specific thinking skills—critical thinking skills that are developed within the context of historical inquiry, which can in turn be transferred to other domains. A review of current research will tell you that, at its very core, critical historical thinking is about our concept of *historical evidence* (Lévesque 2008; Seixas 2004; Seixas & Morton 2013; Wineburg 2001).

Critical historical thinking has been a focus of Australian curricula since the 1970s Wyndham reforms, and was strongly influenced by the British Schools History Project in the 1980s—both of which prompted a move away from the behaviourist understanding of school-based history as the memorisation of facts and towards a more constructivist understanding based on interpretation and inquiry (Parkes & Donnelly 2014). This general momentum was bolstered by Sam Wineburg's (1991) seminal studies on historical thinking conducted in the early 1990s. Wineburg, being an educational psychologist, was interested in the thought processes that occurred during historical evaluation and inquiry, and he identified three reading strategies that were central to disciplinary historical thinking: *sourcing, corroboration* and *contextualisation*. Beyond the identification of particular heuristics, however, the decisive factor identified by Wineburg—the factor that effectively determined the type of analysis taking place—was what he termed an individual's *epistemology of text*, or their concept of historical evidence. Critically, Wineburg found that students tended to think about historical sources as repositories of content rather than contested, problematic and context-bound accounts. The fruit of Wineburg's research can be seen in two areas: first, it reinforced research tradition on historical thinking that spanned the remainder of the 1990s and continues in various forms today; and second, Wineburg's method, with its emphasis on the use of primary sources instead of textbooks in historical inquiry, helped drive the pedagogical shift towards using more sources in the history classroom.

Following Wineburg, the other major contribution to our understanding of historical thinking to be considered here is that of history education scholar Peter Seixas (2004). Seixas's focus was not on cognitive heuristics, as Wineburg's was, but rather on what he called *historical thinking concepts,* which he argued comprised a broader conceptual base designed to demonstrate the many forms that historical thinking can take as individuals grapple with different types of historical questions and content. The concepts include *historical significance, primary source evidence, continuity and change, cause and consequence, historical perspectives* and the *ethical dimension;* as with Wineburg, disciplinary understandings of historical evidence are central to his approach (Seixas 2004; Seixas & Morton 2013).

On the face of it, it appears that it was primarily Peter Seixas's six historical thinking concepts that informed the development of the 'history concepts' in the current Australian Curriculum: History, although Wineburg's work certainly formed part of the broader backdrop. Although the concepts in the history curriculum differ slightly from those of Seixas—comprising *continuity and change, cause and effect, perspectives, empathetic understanding, significance* and *contestability*—they also stress the critical nature of historical inquiry, and direct us towards using historical content to develop critical understandings of historical evidence (NSW Board of Studies 2012).

In sum, the presence of historical thinking concepts in the current history curriculum is the fruit of almost 30 years' worth of research, emerging primarily from the United States and Canada. The depicted function of the concepts within the curriculum—as a lens through which the content should be taught—underscores the importance of adopting a thinking-driven rather than a content-driven approach in Australian history classrooms.

ENGAGING WITH WEBSITES AS HISTORICAL SOURCES

This leads us to the central issue of this chapter: the use of online sources. Following from the discussion above, the primary question to be answered is how Australian history teachers can encourage students to treat websites as rich historical sources. To tackle such a broad topic, I focus my discussion on categories of online sources rather than individual websites, and I include a number of examples of what I consider to be the 'gold standard' of best practice to act as guide for classroom implementation.

Shifting the frame with conventional sources

Conventional sources can be thought of as the textbooks of the internet: they contain narrative content, images, audio, video, relevant questions and often specific guidelines and resources for educators. These are the type of ready-made resource that one can easily slot into part of a lesson or even base a lesson around without too much effort. In an Australian setting, good examples might be the educational resources offered by the Australian War Memorial (AWM) (2018) and the National Library of Australia (NLA) (2018)—both have been expertly curated, contain a strong narrative element, draw upon a range of media and have been aligned to the Australian Curriculum: History. These sites can and will form a part of good history lessons; however, when drawing upon such resources, the temptation might be to fall back into the habit of treating these sites as repositories of content rather than as sources in and of themselves. Indeed, the structure of such sites, and the fact that we appear to have been naturalised into thinking about online content in such ways, makes the temptation hard to resist.

Perhaps the simplest way of encouraging students to view websites as sources is to compare multiple sites with different perspectives on the same topic, which is a variation of traditional source-based activities targeting the concept of *perspectives*. However, such a task has the potential to be richer than existing source-based activities: instead of analysing extracts from text-based sources alone to identify perspectives (as you might find in conventional textbooks), students can explore how a historical perspective can be crafted using multiple modalities, such as hyperlinks (Are they structured to convey a particular meaning? What does the content of the links tell us about the message being sent?) or multimedia elements such as text combined with website design, images and video (How do these non-textual elements of the website combine to help convey a particular perspective? Is the use of colour or certain types of language deliberate?). The great advantage of such activities is that they not only develop deeper understandings of the concept of perspectives, but they also help students to develop critical web literacy skills beyond the traditional URL/author/bias checklists currently in use.

Another particularly rich tool that can be used to analyse a conventional website as a source is the Internet Archive: Wayback Machine (2018), which contains over 299 billion copies of web pages captured from 1996 onwards. Tools of this type are now being utilised by historians who use websites as primary source material in contemporary historical accounts (Brugger & Schroeder 2017). This tool could be harnessed by history teachers in a similar way to explore issues relevant to Australian students—one approach might be to examine news websites such as *The Sydney Morning Herald* or *The New York Times* on the day of historically significant events, such as the 9/11 attacks, the invasion of Afghanistan in 2001 or the Global Financial Crisis in 2008. Unlike traditional static primary sources, the hyperlinks in archived websites are often functional, so students can explore the site and build a more complete picture of how an event was reported and perceived at the time. The Internet Archive: Wayback Machine is free, easy to navigate and can readily be adapted to develop rich source-based activities.

A good example of this can be found in the analysis provided by T. Mills Kelly in *Teaching History in the Digital Age*. Not only does Kelly examine the website itself (including the text, design and images), he also analyses, information external to the website, including locating the site using Google (and issues around Google search results are discussed), finding and examining the physical address of the site owner using Google

Maps (if an address is provided), examining the website metadata (what type of visitors is the page trying to attract?), looking at previous iterations of the site using the Wayback Machine (to examine change over time) and locating any reviews that the page might have. This approach is essentially an application of the heuristics of sourcing, corroboration and contextualisation identified by Wineburg (1991), and embodies the central message that every website should be treated as a rich historical source.

Engage with unconventional sources

In contrast to conventional sources, unconventional sources are those that traditionally have not been accepted as valid in many history classrooms, primarily due to a lack of clear authorship and perceived issues with quality control; the chief example here is Wikipedia. As was mentioned earlier, research indicates that unconventional sources are also the most widely used by students when conducting research online, despite them being told by educators not to use them (Konieczny 2016). This finding alone makes leaving these sources out of the discussion problematic, so this section is concerned with tapping the potential of open-source sites such as Wikipedia to develop rich understandings of historical evidence and shed additional light upon the process of historical inquiry.

Despite the hesitance that many educators feel around the use of Wikipedia for (explicit) academic purposes, current research suggests that the open-source site offers a number of significant educational benefits, including improving students' research skills (their ability to find, critically appraise and include references in their work), improving the quality of student writing and increasing student motivation (Konieczny 2016: 1528). Related to motivation, one key advantage is the authenticity associated with Wikipedia tasks—instead of being marked and discarded, student work represents a genuine contribution to public knowledge and has a real, and sometimes very interested, audience. Wikipedia also contains many of the advantages of collaborative learning in other settings, including motivating students, and moving them from being passive to active participants in the knowledge-construction process (2016: 1529).

A Wikipedia-based assignment in Australian history classrooms does not have to be complex, and can be used to sharpen skills in both research and critical analysis. With regard to research, it might take the form of constructing an article on a topic of local historical interest about which sufficient primary material can be located, or students could be encouraged to draw material from Australian digital archives such as Trove (2018) or the Australian War Memorial (AWM) (2018) to develop an article on a person or event that is not currently in the encyclopaedia. Another task might involve asking students to critically appraise an existing article by examining the sources used, the edits made and the discussion from the editors. A good example of this is the work of Australian history teacher Nigel Davies (2010) who, before permitting students to use Wikipedia for classroom research, 'prepares' them by asking them to analyse the edit history of articles on controversial topics (flat-earth or global warming are fairly benign, but if you want something edgier, perhaps look at a revisionist history). Davies uses the discussion around the edit history to draw attention to both the process of article construction and the important issue of identifying contrasting historical perspectives.

Used in this way, Wikipedia-based assignments provide opportunities to develop critical understandings of historical evidence, the nature of historical inquiry and the process by which historical narratives are constructed from disparate pieces of evidence. Further, the tools contained within Wikipedia render it more transparent and open to critique than many conventional sources. The discussion page of a Wikipedia entry, as mentioned above, reveals the debates between page editors around the sources used or the perspectives taken in the account, and the history page presents a complete edit history from the day the page was first created. Trawling through such an edit history provides unprecedented detail not only on how a historical account is gradually constructed, but also how it shifts and changes over time. Laying bare the mechanisms of knowledge construction in such a space will hopefully shift students' thinking about Wikipedia's use as a rich source instead of an uncitable one, which has the knock-on effect of better equipping them to evaluate such sources in their future research work (and hopefully cite them if they are used). Taken together, these features make Wikipedia a potentially rich historical source that is ready-made for educators to use to develop deep and critical historical understandings of historical evidence.

Utilise the raw material

Letters, maps, photographs, film and artefacts are the 'stuff' of history—the very material through which historians construct their accounts. One of the most celebrated achievements of the internet is the 'democratisation' of access to previously inaccessible (or at least difficult to reach) archival records, and there was a lot of excitement in the 1990s within the history-education community when large institutions such as the US Library of Congress began digitising their material and making it available free of charge (O'Malley & Rosenzweig 1997). Research tools such as these can helpfully (and literally) be thought of as the archives of the internet: they contain the raw historical material (primary sources for the most part) from which quality teaching and learning resources can be developed.

Tools that would be useful for Australian history teachers include the National Library of Australia's (NLA) Trove (2018) archive, which provides access to over 500 million digital resources, including newspaper articles, photos, maps, lists, books and even archived websites. Another significant resource is the National Film and Sound Archive (NFSA) (2018). Not quite as vast as the Trove collection, the NFSA's collection tends to focus more explicitly on video and audio resources (though it does contain documentation and artefacts). The other major archival source worth mentioning is the Australian War Memorial (AWM) (2018), which contains a large collection of searchable primary source material (documents, photographs, video and artefacts) relating to Australian military history. It is possible to simply locate relevant and useful primary sources from these archives and integrate them directly into your lessons—indeed, Wineburg's (2001) approach hinges on exposing students to complex, stimulating and revealing primary sources within the classroom, where educators have an opportunity to model and scaffold the process of historical inquiry for students.

A guiding principle for this type of teaching is to select sources that help to reveal the complex, problematic and often contested nature of historical inquiry. Unfortunately, the sources provided in many textbooks may be chosen because they are illustrative rather than contentious or problematic (I have yet to see a textbook deliberately challenge its own metanarrative). Although it helps to make telling the story a little easier, it may ultimately be doing students a disservice, as the process of historical inquiry is rarely this neat. Accordingly, try to select rich sources that may be open to multiple interpretations, and encourage students to grapple and reason with them as they develop plausible interpretations. If pursuing this type of direct integration, it is important to always provide students with a rich context for the source (both historical and, if appropriate, historiographical) to help them reach warranted conclusions.

An example of teaching with archives done well can be seen in the work of Tona Hangen (2015) from Worcester State University, who argues that it is important not only to teach students how to use existing archives, but also to shift the frame and view the archive itself *as a source*. The best way to teach students the processes, limits and ethics of archival work, Hangen argues, is to ask them to build an archive themselves. This could be as simple as collating digital sources in a site like Pinterest, Flickr or Scoop.it, or as elaborate as collaborating with a local library or university to help digitise a portion of its collection (2015: 1198). An interesting assessment set by Hangen involves asking students to collate a collection of three to five primary sources that shed light upon a recent historical event, then pass them on to another student who is asked to evaluate the quality of the sources, add a new source and include a justification for the addition. The collection of sources, and the reasoning behind their inclusion, become richer as the archive progresses through multiple iterations, and students develop valuable understandings of some of the issues and ethics surrounding the use of digital sources (2015: 1198).

CRITICAL WEB LITERACY

Before concluding our discussion, one area that should be touched upon is the omnipresent issue of website evaluation. Despite the fact that the internet has been in public use for almost 30 years, and the fact that our students have grown up interacting with it, research still suggests that large numbers of students are not engaging critically with the information they find (Hargittai et al. 2010; McGrew, Breakstone, Ortega, Smith & Wineburg 2018). This is clearly an issue that touches upon many areas of the school curriculum, but history educators should be particularly concerned. History is by nature a contested discourse, and it is often used as a tool for communicating, promoting and legitimising a broad spectrum of views, including those that are false and misleading. Given that the typical goal of history educators is to prepare students for democratic citizenship, approaching websites with open yet critical minds is surely another important aspect of our task.

Classical approaches

So how can we help to prepare students to be critical web consumers? The first approach to be considered here is termed the 'classical' model of online source analysis. This represents the tried-and-true checklist-type approaches that contain criteria such as the location of the information, detection of bias, the motivation of the author, checking the URL, examining any links the page contains, and assessing relevance and other factors (Taylor & Young 2003: 136). These scaffolds have a place in the classroom, and they are effective when the type of information on the website mirrors that found in traditional print-based material (headers, titles, indexes, keywords, graphs, etc.); however, most of these scaffolds are adaptations of traditional print-based criteria, and the print-based nature of the scaffolds may limit their effectiveness when approaching web-based text types that do not appear in traditional material. Recent research suggests that in some cases the use of classical checklists may make students more vulnerable to online misinformation, not less, because the developers of such websites design them in such a way as to satisfy all the traditional criteria for credibility (Goulding 2015; Wineburg & McGrew 2017). As such, any use of checklists in the classroom must be accompanied by broader discussions about how websites can manipulate the appearance of their content in order to appear more credible (Goulding 2015; Wineburg & McGrew 2017).

Conceptual approaches

In contrast to the classical approach, the conceptual approach is based around the unique features of web-based information that play into evaluation, such as information design and appearance, information accessibility, the role of search engines, the function of hypertext (as opposed to simply examining where the links lead) and the social practices surrounding internet usage. Such an approach may be oriented around the mechanisms that web designers use to persuade their audience to believe a site's content, and may have involved a shift from asking questions about 'What is the website saying?' to questions related to 'What is the website doing?' (Goulding 2015). For example, reflecting upon questions such as 'How has the site been designed, and how does this make me feel about the content?', 'Have links been used to develop a particular image for the site?' and 'Does the site's ranking on a search engine shape the way I perceive it?' can help to activate critical awareness among students, and help them to notice important features of websites that may previously have gone unnoticed (Goulding 2015).

Modelling

Perhaps the best way of communicating both classical and conceptual approaches to website analysis is through teacher modelling, which can be integrated directly into existing lessons. A rule of thumb here is to start not on the target web page, but with Google—this is where most students will start, and it provides you with an opportunity to discuss issues such as website ranking (which many students use as a proxy for credibility). Recent research undertaken by the Stanford History Education Group with professional fact checkers also stresses the importance of *lateral reading,* where important clues as to the credibility of a particular page are found not within the page itself, but through reading laterally using search engines to locate reviews and corroborating information (Wineburg & McGrew 2017). When integrating such modelling into existing lessons, it may be easier to use legitimate websites that you might expect students to use to complete their work. However, if you want to devote time to the explicit teaching of critical web literacy, another strategy might include the use of hoax websites, as this provides opportunities for you to make explicit the tactics used by website creators to make their content appear legitimate with a source that all students can accept is clearly fabricated.

CONCLUSION

At its core, disciplinary historical thinking is about how we approach historical evidence, and the central challenge considered in this chapter has been to suggest ways to activate student critical thinking when dealing with websites. By moving beyond the binary of viewing websites as either credible or not credible, we can encourage students to treat them not just as the storehouses of historical content, or as hidden sources in the process of historical inquiry, but as the rich and nuanced historical sources they are.

REFERENCES

Australian War Memorial (AWM) 2018, 'Classroom resources', <www.awm.gov.au/learn/schools/resources>, accessed 29 January 2018.

Brugger, N. & Schroeder, R. 2017, *Web as History: Using Web Archives to Understand the Past and the Present*, London: UCL Press.

Davies, N. 2010, 'The uses and abuses of Wikipedia', *Agora*, vol. 45, no. 4, pp. 11–14.

Goulding, J. 2015, 'Improving online source analysis in history education: Trialling the ethos model', *Historical Encounters*, vol. 2, no. 1, pp. 89–101.

Hangen, T. 2015, 'Historical digital literacy, one classroom at a time', *The Journal of American History*, vol. 101, no. 4, pp. 1192–1203.

Hargittai, E., Fullerton, L., Menchen-Trevino, E. & Yates Thomas, K. 2010, 'Trust online: Young adults' evaluation of web content', *International Journal of Communication,* vol. 30, no. 2, pp. 468–94.

Hilligoss, B. & Rieh, S.Y. 2008, 'Developing a unifying framework of credibility assessment: Construct, heuristics, and interaction in context', *Information Processing and Management,* vol. 44, pp. 1467–84.

Internet Archive: Wayback Machine 2018, Website, <https://archive.org/web>, accessed 7 September 2018.

Kelly, T.M. 2013, *Teaching History in the Digital Age.* Ann Arbor: University of Michigan Press.

Konieczny, P. 2016, 'Teaching with Wikipedia in a 21st century classroom: Perceptions of Wikipedia and its educational benefits', *Advances in Information Science,* vol. 67, no. 7, pp. 1523–34.

Lévesque, S. 2008, *Thinking Historically: Educating Students for the Twenty-First Century,* Toronto: University of Toronto Press.

McGrew, S., Breakstone, J., Ortega, T., Smith, M. & Wineburg, S. 2018, 'Can Students Evaluate Online Sources? Learning from Assessments of Civic Online Reasoning', *Theory & Research in Social Education,* vol. 46, no. 2, pp.165–93.

Menchen-Trevino, E. & Hargittai, E. 2011, 'Young adults' credibility assessment of Wikipedia', *Information, Communication & Society,* vol. 14, no. 1, pp. 24–51.

National Film and Sound Archive (NFSA) 2018, Website, <www.nfsa.gov.au>, accessed 29 January 2018.

National Library of Australia (NLA) 2018, *Digital Classroom,* <www.nla.gov.au/digital-classroom>, accessed 29 January 2018.

NSW Board of Studies 2012, *Syllabus for the Australian Curriculum: History K–10,* Sydney: NSW Board of Studies.

O'Malley, M. & Rosenzweig, R. 1997, 'Brave new world or blind alley? American history on the World Wide Web', *The Journal of American History,* vol. 84, no. 1, pp. 132–55.

Parkes, R. & Donnelly, D. 2014, 'Changing conceptions of historical thinking in history education: An Australian case study', *Revista Tempo e Argumento,* vol. 6, no. 11, pp. 113–36.

Seixas, P. (ed.) 2004, *Theorizing Historical Consciousness,* Toronto: University of Toronto Press.

Seixas P. & Morton, T. 2013, *The Big Six Historical Thinking Concepts,* Toronto: Nelson.

Taylor, T. & Young, C. 2003, *Making History: A Guide for the Teaching and Learning of History in Australian Schools,* Melbourne: Curriculum Corporation.

Trove 2018, Website, <https://trove.nla.gov.au>, accessed 7 September 2018.

Wineburg, S. 1991, 'On the reading of historical texts: Notes on the breach between school and academy', *American Educational Research Journal*, vol. 28, no. 3, pp. 495–519.
—— 2001, *Historical Thinking and Other Unnatural Acts: Charting the Future of Teaching the Past*, Philadelphia, PA: Temple University Press.
Wineburg, S. & McGrew, S. 2017, *Lateral Reading: Reading Less and Learning More When Evaluating Digital Information*, Working Paper No. 2017, Stanford, CA: Stanford History Education Group.

CHAPTER 18
Digital technology in the primary classroom

Catherine L. Smyth

This chapter provides insights into the kinds of online digital technologies teachers can use to enable primary students to connect with, and make sense of, the discipline of history in engaging and meaningful ways. The chapter views digital technology not as just another unnecessary classroom gadget or unnecessary resource cluttering a busy lesson, but as an 'epistemic tool' that has the potential to help students generate new knowledge, organise their understanding or help them to engage with historical methods, procedures and skills. By identifying the *capacities* and *functions* of specific digital technologies to help students understand what history is and how to do history, time-poor primary teachers can navigate an increasingly overwhelming online digital world and make effective pedagogical decisions about how they can utilise digital technologies in their teaching.

The chapter first provides a brief overview of history and ICT in the Australian Curriculum (ACARA 2017a). It then establishes a socio-cultural perspective of history as a discipline and makes a theoretical link between history and technology by highlighting the capacities of specific digital technologies and exploring the potential these technologies have to build primary students' disciplinary knowledge. In the final section, various effective digital technologies for teaching and learning history in the primary classroom are identified, and teaching ideas are provided.

CURRICULUM CONTEXT

Disciplinary learning is a cornerstone of the Australian Curriculum. Knowledge of a range of disciplines is viewed as essential in equipping students for the twenty-first century. A key goal of the Australian Curriculum, highlighted in the Melbourne Declaration of Educational Goals for Young Australians (MCEETYA 2008), states:

> The curriculum will enable students to develop knowledge in the disciplines ... and open up new ways of thinking. It will also support the development of deep knowledge within a discipline, which provides the foundation for inter-disciplinary approaches to innovation and complex problem-solving ... and an ability to move across subject disciplines to develop new expertise.

For generalist-trained primary teachers, who are required to teach a broad range of subjects within the primary curriculum, the shift to a disciplinary-based curriculum for each subject has significant pedagogical, practical and conceptual implications. The new curriculum signals new ways of knowing, learning and teaching in the primary classroom.

The disciplinary focus of the Australian Curriculum aligns with international concerns that students enter and leave school with a very limited notion of what the disciplines they study are actually about (Ford & Forman 2006; Shulman & Quinlan 1996; Wineburg 2001). Limited disciplinary knowledge means students are not equipped to build new knowledge and have no way to determine how that knowledge is 'appropriately disseminated, scrutinized, and contested' (Van Bergen & Bahr 2009). Lehman, Lempert and Nisbett (1998) argue that different subjects should expose teachers and students to different disciplines, acculturating them to appreciate particular forms of evidence: what counts as truth and what knowledge is considered of value. Morrison and Collins (1995) suggest that an important goal of school is to help people to become epistemically fluent across a range of disciplines so they might acquire different ways of knowing the world.

SOCIOCULTURAL VIEW OF THE DISCIPLINE

Put simply, a discipline is a branch of knowledge. An academic discipline, such as history, is the study of something in a particular area, and is characterised by the different kinds of questions that are asked, the ways in which different kinds of data are collected and the different ways in which knowledge is formulated and communicated (Schwab 1962). Within sociocultural research, a discipline is conceptualised in four main ways (Brown, Collins & Duguid 1989: 32-4):

1. Disciplinary knowledge is not a collection of isolated facts but *has a structure*. This is a conceptual structure made up of big ideas that together define the nature of the discipline. In history, these include abstract concepts such as significance, evidence, change and continuity, and practical concepts such as historical inquiry. In grasping and applying these concepts, historians make sense of previous events, people, practices and ideas.
2. Disciplinary knowledge is *situated*, being in part a product of the *activity, context and culture* in which it is developed and used (Brown, Collins & Duguid 1989: 32-4). Just as if a discipline were a foreign country, the most effective way to get to know that culture is to go there and experience how things are done. When people observe, imitate and participate in the ordinary practices of the culture, they quickly adopt the complex ways of that culture. In school history, students should be given the opportunity to get to know the unique culture of history—to learn the language and engage in the authentic practices inherent to the discipline.
3. The construction of new knowledge requires *learning how to use the knowledge-building structures (or concepts)* that one's culture makes available (Morrison & Collins 1995). Disciplinary knowledge is constructed through distinctive methods, procedures and processes of inquiry. In history, knowledge is constructed through 'the retrieval, comprehension and interpretation of sources, and judgment, guided by principles that are intrinsic to the discipline. [Historical knowledge] is based on the available evidence, but remains open to further debate and future reinterpretation' (National Curriculum Board 2009).
4. There are numerous ways of constructing knowledge, with some *domain specific* and some *general* (Morrison & Collins 1995). Historical knowledge is constructed by asking questions, applying skills associated with analysing, interpreting and evaluating sources of evidence, developing an explanation and communicating historical knowledge in appropriate forms.

These four assumptions underpin the Australian Curriculum: History (and various state-based syllabuses), where the emphasis is on providing students with the opportunity to learn history through disciplinary approaches.

A key aim of the Australian Curriculum: History (NCB 2009: 7) is for students to:

> Acquire a knowledge and understanding of history, skills associated with the identification, comprehension and interpretation of sources, use of chronology, and research and communication need to be developed. The curriculum should allow for the development of skills through a process of historical inquiry. A key aspect of inquiry in history is the study of primary and secondary sources of evidence. Students comprehend, analyse, interpret and evaluate historical sources and use the evidence provided in the sources to make informed decisions about an inquiry question. Appropriate historical inquiry questions can be framed for students at different stages of development.

TECHNOLOGIES IN THE AUSTRALIAN CURRICULUM

Information and Communication Technology (ICT) is one of seven 'general capabilities' to be addressed across the curriculum. ICTs (referred to as technologies) play an important role 'in equipping young Australians to live and work successfully in the twenty-first century' (ACARA 2017b). Throughout their schooling, students are to 'learn to use ICT effectively and appropriately to access, create and communicate information and ideas' (ACARA 2017c) and, within each subject area, students are to 'make the most of the digital technologies available to them, adapting to new ways of doing things' (ACARA 2017c). Within history, students 'learn how to build discipline-specific knowledge about history ... using a wide range of ICT' (ACARA 2017c), yet the pedagogical and planning implications of this for teachers seem to have been overlooked. What does a 'wide range of ICT' encompass? How do teachers identify and select effective technologies that enable their students to build discipline-specific knowledge? What digital technologies help primary students to understand what history is? What digital technologies enable students to learn to do history? In the next section, we introduce the notion of 'epistemic tools' to address these questions and open up new ways of thinking about the capabilities and affordances of specific digital technologies that help students build new knowledge.

TECHNOLOGY AS AN EPISTEMIC TOOL FOR CONSTRUCTING HISTORICAL KNOWLEDGE

According to Lina Markauskaite and Peter Goodyear (2017: 355), an epistemic tool is something that 'increases the user's *understanding* of the problem and guides them in taking knowledgeable *action*'. By viewing digital technologies as potential epistemic tools, teachers can identify the types of technologies that develop their students' understanding of history as a discipline, or a technology that scaffolds, guides or sequences the historical inquiry process. The two main characteristics of digital technologies that can be used as epistemic tools are discussed below.

The first characteristic of an epistemic tool is that it should increase the user's understanding of the discipline, opening up the opportunity to understand disciplinary culture, customs and practices. A digital technology that builds disciplinary knowledge facilitates an understanding that history is a distinctive subject with a specific purpose, and with its own methods and procedures. The technologies we use in primary history should emphasise the unique nature and culture of the discipline so students understand that history is more than facts and dates. They become aware that history, by its nature, is contested and interpretive. Digital technologies that allow students to consider multiple perspectives and different accounts of historical events reflect the inherent nature of history as a discipline. Another way to evaluate whether a digital technology is a useful epistemic tool is to consider how historical concepts and historical language are embedded in the teaching and learning activities. For example, does the technology expose students to different types of historical language (e.g. specialised terminology, vocabulary to denote time or to communicate historical knowledge) or to historical concepts such as significance, change and continuity, cause and effect or empathy? These are just some of the features to consider when identifying, evaluating and selecting digital technologies for teaching and learning primary history.

The second characteristic of an epistemic tool is that it *guides, scaffolds or structures actions*. In other words, consider digital technology that models or represents the practical activities of a discipline such as history, and carefully evaluate whether the technology enables students to actually *do* history. By viewing the affordances that technology has to scaffold the historical inquiry process or structure a historical activity—for example, analysing a photograph—students have the opportunity to *participate* in disciplined inquiry, and the activities and practices of the discipline. By way of illustration, digital story technology enables students to construct a historical narrative. An important affordance of this technology is the structure it provides. To create their digital story for history, students use, organise and sequence a range of different sources (e.g. photographs, music, text) as they engage with the historical inquiry process. Digital story technology is a useful scaffold for the construction of a historical narrative or explanation, and provides a way for students to engage with the practices of history. Teachers can facilitate the inquiry process by planning learning activities addressing historical skills such as asking questions, gathering evidence, analysing sources and communicating historical knowledge in the form of a historical narrative.

The following section identifies a range of useful, appropriate and engaging digital technologies for school history lessons. Five online technologies are examined and analysed for the ways in which students might use the technology as an epistemic tool to extend their understanding of history and historical inquiry. Each example of a digital technology can be used for a specific purpose in history. For example, one tool might help a student grasp the usefulness of primary and secondary sources, while another might provide the structure for creating a timeline showing key events. Additional ICT resources for teaching history can be accessed on the 'Teaching history with ICT' Scoop.it! site (Smyth 2018).

Death in Rome

In this highly engaging online interactive game (BBC History 2014), the aim is to solve a Roman murder mystery by posing questions, analysing primary and secondary sources, and coming up with an explanation based on evidence. To play the game and solve the mystery, students use and analyse both primary sources (things that were around at the time, such as artefacts or eyewitnesses) and secondary sources (for example, a medical expert). The game requires that students actively engage in the historical inquiry process and use methods and procedures inherent to the discipline. The game enables the user to develop an understanding of evidence, a key concept in history, as they solve the question, 'How did this man die?' The game makes available a range of primary and secondary sources, some of which are useful in answering the question of inquiry, while others are not. Through the interaction with different sources, students begin to piece together evidence to construct a plausible explanation for what happened in the past.

VoiceThread

VoiceThread (2018) is an online application used to create multimedia presentations and conversations. Instructors and/or students can use it to create, share and comment on images, Microsoft PowerPoint presentations, videos, audio files, documents and PDFs, using microphone, webcam, text, phone and audio-file upload.

Source analysis is an important historical skill. In the Australian Curriculum: History, children begin to develop the skills of analysis and use of sources as early as the Foundation/Kindergarten year, where they explore and use a range of sources, and identify and compare features of objects from the past and present. In subsequent years, students not only locate information from sources, but they also compare, analyse and use sources relevant to inquiry questions.

In this example of an activity using VoiceThread, an American fifth-grade teacher records her students as they interpret and make sense of a historical photograph. The black and white photograph depicts a family of newly arrived immigrants to Ellis Island in New York's harbour. It is an image of a mother and father and a large brood of children of varying ages. The fifth-grade students each take on the role of a family member and construct a short narrative about what the experience of the arrival at Ellis Island was like. The recording captures the students' different perspectives, interpretations and analysis of a primary source. It also shows how the students are developing empathetic understanding as they explain how and why people in the past may have lived and behaved differently from today.

A digital technology like VoiceThread can be used to activate new knowledge about the past and, as the fifth-grade example shows, it was an engaging, collaborative and inclusive activity involving every student. It was also a task that required students to use different historical skills, historical language and historical imagination.

Digital storytelling (see appendix A, page 253)

Digital stories (Tech4Learning 2018) are multimedia movies that combine photographs, video, animation, sound, music, text and a narrative voice. The production of a five-minute digital story requires the use of a range of technological tools (e.g. Movie Maker, iMovie, video editing) to organise, sequence, present and communicate ideas.

When used for epistemic purposes, digital stories are powerful tools for helping students to understand what history is and engaging them in doing history. The final product, the digital story, is a historical narrative or explanation about a person, event or place in the past. The construction of the historical narrative requires the user to engage with the concepts as well as the methods and practices inherent in the discipline. For example, a student who constructs a digital story (a historical narrative) about why their grandparents migrated to Australia might develop an understanding of historical concepts such as significance or cause and effect, as well as build new knowledge about what life was like for people in the 1940s. In doing so, students draw on a range of primary and secondary sources as they participate in the historical inquiry process. A key understanding for students includes the interpretive nature of history.

Timeglider

Timeglider (National History Clearing House 2018) is a digital technology that enables students to create, collaborate and publish zooming and panning interactive timelines. It is an example of a web-based timeline software for creating and sharing history.

While timelines play a vital role in organising and representing historical time, primary-aged children make sense of a timeline if they can make connections to their prior knowledge. Initially, students develop an understanding of then and now by making connections with material and social aspects of life (e.g. school, toys, clothes, transport) before being able to sequence more abstract events and people in chronological order, and representing time by creating timelines. According to Levstik and Barton (2005), understanding historical time involves being able to order moments in time, and being able to match moments in time to specific dates. Research shows that children are better at sequencing historical periods (e.g. convict era, colonial Australia) than assigning dates or names to those periods. Dates often don't allow students to visualise the time being referred to. Teachers can therefore facilitate learning by helping students to visualise images of history with the corresponding dates. They can also help students to make distinctions between broad categories of time (close to now, a long time ago, in the 1800s, etc.).

Recording experiences with Year 1 students

Digital photography (National History Clearing House 2018) is an accessible technology that has the potential to enable students to develop understanding of a range of historical concepts. This example demonstrates how a generic technology such as digital cameras can be used for epistemic purposes.

Organised in four parts, the video shows the way a teacher uses the digital photographs, taken by her Year 1 students on a field trip, to activate historical knowledge about significant memorials and buildings. The learning experiences are carefully scaffolded and sequenced to enable students to make connections to prior knowledge and build new conceptual knowledge and historical skills.

Primary sources that are text-based can be a challenge for younger students, so it is often useful for teachers to provide concrete experiences outside the classroom where students can interact with artefacts, statues or places. By using digital photography to capture and record interactions with physical objects, teachers can help younger students to build conceptual knowledge.

CONCLUSION

There are limitless online resources and digital technologies available for teachers to use to teach history. While the main purpose and function of some digital technologies, such as Death in Rome, are pedagogical and disciplinary-based, generic digital technologies such as digital stories, digital photographs or VoiceThread can also be used for epistemic purposes. Some digital technologies are disciplinary in nature because they purposefully and explicitly target history, while others are generic but can be used for epistemic purposes. By identifying and selecting digital technology for the affordances it has to be used as an epistemic tool for students to use to develop an understanding of the discipline of history or as a way to do history, teachers can expose students to disciplinary ways of knowing. By examining the affordances of different technologies to acculturate, structure and guide students in history and historical inquiry, teachers can make pedagogical decisions about how to use ICT to activate historical knowledge and understanding in the primary classroom.

APPENDIX A: DIGITAL STORY TASK

Instructions

Students focus on an aspect of their family or personal history that intrigues or interests them. Discuss different ways to approach the task. For example, students might link back to past events using family generations, tell a family story to introduce ideas about migration, use personal memories as a stimulus for creating or summarising a sense of period (e.g. the Great Depression, the 1980s), trace the impact of war on family, or use family memories to explore changes in everyday life. As family historians, they are to adopt the methods used by historians and engage in the historical inquiry process to create a historical narrative or explanation. The form and function of the digital story scaffold and guide action in the following ways:

- The student initiates their historical inquiry with questions they have about an aspect of their family (e.g. what was childhood like for my mother growing up in China? Why did my grandparents migrate from Macedonia? What was life like for my father who was a refugee from Vietnam?).
- Focusing on the question/s they have posed, students identify and gather a range of primary sources (e.g. family photographs, maps, passports, migration papers, medals, newspaper articles, oral interviews) to help them in their inquiry.
- They gather secondary sources (e.g. reference books) to build contextual knowledge (e.g. significant events, what people wore, what people believed at the time, what technology was used, what they did for leisure, the government, music, schools), situating the story in time and place.
- The student analyses and interprets sources (asks questions, hypothesises, draws conclusions).
- The student sorts and evaluates the sources, and makes decisions about what counts as evidence and what does not. They evaluate which sources are useful to their inquiry and which are not.
- Using the evidence they have gathered, the student constructs a narrative or explanation to answer their question of inquiry.
- The story might be organised in chronological order, or the story might focus on family members' different perspectives or the significance of an event.

APPENDIX B: THE AFFORDANCES OF DIGITAL TECHNOLOGIES

This taxonomy depends upon the following constructs: what sort of knowledge the game produces (its epistemic focus); what the game aims to achieve (its epistemic agenda); the nature of the epistemic object around which the game unfolds; and the sorts of knowledge and skills that expert players of the game use.

Digital technology	Capabilities	Epistemic goals	Constructing historical knowledge	
			Affordance 1: Conceptual knowledge	Affordance 2: Actions Scaffolding, guiding, structuring actions
Digital storytelling	Make 3–5 minute multimedia presentation combining photographs, video, music, text, animation and a narrative voice. Use a range of technological tools (e.g. Movie Maker, iMovie, video editing).	Construct a historical narrative or explanation about family or personal history. Engage with the historical inquiry process to produce new historical knowledge. Historical inquiry is the process of developing knowledge and understanding in history by: asking questions about the past, and applying skills associated with analysing, interpreting and evaluating sources of evidence to develop informed and defensible answers.	The technology has the potential to increase the user's understanding that: History is not a collection of facts. History is interpretive. History is constructed. New historical knowledge is constructed through the historical inquiry process. Historical concepts help organise the past. History is a way to make sense of the past.	The technology scaffolds, guides, structures activity and enables the user to: Participate in the historical inquiry process. Organise, sequence, present and communicate historical ideas. Develop new historical inquiry skills. Communicate new knowledge in historical form (historical narrative).

Digital technology	Capabilities	Epistemic goals	Constructing historical knowledge	
			Affordance 1: Conceptual knowledge	Affordance 2: Actions Scaffolding, guiding, structuring actions
VoiceThread	VoiceThread is a learning tool for enhancing student engagement and online presence. Students can create, share and comment on images, Microsoft PowerPoint presentations, videos audio files, documents and PDFs, using microphone, webcam, text, phone and audio-file upload.	Construct a historical narrative or explanation about people, a place or event.	The technology has the potential to increase the user's understanding of: History as a way to understand the past. Evidence. Historical empathy. Perspectives. Change and Continuity. Historical inquiry skills.	The technology scaffolds, guides, structures activity and enables the user to: Ask questions about the past (e.g. what was life like?). Use the well-established methods and procedures of historians (primary source analysis). Apply skills associated with analysing, interpreting and evaluating sources of evidence. Develop informed and defensible answers, explanations or narratives.

Digital technology	Capabilities	Epistemic goals	Constructing historical knowledge	
			Affordance 1: Conceptual knowledge	Affordance 2: Actions Scaffolding, guiding, structuring actions
Death in Rome	Online interactive 'murder mystery' game.	Construct a historical explanation of why the Roman man died. Ask questions, engage with primary and secondary sources to help answer questions of inquiry.	The technology has the potential to increase the user's understanding of: Evidence, cause and effect. Primary and secondary sources are both useful to me if they answer my questions of inquiry.	The technology scaffolds, guides, structures activity and enables the user to: Ask questions about the past (e.g. how did this man die?). Use the well-established methods and procedures of historians (primary and secondary source analysis). Apply skills associated with analysing, interpreting and evaluating sources of evidence. Develop informed and defensible answers or explanations based on evidence.

REFERENCES

Australian Curriculum and Reporting Authority (ACARA) 2017a, *Australian Curriculum*, <www.australiancurriculum.edu.au>, accessed 1 December 2017.

——2017b, *General Capabilities in the Australian Curriculum*, <www.australiancurriculum.edu.au/f-10-curriculum/general-capabilities>, accessed 10 January 2018.

——2017c, *Information and Communication Technology (ICT) Capability*, <www.australiancurriculum.edu.au/f-10-curriculum/general-capabilities/information-and-communication-technology-ict-capability>, accessed 10 January 2018.

BBC History 2014, *Death in Rome*, <www.bbc.co.uk/history/ancient/romans/launch_gms_deathrome.shtml>, accessed 27 April 2018.

Brown, S.J., Collins, A. & Duguid, P. 1989, 'Situated cognition and the culture of learning', *Educational Researcher*, vol. 18, no. 32, pp. 32–42.

Ford, M.J. & Forman, E.A. 2006, 'Redefining disciplinary learning in classroom contexts', *Review of Research in Education*, vol. 30, no. 1, pp. 1–32.

Lehman, D.R., Lempert, R.O. & Nisbett, R.W. 1998, 'The effects of graduate training on reasoning: Formal discipline and thinking about everyday-life events', *American Psychologist*, vol. 43, pp. 431–42.

Levstik, L. & Barton, K. 2005, *Doing History: Investigating with Children in Elementary and Middle Schools*, 3rd ed., Mahwah, NJ: Lawrence Erlbaum.

Markauskaite, L. & Goodyear, P.M. 2017, *Epistemic Fluency and Professional Education: Innovation, Knowledgeable Action and Working Knowledge*. Springer.

Ministerial Council on Education, Employment, Training and Youth Affairs (MCEETYA) 2008, *Melbourne Declaration of Educational Goals for Young Australians*, <www.curriculum.edu.au/verve/_resources/National_Declaration_on_the_Educational_Goals_for_Young_Australians.pdf>, accessed 1 December 2017.

Morrison, D. & Collins, A. 1995, 'Epistemic fluency and constructivist learning environments', *Educational Technology*, vol. 35, no. 5, pp. 39–45.

National Curriculum Board (NCB) 2009, *Shape of the Australian Curriculum: History*, Canberra: NCB.

National History Clearing House 2018, 'Recording experiences with first graders', 2010–2018, <http://teachinghistory.org/digital-classroom/beyond-the-chalkboard/25640>, accessed 27 April 2018.

Schwab, J.J. 1962, 'The concept of the structure of a discipline', *The Educational Record*, vol. 43, pp. 197–205.

Shulman, L.S. & Quinlan, K.M. 1996, 'The comparative psychology of school subjects', in D.C. Berliner & R.C. Calfee (eds), *Handbook of Educational Psychology*, New York: Simon & Schuster, pp. 399–422.

Smyth, C. 2018, 'Teaching history with ICT', Scoop.it! website, <www.scoop.it/t/teaching-history-with-ict>, accessed 27 April 2018.

Tech4Learning 2018. 'Digital storytelling', <http://creativeeducator.tech4learning.com/digital-storytelling>, accessed 27 April 2018.

Van Bergen, P. & Bahr, N. 2009, 'The awareness and explication of disciplinarity across four senior-secondary subject areas', paper presented at the American Educational Research Association Annual Meeting, San Diego, <http://eprints.qut.edu.au/31759>, accessed 1 December 2017.

VoiceThread 2018, '5th Grade—Ellis Island narratives from Barbara De Santis', <https://voicethread.com/about/library/5th_Grade__Ellis_Is_Narratives_from_Barbara_De_Santis>, accessed 27 April 2018.

Wineburg, S. 2001, *Historical Thinking and Other Unnatural Acts: Charting the Future of Teaching the Past*, Philadelphia, PA: Temple University Press.

CHAPTER 19
History teaching and the museum

Craig Barker

After spending more than a decade in museum education, I am convinced that museums remain one of the most useful resources available for developing historical understanding for students of all ages and levels. In this chapter, I use some of my personal experiences of historical and archaeological education through museum collections and object-based inquiries to explore larger issues relating to the value of good museum-engagement strategies for history teachers and students. Through museums, students are given the opportunity to contextualise their historical learning, engage with historical material culture directly and challenge notions of researching and presenting a historical narrative in ways that are not necessarily possible within a classroom environment.

The museum environment allows students to explore the practicalities of historical investigation, and stimulates curiosity and intellectual development. Museums are unique places for learning and inspiration that can tell local, national and global stories and allow us to explore the world around us and preserve cultural memories. Furthermore, a positive museum experience during a student's school career will encourage a lifetime of gallery and museum visitation, both locally and when travelling abroad. Museums will remain a major connection with historical inquiry that the majority of students will continue to have long after their schooling career has ended: the 62 museums that make up the Council of Australasian Museum Directors had 51 million visits in 2013–14 to the brick and mortar institutions themselves, and higher numbers to collection websites (Greene 2014). The challenge for teachers is to link museum experiences with classroom history teaching in a dynamic and interesting way, and to integrate the learning experiences offered by a museum (both physically and digitally) into the daily routine of history teaching.

In recent decades, there has been considerable growth in the development and delivery of curricula-related museum education programs across a wide range of institutions. The notion of museums as dusty, dull, boring and static institutions has well and truly been shattered, with dynamic and innovative museum programs for visitors of all types, including school students, which also provide for teacher professional development. Increasingly, varieties of resources and pedagogies are being used by museums to encourage choice, discussion, questioning and active involvement within the context of an institution's collections. The model of object-centred learning is at the focus of much of this development—giving students the tools to engage directly with items held within the collections of museums and galleries (Paris 2002). The shift away from content information in the learning agenda of museums actually privileges the students, giving them responsibility for their own learning. Direct engagement with the interpretation of historical material culture allows students to claim ownership of learning, and gives them recognition as being capable and willing to learn when provided with the right opportunities. Good museum educational experiences must be stimulating—whether they are face-to-face experiences or the encounters with online resources.

I write from the perspective of a museum educator with decades of experience in providing ancient Mediterranean-world content to K–12 students and with direct experiential archaeological education. After years of development of object-centred teaching experiences, both through hands-on workshops and discussion-based guiding, I can see firsthand the value of the access to direct historical and archaeological materials for history students in terms broadening their understanding of historical context. In addition, this experience enables the student to develop broader philosophical and ethical questions that they can then apply elsewhere in their historical studies, and leads to the development of critical interpretive skills. The museum experience should enhance and expand upon a student's classroom experience, integrating different knowledges so that students have a more holistic understanding of historical inquiry.

The development of good museum-based education programs is, however, completely dependent upon the growth of strong relationships between teachers and museum education teams, so that both sides know what the other needs and can deliver. On the one hand, teachers should feel emboldened to speak with museums and work collaboratively with them to find interesting approaches to engage their students. On the other, museums are partners in learning processes, not places to merely book routine excursions. They must provide enjoyable and participatory experiences for students, and teachers must provide feedback about what did and didn't work.

MUSEUM EDUCATION: WHY VISIT A MUSEUM?

In the twenty-first century, it is important to think of the museum education experience as no longer the traditional school excursion, but rather a multidisciplinary and multisensory experience for students. Good museum education and exhibition experiences should engage visual, auditory, reading and kinaesthetic modes of learning.

From a pedagogical perspective, there has been a revolution in museum education over the past decades, often led by researchers and developers including John Falk and Lynn Dierking (2000, 2012), George Hein (1998, 2006), Eilean Hooper-Greenhill (2007) and David Anderson (1999). Students are encouraged to immerse themselves in the gallery or education-space experience through participation in interactions that might include drama and role-play, discussion and thoughtful analysis, and online and hands-on experiences (Griffin 2011). Although museums have always presented themselves as educational institutions, it has only been in the last few decades that exhibition designers and curators have considered the needs of teachers and students within their planning phases, and school education was not simply an afterthought (Schäfer 2016). If a worksheet (or digital-format worksheet) is provided now, it is no longer a simple 'fill in the blanks' affair, but rather designed to instigate thought-provoking investigation. As Tim Ambrose and Crispin Paine (2012: 65) write, 'the sign of a good worksheet is that it encourages the user to look at material on display. If the user can answer the questions without really looking, it has been badly constructed ... [a good worksheet] requires deduction from observation.' Good examples abound online, from the Getty Education (2018) team to the Nova Scotia Museum's (2016) 'How to Read a Shoe' activity.

Decades of studies have shown the value of museum experiences for students of history: students clearly remember the experience much longer than they do a classroom learning experience. A pioneering 2002 study of school services of the Museum of Reading in the United Kingdom demonstrated that 92 per cent of teachers viewed object learning as equally or more important than learning from books, and comments from students ten months after the visit highlighted the benefits for memory and imagination. As one primary-aged student told the interviewer, 'If you look at pictures you imagine what it was like for them. But when you have the objects you imagine what it would be like for you and how you would feel' (McAlpine 2002: 26–7).

Kinaesthetic experiences are particularly useful for student engagement and memory, with the experience of object engagement opening up endless possibilities for students. Direct access with material culture also creates accessible learning experiences: history becomes *tangible*. This is particularly the case in museums and cultural institutions that have built object-handling activities, such as those sessions we conduct at the Nicholson Museum (discussed later).

HANDS-ON HISTORY

The museum experience should be participatory and engaging, not passive. The days of 'look but don't touch' and 'sssshhh, be quiet!' have long since passed in terms of school excursions to museums. Most cultural

Figure 19.1 Simulating history engagement with role-playing and object-handling. Courtesy Nicholson Museum, University of Sydney.

institutions have realised the value of positive student engagement, even if only because today's school excursion participant becomes tomorrow's regular museum visitor.

Across the cultural institution sector, museums now regard themselves as centres that want to create a fun environment (educational and entertaining are not mutually exclusive) and centres of participatory creativity. While each institution has different processes of engagement, and that level of engagement will also vary depending upon the age group of the visiting students and the time available, the key is that students are made to feel welcome within a museum and that museums are places to which they feel comfortable about returning.

As previously mentioned, there are a range of methods now used by museums to engage with students beyond the old-fashioned worksheet and a traditional guided tour. These include inquiry-based apps, interactive displays, 'treasure-hunting'-style experiences, drawing classes, empathy-based role-playing and drama exercises, and asking students to film or photograph objects for audiovisual presentations.

However, I believe from my own observations that it is the experience of handling material culture from collections that truly provides

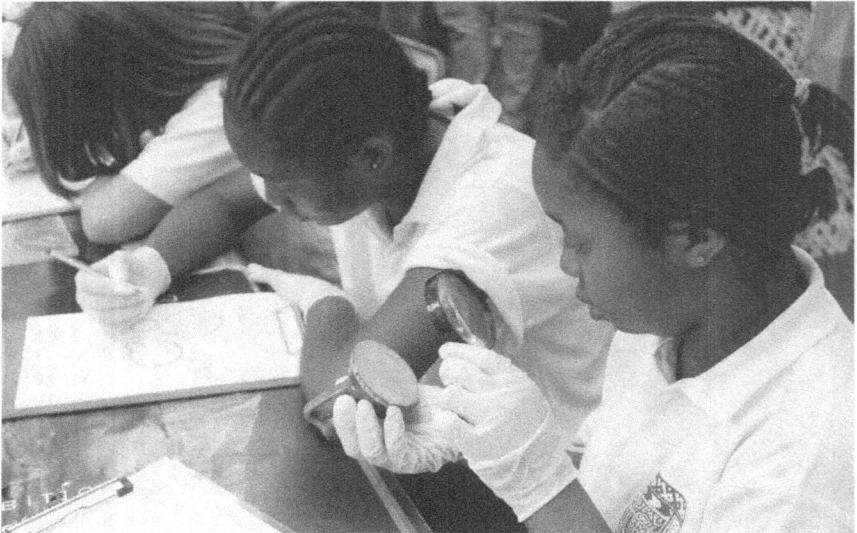

Figure 19.2 Hands-on history in action; close examination of artefacts can stimulate the development of new lines of historical inquiry for students. Courtesy Nicholson Museum, University of Sydney.

the greatest opportunities for students of history—a rare and sometimes unique experience of engaging directly with objects from the past through tactile engagement. Many museums offer experiences of handling genuine collection items for school visitors, or alternatively replicas and increasingly 3D-printed copies of collection items are being used as part of the educational experiences. While the actual material itself doesn't matter so much for the experience (although the knowledge that it is genuine historical material does make the experience even more special), the very process of students holding, touching and turning historical artefacts provides an opportunity to grow an understanding of the past.

The idea of 'hands-on' history has had considerable intellectual conceptualising within museum education and archaeological education over recent decades, including authors such as Russell (1994), Gurian (1999) and Duensing (2002). While a number of approaches can be taken with object-handling sessions, such as an exploration of contrast and comparison issues or integration of archaeological assemblages, I have found it is by encouraging students to ask specific questions of the museum object(s) and integrating the evidence this process provides that students gain the maximum understanding.

Broader questions students may ask of the objects they are handling and examining include:

- What is the artefact? (identification)
- What was the artefact used for? (function)
- What was the artefact made from? Why? How? (manufacturing technique)
- How old is the artefact? How do we know? (chronology)
- Where was the artefact found? (context)
- What does the artefact tell us about the culture that produced it? (interpretation)

This type of 'hands-on history' session can also be used to help develop teamwork and problem-solving skills among the students.

PRE- AND POST-VISIT ACTIVITIES

It is important that teachers think of the broader context of museum engagement. Excursions are time-consuming and can be difficult to organise, so it is essential that maximum benefit is gained for the students. Any museum visit by school students must be approached as part of a larger historical inquiry, so incorporation of pre- and post-visit activities is important. Some institutions offer specific resources for this purpose, but even if they don't, it is advisable for the teacher to visit the institution first or to speak with the museum's education team about expectations; also, give students the opportunity to explore the institution's website and discuss what they will be seeing. Critical analysis of the experience and reflective discussion after the visit are also worthwhile exercises for students, so the museum visit is not seen in isolation, but is rather part of the continuous experience of engaging with historical material.

CRITICAL INTERPRETATION AND REVIEW OF EXHIBITIONS AND MUSEUM COLLECTIONS

One other advantage of direct engagement with museums is the opportunity it allows for students to critically analyse the concept of a museum as historical interpreter. In other words, students can learn and think about the curatorial perspective. Museums are places of storytelling through the objects selected for public display and the labels and signage attached to each exhibition. So how does a curator develop a narrative of the material that they may choose to exhibit? Context is important in that narrative, too; the same object can be displayed within the context of different exhibition narratives. It is a wonderful example to students of the power of multiple interpretations of historical material. It is also essential that students are taught to challenge concepts of museums as authoritative voices.

How can students learn to critique an exhibition? They can do so with the same skills they have developed to analyse and critique any other secondary source. Reviewing exhibitions for content, biases and the tone of narratives is an important skill for students, and is similar to the skills required to review historical material critically. Museums can also provide the opportunity for students to explore a range of issues and ethics associated with historical investigation. There are a variety of collection-related issues and controversies, many of them suitable for history-extension investigative projects as well as general discussion and consideration by students of all ages.

These issues can include emphasising an understanding of the historical development of museums themselves as a concept. The grand historical narrative of the nature of collecting antiquities and other historical items is fascinating: the growth from private collections and *wunderkammer* ('cabinets of curiosities') through to the grand national museums in the nineteenth century, to the more recent developments of specialised museums and local site-specific collections and displays, reflects a changing narrative of the ways in which the general public chooses to engage with historical understanding. It reflects the change in the presentation of history from a colonial perspective to a nationalist narrative to a more nuanced localisation of history. Visits to more than one type of museum can enable a debate about variation in the presentation of historical narratives, and how museums reflect contemporary culture.

The ethics of collecting and displaying material can also be explored by students. What was chosen to be collected by the institution and why? Did the nature of the museum or gallery's collection change over time? If so, why? For archaeological collections, what material has archaeological provenance and what doesn't? Do museums have fakes and forgeries within their collections? These are all valuable historical-inquiry questions that students can use as the basis for larger ideas of the conceptualisation of museums.

Some collections are more contentious than others. Students can explore ethical issues such as the rights and wrongs of the collection and display of human remains and of other culturally sensitive materials, as well as materials known to have been looted from archaeological sites or taken illegally and against the 1970 UNESCO Convention on the Means of Prohibiting and Preventing the Illicit Import, Export and Transfer of Ownership of Cultural Property. Repatriation of heritage items and entire collections is also an area of discussion that students could choose to explore within a museum context—both from larger well-known topics, such as Greece's ongoing attempts at repatriation of the Parthenon marbles from the British Museum, to more regular examples of museums and communities working closely and collaboratively, such as repatriation programs between museums and Indigenous communities (Simpson 1996). The illegal acquisition and repatriation of high-profile objects at one stage in the collections of the National Gallery of Australia and the Getty are valid discussion points.

Museums are political institutions. The narratives they choose to tell and the material they choose to display, as well as the perspectives of temporary exhibitions and the language used in labels and other signage and supportive material (digital content, background images, quotes and so on) within the exhibits are all ripe for critical evaluation.

Students can ponder how museums can deal with confronting or controversial materials. How do they choose to display narratives of the Holocaust or of slavery, for example? How do they choose to reflect nationalist or colonial perspectives through their display of collections and associated interpretive material? These are just some areas that can challenge students' ideas of the aim and purposes of a museum. Good teachers and good museum educators can help students to navigate some of these complex issues through specialised engagement, and by thinking about big ideas of what the exhibitions are saying—and in some cases, not saying.

The very act of visiting a museum and thinking about the role of museums in society in a critical manner will enable students to enter into much larger historical, archaeological, heritage and ethics-based discussions and debates than the mere act of allowing students to see historical artefacts up close.

REPLICATING THE MUSEUM EXPERIENCE WITHIN THE CLASSROOM

While the experience of being in a museum is a unique opportunity for students, it is worthwhile considering parts of the experience that can be replicated within the classroom. Online content of museums (in the form of collection databases) is one way, but specific activities such as a hands-on workshop can at least partly be replicated in the classroom by using replicas of historical items that can be purchased online, or even historical material bought from junk and antique shops. It is essential that educators engage in the purchase of actual antiquities from only reputable sources to prevent participation in the trade of looted or fake materials. Indeed, examples of online sales of antiquities can provide a good example for students to debate the ethics of antiquity collecting and the value of material without provenanced archaeological or historical context. Replicas, however, are sufficient for students to gain experience in the process of handling material culture and developing investigative skills.

Similar techniques are equally applicable to the study of Australian history through family heirlooms, family photographs and material borrowed from local historical societies. Archaeological interpretation is based on recording and interrogating materials, so by using replicas, images and online databases, students can develop their descriptive and visual skills by describing material culture and drawing or photographing it to capture the details (Corbishley 2011). Historic photographs can be analysed as if they were an 'archaeological artefact', too—students can interpret historical 'meaning' in the images. Many schools have their own collections of historical photographs, or students may even be able to access family historical images and materials for the same degree of historical reflection and questioning.

A CASE STUDY: THE NICHOLSON MUSEUM

I have worked as the Manager of Education and Public Programs at Sydney University Museums for over a decade and have been involved in museum education at that institution for longer. A number of the museums on the campus of the University of Sydney are being merged to create the new Chau Chak Wing Museum, which will incorporate collections of visual arts, antiquities, natural history, science and Australian history—both Aboriginal and Torres Strait Islander history, and post-settlement history—when it opens to the public in 2020. In the meantime, the Nicholson Museum, a museum of classical, Egyptian and Near Eastern antiquities, continues to operate its school-education programs (Barker 2014).

The Nicholson Museum is Australia's oldest university museum, opening in 1860. It has the largest collection of Mediterranean-based archaeological material and antiquities in the Southern Hemisphere. Founded by polymath and University of Sydney father Sir Charles Nicholson (1808–1903), the initial collection was acquired during a journey to Egypt and Italy in 1856–7 by Nicholson (Potts & Sowada 2004; Turner 2012). The museum rapidly grew in size through private donations and benefaction, the active acquisition policies of a number of prominent curators through art markets and loans and gifts from other museums, and through University of Sydney sponsorship of archaeological expeditions in the interwar and post-World War II years. The University of Sydney itself conducted historic excavations in Cyprus and Jordan, which added material to the collection. Today, the Nicholson Museum is home to more than 30,000 items.

Community outreach and school education have always been a significant component of the museum—the earliest school visit to the Nicholson Museum appears to have occurred in 1862, and during the 1950s the museum employed its first educational staff specifically for guiding school visitors. The modern curriculum-based, object-learning-focused program for visiting schools was first established at the Nicholson Museum in 1992, and has grown since then—particularly since the creation of the administrative structure of Sydney University Museums. The motivating factor for our development of tactile learning activities has been the strong focus in the NSW syllabuses in recent decades, particularly the ancient history Stage 6 syllabus, on the role of using objects in learning.

Given the nature of the collections of the Nicholson Museum, the main school-student engagement is with students of ancient history, but one interesting aspect is the number of other disciplines that use the collections for education: we have received visits from classes with an interest in visual arts, science, languages and drama.

Much of the broader pedagogical philosophy of the Nicholson Museum's education programs grew and developed from broader global trends in archaeological museum education (Stone 1990; Smardz & Smith 2000), and historically we have focused on kinaesthetic learning programs where visitors are allowed to handle material from the collection as they learn.

The haptic, or tactile sensually, learning experiences created through the hands-on workshop are available to all students who come on an organised excursion. Students are taken to the museum's education room and asked to put on gloves; they are then given the chance to handle genuine archaeological artefacts from the collection. Over 120 individual artefacts have been selected for these education programs—they are displayed in education boxes that cover cultures as diverse as New Kingdom Egypt, Classical Athens and Sparta, Imperial Rome, Pompeii and prehistoric Europe; on occasions, Aboriginal and Torres Strait Islander material culture and that of colonial Sydney is included.

Depending on the workshop, students can analyse in detail individual artefacts or a collection of related objects as an assemblage (a range of objects from an Egyptian tomb, for example, which can be used to discuss the role of grave goods for the afterlife, or the collection of Pompeiian finds to collectively explore the urban context of life in the first century AD). It also provides the opportunity for students to work with the objects individually or as part of a group, sharing ideas and discussing the context of the material. Students will be asked to draw and describe 'their artefact'; they then present their findings and interpretation of the artefact to their peers. Through presenting their ideas and discussing their own interpretations of the objects with their peers and museum educators, students are developing key observational and identification skills necessary for historical inquiry.

The value of such experiences can be seen in the feedback we receive from students, including a Year 7 student who told us he 'didn't like history until he came to the Nicholson Museum and handled artefacts'. We find that getting the students to present their own research findings to their peers by analysing the object they have chosen gives them ownership of the information they have observed and deduced.

A key component of any history hands-on workshop is asking students to draw the material they handle. The focus on illustration in this context is to teach students the skills of observation through recording the artefact on paper. Senior groups are often able to engage in a discussion about the historical role of scientific illustration, and of archaeological drawing as a method of recording. As the students are drawing the artefact, they are able to engage in the idea of accurate reproduction of the object as opposed to a creative and artistic depiction of the piece, and the values that both types of drawing have to both archaeological and art historical researchers. Concepts that can be considered include why archaeologists would need accurate drawings in an era of photography and 3D scanning, and how this type of illustration trains one's eye to make careful observation of the material being examined. Exercises where students describe objects verbally after looking at an artefact as opposed to examples of students describing the artefact that they have just sketched are very telling, as the level of comprehension of details is profoundly different. Illustration opens up new insights into the processes of research.

Much of the intellectual framework of the Nicholson's program sits within broader educational models for archaeological teaching (Fagan 2000; Lea 2000). The five main ideas of the program are:

1 Tangible learning experiences are developed through a 'hands-on' approach by using genuine evidence from the past.
2 The study of material culture can develop key skills of critical analysis and helps students develop the concept of multiple levels of interpretation of raw data more easily. Interrogation of artefacts helps develop an understanding of historical processes.
3 Students will gain direct experience of learning to think and act in the way a professional historian/archaeologist/art historian does.

4 The museum provides a memorable and fun learning experience for students outside of the classroom environment.
5 Sessions are designed to develop lifelong learning concepts.

All students who visit the Nicholson Museum, irrespective of age and level of study, are encouraged to think about what archaeology and ancient history are, and what these disciplines aim to achieve. The key focus is for students to comprehend the broader processes of archaeological investigation along with the questions of 'who, what, where, how, and why' of history and material culture. From these questions, more specialised and detailed study of particular cultures, time periods, archaeological sites or assemblages of materials may be possible, with increasing levels of sophistication depending upon the age of the visiting students and their previous knowledge (Barker 2011).

Guided school tours of the gallery spaces are not conducted as lectures; instead, education officers act as facilitators for school groups in discussion about what they see. Our policy is to focus on discussion-based activities, encouraging students to ask questions, describe their observations and express their thoughts and interpretations of the objects. The discussion can alternate according to curricula content, and range from the ethics of displaying mummies, through to the scientific processes used to date objects, onto how the artefact reflects the society that produced it.

Younger students are often encouraged to empathise with the past through role-playing and costume wearing. The Nicholson Museum has a range of options of togas for ancient Rome, and hoplite armour for ancient Greece; re-enacting the stories of Greek mythology in costume is an incredibly popular activity.

Even more popular for primary-aged students in the Nicholson Museum is the session focusing on mummy wrapping. Once they have had the chance to engage with real Egyptian material, students undertake the process of wrapping one of their cohorts in bandages and 'mummifying' them. All students get involved, role-playing as embalmers, priests or worshippers, and the students wrap themselves up using bandages, replica amulets and death masks. During the activity, the guides explain the process of ancient mummification and its importance for Egyptian society. It is an activity that is possible to replicate in a classroom environment, too, using bandages or even toilet paper.

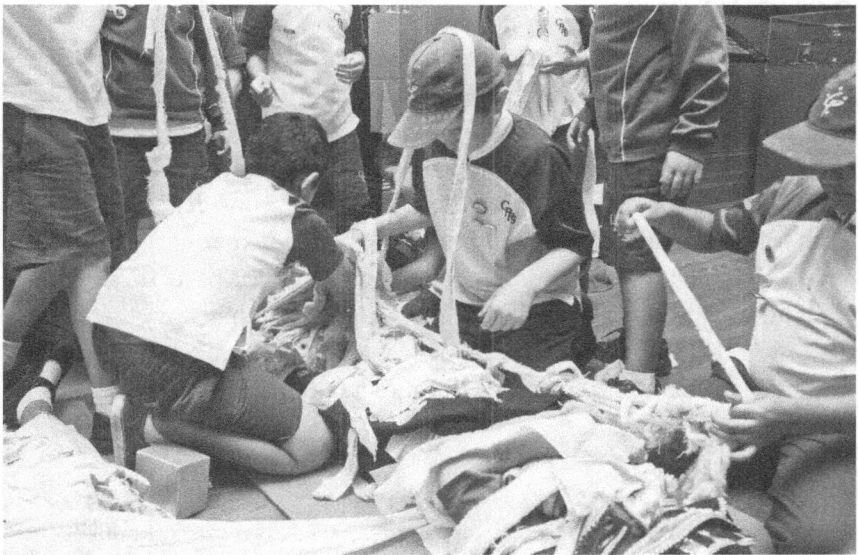

Figure 19.3 Mummy wrapping is a messy, but entertaining, means of allowing students to contextualise the Egyptian mummies displayed in the exhibition space. Courtesy Nicholson Museum, University of Sydney.

SCHOOL–MUSEUM PARTNERSHIPS

The key to any good school–museum interaction is the development of a partnership, and this must be based upon meaningful communication between the school teacher and the museum educator regarding student needs, desired outcomes, educational options and the accessibility to relevant collection materials.

The logistical practicalities of excursion organisation are stressful enough for teachers, so a good relationship with the museum that the students are to visit is essential to help ease the experience. Until recently, there was often a disconnect between the teacher and the museum, but this can be changed very easily.

The way forward is for teachers to engage with museums themselves. Speak with museum education staff about needs, visit the museum or cultural institution, and spend time on the museum's website before the excursion. Discuss pre- and post-visit content that the museum can provide and that can be incorporated into lesson plans.

CONCLUSION

Museums will always remain the best complementary learning experience to classroom history teaching. The challenge for teachers and for museum educators is to continue to build the partnerships so the two are seen as answering the same learning outcomes: students with a good knowledge of historical processes and the ability to think, consider and critically analyse information. There is nothing quite like the experience of handling genuine artefacts to spark students' curiosity about the past. These curious students are the ones who will continue to engage with history throughout the rest of their lives; part of that engagement will be a lifetime of visiting museums for stimulus, inspiration and reflection.

REFERENCES

Ambrose, T. & Paine, C. 2012, *Museum Basics*, 3rd ed., New York: Routledge.

Anderson, D. 1999, *A Common Wealth: Museums in the Learning Age*, London: Department of National Heritage.

Barker, C. 2011, 'Hands-on history: Teaching archaeology to Australian school students; experiences from the classroom, from the field and from museums', paper presented to the national symposium Building Bridges for Historical Learning: Connecting Teacher Education and Museum Education, University of Canberra, 28–29 March, <www.learnonline.canberra.edu.au/course/view.php?id=5882>, accessed 10 October 2017.

—— 2014, 'Materials-based teaching in museums: The experiences of education programs at Sydney University Museums', *Journal of Artistic and Creative Education*, vol. 7, no. 1, pp. 166–91.

Corbishley, M. 2011, *Pinning Down the Past: Archaeology, Heritage, and Education Today*, Woodbridge: The Boydell Press.

Duensing, S. 2002, 'The object of experience', in S.G. Paris (ed.), *Perspectives on Object-Centered Learning in Museums*, Mahwah, NJ: Lawrence Erlbaum, pp. 351–63.

Fagan, B. 2000, 'Education is what's left: Some thoughts on introductory archaeology', *Antiquity*, no. 74, pp. 190–4.

Falk, J.H. & Dierking, L.D. 2000, *Visitor Experiences and the Making of Meaning*, Walnut Creek, CA: AltaMira Press.

—— 2012, *The Museum Experience Revisited*, Walnut Creek, CA: Left Coast Press.

Getty Education 2018, *Resources for the Classroom*, <www.getty.edu/education/teachers/classroom_resources>, accessed 7 September 2018.

Greene, J.P. 2014, 'Visits to Australia's museums rise on the back of a digital experience', *The Conversation*, 23 October, <https://theconversation.com/visits-to-australias-museums-rise-on-the-back-of-a-digital-experience-32699>, accessed 10 October 2017.

Griffin, J. 2011, 'The museum education mix: Students, teachers and museum educators', in D. Griffin & L. Paroissien (eds), *Understanding Museums: Australian Museums and Museology*, Canberra: National Museum of Australia.

Gurian, E.H. 1999, 'What is the object of this exercise? A meandering exploration of the many meanings of objects in museums', *Daedalus*, vol. 128, no. 3, pp. 163–83.

Hein, G. 1998, *Learning in the Museum*, London: Routledge.

—— 2006, 'Museum education', in S. MacDonald (ed.), *A Companion to Museum Studies*, Malden, MA: Blackwell, pp. 340–52.

Hooper-Greenhill, E. 2007, *Museums and Education: Purpose, Pedagogy, Performance*, London: Routledge.

Lea, J. 2000, 'Teaching the past in museums', in K. Smardz & S.J. Smith (eds), *The Archaeology Education Handbook*, Walnut Creek, CA: AltaMira Press, pp. 315–27.

McAlpine, J. 2002, 'Loan star', *Museums Journal*, vol. 102, no. 1, pp. 26–7.

Nova Scotia Museum 2016, 'Activity: How to Read a Shoe', *Toolbox for Museum School Projects*, p. 170, <https://museum.novascotia.ca/sites/default/files/inline/documents/toolbox2016/nsm_toolbox_-_appendix_f_2016.pdf>, accessed 8 September 2018.

Paris, S.G. (ed.) 2002, *Perspectives on Object-Centred Learning in Museums*, Mahwah, NJ: Lawrence Erlbaum.

Potts, D.T. & Sowada, K.N. (eds) 2004, *Treasures of the Nicholson Museum*, Sydney: Nicholson Museum.

Russell, T. 1994, 'The enquiring visitor: Usable learning theory for museum contexts', *Journal of Education in Museums*, no. 15, pp. 19–21.

Schäfer, J. 2016, 'Education as curatorial practice', in C. Mörsch, A. Sachs & T. Siber (eds), *Contemporary Curating and Museum Education*, Bielefeld: Transcript-Verlag, pp. 53–64.

Simpson, M.G. 1996, *Making Representations: Museums in the Post-colonial Era*, London: Routledge.

Smardz, K. & Smith, S.J. (eds) 2000, *The Archaeology Education Handbook*, Walnut Creek, CA: AltaMira Press.

Stone, P. 1990, *The Excluded Past. Archaeology in Education*, London: Routledge.

Turner, M. 2012, *50 Objects 50 Stories: Extraordinary Curiosities from the Nicholson Museum, the University of Sydney*, Sydney: Nicholson Museum.

PART 4
KEY ISSUES IN AUSTRALIAN HISTORY TEACHING

CHAPTER 20
Classroom perspectives on Australia's contact history

Nina Burridge

INTRODUCTION

Reflections on being a history teacher

As a young, passionate teacher of history, the beginning of my understanding of what was missing from our nation's historical record occurred at a History Teachers' Association of Australia (HTAA) conference in Darwin in 1982. It was there that my eyes were opened to the 'other side of the frontier' as I listened to Aboriginal women tell of the search for their stolen children, and to Aboriginal men tell their stories of being taken away as children and the anguish of the search for their mothers, their families, their country.

I returned to my classroom in my city high school dumbfounded that this aspect of our Australian story had not been part of my school or university education in the 1970s. The significance of the Stolen Generations came home to me most clearly in early 1984 when I gave birth to my first child, a little girl called Emma. I pondered with total horror the idea that some government official would dare take my child away for no other reason than my race. It left an indelible impression on my role as a teacher of Australian history.

As a non-Aboriginal person teaching in mainstream classrooms, I realised the need to ensure that the experiences and voices of Aboriginal peoples were heard. It became a journey of discovery and learning as I sought to work with Aboriginal education officers and reach out to Aboriginal community networks around Sydney to try to incorporate their stories into my classes.

This chapter discusses some of the main historical themes in Australia's contact history, including the Frontier Wars, Aboriginal activism, aspects of the education of Aboriginal children, and approaches towards reconciliation. The perspectives presented are not only through the lens of those making their way onto the shore of Sydney Harbour seeking to settle, but also from the eyes of the Aboriginal clans watching from the banks, wondering who these invaders were. This capacity to engage in an empathetic process in history—to see it from the other side—is an important aspect of historical thinking and historical understanding that all teachers and students of history need to acquire.

DISCUSSING CONTESTED HISTORY IN THE CLASSROOM

One of the over-arching aims of the Australian history curriculum is the development of 'understanding and use of historical concepts, such as evidence, continuity and change, cause and effect, perspectives, empathy, significance and contestability' (ACARA 2017). The capacity to evaluate evidence, to see history from the perspective of others and to appreciate that the nature of historical evidence is subject to variations in interpretation can result in important understandings of the historical process. Enabling students to gain these skills and understandings requires an investigative approach that examines evidence in detail and asks questions—whether it be in relation to a historical image or a representative text in a history book.

The two images shown in Figures 20.1 and 20.2 are often used to portray the differing representations of 'contact' or 'invasion' history. Figure 20.1 is a drawing by Samuel Calvert from the State Library of New South Wales and Figure 20.2 is a painting by R. Caton Woodville in Ida Lee's (1906) *The Coming of the British to Australia*.

These images provide a rich platform for discussing differing perspectives, the accuracy in historical writing, interpretation vs real images and how the writing of history must be scrutinised in order to peel away the layers to ensure that we have the most authentic representation of the past that is possible. From these images emerge discussions about the use of terms such as 'settlement', 'colonisation' and 'invasion' in the interpretation of 26 January 1788, leading to the contemporary debate about whether 26 January should be a day of celebration or a day of mourning. There are many other examples of contestation in the Australian historical record. Teachers need to reflect on how these images can be utilised in the history

CLASSROOM PERSPECTIVES ON AUSTRALIA'S CONTACT HISTORY 281

Figure 20.1 *Fight between Aborigines and Mounted Whites* by Samuel Calvert, 1870s, State Library of New South Wales, SSV/101.

Figure 20.2 *Captain Cook Landing at Adventure Bay* by R. Caton Woodville, in Ida Lee's *The Coming of the British to Australia, 1788 to 1829* (1906).

classroom to illustrate how history can be portrayed and interpreted very differently, depending upon what sources are used and how they are interpreted.

CONTACT HISTORY

As noted above, much has been written about the nature of early frontier contact on Australian shores. Early Australian history books and school textbooks consistently wrote about a 'peaceful settlement' based on the legal premise of *terra nullius*—'a land belonging to no one' (Fitzmaurice 2007). This view of the Aboriginal response to European contact remained part of the Australian historical narrative for many decades into the twentieth century, as even the most renowned historians neglected to focus on Aboriginal perspectives of Australia's history.

Anthropologist W.E.H. Stanner, in the 1968 Boyer Lectures series *After the Dreaming*, spoke of the 'Great Australian Silence'. After listing the titles of key accounts of Australian history up to 1968, he noted (1969: 18):

> I need not extend the list. A partial survey is enough to let me make the point that inattention on such a scale cannot possibly be explained by absent-mindedness. It is a structural matter, a view from a window which has been carefully placed to exclude a whole quadrant of the landscape. What may well have begun as a simple forgetting of other possible views turned under habit and over time into something like a cult of forgetfulness practised on a national scale.

Perspectives did change, however—perhaps in conjunction with the rise of Aboriginal and Torres Strait Islander activism and in the aftermath of the 1967 referendum—as historians, including Henry Reynolds (1981), Lyndall Ryan (2001), Bain Attwood (1989) and Aboriginal writers such as Marcia Langton (Langton & Peterson 1983), began rewriting the history of frontier conflict. These differing perspectives on Australian history have not come without an extensive backlash and acrimonious accusations by more conservative historians, who felt that Australia's contact history was taking a very negative turn and was being mired in the political ideologies of the left. The more prominent historians associated with this view include Geoffrey Blainey (1993: 10–15), who coined the term 'black armband' history in his 1993 Latham Memorial Lecture, and Keith Windschuttle (2002), who wrote *The Fabrication of Aboriginal History* (and prior to that contributed many articles to the conservative magazine *Quadrant*).

This ongoing contestation of Aboriginal and Torres Strait Islander and settler history has come to be known as the History Wars between those who want a more positive, 'three cheers' representation of the achievements of settlers, and those who lay claim to a more realistic portrayal of post-1770 contact history—one where Aboriginal people are seen to have a vibrant cultural heritage with strong links to their ancestral lands, which they sought to defend as warriors against the invaders. Figures 20.3 and 20.4 serve to illustrate some of the differing perspectives on the History Wars and the role of historians.

RECOGNITION OF THE FRONTIER WARS

The next phase of the debate about contact history surrounded the discussion of whether Aboriginal warriors should be commemorated as soldiers of the war front, just like the heroes of Gallipoli and those who are justly acknowledged for their sacrifices in all our wars. Historians such as

Figure 20.3 *How to Remove Your Black Armband* by Henrich Hinze (David Pope), *The Republican*, 22 August 1997.

Figure 20.4 *Stand Back! I'm a Doctor. I Have a PhD in History* by P. Nicholson, *The Australian*, 27 September 2003.

John Connor (2002), Alan Stephens (2014) and Lyndall Ryan (quoted in Brennan 2017), who has recently published a map of Australia's frontier conflicts, advocate for these conflicts to be commemorated as civil wars by the Australian War Memorial (AWM) in Canberra. Stephens (2014) maintains that:

> The establishment of a Frontier Wars wing at the AWM—not a gallery, or a hall, or some other token affair, but a separate, comprehensive wing—would be the single most powerful action official Australia could take to promote reconciliation and honesty.

The AWM does acknowledge Aboriginal soldiers who fought in Australian wars since Federation. While it sees the need for some form of commemoration of frontier conflicts, Dr Brendan Nelson, Director of the AWM, claims that its focus is on wars fought overseas on behalf of Australia. During the 2017 Anzac Day commemoration, Dr Nelson did praise a new exhibition titled *For Country for Nation* at the AWM that 'looks closely at the horrendous treatment Indigenous Australians received at the hands of European settlers and the fact that, despite this, many still wanted to volunteer to fight for Australia' (quoted in Burton-Bradley, Quartermaine & Lawford 2017). The varying perspectives noted above exemplify the nature of history and its contestability, as historians research, discover and interpret historical events to shed light on the past.

ABORIGINAL ACTIVISM

Another important aspect to consider is the history of Aboriginal activism. By the 1920s in New South Wales and Victoria in particular, Aboriginal people began to organise and speak out for their rights. The first prominent politically active Aboriginal group was the Australian Aboriginal Progressive Association (AAPA). Formed by Frank Maynard in 1924, the AAPA set out to fight the NSW Protection Board and its role in the taking of Aboriginal reserve lands, and to secure basic civil rights for Aboriginal people. The AAPA was well organised and publicly vocal for about three years, holding street rallies, meetings and conferences, writing letters and even sending petitions to the NSW government and the King of England (Cadzow 2007). Among its concerns was the struggle against the removal of children from their families and the exclusion of Aboriginal children from schools (Burridge & Chodkiewicz 2012). The most famous protest of this period was the Day of Mourning protest on 26 January 1938, organised by the AAPA to highlight that what was a celebration for non-Aboriginal people was a day of deep sadness for Aboriginal peoples.

After World War II, Aboriginal and Torres Strait Islander activism continued in many parts of Australia. Activists came together in 1958 to form the Federal Council for the Advancement of Aboriginals and Torres Strait Islanders (FCAATSI). Its primary role was to campaign for a referendum to recognise Aboriginal people as citizens of Australia. The 1967 referendum is an example of Aboriginal and non-Aboriginal people working together to pressure the federal government to instigate the process. Many other campaigns occurred: the Freedom Rides in 1965; the Gurindji Wave Hill Walk Off in 1966 as Aboriginal stockman fought for fair pay; the establishment of the Tent Embassy at the front of Parliament House in 1972 (which is still in existence on the grounds of old Parliament House); and the land rights campaign against the growth of mining in the northern regions of Australia.

The struggle for land rights saw the passing of the *Northern Territory Land Rights Act* in 1976, and this ongoing battle against *terra nullius* finally culminated in the historically important *Mabo* High Court decision in 1992. This was followed by the now famous Redfern Speech by then

Prime Minister Paul Keating and the passing of the *Native Title Act 1993*. Other important milestones include the release of the *Bringing Them Home* report (HREOC 1997) at the Australian Reconciliation Convention in 1997. In part, this led to calls by Aboriginal peoples for a national apology for past acts of dispossession. At the Convention, a number of delegates turned their back on Prime Minister John Howard as a sign of protest at his refusal to make a formal apology to the Stolen Generations (Figure 20.5).

Today the struggle continues in terms of Aboriginal and Torres Strait Islander peoples gaining full recognition, not only as part of a preamble to Australia's Constitution, but also through a formal treaty. Struggles are also ongoing for a new Aboriginal representative body to replace the Aboriginal and Torres Strait Islander Commission (ATSIC) and what to do about Australia Day. This very brief summary of Aboriginal activism illustrates the rich sources of evidence available for teachers to build classroom activities that focus on key concepts of the Australian history curriculum.

Figure 20.5 Delegates turn their backs to Prime Minister John Howard. Australian Reconciliation Convention, Melbourne, *The Age*, 27 May 1997. Photograph by Rick Stevens.

ABORIGINAL EDUCATION: SEPARATE AND INFERIOR SCHOOLING

In order to fully understand the current policies and issues related to the education of Aboriginal and Torres Strait Islander students, it is important to delve into the history of government policies that impacted on Aboriginal people's lives from their very early years. This history dates from the colonial years and covers periods of state and later federal government policies that, until the late 1960s, saw Aboriginal children suffer under a system of discrimination. That system variously segregated, excluded, 'protected' or removed them from their families. Beyond the 1960s, the movement for Aboriginal rights took hold and governments were required to respond with greater focus on policies for self-determination.

A feature of the nineteenth-century education of Aboriginal peoples was the mission schools, which were largely run by the Christian churches and linked to a missionary zeal to 'Christianise' and 'civilise'. The passing of the *Public Instruction Act* in 1880 enabled the NSW government to take over the administration of these schools and to introduce restrictive regulations; this was known as the protection era (Partington 1998). During this period, policies were also put in place that allowed for the forcible removal of Aboriginal children from their families and the removal of Aboriginal children from schools under the essentially racist 'clean, clad and courteous' and 'exclusion on demand' policies (Fletcher 1989).

In New South Wales, the removal of children was sanctioned further under the *Aborigines Protection Act 1909* and, together with the ability to exclude Aboriginal children from schools, this led to the creation of a separate and inferior system of education for Aboriginal children across New South Wales. This system sanctioned a debased curriculum that focused on teaching manual skills under the assumption that Aboriginal people would be better suited to working as domestic labour for 'white' masters or employers. It is important to note here that the capacity for principals to exclude Aboriginal children from schools was in place in New South Wales until 1972, when it was finally removed from the *NSW Teachers Handbook* (Parbury 2005).

An assimilation policy was introduced in 1940 in an attempt to immerse Aboriginal people into the 'mainstream'. Exemption certificates were introduced so that holders 'disassociated themselves from Aboriginal communities and assimilated to access housing and education opportunities that non-Aboriginal people have' (Cadzow 2007: 20). For children to access state schools, they were certified as honorary whites. In Aboriginal communities, the certificate (Figure 20.6) became known as the 'dog tag'.

From the mid-1940s until the early 1960s, resistance to segregation, which had begun in regional communities in New South Wales and Victoria in the 1920s, continued to grow, and governments slowly began a policy of integration of children into mainstream schools. Following the 1967 referendum, the federal government, through the Australian Schools Commission (ASC), took an increasing role in the administration of funding for Aboriginal education. In New South Wales, the first Aboriginal Education Policy (AEP) was issued in 1982, and in 1987 it was made mandatory for schools to incorporate the policy into the curriculum (Parbury 2005). This state initiative was followed by the National Aboriginal Education Policy (NAEP) released by the Australian government in 1989, which sought to coordinate responsibility for Aboriginal education among the various states through cooperative long-term strategies that were linked to federal funding (Burridge & Chodkiewicz 2012). There

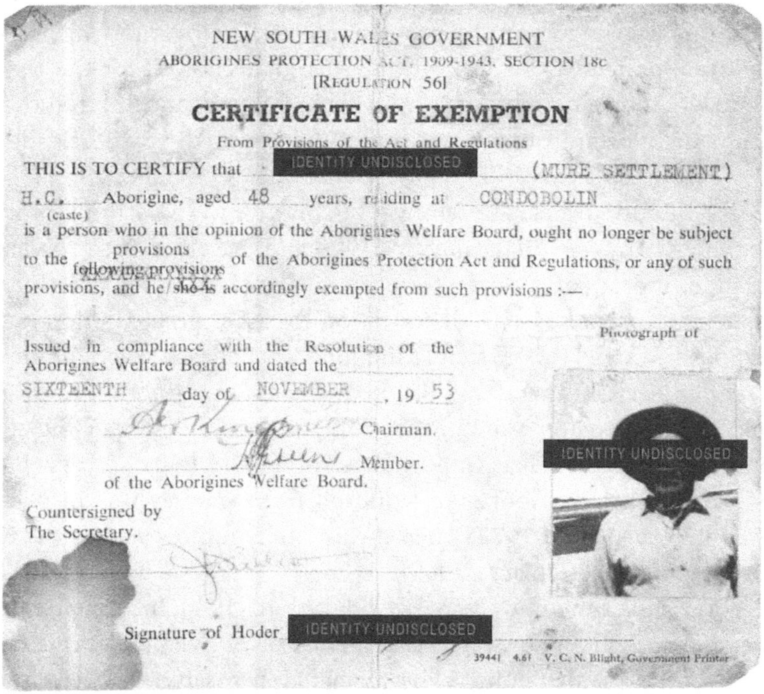

NEW SOUTH WALES GOVERNMENT
ABORIGINES PROTECTION ACT, 1909-1943, SECTION 18C
[REGULATION 56]

CERTIFICATE OF EXEMPTION

From Provisions of the Act and Regulations

THIS IS TO CERTIFY that IDENTITY UNDISCLOSED (MURE SETTLEMENT)
H.C. Aborigine, aged 48 years, residing at CONDOBOLIN
(caste)
is a person who in the opinion of the Aborigines Welfare Board, ought no longer be subject to the ~~following provisions~~ provisions of the Aborigines Protection Act and Regulations, or any of such provisions, and he/~~she~~ is accordingly exempted from such provisions :—

Issued in compliance with the Resolution of the Aborigines Welfare Board and dated the SIXTEENTH day of NOVEMBER, 19 53

Chairman.

Member.

of the Aborigines Welfare Board.

Countersigned by
The Secretary.

Photograph of

IDENTITY UNDISCLOSED

Signature of Hoder IDENTITY UNDISCLOSED

39441 4.61 V. C. N. Blight, Government Printer

Figure 20.6 Certificate of Exemption, published in Sovereign Union: First Nations Asserting Sovereignty.

have been many reviews and updates of Aboriginal education policies since the 1980s. They were designed to both gather data and to further develop policy frameworks that could be used by academics, teachers and school leaders to implement successful culturally responsive programs that value what Aboriginal and Torres Strait Islander students bring into the classroom, Aboriginal and Torres Strait Islander knowledge, and local Aboriginal and Torres Strait Islander communities.

RECONCILIATION: ACKNOWLEDGING A SHARED HISTORY

The struggle for formal Aboriginal and Torres Strait Islander recognition either through a treaty or through amendments to the Constitution has been a long and convoluted process. Indeed, it is still seen as the 'unfinished business' of the Australian nation by many Aboriginal and Torres Strait Islander people and other Australians. If a constitution is considered the 'birth certificate' of a nation, yet it does not recognise the histories and culture of the original inhabitants, then the story is incomplete.

The focus on a policy of reconciliation emerged as a response to a greater public awareness of Aboriginal and Torres Strait Islander issues as the Bicentenary of European settlement approached. In the initial stages of the Hawke Labor government's first term, Aboriginal affairs strategists held hopes for creating a binding document, such as a treaty, to be discussed if not realised by 1988. However, given the mining boom of the 1980s, some states objected to fulsome discussions of a treaty. Political pragmatism won the day, and any thoughts of a treaty were sidelined for more politically palatable terms such as a 'compact' or a 'makarrata', and finally reconciliation.

The creation of the Council for Aboriginal Reconciliation in 1991 was supported by all sides of politics and by many in the wider community. The expectation was that in ten years, at the Centenary of Federation, the nation would be able to reach some resolution of many of the issues affecting Aboriginal and Torres Strait Islander Australians. The prospect for reconciliation was substantially enhanced by Paul Keating's Redfern Park speech in December 1992 at the launch of the United Nations Year of Indigenous People (Keating 1992). It has become known as the 'Redfern Speech' and is regarded by many as the most significant speech ever made by a Prime Minister on Aboriginal and Torres Strait Islander issues. Prime Minister Keating spoke of the need for recognition:

> Recognition that it was we who did the dispossessing ... We brought the diseases and the alcohol. We committed the murders. We took the children from their mothers. We practised discrimination and exclusion. It was our ignorance and our prejudice and our failure to imagine these things being done to us.

In making such a speech, Keating gave strength to the government's position on reconciliation. Further, in seeing the High Court *Mabo* decision on native title as 'an historic turning point, the basis of a new relationship between Indigenous and non-Indigenous Australians' (Keating 1992), he signalled that there was a real connection between land rights and reconciliation.

With its focus on nation building and the search for better relations between Aboriginal and Torres Strait Islander and settler cultures, reconciliation has generally been interpreted as a very positive movement towards a shared history. In reality, its interpretation and meaning were often based on cultural and socio-political divides, and this is one reason why the discourse on what constitutes 'true reconciliation' is still ongoing. There is insufficient space in this chapter to discuss these variations in meanings. Suffice to say that discussions of terms such as 'symbolic' reconciliation, or 'practical' reconciliation, and 'substantive or deep' reconciliation involve an analysis of the terms in their historical and political contexts, and also in relation to the symbolic connotations of a shared sense of history (Burridge 2011). Reconciliation Australia was set up in 2001 at the end of Council for Aboriginal Reconciliation's ten-year term. It has continued to advocate for Aboriginal recognition in the Constitution, and produces a range of excellent resources and reports on the implementation of reconciliation policy in the community. Yet the call for a treaty continues, as Australia—unlike our neighbour, New Zealand, at Waitangi in 1840 (Orange 2011)—has yet to sign a treaty with its first nations peoples.

In summary, are Australians merely satisfied with the symbolic aspects of reconciliation? Was the formal apology to Aboriginal and Torres Strait Islander peoples by Prime Minster Kevin Rudd in February 2008 merely a symbolic act? Was the walk across the Sydney Harbour Bridge in Sydney and bridges in other parts of Australia in 2000, and the waving of Aboriginal flags when Cathy Freeman won Olympic gold in September 2000—described as '400 metres of Reconciliation' (Rintoul 2000: 10)—the

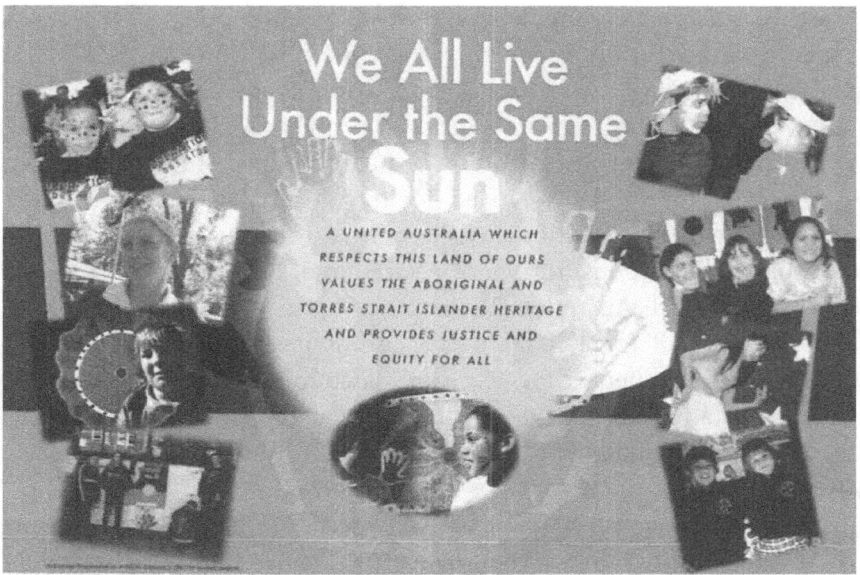

Figure 20.7 *We All Live Under the Same Sun*, poster from N. Burridge (ed), 'Nullawa' Achieving Reconciliation in NSW Schools, Macquarie University, 1997.

limit of what non-Aboriginal and Torres Strait Islander people would do for reconciliation?

THE ULURU STATEMENT: SEEKING TO BE HEARD

The Referendum Council of Australia, a sixteen-member body set up on 30 June 2017 to advise the Australian government on the way ahead for reconciliation, delivered its last report later the same year. The report followed a series of dialogues in each state with Aboriginal and Torres Strait Islander communities and a national Constitutional Convention, which was held at Uluru, the heart of Australia, in May 2017. Part of the *Uluru Statement from the Heart* (Referendum Council 2017) is reproduced below:

> We seek a Makarrata Commission to supervise a process of agreement-making between governments and First Nations and truth-telling about our history.
>
> In 1967 we were counted, in 2017 we seek to be heard. We leave base camp and start our trek across this vast country. We invite you to walk with us in a movement of the Australian people for a better future.

The Final Report of the Referendum Council supported these key aspects of the *Uluru Statement from the Heart*; however, it did not endorse the setting up of the Makarrata Commission because, as a legislative process, it was outside its jurisdiction (Hobbs 2017). The Council did recommend that 'a referendum be held to provide in the Australian Constitution for a representative body that gives Aboriginal and Torres Strait Islander First Nations a Voice to the Commonwealth Parliament' and that an 'extra-constitutional Declaration of Recognition be enacted and passed by all Australian Parliaments' (Anderson & Leibler 2017). Initially, the call for a Makarrata Commission was interpreted as 'a very big idea' by then Prime Minister Malcolm Turnbull. Subsequently, however, the government refused to consider the recommendations as viable and left hanging the future of both a treaty and a new representative body for Aboriginal peoples (Wahlquist 2017).

Whether substantive action is taken by future federal governments on the recommendations of this report will again determine the type of reconciliation process Australians are willing to undertake with Aboriginal and Torres Strait Islander peoples. Will it be delayed and merely be seen as another symbolic step in the process, or will it achieve lasting change and embed true recognition of Aboriginal and Torres Strait Islander peoples in our Constitution and legislative process? As the co-chairs of the Referendum Council note in their introductory letter presenting the report to the federal government: 'Constitutional recognition is longstanding and unfinished business for the nation' (Referendum Council 2017). From an Aboriginal perspective, this history is eloquently captured by Referendum Council member Galarrwuy Yunupingu (2016) in his essay 'Rom Watangu':

> What Aboriginal people ask is that the modern world now makes the sacrifices necessary to give us a real future. To relax its grip on us. To let us breathe, to let us be free of the determined control exerted on us to make us like you. And you should take that a step further and recognise us for who we are, and not who you want us to be. Let us be who we are—Aboriginal people in a modern world—and be proud of us. Acknowledge that we have survived the worst that the past had thrown at us, and we are here with our songs, our ceremonies, our land, our language and our people—our full identity. What a gift this is that we can give you, if you choose to accept us in a meaningful way.

TEACHING ABORIGINAL HISTORY AND CULTURE: EFFECTIVE TEACHERS

There is no doubt that good teaching makes a difference to students' engagement and learning. Historian Anna Clark, in an interview for *The Australian* after the publication of her book *History's Children: History Wars in the Classroom* (2008), noted that 'generally it is not *what* is taught in classrooms that engages students, but it is *how* it is taught'. Clark commented (in Guilliatt 2008):

> History isn't just something you get taught, it's a process whereby the student becomes the historian. It's surprising that, despite all the efforts to make history teaching more engaging and connected for students, many of them describe it as a traditional, staid sort of experience.

Clark's research into students' perceptions of Australian history revealed a pattern of disenchantment and boredom with many topics, including Federation and Aboriginal and Torres Strait Islander issues. Approaches to history were seen as repetitive, lacking in creative strategies and authenticity. Commenting on the teaching of Indigenous history, Clark notes (in Guilliatt 2008) that teachers were:

> scared of speaking for Aboriginal people because they're aware, from what has happened in the past, that it might not be the whole story. There's a sense of, 'Am I perpetuating inequality by being another non-indigenous person telling indigenous history?'

Effective teaching is central to effective classroom practice. So what makes an effective teacher? There is extensive research on this issue. Good teachers have deep knowledge of their subject field, and are creative, innovative and passionate about their profession. They recognise that students bring individual learning experiences and backgrounds to their classroom, and they cater for individual needs. They enjoy working with students, giving clear instructions, being flexible as well as authoritative if needed, and providing safe working environments that engage students in learning (NSW Department of Education and Communities 2013).

The metadata studies on this issue by leading education researchers such as John Hattie (2003) and Ken Rowe (2003) have been praised for their data-based analysis of what works in improving student learning.

They have also been criticised for their incapacity to relate this data to authentic culturally diverse contexts, particularly Aboriginal and Torres Strait Islander cultural contexts (Lewthwaite et al. 2015).

Results from the Quality Teaching Indigenous Project (Burridge, Whalan & Vaughan 2012), a study of how schools with significant populations of Aboriginal students approached teaching and learning, illustrated that a number of factors in school communities were crucial to promoting quality teachers. Themes that capture good practice, both in teaching and in policy development, are:

- supporting teacher professional learning in a collaborative learning environment
- active and supportive leadership within the school
- understanding contexts and the complexities of student learning
- applying technologies and new learning projects in a culturally responsive way
- understanding and valuing Aboriginal and Torres Strait Islander knowledge(s) and expertise, and
- connecting and engaging with local Aboriginal communities.

These themes should inform future pathways and strategies in Aboriginal and Torres Strait Islander education.

CULTURALLY RESPONSIVE PEDAGOGIES

Engaging in culturally responsive pedagogies (CRP) (Perso 2012) involves many of the characteristics of effective teachers noted above, with the added dimension of understanding the cultural contexts in which the teaching and learning is embedded. This means understanding Aboriginal and Torres Strait Islander ways of seeing the country, and understanding Indigenous cultural knowledge and its place in Aboriginal and Torres Strait Islander identity (Nakata 2007). It also requires knowledge of the contested nature of aspects of the Australian historical narrative and the importance of incorporating the voices of elders, of parents and of the local Aboriginal community. This helps to build an inclusive whole-school approach when working with Aboriginal and Torres Strait Islander students. It means building a culture of collaboration in the classroom and ensuring that students are provided with safe spaces where they can speak their mind. They do so in the knowledge that their views will be discussed and critiqued in a respectful manner, using evidenced-based approaches that illustrate the differing perspectives that exist in the historical record.

There are therefore several aspects to culturally responsive pedagogies, which are not just focused on teacher competencies. They include an institutional dimension, where policy-makers, schools and school leadership teams are aware and embed responsive practices in policy procedures and governance documents, as well as ensuring that school practices are much more than simple rhetoric. Figure 20.8 captures the various components of this holistic approach (ACER 2016).

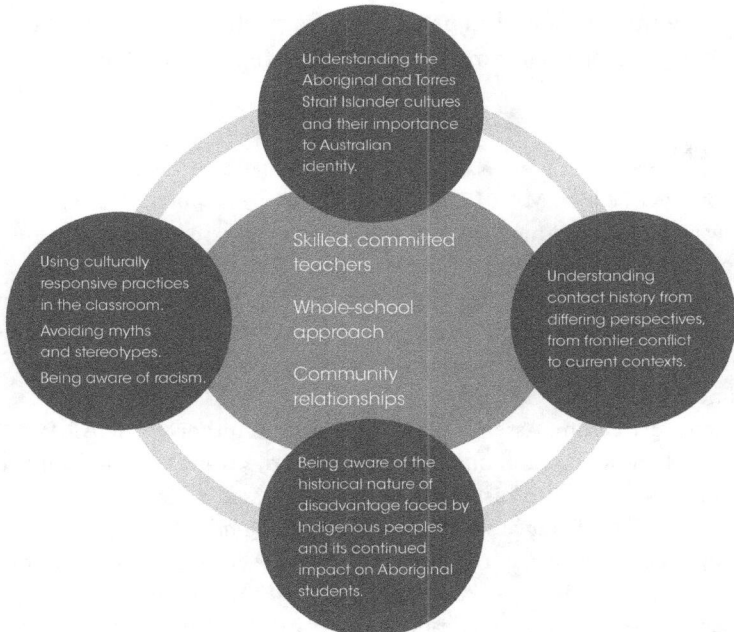

Figure 20.8 Schools as learning communities: best-practice approaches to teaching contact history.

CONCLUSION

The teaching of contact history in schools provides an excellent opportunity to incorporate all the aspects of effective teaching practices to engage students in a full understanding of the nation's past from a variety of perspectives. The role of the individual teacher who is willing and ready to learn, and who has the confidence to incorporate Aboriginal and Torres Strait Islander perspectives into the curriculum, is crucial. Specifically, we need to create schools as learning communities where the teacher and the school, together with the community, engage in the actual process of effective implementation of these strategies in the classroom. This requires the teacher to be skilled, passionate, engaging and willing to put in the time and effort to incorporate local Aboriginal and Torres Strait Islander community knowledge, and so 'make a difference' to the lives of children and young people they teach. The underlying philosophy here is based on a collective spirit of reconciliation and acceptance of a shared history and a common future between Aboriginal and non-Aboriginal Australians, which seeks to address the inequities and injustices that currently exist in many facets of Aboriginal people's lives compared with those of all Australians.

REFERENCES

Anderson, P. & Leibler, M. 2017, *Referendum Council Report*, 30 June, <www.referendumcouncil.org.au/final-report>, accessed 20 June 2018.

Attwood, B. 1989, *The Making of the Aborigines*, Sydney: Allen & Unwin.

Australian Council for Education Research (ACER) 2016, 'Collaborating for culturally responsive teaching', *Research Developments*, <https://rd.acer.edu.au/article/collaborating-for-culturally-responsive-teaching>, accessed 20 June 2018.

Australian Curriculum, Assessment and Reporting Authority (ACARA) 2017, 'Historical knowledge and understanding strand', <www.australiancurriculum.edu.au/f-10-curriculum/history/structure>, accessed 3 July 2017.

Blainey, G.A. 1993, 'Balance sheet on our history', *Quadrant*, July, pp. 10–15.

Brennan, B. 2017, 'New map records massacres of Aboriginal people in frontier wars', *ABC News*, 5 July, <www.abc.net.au/news/2017-07-05/new-map-plots-massacres-of-aboriginal-people-in-frontier-wars/8678466>, accessed 20 July 2017.

Burridge, N. (ed) (1997) 'Nullawa' Achieving Reconciliation in NSW Schools, Macquarie University.

—— 2011, 'Reconciliation matters', in R. Craven (ed.), *Teaching Aboriginal Studies*, 2nd ed., Sydney: Allen & Unwin, pp. 152–71.

Burridge, N. & Chodkiewicz, A. 2012, 'The journey continues', in N. Burridge, F. Whalan & K. Vaughan (eds), *Indigenous Education: A Learning Journey for Teachers, Schools and Communities*, Rotterdam: Sense Publishing, pp. 239–54.

Burridge, N., Whalan, F. & Vaughan, K. 2012, *Indigenous Education: A Learning Journey for Teachers, Schools and Communities*, Rotterdam: Sense.

Burton-Bradley, R., Quartermaine, C. & Lawford, E. 2017, *Remarkable Indigenous Diggers Take the Lead on Anzac Day at Last*, SBS NITV, 25 April, <www.sbs.com.au/nitv/nitv-news/article/2017/04/25/remarkable-indigenous-diggers-take-lead-anzac-day-last>, accessed 20 February 2018.

Cadzow, A. 2007, *A NSW Aboriginal Education Timeline 1788–2007*, Sydney: Board of Studies NSW.

Clark, A. 2008, *History's Children: History Wars in the Classroom*, Sydney: UNSW Press.

Connor, J. 2002, *The Australian Frontier Wars 1788–1838*, Sydney: UNSW Press.

Fitzmaurice, A. 2007, 'The genealogy of *terra nullius*', *Australian Historical Studies*, vol. 38, no. 129, pp. 1–15.

Fletcher, J.J. 1989, *Clean, Clad and Courteous: A History of Aboriginal Education in NSW*, Sydney: Southwood Press.

Guilliatt, R. 2008, 'Why kids hate Australian history', *The Australian*, 23 February.

Hattie, J. 2003, 'Teachers make a difference: What is the research evidence?', paper presented at the ACER Annual Conference on Building Teacher Quality, Melbourne 19-21 October.

Hobbs, H. 2017, 'Response to Referendum Council report suggests a narrow path forward on Indigenous constitutional reform', *The Conversation*, 18 July.

Human Rights and Equal Opportunity Commission (HREOC) 1997, *Bringing Them Home: Report of the National Inquiry into the Separation of Aboriginal and Torres Strait Islander Children from Their Families*, Sydney: HREOC.

Keating, P. 1992, 'Redfern Speech: Year for the World's Indigenous People', delivered in Redfern Park, Sydney, by Prime Minister Paul Keating, 10 December.

Langton, M. & Peterson, N. (eds) 1983, *Aborigines, Land & Land Rights*, Canberra: AGPS.

Lee, I. 1906, *The Coming of the British to Australia*, 1788 to 1829, London: Longmans Green and Co. <http://gutenberg.net.au/ebooks09/0900091h.html>, accessed 30 January 2018.

Lewthwaite, B.E., Osborne, B., Lloyd, N., Boon, H., Llewellyn, L., Webber, T., Lan, G., Harrison, M., Day, C., Kemp, C. & Wills, J. 2015, 'Seeking a pedagogy of difference: What Aboriginal students and their parents in North Queensland say about teaching and their learning', *Australian Journal of Teacher Education*, vol. 40, no. 5, pp. 130–59 <http://ro.ecu.edu.au/cgi/viewcontent.cgi?article=2687&context=ajte>, accessed 8 September 2018.

Nakata, M. 2007, *Disciplining the Savages: Savaging the Disciplines*, Canberra: Aboriginal Studies Press.

NSW Department of Education and Communities 2013, *Great Teaching Inspired Learning: What Does the Evidence Tells Us About Effective Teaching?* Sydney: NSW Department of Education and Communities.

Orange, C. 2011, *The Treaty of Waitangi*, Wellington: Bridget Williams.
Parbury, N. 2005, *Survival*, Sydney: NSW Department of Aboriginal Affairs.
Partington, G. 1998, '"In those days it was rough": Aboriginal and Torres Strait Islander history and education', in G. Partington (ed.), *Perspectives on Aboriginal and Torres Strait Islander Education*, Katoomba: Social Science Press, pp. 27–54.
Perso, T.F. 2012, *Cultural Responsiveness and School Education: With Particular Focus on Australia's First Peoples—a Review & Synthesis of the Literature*, Darwin: Menzies School of Health Research, Centre for Child Development and Education.
Referendum Council 2017, *Uluru Statement from the Heart*, Statement of the First Nations Constitutional Convention, 26 May, <www.referendumcouncil.org.au/event/uluru-statement-from-the-heart>, accessed 14 March 2018.
Reynolds, H. 1981, *The Other Side of the Frontier: Aboriginal Resistance to the European Invasion of Australia*, Sydney: UNSW Press.
Rintoul, S. 2000, 'Beyond the Games, nursing the flame', *The Australian*, 21 October.
Rowe, K. 2003, 'The importance of teacher quality as a key determinant of students' experiences and outcomes of schooling', paper presented to ACER Research Conference, Melbourne, 19–21 October.
Ryan, L. 2001, 'Aboriginal History Wars', *Australian Historical Association Bulletin*, vol. 92, pp. 31–7.
Sovereign Union: First Nations Asserting Sovereignty, <http://nationalunitygovernment.org/governments-attempting-to-steal-our-original-sovereign-citizenship-and-independence>, accessed 29 October 2018.
Stanner, W.E.H. 1969, *After the Dreaming: The 1968 Boyer Lectures*, Sydney: New Century Press.
Stephens, A. 2014, 'Reconciliation means recognising the frontier wars', *The Drum*, 7 July, <www.abc.net.au/news/2014-07-07/stephens-reconciliation-means-recognising-the-frontier-wars/5577436>, accessed 20 February 2018.
Wahlquist, C. 2017, 'Turnbull's Uluru statement rejection is "mean-spirited bastardry"—legal expert', *The Guardian*, 26 October.
Windschuttle, K. 2002, *The Fabrication of Aboriginal History*, Sydney: Macleay Press.
Yunupingu, G. 2016, 'Rom Watangu: An Indigenous leader reflects on a lifetime following the law of the land', *The Monthly*, July, <www.themonthly.com.au/issue/2016/july/1467295200/galarrwuy-yunupingu/rom-watangu>, accessed 20 September 2017.

CHAPTER 21
Approaches to teaching Aboriginal history and politics

Heidi Norman

INTRODUCTION

This chapter offers insights into and reflection about approaches to teaching and learning Aboriginal history and politics at Australian universities to improve understandings of Aboriginal lives, inform practice and contribute to 'truth-telling' of local and national histories.

A recent national gathering of Aboriginal and Torres Strait Islander peoples to discuss priorities for achieving constitutional recognition identified *truth-telling about our history* as a leading aspiration. For Aboriginal people, a persistent grief endures that the past is yet to be truly comprehended by fellow Australians. The 2017 *Uluru Statement from the Heart* makes the key point that the lack of comprehension of the past is manifest in Aboriginal people's futures; it is jeopardised by alarming rates of incarceration and is currently undermined by a marginalised Aboriginal polity and a return to policy paternalism.

Over the last half-century, the history of Aboriginal people in Australia has transitioned from uncomfortable 'silence' (Stanner 1969) in the public and academic history spheres to much greater awareness through the culmination of an incredible burgeoning of scholarship, activism and creative production. This body of work, informed by considerable social and cultural change, has underpinned the social justice claims of the state, and has challenged accepted historiography and recast national narratives. Creating awareness of the once 'forgotten' Aboriginal history has been a national priority in several key areas: schools across the country have been mandated to teach Aboriginal history since the late 1980s and, at the community level commencing in 1990, a decade-long process of 'reconciliation', organised around 'learning circles' and dialogue, set out to build awareness of Aboriginal and Torres Strait Islander history and culture to develop a 'shared sense of history'.

Perhaps predictably, this new body of work and the interlinked cultural and social change placed Aboriginal worlds and experience at the centre of a brutal contestation about the nation's history. On one hand, this is a settler story of peaceful settlement and battlers making good; on the other, the Aboriginal story 'casts long, dark shadows over those sunny narratives' (Reynolds 2006). Differences between historians regarding the past—and the public policy and resource redistribution this entails—have become the site for major political contestation, debate and anxiety as the very foundation of the nation is called into question. 'Truth-telling', as Aboriginal people have asserted in many forums—including most recently at Uluru—turns out to be a far more complex undertaking than once thought, and continues to disrupt accepted national narratives and the extrinsic purpose of rights to land and governance.

REFLECTION ON APPROACHES TO ENGAGING STUDENT LEARNERS

Appreciating 'truth-telling', or Aboriginal history as a purposeful activity, this chapter offers a reflection on pedagogical practice, integration with content and assessment activities. A little-explored area of Aboriginal history is how we approach the challenge of facilitating student learning in order to develop the necessary undergraduate attributes: discipline knowledge; critical analysis; communication; and professional capacity. The approach I have taken to teaching Aboriginal political history is to frame approaches about understanding Aboriginal worlds and the spheres of contact with settler institutions, ideas and actions in time and space. This historically inflected framework is necessarily interdisciplinary, drawing on archaeology, history, anthropology, cultural studies, politics, philosophy and Indigenous knowledges.

Contested histories pose particular learning challenges for our students, and the creation of spaces becomes vital to support and sustain robust critique about knowledge and power, and how to be effective agents for change. Often the material we cover can be confronting and challenging; some issues resonate deeply with students, who identify their own or others' similar experience. Some students find themselves confronting accepted family views, while others find their parents eager to shadow the subject, doing the readings and explaining the debates for them. On occasion, Aboriginal students are keen to piece together family stories and experiences as part of a larger narrative or framework. Most students feel disappointed by the way Aboriginal history was taught to them at school; some reject the complexity and nuances of academic learning in favour of a radical position. All, in my experience, are anxious about speaking aloud and debating Aboriginal history: they fear causing offence and are aware that their views, however deeply held, are unexamined. Students also come from a range of professions and disciplines. Together, these factors make it necessary to innovate. Learning approaches must simultaneously engage students while maintaining intellectual rigour; they must give students access to existing debates and core learning, but also allow them to explore their own interests and, above all, allow for kindness and care. Below I set out some approaches that could be taken to the weekly introduction of content and to student assessment.

CONTENT: HISTORY, IDEAS AND CHANGE

In this section, I reflect on approaches to learning and curriculum in the elective subject 'Aboriginal Political History: Ideas, Action and Agency'. To begin the subject, students are required to watch the first episode of *First Footprints: Super Nomads* (Butler et al. 2013), then to answer questions about the documentary and embark on a reflective, place-based exercise. This includes a field trip with teaching staff to a nearby locality or self-directed site visit. Students are asked to reflect on Australia's 50,000-year history, and the disciplines and methods that might be required to produce historical narratives of the deep past. They are encouraged to consider how they know what they know about the country on which they live, its original people and the relationships to place that endure today. By this means, we hope to make them aware, as they begin the semester, of their own experience and views and where they lie in a wider context. This process has come to be known as *deep history* (McGrath & Jebb 2015). Aboriginal history has been the other side of Australian history—at times embattled and silenced, at others entangled with the state, colonial power and relations between British and Indigenous peoples. By contrast, deep history seeks to explore the full range of human experience, or what historian Lynette Russell (2017) summarises as 'from arrival, changes in climate, technologies and belief systems to interactions with Macassans, Portuguese, Dutch, French and finally the British', which stretches 'across 2500 unbroken generations of people birthed, nurtured and sustained: people who modified landscapes, hunted, sang songs, practised religion and buried their dead'.

We then commence our lecture series with the first of three themes: the battlefields of Aboriginal history, ideas and change. For three weeks, students explore the issues and debates central to the emergence of Aboriginal history in Australia (Attwood 1992; Morris 1992; Reynolds 1984), the influence of wider international movements (Maynard 2005) and ideas, trade and access to land and resources (Goodall 1996) as critical to understanding colonisation and dispossession.

This opens up wider discussions about how we interpret the past and make sense of the present. We look at the key scholars in the field who questioned the cult of forgetfulness, and whose work heralded the end of the great Australian silence (Curthoys 2008; Stanner 1969). Students consider the various forms that the invasion took at different times and in different places, and the complex relationships between colonisers and colonised (Goodall 1995; Nugent 2008). Debates on historiography and how innovative methods have produced different accounts of the frontier encourage our students to grasp the ways the past has been narrated (Attwood 2001; Dwyer & Ryan 2016). Henry Reynolds' influential work *The Other Side of the Frontier: Aboriginal Resistance to the European Invasion of Australia* (2006) introduced the previously omitted account of Aboriginal resistance to invasion. By drawing on fragmentary sources—archival information, diaries, journals, newspapers, official documents and oral narratives—that describe the many and varied acts of resistance at the frontier from the opening months at Sydney Cove until the start of the twentieth century, Reynolds (2006) compiled a radical retelling of Australia's history. He showed that all over the continent, Aboriginal people 'bled as profusely and died as bravely' as white soldiers in Australia's twentieth-century wars.

One classroom activity that has elicited productive debate, and that students have said has helped their understanding, is to do with the use of language. Stimulus material includes a front-page story from Sydney's *The Daily Telegraph* condemning a University of New South Wales language guide that recommended, among other things, that staff and students use the word 'invasion' instead of 'discovery' (*The Daily Telegraph* 2016).

Students are asked to consider why describing the frontier, and colonial violence and dispossession, has been so fraught in Australia. A key point that we want our students to appreciate is that colonisation and dispossession are less an event or a moment than a series of violent conflicts that have varied across space and time over more than 100 years, and that require careful consideration of local conditions and changing circumstances.

Reynolds' methodological innovation showed the way for other scholars and heralded a revision of Australia's history from the dominant narrative of 'peaceful settlement of the colonial frontier to one of violent conflict between colonial settlers and Aborigines' (Ryan 2012). These two versions soon came into conflict, with the standard Australian story of peaceful settlement and battlers making good contrasting with the Aboriginal story, which told a very different version of events (Reynolds 2001).

Moving on to the second subject theme, we consider the ideas that influenced the emergence of the administrative regimes that, over time, came to control Aboriginal lives in New South Wales from the start of the twentieth century. The various strategies Aboriginal people deployed to resist authoritarian rule, and their occasional supporters, are studied (Broome 1982; Maynard 2005). Students consider how race science shaped those administrative regimes, along with international solidarity movements and Aboriginal modernity (McGregor 2012). In the third section of the course, we consider how change happens with reference to wider social movements, including decolonisation, feminism, environmental justice and anti-racism (Bandler 1989; Curthoys 2002; Rowse 2000). Students study the movement for the 1967 referendum (Peters-Little 1997); contestation following the referendum that saw land rights emerge as a focused, culturally inflected claim to the colonial state; and the emergence of the pan-Aboriginal national political movement alongside the assertion of place-based, connected-to-country identity (Cook & Goodall 2013; Norman 2015). In this, students consider the influences from the local, national and international in the emergence of the Aboriginal polity from the 1970s and the eventual response by governments (McGregor 2009).

Students study examples of how Aboriginal people's engagement with history can be seen in many works produced in this period that sought to renegotiate power and reimagine identities and futures. They are exposed to poetry, street theatre, biographies and stage plays that were written and performed on political and historical themes (Shoemaker 2004).

Aboriginal history and the emerging body of Aboriginal creative work not only offered more adequate accounts of Australia's past, but also formed the moral basis for remedying past damage to Aboriginal society. The 1992 Redfern Speech of Prime Minister Paul Keating captured this idea. He described the challenge of extending 'opportunity and care, dignity and hope' to Australia's Aboriginal and Torres Strait Islander peoples as

> a fundamental test of our social goals and our national will, our ability to say . . . that Australia is a first-rate social democracy, that we are what we should be—truly the land of the fair go and the better chance . . . It is a test of our self-knowledge, of how well we know the land we live in, how well we know our history (Keating 1992).

An important consideration in the curriculum is to frame Aboriginal social justice claims of the state in the wider context of power and factors—perhaps structural—that mitigate against decolonisation. Rather than narrating a story over the semester of progress towards enlightenment or of ongoing improvement in the life opportunities for Aboriginal people, students are introduced to the contestation of Aboriginal history from 1996, and are therefore alerted to the way change rarely occurs in straight lines.

The 1996 election of a conservative government reluctant to recognise Aboriginal rights stimulated hostility to the emerging consensus that past injustices underpinned Aboriginal Australians' present disadvantage. Conservative historian Geoffrey Blainey (1993) was a central figure opposing the New History, which he dubbed 'black armband'. Blainey's charge was that the New History, with its emphasis on Aboriginal lives, was sustained by a revised and unduly sorrowing account of Australia's history; that Australia had a fairer society in the past than the revisionists conceded; and that the loss of Aboriginal populations was due more to disease than to genocidal violence. Keith Windschuttle (2002) went further. His *The Fabrication of Aboriginal History* (2002) claimed that historians had fabricated the evidence of massacres of Aboriginal people, and therefore of violence on the frontier. Whereas Aboriginal history scholarship draws on a range of sources, conservative historians continue to claim that sources must be 'direct evidence'—firsthand 'genuine eyewitnesses'. For example, Windschuttle questions estimates of the Gomeroi people killed at the Waterloo Creek massacre. If sources are limited to printed accounts (a judicial inquiry and the papers of the missionary Lancelot Threlkeld), the toll is far less than that put forward by scholars of Aboriginal history. Such a limited use of primary sources, as Dwyer and Ryan (2016) argue, reveals 'little understanding of how the colonial frontier worked'.

The History Wars that commenced from the early 1990s were marked by heated public debate that largely took place about us, without us. I vividly recall a debate in the late 1990s in a crowded lecture theatre in the University of Sydney's Woolley Building, in which the usual adversaries (Windschuttle, Reynolds) argued over the details and motives for the removal of Aboriginal children and the extent of frontier violence. As they argued, agitation steadily grew among the crowd gathered to hear them. One Aboriginal woman yelled from the audience her story of being taken from her family as a baby from the hospital, which was a stone's throw away from where this debate over evidence and methodology was proceeding, as though the issues were remote from human experience. It really was a horrible and debasing flashpoint in time that held injured lives up to careless scrutiny at a time when Aboriginal people were engaged in new ways of comprehending the past and its impact in the present—myself included.

The *Yorta Yorta* native title decision was emblematic of this process. The Federal Court found against the claimants—its first negative native-title decision—ruling that 'the tide of history' had 'indeed washed away any real acknowledgment of their traditional laws and any real observance of their traditional customs'. One study stated that, in reaching his decision, Justice Olney had privileged documentary over oral evidence—that is, evidence from the past over evidence from the present about the past (Genovese & Reilly 2004).

The History Wars thus amounted to more than a debate over historiography and the role of historians in public discourse. For students, it is essential—although it may be challenging—to learn how Aboriginal perspectives on events of the past are disavowed, and to consider the effects of that process. Aboriginal history has spawned heated, highly politicised debates over the ways that colonisation should be recognised and collectively remembered in Australia's national narrative. That debate is more than a mere competition between two accounts of the past—'black armband' versus 'white blindfold'. If we see it as only that, we will fail to comprehend not only how a settler society such as Australia represents its past, but also how the past and debates over the past inform the present. Our students need to be introduced to a nuanced view of that history, which avoids such over-simplifications.

Our Aboriginal history classrooms are therefore critical places: it is there that the evidence is studied, the discussions are conducted and the controversies are engaged in that in time form future public intellectuals. It is there that individuals are educated in the traditions of scholarship, the analysis of the past and the understanding of power that will enable them to be agents for change.

ASSESSMENT: REFLECTIVE LEARNERS AND PUBLIC INTELLECTUALS

In my teaching I have tried, above all, to create opportunities for students to engage actively in Aboriginal worlds as intellectuals and future professionals. I have long believed that if the material conditions of Aboriginal people are to change, new conversations must take place. University classrooms are ideal places to begin those conversations, and to create opportunities to move beyond what now exists. Exercises such as field trips, case-study role-plays, classroom debates and public intellectual activities can achieve this. To illustrate these points, I refer to two assessment activities for the subject 'Aboriginal Political History'.

In one assessment, students are encouraged to imagine themselves as public intellectuals in the Aboriginal social and political sphere. The rationale is to show students their responsibility to engage both constructively and in an informed way in debates and to be agents for change. One form that this assessment can take is a review of a recent book or creative production in the fields of Aboriginal politics and history. Students are required to write the review and nominate a publication in their professional practice or discipline in which it might appear. They tend to nominate a wide range of newspapers, creative-industry journals and academic journals. From 2015, a student journal, *NEW: Emerging Scholars in Indigenous Studies* (Norman & Morrissey 2015), has also been publishing students' work of this kind. The point is to get students to imagine communicating ideas to their peers as a public intellectual activity, taking forward serious scholarship in Aboriginal history and debates about Aboriginal futures, and then to encourage them to think about how their future profession communicates with and about Aboriginal worlds.

A second assessment requires students to write a reflective blog about a self-directed site visit in Sydney. The purpose is to allow students to move beyond the classroom and to apply ideas about place, belonging and change over time. The responses to this task have been exceptional, and students themselves have said the exercise has changed how they see and experience Sydney: they now view it as an always 'Aboriginal place' with a deep history.

CONCLUSION

Debate among historians about historical truth, the relationship between the historian and the past, and questions of fact, value and interpretation are more than mere intellectual jousting. These are the stories of our lives, our communities and our country; they form the framework through which we can understand the world around us and evoke the sentiments that enable us to imagine a shared identity. Aboriginal history as a discipline, however embattled and marginal it may be in Australian universities, is one arena in which cultural competence may be developed. Moreover, broader claims may be made for it. Aboriginal history can guide wider curriculum developments, such as professional service, and bring together scientists, social scientists, practitioners and community to tell stories of much longer time periods.

Ann Curthoys and John Docker (2010) caution against declaring 'that the historian can objectively establish the truth about the past'. Instead, they say, 'There always has to be a question mark hovering over any claim to having attained an objective, let alone scientific, status for one's findings.' The demand for *truth-telling about our history* exposes a constructive paradox: the necessity for, and difficulty of, finding truth in history. Although the demand may never be satisfied in full, the task must nonetheless be attempted. It is the duty of universities, which are uniquely placed to take up this plea from Aboriginal community leaders, to make that attempt. The *Uluru Statement from the Heart*, and many statements that came before it, are ultimately optimistic: that optimism lies in the hope that, by embracing our ancient sovereignty, Australia's nationhood may be enriched.

REFERENCES

Attwood, B. 1992, 'Introduction' in B. Attwood and J. Arnold (eds), 'Power, Knowledge and Aborigines', special issue of the *Journal of Australian Studies*, vol. 16, no. 35, pp. 1–16.

—— 2001, '"Learning about the truth": The Stolen Generations' narrative', in B. Attwood & F. Magowan (eds), *Telling Stories: Indigenous History and Memory in Australia and New Zealand*, Wellington: Bridget Williams, pp. 183–212.

Bandler, F. 1989, *Turning the Tide: A Personal History of the Federal Council for the Advancement of Aborigines and Torres Strait Islanders*, Canberra: Aboriginal Studies Press.

Blainey, G. 1993, 'Drawing up a balance sheet of our history', *Quadrant*, vol. 37, nos 7–8, pp. 10–15.

Broome, R. 1982, *Aboriginal Australians*, Sydney: Allen & Unwin.

Butler, M., Dean, B., Dingo, E. & Nehme, T. 2013, *First Footprints*. Episode 1: 'Super Nomads'; Episode 4: 'The Biggest Estate' [Video and DVD], Sydney: Flame Distribution.

Cook, K. & Goodall, H. 2013, *Making Change Happen: Black and White Activists Talk to Kevin Cook About Aboriginal, Union and Liberation Politics*, Canberra: ANU e-Press.

Curthoys, A. 2002, *Freedom Rides: A Freedom Rider Remembers*, Sydney: Allen & Unwin.

—— 2008, 'W.E.H. Stanner and the historians', in M. Hinkson & J. Beckett (eds), *An Appreciation of Difference: W.E.H. Stanner and Aboriginal Australia*, Canberra: Aboriginal Studies Press, pp. 233–50.

Curthoys, A. & Docker, J. 2010, *Is History Fiction?* Sydney: UNSW Press, p. 5.

The Daily Telegraph 2016, 'Whitewash: UNSW rewrites the history books to state Cook "invaded Australia"', 29 March.

Dwyer, P.G. & Ryan, L. 2016, 'On genocide and settler-colonial violence: Australia in comparative perspective', in D. Mayersen (ed.), *The United Nations and Genocide*, Basingstoke: Palgrave Macmillan, pp. 32–53.

Genovese, A. & Reilly, A. 2004, 'Claiming the past: Historical understanding in Australian native title jurisprudence', *Indigenous Law Journal*, vol. 3, pp. 19–41.

Goodall, H. 1995, 'New South Wales', in A. McGrath (ed.), *Contested Ground: Australian Aborigines Under the British Crown*, Sydney: Allen & Unwin, pp. 55–120.

—— 1996, *Invasion to Embassy: Land in Aboriginal Politics in New South Wales, 1770–1972*, Sydney: Allen & Unwin.

Keating, P. 1992, 'Redfern Speech: Year for the World's Indigenous People', delivered in Redfern Park, Sydney, by Prime Minister Paul Keating, 10 December.

Maynard, J. 2005, 'In the interests of our people: The influence of Garveyism on the rise of Australian Aboriginal political activism', *Aboriginal History*, vol. 29, pp. 1–22.

McGrath, A. & Jebb, M. 2015, *Long History, Deep Time: Deepening Histories of Place*, Canberra: ANU Press.

McGregor, R. 2009, 'Another nation: Aboriginal activism in the late 1960s and early 1970s', *Australian Historical Studies*, vol. 40, no. 2, pp. 343–60.
—— 2012, 'Aboriginal activists demand acceptance', in *Indifferent Inclusion: Aboriginal People and the Australian Nation*, Canberra: Aboriginal Studies Press, pp. 37–54.
Morris, B. 1992, 'Frontier colonialism as a culture of terror', in B. Attwood (ed.), *Power, Knowledge and Aborigines*, Melbourne: La Trobe University Press in association with the National Centre for Australian Studies, Monash University, pp. 72–87.
Norman, H. 2015, *'What Do We Want?': A Political History of Land Rights*, Canberra: Aboriginal Studies Press.
Norman, H. & Morrissey, P. (eds) 2015, *NEW: Emerging Scholars in Australian Indigenous Studies*, University of Technology Sydney e-press, <https://epress.lib.uts.edu.au/student-journals/index.php/NESAIS>, accessed 20 June 2018.
Nugent, M. 2008, 'The encounter between Captain Cook and Indigenous people at Botany Bay in 1770 reconsidered', in P. Veth, P. Sutton & M. Neale (eds), *Strangers on the Shore: Early Coastal Contacts in Australia*, Canberra: National Museum of Australia Press, pp. 198–207.
Peters-Little, F. 1997, *Vote Yes For Aborigines*, Canberra: Ronin Films.
Reynolds, H. 1984, *The Other Side of the Frontier: Aboriginal Resistance to the European Invasion of Australia*, Sydney: UNSW Press.
—— 1998, *This Whispering in Our Hearts*, Sydney: Allen & Unwin.
—— 2001, *An Indelible Stain? The Question of Genocide in Australia's History*, Ringwood: Penguin.
—— 2006, *The Other Side of the Frontier: Aboriginal Resistance to the European Invasion of Australia*, Sydney: UNSW Press, p. 200.
Rowse, T. 2000, 'The modest mandate of 1967', in *Obliged to Be Difficult: Nugget Coombs' Legacy in Indigenous Affairs*, Cambridge: Cambridge University Press, pp. 17–33.
Russell, L. 2017, '50,000 years of Australian history: A plea for interdisciplinarity', Second Bicentennial Australian History Lecture, University of Sydney, October.
Ryan, L. 2012, *Tasmanian Aborigines: A History Since 1803*, Sydney: Allen & Unwin.
Shoemaker, A. 2004, *Black Words, White Page: Aboriginal Literature 1929–1988*, Canberra: ANU e-Press.
Stanner, W.E.H. 1969, 'The Great Australian Silence', 1968 Boyer Lecture: *After The Dreaming*, Sydney: ABC Enterprises.
Windschuttle, K. 2002, *The Fabrication of Aboriginal History, Vol. 1—Van Diemen's Land 1803–1847*, Sydney: Macleay Press.

CHAPTER 22
Teaching citizenship in the history classroom

Yeow-Tong Chia and Kieren Beard

The advent of history as a school subject was associated with the rise of the nation-state and nationalism (Green 1990, 1997). Consequently, the inculcation of citizenship values—especially in the forging of national identity—has been a key aim of schooling, performed primarily through the teaching of history (Osborne 1991, 1995). Indeed, as early as 1920, Helen Madeley (1920: 10) argued that the key aim of history teaching should be 'the making of the citizen'.

This chapter discusses what many argue is the ultimate goal of history education in the classroom: citizenship. It discusses the relationship between history education and citizenship, and reviews some of the research literature on citizenship education. This provides the context for the key aim of the chapter, which is to examine the notion of Asia in the teaching of citizenship in the Australian history classroom. The emphasis is on Australia's engagement with Asia and 'Asia literacy' in history education, which has clear citizenship implications. We argue that while it is important to teach Asian history, it is equally important that Asian Australian history is not inadvertently neglected.

HISTORY EDUCATION AND CITIZENSHIP

History and history education are often sites for political contestation, both in schools and in society at large (Clark 2008, 2009; Davies 1995; Hong & Yap 1983; Osborne 2003; Symcox 2002). Governments often use history as a tool for legitimisation (Chia 2012; Vickers & Jones 2005). In instilling a sense of pride in the common past, history writing and teaching of a nation's history contribute to the creation and strengthening of nationalism. History frequently becomes subservient to the cause of nation-building and political legitimisation, and to the ends of citizenship education. In the 1950s and 1960s, history thus played a central role in the inculcation of citizenship values in the West, with the teaching of national grand narrative history, which was positivist and teleological.

The flowering of social history since the 1960s, however, has served to broaden the historian's perspectives on the past. History was no longer seen as an integrated body of knowledge (Evans 2000). The broadening, diversification and expansion of the historical discipline went alongside the fragmentation of history. These 'new histories' in academe challenged the idea of progress in history, and the debate spread across to school history as well. Since the 1960s, debates over the nature and purpose of history, as well as history teaching in schools in the West, have had the unintended effect of diminishing the role of history education in schools.

The same period in Australia saw the dilution of history in the compulsory years of schooling into an integrated course of studies, once known as Social Studies, but more commonly known nationally as Studies of Society and Environment (SOSE). One outcome of instituting Social Studies in the compulsory years of schooling has been a failure among the school population to identify the discipline of history. The result is that history has become increasingly unpopular in the post-compulsory years of schooling, where the subject is just one elective in an increasingly wide range of choices (Barcan 1997). Other scholars regard the introduction of an increasing skills orientation as leading to the decline of history in schools (Macintyre 1997). New South Wales bucked the trend that began in the 1990s of the decline of history as a school subject nationally, with history continuing to be taught as a compulsory subject from Years 7 to 10. Pedagogically, the syllabus aims to encourage student interaction and vested interest in history as a discipline through skills-based and biographical praxes. The key objectives of the K–10 syllabus are 'to stimulate students' interest in and enjoyment of exploring the past . . . [and] to develop the critical skills of historical inquiry . . . to [nurture them] as active, informed and responsible citizens' (Board of Studies NSW 2012: 12).

Prominent Canadian history educator Ken Osborne (1995: 25) observed that 'paradoxically, at the same time history was declining in status, interest in citizenship education—variously called civic or political education—was rising, in Canada and elsewhere'.

CITIZENSHIP AND CITIZENSHIP EDUCATION

Both citizenship and citizenship education are contested concepts, and because of competing definitions, conceptualisations and contexts of what the term 'citizenship' entails, citizenship education is often not easy to define (Kerr 2003: 6–8). Broadly speaking, citizenship education places strong emphasis on 'civic education', which involves students learning about the country's political, legal and economic systems, their rights and responsibilities as citizens, and how their government works (Callan 2004; Freeman Butts 1980; Heater 2004; Marshall 1950; Osborne 2001). Kennedy (1997: 3) reiterates that this kind of civic knowledge 'is interdisciplinary and integrated while the values must be firmly embedded in a vision that focuses on the good of all rather than the selfish demands of individuals'. Civics also teaches students about decision-making and leadership. In short, citizenship involves participation in and awareness of the benefits, privileges and responsibilities of community life. The process develops decision-making skills, values, attitudes and understanding to allow young citizens to participate actively in society.

Historically, national education systems played an important role in citizenship education—particularly in education for nation-building (Green 1997)—and in the rise of the nation-state. In doing so, citizenship education 'act[s] as a vehicle of social integration through the transmission of culture' (Green 1990: 36)—a socialising function and the maintenance of social order. Over the past century, the aims and motivations for education, and citizenship education in particular, have oscillated between nation-building and national identity-formation (Anderson 1991), and education for democratic participation (Osborne 1991). For the past few decades, and until relatively recently, the emphasis of citizenship education in the West, including Australia, has largely shifted from the forging of national identity to the cultivation of democratic and civic values (Barton & Levstik 2004; Osborne 1991, 1995). This was partly due to the devastating experiences of the two world wars, which 'made the advanced nations . . . cautious about promoting national identities through education' (Green 1997: 3).

In recent decades, there has been increasing global policy interest in citizenship education, particularly in the role of schools in equipping younger generations with the necessary knowledge, skills and attitudes for participation in modern democracies as informed, responsible, committed and effective citizens (Franzosa 1988; Niemi & Junn 1988;

Print, Ellickson-Brown & Baginda 1999; Print & Milners 2009). This increased interest in citizenship education by policy-makers and politicians is fuelled by a perceived decline in civic engagement from around the late 1970s, as evidenced in decreased participation in civil society and declining voter turnout, especially among youths. This gave rise to a renewed emphasis on civics and citizenship education in the West, and in Australia in particular, with programs such as Discovering Democracy and the recent Civics and Citizenship Education syllabus (Print 2017). Such initiatives highlight the role and aims of citizenship education as democratic learning and inculcation. The national identity and nation-building dimension appears to be implicitly de-emphasised in the citizenship education curricula. Nonetheless, some politicians and scholars continue to regard nation-building and national identity as key goals of history teaching. Consequently, the History Wars of the 1990s and their brief resurgence in 2014 centred on the debates over Australian national identity (Taylor 2013).

AUSTRALIA AND ASIA

Discussions over national identity often involve a selective understanding and use of history, and Australia is no exception. A key to unpacking the notion of Australian national identity is to understand the history of Australia and 'Asia'. Indeed, Australia has consistently been fascinated with the ascendency of Asia, both politically and economically, as well as its influence over and role in Australia's future. David Walker has featured prominently in the academic debates surrounding the Asian anxieties evident throughout Australian history (most notably Australia's 'yellow peril'), and how they have influenced the present social, economic, political and cultural landscape of Australia (Walker 2002a: 63–75; Walker 2010, 2012). There is a consensus among 'Asia literacy' academics that the history of Australia's prior engagement with Asia has been blemished with racial intolerance and anxieties that derive from colonial insecurities within its geographical proximity to Asia (Jayasuriya, Walker & Gothard 2003; Peacock 1968: 308–9; Walker 2002a; Walker & Sobocinska 2012: 4). However, attitudes are shifting due to new and informed curiosities as Australia is arguably firmly positioned in the 'Asian century'. Throughout the nineteenth and twentieth centuries, some Asianists have braved the Eurocentric settlers' attitudes towards Asia in promoting greater engagement through studies of Asia and its languages. Despite the recent emboldened attitudes of Rudd and Gillard, Australia's education system is lacking a key aspect of Asian studies for building adept 'Asia literacy' (AACTF 2012: 15–16).

A major obstacle in ascertaining Asia literacy has been the way Asia is viewed within the public consciousness. There has been an insistence on forging Australia's Western democratic identity around Anglo-European ancestry. Australia's connections with Asia are consequently interwoven with fear, anxiety and threats of invasion—an irony considering the initial 'invasion' ethos of European colonists. Nonetheless, with Asia literacy slowly becoming a new buzzword surrounding multicultural educational outcomes—particularly in previous efforts towards languages in schools from 2012—Asia has been thrust to the forefront of public consciousness.

Walker and Sobocinska's book *Australia's Asia: From Yellow Peril to Asian Century* (2012) provides a vivid historical account of Australia's long and tumultuous engagement with Asia. According to Walker and Sobocinska, Asia appears throughout Australian history as a source of both anxiety and hope. During the nineteenth and twentieth centuries, there were numerous examples of anti-Asian attitudes plaguing the image and recognition of Asia's influence and future importance to Australia. In 1888, Queensland labour activist William Lane, an anti-Chinese zealot, publicly challenged citizens to consider whether Australia's future would be 'white or yellow' (Walker 2002a, 2002b; Walker & Sobocinska 2012: 45). Moreover, during the nineteenth century, and leading into the twentieth century, there were already tensions with our local Asian communities that brought about the 'White Australia' rhetoric. Examples include the restriction of Chinese immigrants from working in the goldmines during the 1850s, and the bubonic plagues of the 1900s, which saw 'Asian' or Chinese communities in particular quarantined out of fear of their apparent detrimental influence in Australia (Walker 2012: 36; Walker & Sobocinska 2012: 45). As Federation approached, it was clear Australia would define its identity through the racial purification model of the White Australia policy, formally known as the *Immigration Restriction Act 1901*. Through this Act, immigration could be controlled to protect the colonialists' image of an Anglo-European Australia (Jayasuriya, Walker & Gothard 2003: 58). As a result, an embedded anxiety about Asia swept the national consciousness. Walker notes that Australian history displays cycles of ignorance, which are swiftly followed by exhortations to 'wake up' in its attitudes towards Asia (Walker & Sobocinska 2012: 3).

In 1963, Donald Horne, an Australian journalist and academic, travelled through Asia and detailed his experiences in his book *The Lucky Country* (Horne 1964). As an evaluation of Australia's traditional colonial attitudes towards Asia, Horne criticised the 'second-rate people' who shared the luck Australia held; Australia's proximity to Asia gave it a political significance that it did not already own (Walker 2002b: 324). Walker supports these claims, as the world was shrinking and Australia appeared to be heading towards an increasingly Asian future (2002b: 321). The 1950s marked a significant political derivation that manifested the shift in attitudes towards Asia-readiness, which Walker (2002b: 319) describes as 'a new era of cultural receptivity and developing Asia awareness'. The defining moment came through the Menzies-led Liberal government, which was aware that there was a restructuring of European and Western power presence in the East. Menzies aimed to place Australia on good terms with Southeast Asia; he initiated the Colombo Plan, through which students from the Asian region could study in Australia. Moreover, trade and commerce agreements were struck with an ever-growing Japanese power in 1957 that signalled new political relations, and the *Migration Act 1958* changed Australian immigration laws. Australia's history of race relations developed further as the 1972–5 Whitlam-led federal government rescinded the *Immigration Restriction Act 1901*, opening up our borders for global immigration. Although it would have been highly controversial at the time, this has shaped Australia's present multicultural status.

Prior to the abolition of the White Australia policy, the Auchmuty Report (Auchmuty 1971: 89–90) identified that Australian students did not experience any 'systematic study of Asian affairs' and were offered limited opportunities for the study of Asian languages (Halse 2015: 15). The overall theme of the report was a reappraisal of Australia's traditional attitudes towards Asia (Halse 2015: 11). Following the Auchmuty Report, many other reports were published that aimed to evolve the Asia-consciousness debate. The Basham Report targeted the long-term benefits of Asian studies for Australia (ASAA 1978) and the Fitzgerald Report (ASAA 1980) challenged Australia's Eurocentrism while promoting further study of Asian languages and cultures to enhance global knowledge. On an economic level, the Garnaut Report (Garnaut 1989; see also Henderson 2008b: 173) argued that Asian studies would be part of the process of macroeconomic reform. However, Stivens (cited in Henderson 2008a: 36–7) argues that the Garnaut Report, while a significant study that threw Asian studies firmly into the national political spotlight, suggested that Asian studies (through a focus on languages) would equate to trade success at the expense of other key areas for Asian studies. This provocation is mirrored in the 2012 White Paper released during Julia Gillard's ministership, which maintains that Asian studies can only serve as economic value for Australia's future in the Asian consciousness.

In the twenty-first century, Australia has made positive strides towards ensuring Australian students are competent in Asian studies and languages. Kevin Rudd's rise to power in 2007 was a defining moment for the Asia-centric focus for education. Rudd showed how Asia-literate he was, as a bilingual politician who was fluent in [Chinese] Mandarin, a skill reflected in the 1994 *Asian Languages and Australia's Economic Future* report (also known as the Rudd Report), which was produced while he was chairperson of the Council of Australian Governments (COAG), insinuating the importance of language education in contributing to Asia literacy and Australia's economic future. Johnson, Ahluwalia and McCarthy (2010: 66) note the overall public amazement that an Anglo-European male could speak Mandarin so fluently was a sign of how Western and Anglo-centric Australia still is. Julia Gillard continued the focus on Asia through the White Paper (AACTF 2012). Significantly, of the five pillars for Australia evolving in the Asian century, skills and education were at the forefront of change; this was seen later in the report: 'our skills and education system play a fundamental role in ensuring that all Australians can develop the right capabilities to take advantage of the Asian century' (AACTF 2012: 2, 162).

CITIZENSHIP THROUGH HISTORY EDUCATION: ASIAN PERSPECTIVES

In sum, the above discussion outlines Australia's approach to engaging with Asia, which goes under the notion of 'Asia literacy'. This term is both highly problematic and ambiguous, and it could be argued that it essentialises Asia, ignoring the many different nations and diverse cultures in the Asian region. For a more in-depth discussion and critique of this notion, see Salter (2013). While this is driven primarily by economics, there is also a crucial citizenship dimension in the history of Australia's engagement with Asia, as Australia's national identity is partly shaped in contrast to its Asian 'other'. The cross-curricular priority of 'Asia and Australia's engagement with Asia' in the history curriculum focuses more on a cultural rather than an economic dimension of Australia and Asia (Board of Studies NSW 2012: 29–30). Even though Asian Australians are mentioned, this reads like an appendage and afterthought. It implicitly suggests the continued ambivalence of Australia's position regarding Asia and Asians. There is therefore a risk of perpetuating Asia and Asians as the 'other'. Despite this, several depth studies in the existing Australian Syllabus: History 7–10 provide opportunities for a greater and richer understanding of Australia and Asia in terms of the content to be taught (Beard 2017).

Beyond teaching and understanding Asian history, and the contributions of Asian Australians, there is a need to regard Asian Australian history as a key part of Australian history and not as an aside, thereby potentially enriching and deepening Australian multiculturalism and diversity. The Stage 5 history syllabus offers many possibilities to bring Asian perspectives into the classroom, such as the White Australia policy (Depth Study 2), the role of Asian Australians in the world wars (Depth Study 3) and Asian-Australian activism (Depth Study 4) (Board of Studies NSW 2012). Teachers could also explore the invisibility of Asia and Asians in *all* the depth studies. We are not advocating teaching Asian content in every class, but to integrate 'Asia' and 'Asians' into the teaching of Australian history whenever possible.

Other than the teaching of Asian and Asian Australian history, it would be good for teachers to have an understanding of Asian notions of citizenship and history. For instance, the East Asian conception of education has a long history, which is rooted in Confucian tradition. Education was highly valued throughout Chinese Imperial history, with the long tradition of imperial examinations (科举) from the Han Dynasty, which were based on Confucian classics. It served two functions: 'self cultivation and recruiting of "men of talent" to administer the affairs of the state' (Peterson, Hayhoe & Lu 2001: 2). Values education has a long history in the East Asian and particularly Chinese intellectual tradition. In this context, Cummings, Gopinathan and Tomoda (1988) argue that the West tends to emphasise education for democracy and civic values, while East Asia emphasises 'good' citizenship and moral education. Unlike in the West, where citizenship education and moral education are regarded as related but mutually exclusive, the Asian conception of citizenship tends to conflate civics with morality (Lee 2008). While Professor Wing On Lee is widely acknowledged as the doyen in the field of Asian citizenship education, he draws primarily on Confucian philosophy and epistemology in his conceptions of Asian citizenship (even though he acknowledges the diverse faith and philosophical traditions of Asia). His notion of 'Asian citizenship' therefore tends to neglect the complexities and diversities of the region and its cultural traditions. For a more nuanced discussion of citizenship and education in Asian contexts, see Vickers and Kumar (2015).

Western historiography tends to regard the past as a foreign country that is separate from the present, and as dissimilar to history (Sandwell 2003; Seixas 2006). History is interpretive and constructed, while the past is everything that has happened. In contrast, East Asian conceptions of history, and the Confucian view of history in particular, place importance on the past as a mirror to the present. The past is seen as in dialogical relationship and connected with the present, and as providing lessons to the present (Huang 2010).

CONCLUSION

This chapter examined the notion of Asia in the teaching of citizenship in the Australian history classroom. The preceding discussion on Asian perspectives in Australian history education suggests some limitations in the historical-thinking approach to history education. The existing historical-thinking approach is based on a Western approach, which regards the past as separate from the present and, by extension, citizenship as related but mutually exclusive to history education. The preliminary discussion on East Asian conceptions of history and citizenship reveals a dialogic, integrated and embodied relationship between the past and present, as well as history and citizenship—as they point to the ultimate aim of being *human*. This corresponds to the notion of humanistic education and deliberation as proposed by Keith Barton (2006, 2012). With the tumultuous global milieu in which we find ourselves today, perhaps dialogue and deliberation are the key insights that an Asian perspective offers to enrich the history classroom.

REFERENCES

Anderson, B. 1991, *Imagined Communities: Reflections on the Origin and Spread of Nationalism*, rev. ed., London: Verso.

Asian Studies Association of Australia (ASAA) 1978, *The Teaching of Asian Languages in Australian Tertiary Institutions*, Canberra: ASAA (Basham Report).

—— 1980, *Asia in Australian Education* (3 vols), Canberra: ASAA (Fitzgerald Report).
Auchmuty, J. 1971, *The Teaching of Asian Languages and Cultures*, Canberra: AGPS (Auchmuty Report).
Australia in the Asian Century Task Force (AACTF) 2012, *Australia in the Asian Century: White Paper*, <www.asiaeducation.edu.au/verve/_resources/australia-in-the-asian-century-white-paper.pdf>, accessed 4 August 2017.
Barcan, A. 1997, 'History in a pluralist culture: response of Macintyre', *Australian Journal of Education*, vol. 41, no. 2, pp. 199–212.
Barton, K. 2006, 'History, humanistic education and participatory democracy', in R. Sandwell (ed.), *To the Past: Public Memory, Citizenship, and History Education*, Toronto: University of Toronto Press.
—— 2012, 'Agency, choice and historical action: How history teaching can help students think about democratic decision-making', *Citizenship Teaching and Learning*, vol. 7, no. 2, pp. 131–42.
Barton, K. & Levstik, L. 2004, *Teaching History for the Common Good*, Mahwah, NJ: Lawrence Erlbaum.
Beard, K. 2017, '(In)Visibility of Asian history in the Australian history curriculum', unpublished Honours thesis, University of Sydney.
Board of Studies NSW 2012, *History K–10 Syllabus*, Sydney: Board of Studies NSW.
Callan, E. 2004, 'Citizenship and Education', *Annual Review of Political Science*, vol. 7, pp. 71–90.
Chia, Y.-T. 2012, 'History education for nation-building and state formation: The case of Singapore', *Citizenship Teaching and Learning*, vol. 7, no. 2, pp. 191–207.
Clark, A. 2008, *History's Children: History Wars in the Classroom*, Sydney: UNSW Press.
—— 2009, 'Teaching the nation's story: Comparing public debates and classroom perspectives of history education in Australia and Canada', *Journal of Curriculum Studies*, vol. 41, no. 6, pp. 745–62.
Cummings, W.K., Gopinathan, S. & Tomoda, Y. (eds) 1988, *The Revival of Values Education in Asia and the West*, Oxford: Pergamon Press.
Davies, B. 1995, *Whatever Happened to High School History? Burying the Political Memory of Youth. Ontario: 1945–1995*, Toronto: James Lorimer.
Evans, R. 2000, *In Defence of History*, London: Granta Books.
Franzosa, S.D. (ed.) 1988, *Civic Education: Its Limits and Conditions*, Ann Arbor, MI: Prakken Publications.
Freeman Butts, R. 1980, *The Revival of Civic Learning: A Rationale for Citizenship Education in American Schools*, Arlington, VA: Phi Delta Kappa Education Foundation.

Garnaut, R. 1989, *Australia and the Northeast Asian Ascendancy*, Canberra: AGPS (Garnaut Report).

Green, A. 1990, *Education and State Formation: The Rise of Education Systems in England, France, and the USA*, New York: St Martin's Press.

—— 1997, *Education, Globalization and the Nation State*, New York: St Martin's Press.

Halse, C. (ed.) 2015, *Asia literate Schooling in the Asian Century*, New York: Routledge.

Heater, D. 2004, *A Brief History of Citizenship*, Edinburgh: Edinburgh University Press.

Henderson, D. 2008a, 'Meeting the national interest through Asia literacy: An overview of the major stages and debates', *Asian Studies Review*, vol. 27, no. 1, pp. 23–53.

—— 2008b, 'Politics and policy-making for Asia literacy: The Rudd Report and a national strategy in Australian education', *Asian Studies Review*, vol. 32, no. 2, pp. 171–95.

Hong, L. & Yap, J. 1983, 'The past in Singapore's present', *Commentary*, vol. 11, no. 1, pp. 31–8.

Horne, D. 1964, *The Lucky Country*, Ringwood: Penguin.

Huang, C. 2010, *Humanism in East Asian Contexts*, New York: Columbia University Press.

Jayasuriya, L., Walker, D. & Gothard, J. 2003, *Legacies of White Australia: Race, Culture and Nation*, Perth: UWA Publishing.

Johnson, C., Ahluwalia, P. & McCarthy, G. 2010, 'Australia's ambivalent reimagining of Asia', *Australian Journal of Political Science*, vol. 45, no. 1, pp. 59–74.

Kennedy, K. (ed.) 1997, *Citizenship Education and the Modern State*, London: Falmer Press.

Kerr, D. 2003, 'Citizenship: Local, national and international', in L. Gearon (ed.), *Learning to Teach Citizenship in the Secondary School*, London: RoutledgeFalmer, pp. 6–8.

Lee, W.O. 2008, 'Tensions and contentions in citizenship curriculum in Asia and the Pacific', in D. Grossman, W.O. Lee & K. Kennedy (eds), *Citizenship Curriculum in Asia and the Pacific*, Dordrecht: Springer, pp. 215–31.

Macintyre, S. 1997, 'The genie and the bottle: Putting history back into the school curriculum', *Australian Journal of Education*, vol. 41, no. 2, pp. 189–99.

Madeley, H.M. 1920, *History as a School of Citizenship*, Oxford: Oxford University Press.

Marshall, T.H. 1950, *Citizenship and Social Class and Other Essays*, Cambridge: Cambridge University Press.

Niemi, R.G. & Junn, J. 1988, *Civic Education: What Makes Students Learn*, New Haven, CT: Yale University Press.

Osborne, K. 1991, *Teaching for Democratic Citizenship*, Toronto: Our Schools/Our Selves.

—— 1995, *In Defence of History: Teaching the Past and the Meaning of Democratic Citizenship*, Toronto: Our Schools/Our Selves.

—— 2001, 'Democracy, democratic citizenship and education', in J. Portelli & R.P. Solomon (eds), *Democracy in Education: From Critique to Possibilities*, Calgary: Detselig Enterprises.

—— 2003, 'Teaching history in schools: A Canadian debate', *Journal of Curriculum Studies*, vol. 35, no. 5, pp. 585–626.

Peacock, A. 1968, *Australian House of Representatives Debates*, 26th Parliament, Second Session, vol. 12 [20 March 1968], pp. 308–9.

Peterson, G., Hayhoe, R. & Lu, Y. (eds) 2001, *Education, Culture and Identity in Twentieth-Century China*, Ann Arbor, MI: University of Michigan Press.

Print, M. 2017, 'The recent history of teaching civics and citizenship education in Australia, 1989–2015', in A. Peterson & L. Tudball (eds), *Civics and Citizenship Education in Australia: Challenges, Practices and International Perspectives*, London: Bloomsbury, pp. 7–22.

Print, M., Ellickson-Brown, K. & Baginda, A.R. (eds) 1999, *Civic Education for Civil Society*, London: ASEAN Academic.

Print, M. & Milners, H. 2009, *Civic Education and Youth Political Participation*, Rotterdam: Sense.

Salter, P. 2013, 'The problem in policy: Representations of Asia literacy in Australian education for the Asian Century', *Asian Studies Review*, vol. 37, no. 1, pp. 3–23.

Sandwell, R. 2003, 'Reading beyond bias: Teaching historical practice to secondary school students', *McGill Journal of Education*, vol. 38, no. 1, pp. 168–86.

Seixas, P. 2006, 'What is historical consciousness?', in R.W. Sandwell (ed.), *To the Past: History Education, Public Memory, and Citizenship in Canada*, Toronto: University of Toronto Press, pp. 11–22.

Symcox, L. 2002, *Whose History? The Struggle for National Standards in American Classrooms*, New York: Teachers College Press.

Taylor, T. 2013, 'History in politics: Neoconservative progressivism, knowledgeable ignorance and the origins of the next history war', *History Australia*, vol. 10, no. 2, pp. 227–40.

Vickers, E. & Jones, A. (eds) 2005, *History Education and National Identity in East Asia*, New York: Routledge.

Vickers, E. & Kumar, K. (eds) 2015, *Constructing Modern Asian Citizenship*, London: Routledge.

Walker, D. 2002a, 'National narratives: Australia in Asia', *Media History*, vol. 8, no. 1, pp. 63–75.
—— 2002b, 'Survivalist anxieties: Australian responses to Asia, 1890s to the present', *Australian Historical Studies*, vol. 33, no. 120, pp. 319–30.
—— 2010, 'The "flow of Asia"—vocabularies of engagement: A cultural history', *Australian Journal of Political Science*, vol. 45, no. 1, pp. 45–58.
—— 2012, *Anxious Nation: Australia and the Rise of Asia, 1850–1939*, Perth: UWA Publishing.
Walker, D. & Sobocinska, A. 2012, *Australia's Asia: From Yellow Peril to Asian Century*, Perth: UWA Publishing.

CHAPTER 23
Navigating professional identity as a teacher of history

Nicole Mockler

Becoming any kind of teacher is a difficult business. Graduating from an initial teacher education program certainly sets you on the path to 'becoming', but the process of developing a professional identity—a strong sense of yourself as a teacher—is a longer-term exercise. This chapter examines the factors that mediate and shape teacher professional identity, particularly in the beginning years of teaching. It draws on a life-history study of an early-career history teacher to highlight the interwoven nature of professional, personal and political contexts in the shaping of teacher identity, and it argues that understanding and coming to grips with your own professional identity is a critical 'project' in the first few years of teaching.

Before we begin, a couple of caveats are required. It is important to recognise that the development of teacher professional identity is deeply individual. Some come to history teaching with a significant investment in the 'history' part of the equation and, initially at least, less in the 'teaching' part. Some come with an equal investment in both, while others might come with more investment in the 'teaching' part and less in the 'history' part. Taking account of this variety of starting places, this chapter explores the processes around developing teacher professional identity, rather than suggesting there is only one way (or even a limited number of ways) to get there. Second, and related to this, it is important to recognise that there is no one way to *be* a teacher. While professional standards and other education policy documents might suggest otherwise, *becoming* a teacher isn't about learning to conform to a single ideal prototype or exemplar. In a nutshell, it is about understanding your own orientation to education, to schooling, to your students and to your subject area, and connecting and aligning these to your *practices*. Recognising that teaching is *practised* rather than *embodied* (Gore, Ladwig & King 2004) is an important part of this, while developing a robust teacher professional identity can help you align 'who I am' with 'what I do'—the two are not one and the same, and this notion will be explored in more depth later in this chapter.

WHAT IS TEACHER PROFESSIONAL IDENTITY AND WHY SHOULD WE CARE?

Identity is a slippery concept. There are whole fields of research across the disciplines of psychology (e.g. Erikson 1968), philosophy (e.g. Derrida 1981; Hall 1996) and sociology (Bernstein 1996; Wenger 1998) that focus on identity-formation. While these different approaches have their own nuances, the general consensus is that identity-formation is dynamic rather than static; emergent and constantly evolving rather than fixed; multidimensional as opposed to linear; and fluid rather than compartmentalised. American philosopher Judith Butler (1993: 105) says of identity-formation that 'identifications are never fully and finally made; they are incessantly reconstituted.'

What we can take from this in relation to understanding teacher professional identity is that identity-formation isn't something that happens during and shortly after initial teacher education; rather, it is an ongoing process that occurs over the course of a career. Teacher professional identity is formed out of the narratives of teachers' lives as teachers—what F. Michael Connolly and D. Jean Clandinin (1999; see also Clandinin & Huber 2005) have called teachers' 'stories to live by'. This is in some ways consistent with Michael Huberman's (1989) classic work on the seven stages of the 'life cycle' of the teacher: survival and discovery; stabilisation; experimentation/activism; self-doubts; serenity; conservatism; and disengagement. While Huberman characterises the progression through the stages as a linear one, he also notes that they are 'tentative, often fragmentary' (1989: 36) in the way they play out. His point is that teachers continue to shift and change in their orientations to teaching over the course of their careers, regardless of how long those careers may be.

Elsewhere (Mockler 2011), I have posed a way of thinking about the development of teacher professional identity that makes use of these ideas, but understands the formation and mediation of teacher professional identity to be less linear and more complex than Huberman's model might suggest. Figure 23.1 represents the various domains and processes associated with becoming and 'being' a teacher (2011: 521).

Within this model, the essence of being a teacher is said to lie somewhere at the confluence of personal, professional and political dimensions, with teacher professional identity 'anchored' in different places at different times over the course of a career. Teachers' professional identities are formed and mediated by catalysts that emerge from the three domains over the course of a career, either as the result of intentional engagement with professional learning, personal development or 'activist' activities (engagement within and/or beyond the profession), or by virtue of events, occurrences or experiences that take place within an individual domain. The identity 'anchors' that emerge out of this interplay serve to secure teachers' professional identities and provide a touchstone for professional development and formation, and a frame of reference for professional practice at a particular time.

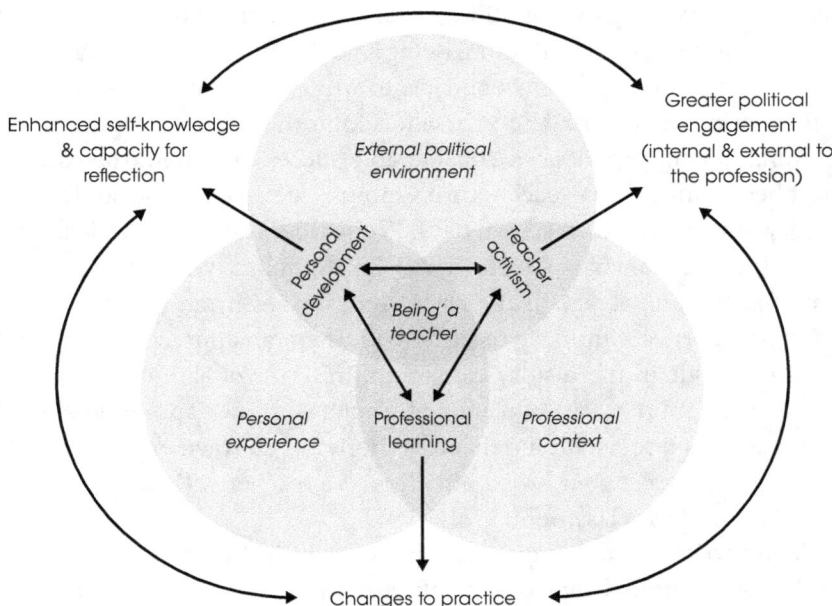

Figure 23.1 Becoming and 'being' a teacher. Mockler, N. 2011, 'Beyond "what works": Understanding teacher identity as a practical and political tool', *Teachers and Teaching*, vol. 17, no. 5, p. 521.

Why should we care?

Thinking explicitly about your own professional identity, who you are as a teacher and who you want to be is an important reflective strategy. Lortie (1975) wrote of the power of the 'apprenticeship of observation', the phenomenon by which pre-service teachers have already spent thirteen years observing other teachers by the time they engage in their own teacher education. He wrote (1975: 62):

> The student . . . sees the teacher front stage and centre like an audience viewing a play. Students do not receive invitations to watch the teacher's performance from the wings; they are not privy to the teacher's private intentions and personal reflections on classroom events. Students rarely participate in selecting goals, making preparations, or post-mortem analyses. Thus they are not pressed to place the teacher's actions in a pedagogically oriented framework.

The apprenticeship is notoriously strong in shaping beginning teachers' ideas about teaching, and part of the aim of initial teacher education is to make students privy to those things that have remained obscured during the apprenticeship of observation. Being able to articulate why you are here and how what you are doing connects to why you are here, beyond what you experienced as a student yourself, is important. Most people go into teaching having experienced considerable success at school themselves: most beginning history teachers, for example, were very good students of history during their own school days. While this is absolutely as it should be, in that we want people with excellent disciplinary knowledge to be working that knowledge in the classroom, it does mean that most new history teachers are unlikely to bring with them an appreciation of what it is to struggle in the history classroom, in terms of skill development, engagement or both. Part of pushing through your own apprenticeship of observation is understanding the limitations of your own experience and learning to connect your broad intention as a teacher with your practices in and beyond the classroom.

Many writers who historically have worked in the space of teachers' work have identified the concept of 'moral purpose' as a key driver for teachers, in terms of both entering and staying in the profession. Christopher Day (2004: 24), for example, notes that 'moral purposes are at the heart of every teacher's work', and in recent research has explored the links between moral purpose and resilience (Day & Hong 2016). Michael Fullan (1993: 12), who has built a body of work in this area over several decades, invokes us to 'scratch a good teacher and you will find a moral purpose'.

Writing about teachers' moral purpose often makes the implicit assumption that, as a teacher, a desire to 'do good' or 'make a difference' will almost automatically drive a particular type of professional practice. The truth is, however, that moral purpose—no matter how strongly held or deeply felt by teachers—is not enough on its own to ensure good practice. Sometimes moral purpose itself can become a 'blocker' to robust debate and professional dialogue, in that it can be very difficult to argue against. In their work on school reform, Grant Wiggins and Jay McTighe (2007), two American teacher professional learning experts who developed the understanding by design approach to curriculum design, argue that there is often a disconnect between teachers' moral purpose and their practice. They write (2007: 128):

> Over the years, we have observed countless examples of teachers who, though industrious and well meaning, act in ways that suggest that they misunderstand their jobs. It may seem odd or even outrageous to say that many teachers misconceive their obligations. But we believe this is the case. Nor do we think this is surprising or an aspersion on the character or insight of teachers. We believe that teachers, in good faith, act on an inaccurate understanding of the role of 'teacher' because they imitate what they experienced, and their supervisors rarely make clear that the job is to cause understanding, not merely to march through the curriculum and hope that some content will stick.

Wiggins and McTighe highlight the power of the apprenticeship of observation and the tendency that we have as a profession to not spend time exploring how we can and should connect our 'industriousness' and 'well meaning-ness' to what we actually do. While it is not the case that bringing about greater alignment between these and understanding and claiming our own professional identity will magically banish the challenges of being a teacher, research certainly suggests that it might help.

It has long been recognised that teachers' work has been increasingly intensified over the past two decades, and more recent work has suggested that this intensification has exponentially increased with the rise of regimes of accountability in education (Apple 2013; Stone-Johnson 2016). In the midst of these challenges, teachers rarely have permission to take time to reflect on their practice in this way. While we talk a lot about the notion of reflective practice in teaching, rarely are we offered a set of useful conceptual tools for engaging in the kinds of reflection that might be useful. In articulating their professional identity, teachers engage in a process whereby they construct themselves in their own minds as teachers—what Margaret Archer (2007) refers to as the 'internal conversation'—but, importantly, also within their school communities. This is essentially about drawing links between moral purpose and practices—it is about congruence between word and deed, and pushing ourselves to articulate what that congruence might look like and then pursuing it through actions.

Figure 23.2 sets out a way of thinking about how this might work in practice. The key challenge is for teachers to push beyond their sense of moral purpose into the territory of practice, where decisions are made about the pedagogical approaches to take, the teaching and learning strategies to employ, and the ways in which we interact with students and other members of the community.

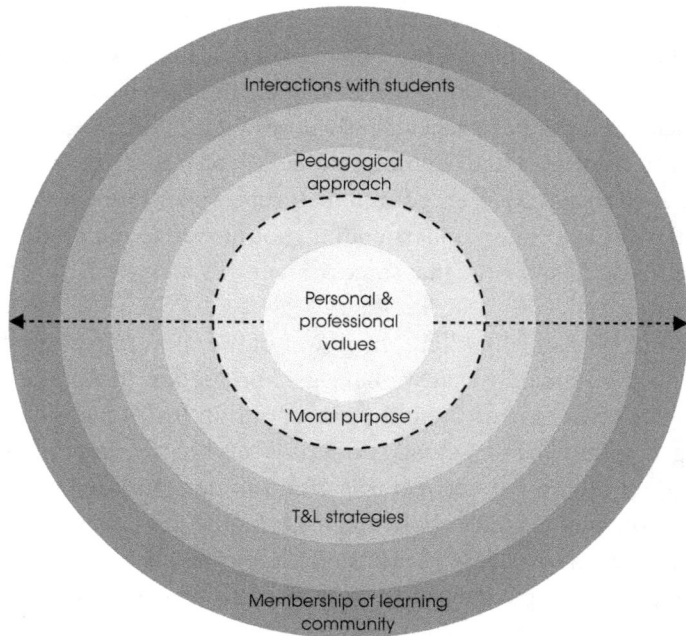

Figure 23.2 Enactment of teacher professional identity, Mockler, N. 2008, 'Beyond "what works": Teachers and the politics of identity', PhD thesis, University of Sydney.

The 'project' of articulating our professional identity is thus one of developing and maintaining congruence between personal and professional values and moral purpose, then pushing through the border between moral purpose and on-the-ground action to create congruence between word and deed. It matters because all the moral purpose in the world will not bring about transformation if it is not followed through with action.

PROFESSIONAL IDENTITY AND BEGINNING HISTORY TEACHERS

Having established that articulating a robust professional identity is important, let's return to Figure 23.1 to think about how the development and mediation of teacher professional identity might commonly work for beginning history teachers. Here we will draw on some general observations about the interplay of the personal, political and professional dimensions of beginning history teachers' identities and explore the experience of Liana, a history teacher who was interviewed over her second and third years of teaching in a comprehensive public secondary school in New South Wales, Australia.

Personal experience: How did I get here?

Teaching is a popular career choice for talented history students wanting to use their love of history in their everyday lives. While there is no doubt that the skills of the historian are eminently transferrable and useful in a range of careers, for those wanting history to be 'front and centre' in their professional lives, the occupations are more limited. Liana is probably quite typical of many beginning history teachers when she says:

> I love history, always have as long as I can remember and I had some really good role models as my teachers so I wanted to be the kind of teacher that shared my passion for the subject with students . . .

Other aspects of personal experience are also important in shaping our orientation to teaching. Often, teaching is a 'first in family' career, where prospective teachers might be the first member of their family to attend university, while conversely some prospective teachers come from families where teaching has historically been a common profession. For all, there is a personal story that has brought them into teaching. Some embark on initial teacher education with the expectation that teaching and education will be a lifelong career, while others come into the profession expecting to teach for a period of time before pursuing other things.

As passionate history students themselves, beginning history teachers often come into the profession with highly developed skills of critical thinking, analysis and synthesis, and these interact with personal experience to produce particular orientations to the world. Many beginning history teachers are knowledgeable about, and have a particular interest in, not only history but also current affairs, political and human geography, and other related areas. In some cases, these interests have been fostered through life experiences involving travel and exploration of other cultures, which again can often produce particular dispositions and orientations to the world. It would be fair to say that many beginning history teachers share a 'big picture' orientation to the world, a desire to understand the antecedents of what's going on in the world and a sense of empathy with others across space and time.

Furthermore, along with their counterparts in other subject areas, beginning history teachers experience the effects of societal attitudes to teacher and teaching both from people they know and more broadly:

> I feel a lot of the time that when I tell people that I'm a teacher I almost need to justify the choice. So people might ask what I did at uni and because I did an Arts degree they'll assume that you know, well what else are you going to do with it? Work at McDonalds or teach? . . . and it's hard for me because when I was at school . . . I was always a high achiever. I was the Vice-Captain. You name it, I did it at school and I got really good results for my own Higher School Certificate and so . . . I don't know I guess being in a profession where it doesn't feel as if there is as much respect then becomes a challenge.

Here Liana points to the disconnect between her own level of commitment to the profession, born of a genuine desire and choice to be a teacher, and the potential for this to be undermined by the status of teachers within society more broadly. Elsewhere, she says:

> My parents were pretty supportive but . . . they both chose the love of the job over money [in their own careers]. I did have a lot of people try and talk me out of it. Saying, you know, 'You're too smart', 'You'll

get bored'. 'You've got this [ATAR] in the 90s, use it.' That's sort of been the mentality. But then this year I was thinking maybe I was just a bit idealistic. You know maybe I could have tried journalism or something first. And it's not that I could ever see myself doing anything else but there's also I think the reality has set in that now I'm a teacher it's going to be really hard to do anything else if I want to . . . because of the way I guess that teachers are perceived as a profession outside. You know, I could never go back and do law . . . It's not as if I'm not enjoying it. I guess I'm just thinking about it more now in terms of like a long-term career than I probably did in the beginning.

Liana underlines here how, in the first few years of teaching, the damaging attitudes that can be expressed by others, which fit into the realm of personal experience, can be stirred up by the realities of the newly embraced professional context. In her case, this has brought her to contemplate the challenges in being and remaining a teacher for the long term.

Professional context: Where am I now? Where am I going?

Quite obviously, professional context is different for every beginning teacher. Furthermore, professional context might be thought of as existing on a range of different scales. For example, national, state and system contexts form part of every beginning history teacher's professional context, as do more immediate contexts such as their school and faculty/department. In the first few years, the elements that are more likely to have an important impact on beginning teachers' professional experiences are those related to staff and student relationships, professional learning experiences and workload issues, including externally imposed requirements such as those related to curriculum or leaving credentials.

For Liana, it was challenging to be a young teacher within a faculty of older teachers approaching retirement and uninclined to encourage innovation:

I see some of the people in my staffroom and just think I never want to end up like that. You know if you don't enjoy what you're doing, then it can make you a very unhappy person and not a very pleasant person in a lot of ways. But it just means that a lot of what I do is sort of very underhanded and I don't talk about the things that I try in the classroom.

On the other hand, her head teacher not only provided her with support as a beginning teacher but was also a powerful role model as someone who had been teaching history for a long time but was still a highly committed and motivated classroom practitioner:

> She's nearly 50 and she's been teaching since she was 21 and she still loves it and she's still really passionate about teaching in general and about the kids and a lot of people I see of her age are kind of sitting there waiting for retirement, especially at my school . . . and so I sometimes get a bit frustrated with things and I look at her and think, 'Oh you can do it for 25 years and still care . . . about the kids and care about the job and take it seriously' . . . The kids really respect her because they know that she teaches them well and cares about their HSC and puts a lot of effort in.

Good professional learning experiences can support beginning history teachers to navigate the difficult terrain of becoming a history teacher. Sometimes this comes in the form of support for developing teaching and learning strategies that authentically engage students who are potentially 'switched off' from history. At other times, it might come in the form of supporting beginning teachers who feel a level of anxiety around 'covering' curriculum content to take a step back and focus on the 'bigger picture'. For Liana, a turning point came in her third year of teaching, when she attended a History Teachers' Association conference and heard one of the 'elders' of the history teaching community speak:

> It was so interesting to hear her say that 30 years on she speaks to ex-students and they're like, 'Oh didn't you teach us about, you know, some war?' and she said, 'Students remember a lot about my classroom but they don't necessarily remember anything about the Peloponnesian War . . . it's the other lessons that they take out of it', and that made me think a lot more about it in broad terms like the leadership opportunities and valuing learning—and those sort of things are going to have a lot more value than . . . remembering who Heracles was.

She recognised that experience and exposure to ideas such as these had helped to orient her slightly differently after a couple of years of teaching, although the relentlessness of the workload remained. What had shifted for her, however, was that:

> I think maybe I've become a little bit more, what's the word, maybe a little bit less tough on myself about it. Like I think I always used to feel when I started teaching quite stressed out if I wasn't on top of everything all the time. And I think now maybe I realise that I just have to use my time effectively and be a bit more flexible about things and if I don't get the marking back to the kids in a week it's okay . . .

Learning to live with the realities of teaching—to make decisions about what can safely be compromised on and how—is an important part of becoming a teacher.

External political environment: Navigating complexity

Australian education has arguably never been such an important political issue as it is in the early twenty-first century. Issues related to school funding, curriculum, standardisation of assessment and 'teacher quality', among other factors, have come to the fore over the past decade, and the debate over these issues in the public space shows no signs of abating. As noted above, many beginning teachers of history have knowledge and interest in not only history, but also current affairs, politics and human or political geography, and this can bring a heightened sense of the complexity of education as a policy field. Liana recognised this:

> The whole debate actually just really frustrates me because obviously you know that technically the federal government has no jurisdiction over education anyway so the whole debate at the moment [over the national curriculum] is unconstitutional and yet, you know, we're having the discussion . . . [Governments] do seem to use education in a way that they don't use the police force and they don't use hospitals. Um, as a pawn for elections.

The introduction of history as a discrete discipline in secondary schools across Australia that came with the implementation of Phase 1 of the Australian Curriculum forms a very tangible part of the external political environment that has impacted the work of history teachers, and created new possibilities for the development of robust history teacher professional identity nationwide. Meanwhile, research suggests that other contemporary developments, such as the implementation of national standardised testing and national teaching standards, have had significant shaping and narrowing impacts on teachers' work and education more broadly (e.g. see Lingard & Seller 2013: 634–56). While these reforms relate to the work of all teachers, it is within the complexity created by this external political environment that beginning history teachers' practice is enacted and professional identity is formed.

CONCLUSION: NAVIGATING A PROFESSIONAL IDENTITY AS A BEGINNING HISTORY TEACHER

The first years of teaching are often tumultuous: while initial teacher education can provide a rich foundation of knowledge and skills to underpin professional practice, the realities of teaching five days a week for 40 weeks a year have to be experienced to be fully understood. It is only natural for beginning teachers to move into 'survival mode', but it is important to build in regular moments to take a step back and reflect on the 'big picture'. Recognising where your own teacher professional identity is anchored as a beginning teacher, and what has contributed to this anchoring, is a good start. Being clear about your own moral purpose and the kinds of practices that align with this purpose and remembering that some of these might be aspirational in the beginning is another. Most important, however, is remaining open to learning. Those things that anchor your teacher professional identity, that shape your understanding of yourself as a teacher, will—and should—change over time. Seeking out spaces for learning, whether through formal professional development, sourcing a wise mentor or cyclically inquiring into your own practice, will support your ongoing formation as a teacher.

Teaching is difficult but enormously rewarding and important work. Having a strong sense of who you are and who you want to be as a teacher, and allowing this to evolve over time, will not magically banish the difficulties, but it will support beginning teachers to be more grounded and confident in their orientation to their work. Over time, a robustly articulated sense of professional identity can work as a useful tool for shaping professional growth and professional activism, supporting teachers to individually and collectively contribute to the project of educational transformation.

REFERENCES

Apple, M.W. 2013, *Teachers and Texts: A Political Economy of Class and Gender Relations in Education*, London: Routledge.
Archer, M. 2007, *Making Our Way Through the World: Human Reflexivity and Social Mobility*, 2nd ed., Cambridge: Cambridge University Press.
Bernstein, B. 1996, *Pedagogy, Symbolic Control and Identity*. London: Taylor & Francis.
Butler, J. 1993, *Bodies That Matter: On the Discursive Limits of 'Sex'*. New York: Routledge.
Clandinin, D.J. & Huber, M. 2005, 'Shifting stories to live by: Interweaving the personal and professional in teachers' lives', In D. Beijaard, P. Meijer, G. Morine-Dershimer and H. Tillema (eds), *Teacher Professional Development in Changing Conditions*, Dordrecht: Springer, pp. 43–60.
Connelly, F.M. & Clandinin, D.J. 1999, *Shaping a Professional Identity: Stories of Educational Practice*. New York: Teachers' College Press.
Day, C. 2004, *A Passion for Teaching*. London: RoutledgeFalmer.
Day, C. & Hong, J. 2016, 'Influences on the capacities for emotional resilience of teachers in schools serving disadvantaged urban communities: Challenges of living on the edge', *Teaching and Teacher Education*, vol. 59, pp. 115–25.
Derrida, J. 1981, *Positions*. Chicago: University of Chicago Press.
Erikson, E.H. 1968, *Identity: Youth and Crisis*. New York: W.W. Norton.
Fullan, M. 1993, 'Why teachers must become change agents', *Educational Leadership*, vol. 50, no. 6, pp. 12–17.
Gore, J., Ladwig, J. & King, B. 2004, 'Professional learning, pedagogical improvement, and the circulation of power', Paper presented to the Australian Association for Research in Education Annual Conference, The University of Melbourne.
Hall, S. 1996, 'Introduction: Who needs identity?', in S. Hall and P. du Gay (eds), *Questions of Cultural Identity*, London: Sage, pp. 1–8.
Huberman, M. 1989, 'The professional life cycle of teachers', *Teachers' College Record*, vol. 91, no. 1, pp. 31–80.
Lingard, B. & Sellar, S. 2013, '"Catalyst data": Perverse systemic effects of audit and accountability in Australian schooling', *Journal of Education Policy*, vol. 28, no. 5, pp. 634–56.
Lortie, D. 1975, *Schoolteacher: A Sociological Study*. Chicago: University of Chicago Press.
Mockler, N. 2011, 'Beyond "what works": Understanding teacher identity as a practical and political tool', *Teachers and Teaching*, vol. 17, no. 5, pp. 517–28.

Stone-Johnson, C. 2016, 'Intensification and isolation: Alienated teaching and collaborative professional relationships in the accountability context', *Journal of Educational Change*, vol. 17, no. 1, pp. 29–49.

Wenger, E. 1998, *Communities of Practice: Learning, Meaning and Identity*, Cambridge: Cambridge University Press.

Wiggins, G. & McTighe, J. 2007, *Schooling by Design*. Alexandria, VA: ASCD.

INDEX

Abbott, Tony 26
Aboriginal and Torres Strait Islander peoples 21
  1967 referendum 282, 285, 288, 291
  activism 282, 285–6, 299, 303
  Constitutional recognition 286, 291–2
  education 287–9
  film, in 227
  frontier wars 283–5, 302–3
  history of 10, 24, 108, 149, 279–96, 299–307
  Indigenous perspectives xxix, 148, 149, 282–3, 289, 294–5, 303–4
  recognition, struggle for 286, 289–91
  'silence' and 'forgotten' history 299, 301, 302
  Stolen Generations 279
  teaching about 293–4, 299–307
  'truth-telling' xxix, 299–300, 307
  Uluru Statement from the Heart 291–2, 299, 307
academic history
  popular history, relationship with 161–2
'Adopt a Soldier' 183–91
adventure novels 197–8
Alexander, Nicole 197
  Absolution Creek 197
alternate histories 199
Anastasia 223
Ankersmit, Frank 78
Annales School 146
antiquarian historical discourse 76

Anzac Cove, landing at 63–8, 109–10
  alternative sources 65–6
  sources, understanding 63–5, 110
Anzac legend 65, 67–8, 110, 150, 198
archival footage 221
art
  critical questions, asking 39
Ashby, Roslyn 50, 60
Ashmead-Bartlett, Ellis 63–5, 66
Asia literacy 314, 316
  public consciousness, and 314
Asian perspectives xxix, 24, 25, 314, 316–18
  colonial narratives, and 315
assessment 142
  Aboriginal history and politics, teaching 306–7
  assessment for learning (AfL) 129, 131–2, 134
  assessment of learning (AoL) 129, 132
  authenticity 139
  Canadian system 131
  classifying student achievement 130–1
  classroom 132–4
  current trends 129–31
  diagnostic testing 130, 131
  effective xxvii–xxviii, 140–2
  equitable marking 140–2
  external testing, problems associated with 130, 171–2
  feedback 139, 140–2
  Finland, in 133–4
  formative and summative 33–7, 131–2, 139–40

assessment *continued*
  informal 131
  inquiry learning approaches 135–40
  marking criteria 141
  modalities xxvi, 135
  New Zealand, in 132–3
  peer 140
  practical aspects 131
  practice, in 134–5
  process, as 34
  purpose of 131–2, 142
  qualitative assessment tools, requirement for 133
  reflective learning 306–7
  self 140
  source-based 120, 138–9
  United States system 130–1
Attwood, Bain 282
Auchmuty Report 315
Australian Aboriginal Progressive Association (AAPA) 285
Australian Council for Education Research (ACER) 20, 48
Australian Curriculum xxvi, 3, 31–2, 43, 56, 173, 248, 333
  adoption by states 28
  debates xxvii, 15, 18–20
  development of 21–4, 26, 28–9, 234–5
  disciplinary studies, and 20, 245–6
  general capabilities 37–41
  humanities and social sciences (HaSS) 32, 33–4
  review (2013) 27–8
  right-wing criticisms 24–5, 26–7
  structural issues 25–6
  technology, and *see* online digital technologies
  values teaching, and 105–6

Australian Curriculum, Assessment and Reporting Authority (ACARA) 14–15, 20, 22–4, 26, 56
  criticisms 27
Australian Reconciliation Convention 286
Australian War Memorial (AWM) 235, 238, 239
  frontier wars, recognition of 284
Australia's Asia: From Yellow Peril to Asian Century 314
Aykut, Susan 11

Ballard, Martin 6
  New Movements in the Study and Teaching of History 6
Barthes, Roland 78
Barton, Edmund 48, 54
Barton, Keith 121, 125–6, 318
Basham Report 315
Bendle, Mervyn 24
Bishop, Julie 14
'black armband' history 10, 24, 75–6, 84, 161, 282–3, 304–5
Blainey, Geoffrey 14, 75, 282, 304
Bloom, Benjamin 6
Boddington, Tony 8
boredom 118, 120–1, 125, 183
  see also student interest/engagement
Bringing Them Home report 286
Brock, Claire 194, 195
Brown, Nick 14

Cambridge Group for the History of Population and Social Structure 146
Canadian system 189
  assessments 131
  citizenship education 311

Carey, Peter 198
  True History of the Kelly Gang 198
Carr, Bob 9
Cato, Nancy 197
  All the Rivers Run 197
cause and effect/consequence xxiv, 15, 33, 52, 56, 234, 280
  analysis of 61
  values teaching, and 105
celebratory pluralism 81, 82–3
celebratory reconstructionism 81, 82
Centre for the Study of Historical Consciousness 51
character education 104
Chau Chak Wing Museum 269
Christian novels 199
citizenship
  Asian perspectives 316–18
  citizenship education and 312–13
  civic knowledge 312
  history education and 310–11
  national narratives/memory xxi, 3, 9, 15, 26, 75, 110, 311
  nationalism 310
  teaching xxix, 175–6
civic comprehension and engagement 49
Civics and Citizenship Education syllabus 313
Clark, Anna 24, 75, 147, 293
Clark, Ronald W. 199
  Queen Victoria's Bomb 199
Cleese, John 123
'cloze' exercises 187
Cochrane, Dr Peter 12
cognitive apprenticeship 73, 225
cognitive dissonance 185
Cold War 27
collective memory 79–80, 81, 82, 109–9
Collingwood, R.G. 7, 92, 96, 97, 98

Colombo Plan 315
colonial narratives 10, 75–6, 78, 102, 108–9, 303
  Asia, and 315
Coltham, Jeanette 6
  The Development of Thinking and the Learning of History 6
  Educational Objectives for the Study of History 6
Commonwealth History Project (CHP) 4, 11, 21
  historical consciousness, and 11–13
conceptual understanding 32–3
Confucian tradition 317–18
Connor, John 284
Constable, Kate 202, 203
  Crow Country 202
'constructionist' epistemology 80
constructivism 122, 129, 135, 225, 234
contact history 161, 176, 279–96
content 121
  knowledge *see* knowledge
  skills versus 73–5, 123–4
contestability 12, 15, 56, 105, 235, 280
  classroom exchanges and 164–5
contested history xxi, 109, 189, 239, 240, 294, 300–1, 304
  classroom, in the 280–2
context bounded credibility 232
contextualisation xxv, 97–9, 111–13, 234, 237
  online resources, and 232–3
  social history, role of 145–6
contextualism xxx, 93
continuity and change xxiv, 15, 33, 51, 56, 234, 280
  identification of 61
  values teaching, and 105

Convention on the Means of Prohibiting and Preventing the Illicit Import, Export and Transfer of Ownership of Cultural Property (UNESCO) 267
cooperative learning activities 68
corroboration 234
Council for Aboriginal Reconciliation 289, 290
Counsell, Christine 123–7
'crisis of representation' 77
critical engagement xxiii, 38–40
critical historical discourse 76
critical historical thinking 233–4, 238
critical pluralism 81, 83
critical reconstructionism 81, 82
critical web literacy 240
  classical approaches 240–1
  conceptual approaches 241
  modelling 241–2
cross-mentoring 168
Cuban Missile Crisis 160, 163–8, 171
cultural memory 109–11
cultural studies 173
culturally responsive pedagogies (CRP) 294–5
Curriculum Corporation 12
curriculum knowledge 3
  explicit curriculum 60
  implicit curriculum 60
  null curriculum 60

Davies, Nigel 238
Day of Mourning protest 285
de Gaulle, Charles 98–9
Death in Rome (game) 250, 253, 257
debate and class discussion 55
debriefing 213
'deconstructionist' epistemology 81
'deep history' xxix, 301

depth studies 22–3, 25, 26, 28, 29, 317
digital technologies *see* online digital technologies
Dilthey, Wilhelm 96
direct instruction 121–3, 126
disciplinary approach 80, 81, 84, 114
  Australian Curriculum: History 245–6
  conceptualisation of discipline 247
  discipline, definition 246
  domain-specific knowledge 247
  general knowledge 247
  interdisciplinary/integrated studies, and 20, 32–3, 76–7
  knowledge-building structures, using 247
  situating disciplinary knowledge 247
  structure of disciplinary knowledge 247
disciplinary distillation 92
Discovering Democracy program 21, 25, 313
distance education 141
docudramas 221, 224
documentaries 221
Donnelly, Kevin 24, 27
drama
  elements of 209–10, 217
  history teaching, in 210–11
drama pedagogy xxviii, 208–10, 218–19
  critical empathy 211–13
  debriefing 213
  dramatic tension 209
  freeze frames 212
  gallery walk 215
  human context 209
  overheard conversations 218
  'performance frame', use of 210

role protection 210
soundscapes 215–16
space, stories and sources 216–18
teacher in role 213
understanding historical events 213–16
A Dramatic Bus Journey Touring Hong Kong Heritage 216–18
Dunlop, Beverley 201
Spirits of the Lake 201

'education revolution' 14, 19–20
educational drama *see* drama pedagogy
Edwards, Rachel 194–5, 204, 205
'effective history' concept 95
effective questioning xxvii
Einfühlung 96
empathy xxiv, xxv, xxvii, 12, 15, 33, 50, 56, 74, 89, 96, 234–5, 280
  critical 211–13
  defining 90–1, 96
  disciplinary conceptions 93
  drama pedagogy, and 211–13
  emotional capacity, as 90
  historical context, and 91
  historical judgement, and xxii, 90
  location of human meaning 94
  need for 91–3
  past and present, balancing 93–5
  problems with 96–7
  social history, and 152–3
  teaching 89–91, 175–7
  values teaching, and 105
empiricist history 77
epistemic tools
  guiding, scaffolding or structuring actions 249–50
  technological 245, 248–53
  understanding, increasing 249
epistemology of text 234

ethics 104
  antiquity collecting 268
  empathy, and 89
  ethical dimensions 52, 234
  museum collections 267–8
  understanding 61
Eureka Stockade 149–50
evidence xxiv, 15, 19, 33, 51, 56, 234, 280 *see also* sources
  critical historical thinking, and 233–4
  empathy, and 90
  personal narratives, role of 166–9
  social history, and 151
  values teaching, and 105
evidence-based and concept-led approach 11, 23
exhibitions 266–8

Facey, Albert 65–6
fantasy novels 199
feature films 221
  values, teaching 227
Federal Council for the Advancement of Aboriginals and Torres Strait Islanders (FCAATSI) 285
Federation 33, 47–8, 54, 293, 314
feedback 139, 140–2
  levels of 141
feminist history xxvi, 77
Fenton, Edwin 4, 5
field-based learning 183
film
  archival footage 221
  cognitive apprenticeship instruction 225–6
  conceptual framework 223–4
  'Disney effect' 222–3
  docudramas 221, 224
  documentaries 221
  feature films 221, 227

film *continued*
  genre, exploring 224
  graphic organisers 224–5
  issues and challenges in using 222–3
  learning scaffolds 224–5
  performative tasks 228–9
  presentism 222
  source, as 226–7
  use of xxviii, 221–9
  values dimension 227
Fines, John 6
  Educational Objectives for the Study of History 6
Finland
  external testing 133
First Fleet database 35, 41
First Footprints: Super Nomads 301
Fitzgerald Report 315
food, history of 154
For Country for Nation 284
formative assessment 33–7
Forrest Gump 222
frame of reference, expanding 67–8
Freedom Rides 285
freeze frames 212
French, Jackie 202, 203
  Somewhere Around the Corner 202
frontier wars 283–5, 302–3
Furst, Alan 198
  The Foreign Correspondent 198
The Future of the Past: The Final Report of the National Inquiry into School History 11
'futures orientation' 23

Gadamer, Hans-Georg 95, 96, 97
gallery walk 215
Gallipoli 63–8, 109–11, 133, 283
  alternative sources 65–6
  place and representation of 75
  sources, understanding 63–5, 110

Gallipoli 227
Garnaut Report 315
Geisteswissenschaften 96
Getty Education 262
Gillard, Julia 14, 18–19, 20, 26, 314, 316
Global Financial Crisis (GFC) 19, 236
globalisation 173, 198
Google 137, 236, 242
Google Earth 41
Google Maps 237
graphic organisers 224–5
Great War 23, 66, 67–8, 153, 214–16
  'Adopt a Soldier' project 183–91
  Anzac Cove, landing at 63–8, 109–10
  Anzac legend 65, 67–8, 110, 150, 198
  Gallipoli *see* Gallipoli
Grenville, Kate 196
  The Secret River 196
group work 168–9
Gurindji Wave Hill Walk Off 285

hands-on history 263–5, 270–1
Hangen, Tona 239–40
Harding, Traci 199
  Chronicle of the Ages 199
Hasluck, Nick 199
  Dismissal 199
Hattie, John 122, 293
Henderson, Gerard 14
heritage
  history, distinguished 181
  time-slip fiction and issues associated with 202–3
heritage items, repatriation of 267
hermeneutics 94, 97
  conservative 94
  moderate 94–5
  radical 94
Heyer, Georgette 197
  These Old Shades 197

INDEX

higher-order thinking xxviii, 138, 165, 169, 170
  fiction, using 194–5, 204, 205
Higher School Certificate (HSC) 129, 130
  markers' notes 137–8
Hill, Ernestine 197
  My Love Must Wait 197
Hirst, John 10, 21, 25
Hirst, Paul 6
historical consciousness xxiii–xxv, 3, 52, 96
  Commonwealth History Project, and 11–13
  Howard government, under 13–15
  human rights, and 112
  nature of xxv
'historical distance' 80
historical fiction
  adventure novels 197–8
  alternate histories 199
  Christian novels 199
  enhancement, processes of 204
  fantasy 199
  literary novels 198
  multi-period epics 196
  mysteries 197
  outback novels 197
  pedagogical engagement 204
  romantic novels 197
  sagas 196–7
  sample classroom questions 204–5
  steampunk 199
  thrillers 198
  time-slip novels 194–5, 199–203
  time-travel novels 200
  traditional historical novels 196
  using xxviii, 39–40, 65–7, 194, 205
  Western novels 197
historical judgement
  empathy, and xxii

historical literacy *see* historical thinking
historical thinking xxv, 14, 173
  application in classroom environment 119–20
  assessment, role of 132–3
  choices, making 67
  classroom, in the 53–6
  competencies 51–2
  concepts of 234–5
  content and context 52–3
  'cultural tools' 52
  defining 48, 52–3, 119, 181
  emergence of 119
  interrelated concepts 68
  method, issues of 60
  national literacy, and 49–53
  questions, asking 61–2
  social history 149–51
  strategies 234
  teaching xxvii–xxviii, 233
Historical Thinking Project 51, 60, 69, 74
historical understanding *see* understanding
historicism 83
historiography xxvi, 77, 83, 198, 318
  Aboriginal history, teaching 302, 305
  multifunctional questioning, and 163
  social history 153–4
  'troubling questions', and 108–9
  values teaching, and 108
history 136
  anxiety 47–9, 56, 77, 314–15
  discipline, as xxi, 37, 50–1, 121, 172, 333
  heritage, distinguished 181
  literacy and numeracy capabilities 37–41

History Advisory Group 32
History Teachers' Association of
    Australia (HTAA) 8, 13, 22, 26,
    27, 76, 279
Teaching History journal 118
history teaching xx, xxii–xxiii, 28–9,
    72–3
  Aboriginal history and culture
    293–4, 296–7
  Aboriginal history and politics
    299–300, 307
  anecdotal diversions 171
  approaches to xviii–ix
  Australia, background in 4–5
  content xxii–xxiii
  culturally responsive pedagogies
    (CRP) 294–5
  direct instruction 121–3, 126
  framework, developing a 81–4
  indoctrination, and 25
  professional discretion 162, 171–2
  professional identity, and 323–34
  proximity and distance, tension
    between 180–1
  regional 182–3
  regurgitation of facts 118, 122
  research xx, xxii
  skills xxii
  'teacher talk' xxviii, 159–77
  'what to teach' debate xxii
History Wars 10, 13, 18, 19, 24, 75,
    108–9, 283, 293, 305, 313
HiTCH (Historical Thinking–
    Competencies in History) project
    51
Hobart Declaration on Schooling
    (1989) 5
Hoepper, Dr Brian 11
Holocaust 106–7, 113, 162
Horne, Donald 315
  The Lucky Country 315

Howard, John 9–10, 13–14, 18–19, 48,
    75, 110, 286
Huberman, Michael 324–5
human rights 112–13
Human Society & Its Environment
    (HSIE) 76, 208
Husserl, Edmund 96

identity-formation xxi, 76, 324
  professional *see* professional identity
imaginative texts, using 39–40
Indigenous perspectives xxix, 148,
    149, 282–3, 289, 294–5, 303–4
Information and Communication
    Technology (ICT) 41, 248
  see also online digital technologies
Inquiry and Skills strand 33–5, 41
inquiry-based approach 7, 15, 21,
    50–1, 135–7
  assessments, and 133, 135–40
  background 117–18
  phases of inquiry 42
  primary teaching, and 32, 34–6,
    41–3
  scaffolding 137–9
  values teaching, and 105–6
Institute of Public Affairs (IPA) 27
intercultural understanding 39
interdisciplinary/integrated approach
    84
  Aboriginal history, teaching 300
  disciplinary studies, and 20, 32–3,
    76–7
International Baccalaureate
  Theory of Knowledge (TOK) course
    76
Internet Archive: Wayback Machine
    236, 237
interviews
  drama pedagogy 217
  oral history 154

Jones, Dr Adrian 11
Judeo-Christian tradition 27–8
Junior Secondary Syllabus (1992) 8–9

Karskens, Grace 147
Keating, Paul 48, 110, 286, 289–90, 304
Kelly, Ned 198
Kelly, T. Mills 236
   Teaching History in the Digital Age 236
Kemp, David 10
key history concepts, assessing 33–7
Kiem, Paul 22, 74
Kingdom of Heaven 224
Klein, Joel 20
knowledge 23, 28, 34, 56
   cumulative acquisition 124–5
   domain specific 247
   frameworks, role of 123–4
   general 247
   importance of 124–5
   procedural 60, 69
   situating disciplinary 247
   skills, versus 73–5, 123–4
   structure of disciplinary 247
   substantive 60, 69
   technology and construction of 249–53
'knowledge-in-use' 61
Kokoda 110–11

Lambert, John 8
L'Amour, Louis 197
   Hondo 197
Lane, William 314
Langton, Marcia 282
language 209
   Aboriginal history, teaching 302–3
   influence of 67
lateral reading 242

Lee, Peter 50, 60, 98
literacy capabilities, history and 37–40, 162
literary artefact, history as 78
literary novels 198
Little, Norm 8
   A New Look at History Teaching 8
local history
   'truth-telling' 299–300
   using 31, 35, 38, 40, 154–5

Mabo High Court decision 285, 290
McCrae, John 214
   'In Flanders Fields' 214–16
McCullough, Colleen 196
   The First Man in Rome 196
McGaw, Professor Barry 20–1, 24
Machiavelli 97–8
Macintyre, Stuart 10, 24–5, 75
Mackinolty, Judy 8
   A New Look at History Teaching 8
Magna Carta 25, 26–7
Mahy, Margaret 201
   The Tricksters 201
Makarrata Commission 291, 292
Making History publications 12, 139
Manning, Dr Corinne 11
maps, using 184–5, 191
Marshall, Catherine 199
   Christy 199
Marxist history 77, 83
Mauldon, Private Joseph 185–6, 189–90
Maynard, Frank 285
The Melbourne Declaration 111, 246
Melleuish, Gregory 25
metanarratives 77–8, 84
Ministerial Council on Education, Employment, Training and Youth Affairs (MCEETYA) 48
Mink, Louis 78

Mitchiner, James 196
　Chesapeake 196
　Hawaii 196
　Poland 196
monumental historical discourse 76
mood 209
moral dimension xxiv, 33, 76
　values teaching, and 105
Moral Majority 27
moral reasoning 113
movement 209
multiculturalism
　values teaching, and 111
multi-period epics 196
Murrell, Belinda 203
　Lulu Bell series 203
museums
　classroom replication of museum experience 268–9
　critical interpretation 266–8
　educational experiences 262–3
　hands-on history 263–5, 270–1
　historical development 266–7
　history teaching, and xxix, 260–74
　Nicholson Museum 269–73
　post-visit activities 265–6
　pre-visit activities 265–6
　school–museum partnerships 273
mystery novels 197

narratives
　fictive discourse 78
　historical fiction *see* historical fiction
　implied 188
　maps, and 184
　multiple, recognition of 84
　'patterned stories' 183
　progress 80
　storytelling 166–70

National Archives of Australia (NAA) 41, 185, 187, 189–90
National Assessment Program—Literary and Numeracy (NAPLAN) 19–20, 129, 130, 133
National Centre for History Education (NCHE) 11–12
　publications 12
National Certificate of Educational Achievement (NCEA) 133
National Council for the Centenary of Federation 48
National Curriculum Board (NCB) 14, 20
National Curriculum (UK) xxi, 8
National Declaration on Educational Goals for Young Australians 104
National Film and Sound Archive (NFSA) 239
National History Curriculum Framing Paper 105
National History Inquiry (2000–01) 4
National History Standards (US) xxi
National History Summit (2006) 4
national identity 10, 310 *see also* citizenship
　Australia and Asia 313–16
　national narratives/memory xxi, 3, 9, 15, 26, 75, 110
National Inquiry (Australia) 10–11
　findings 11
National Library of Australia (NLA) 235, 239
　Pandora archive 13
national literacy
　historical literacy, and 49–53
nationalism 310
　social history, and 148, 311
nationhood 109–10
native title 286, 290, 305
Nelson, Dr Brendan 284

neoliberalism 173
NEW: Emerging Scholars in Indigenous Studies 306
New History movement 5–6, 124, 126, 304, 311
  source-based work, criticisms of 120–1
New Social Studies movement 4
New Zealand 132–3
Nicholson Museum 269–73
  mummy wrapping 272–3
Nietzsche, Friedrich 76
nominalism 90
Nova Scotia Museum
  'How to Read a Shoe' activity 262
numeracy capabilities, history and 37, 40–1

object-centred learning 261, 263
online digital technologies 245
  affordances 254–7
  Australian Curriculum, and 245–6, 248
  capacities 245
  Death in Rome (game) 250, 253, 257
  devaluing knowledge 124
  digital photography 252–3
  digital storytelling 251–2, 253–4, 255
  epistemic tool, as 245, 248–53
  functions 245
  maps 184
  museums 268
  scaffolding historical inquiry 249–50
  Timeglider 252
  use of xxviii, 41, 154
  VoiceThread 251, 253, 256
  websites *see* websites
oral history interviews 154

outback novels 197
overheard conversations 218
Ozhistorybytes 12

Pacific War 110
Papua New Guinea 110
Park, Ruth 195, 200, 201, 202, 203
  Playing Beatie Bow 195, 200, 201, 202, 204
passive learning 122, 223
Pearce, Philippa 201
  Tom's Midnight Garden 201
Pearson, Lester B. 98–9
pedagogy of inquiry xxvi
performative tasks 228–9
'personalising' xxviii, 166–9, 190–1, 214–16
'perspective-taking' 98–9
perspectives xxiv, 15, 33, 52, 56, 61, 234, 236, 280
  Asian xxix, 24, 25, 314, 316–18
  'circle of viewpoints' 42
  classroom exchanges and 164–5
  critical literacy, and 38–9
  film, using 227
  Indigenous xxix, 148, 149, 282–3, 289, 294–5, 303–4
  social history, and 149–50
  values teaching, and 105
  world history 21, 22, 25
phenomenology 96
philosophy of history 92
Piaget 91, 173
place and time 209, 216–18
plan of action 113
pluralism xxvii, 81, 83
  celebratory 81, 82–3
  critical 81, 83
Pocahontas 223
poetry, using 214–16
political history xxvi

politics 102, 123
  Asia, attitudes towards 315
  citizenship *see* citizenship
  conservatives and patriotic pride 26
  museums, and 267–8
  national narratives/memory, and
    xxi, 3, 9, 15, 26, 75, 110, 310
  professional identity, and 333–4
  reconciliation and shared history
    289–91, 292, 300
  White Australia 314, 315
Pompeii: The Last Day 224, 229
popular culture, importance of 187
popular history
  academic history, relationship with
    161–2
positionality xxiv, 80
'possibility thinking' 39–40
postmodern history 73, 77–9, 80–1
presentism xxv, 181–2, 187
  film, in 222
primary history, teaching 31–2
  conceptual understanding 32–3
  inquiry, role of 34–6
The Prime Minister's Guide to the Teaching of Australian History in Schools 14
problem-solving approach 7, 104, 105, 168, 183–4, 246, 265
Professional Digest 12
professional identity xxix, 323–34
  'apprenticeship of observation' 326, 327
  beginning history teachers 329–34
  formation and mediation 324–5, 329
  moral purpose, and 326–7, 334
  nature of 324–5
  personal, political and professional dimensions 325, 329
  political environment, and 333–4
  professional context 331–3
  reflecting on 326–9, 334
Project Zero 36, 37, 42
Pulman, Felicity 195, 203
A Ring Through Time 195
Pyne, Christopher 26, 27, 28

Quality Teaching Indigenous Project 294
questioning skills 61–2
questions 68–9
  causal 61
  comparative 61
  constructive questioning 183
  descriptive 61
  evaluative 61
  interactive classroom exchanges 163–6
  open and closed 61
  textual and intellectual 61–2

Rabbit-Proof Fence 227
racism 194, 227, 295, 303, 313, 314
  Aboriginal and Torres Strait Islander people, against 287
Rantzen, Scilla 12
Rapkins, Eric 67
Reagan, Ronald 27
'real world'
  epistemic gap between classroom and 231–3
'reality effect' 78
reasoning, historical xxv, 61, 74, 79
  values teaching, and 105
reconciliation 289–91, 300
  practical 290
  substantive or deep 290
  symbolic 290
  true, nature of 290
Reconciliation Australia 290

reconstructionism 81–2
  celebratory 81, 82
  critical 81, 82
Redfern Speech 285, 289–90, 304
re-enactment, theory of 92
Referendum Council of Australia
  291–2
reflection on practice 113, 119, 170,
  328, 334
relativism 78–9, 83
  cultural 82
Remembering Australia's Past (RAP)
  project 75
remembrance and commemoration
  82
Republican Rome 160, 169, 171,
  175–6
revisionist history xxvi, 78, 238, 304
  multifunctional questioning, and
  163
Reynolds, Henry 282, 302–3, 305
  The Other Side of the Frontier:
    Aboriginal Resistance to the
    European Invasion of Australia
    302
The Rocks 147–8, 195, 204
Rodwell, Grant 200
  Saving Sydney 200, 201
romantic novels 197
Rudd, Kevin 14, 19, 26, 290, 314, 316
Ryan, Lyndall 282, 284

sagas 196–7
Saylor, Steven 197
  Roma Sub Rosa series 197
Schindler's List 222
Schools Council History Project
  (SCHP) (UK) 3–4, 6–7, 50,
  117–18, 126, 135, 172, 233
  Australia, impact in 7–8, 118–20
'see, think, wonder' routine 42

Seixas, Peter 21, 33, 49, 50, 51, 73, 79,
  98, 107, 188, 234
  approaches to history teaching
    79–81
The Shape of the Australian
  Curriculum 105
Shek Kip Mei Estate 217
Shemilt, Denis 7, 50, 74, 173
  History 13–16 Evaluation Study 7
significance xxiv, 15, 33, 51, 56, 234,
  235, 280
  determination of historical 67
  establishing 60
  values teaching, and 105
skills 15, 23, 34, 82, 127
  content, versus 73–5, 117, 123–4
  development of skills-based
    approach 117–18
  testing higher-order 170
Skinner, Quentin 97
Smith, Wilbur 198
  The Power of the Sword 198
social history xxvi, 145–6, 155, 190
  belonging 148–9
  classroom, in the 151–5
  conceptualising history 154
  empathy, importance of 152–3
  entry point, usefulness as 153
  evidence 151
  experiencing history 154–5
  historical thinking, and 149–51
  historiography, and 153–4
  identity 148–9
  nationalism 148, 311
  nuanced context 150
  personal understandings 148–9
  perspectives, and 149–50
  'reading about' versus 'encountering'
    151
  'realness', promoting 146–8
social movements, impact of 303

social studies approach 4
soundscapes 215–16
source-based assessment 120
sources 33, 50, 126 *see also* evidence
　analysis, four-stage model of
　　62–3
　attribution of 63, 64
　bias 112, 185
　contested history 280–1
　critical web literacy 240–2
　curriculum 'content', and 74
　depersonalisation, and 186–7, 188
　drama pedagogy, and 216
　evidence, as 62–3, 69
　film as 226–7
　first-order 62
　identification of 62, 63
　interpreting 112, 186–8
　judging perspective 63, 64
　maps 183–5, 191
　misunderstandings about primary
　　121
　multiple, using 65–7
　narrativity and textuality 80
　online 235–40
　reliability assessment 63, 65
　second-order 62
　source-based work, criticisms of
　　120–1
　third-order 62
　types of 62
　using 60–1, 120, 126, 137–8
　WWI soldier's military record
　　185–6
sourcing 234
steampunk 199
Stephens, Alan 284
Stolen Generations 279
storytelling 166–9
　digital 251–2, 253–4, 255
　museums, in 266

student interest/engagement 54–5,
　160–1, 205
　Aboriginal history, teaching 293–4,
　　306–7
　'Adopt a Soldier' project 183–91
　destabilising student assumptions
　　161
　fiction, using *see* historical fiction
　film, using *see* film
　hands-on history 263–5, 270–1
　maintaining xxi, 125
　museums 260–1
　national history, and 50
　social history 145–6, 147, 154–5
　student-initiated questions 165–6
　'truth-telling' 300–1, 307
　untangling student understandings
　　161
Studies of Society and Environment
　(SOSE) 5, 9–10, 12, 76, 311
summative assessment 33–7
survey-histories 182
sustainability 24
symbols 209

tableaux 212
Taylor, Tony 21, 22, 27, 28, 48, 53,
　122, 139
teacher-centred learning 121–3,
　126
teacher in role 213
'teacher talk' xxviii, 159–77
　activity structures 170–1
　citizenship, teaching 175–6
　empathy, teaching 175–7
　interactive classroom exchanges
　　163–6
　knowledge base, describing
　　172–5
　telling the story 166–70
teacher voice 162

Teaching for Understanding
  Framework 36, 37, 42
teaching history *see* history
  teaching
Teaching the Truth about Refugees
  212–13
Team Jigsaw 68
technology *see* online digital
  technologies
Tent Embassy 285
terra nullius 282, 285
thought, history of 92
thrillers 198
Time, Continuity and Change 5, 12,
  15
time-slip novels 194–5, 199–203
  Australian 200–1
  popularity of 201–2
  time-slip, definition 200
  time-travel fiction, distinguished
    200
Timeglider 252
traditional historical novels 196
transdisciplinary teaching 77, 84
transnational critiques 173
Trove 154, 238
'truth-telling' xxix, 299–300, 307
  engaging student learners 300–1
Turnbull, Malcolm 26, 292

Uluru Statement from the Heart
  291–2, 299, 307
understanding 15, 21, 23, 28, 34, 56
  conceptual 32–3
  context of historical understanding
    97–9
  culminating tasks, and 34
  drama pedagogy, and 213–16
  intercultural 39
  past and present, contrasting and
    untangling 97
  re-enactment conceptions 96–7
  through the past 95
United Kingdom 5
  National Curriculum (UK) xxi
  Schools Council History Project
    (SCHP) 3–4, 6–8, 50, 117–18,
    126, 135, 172, 233
United States
  assessment system 130–1

V for Vendetta 226
values 103, 114, 174
  analysing and engaging with 107
  Australian Curriculum: History
    Years 7–10 105–6
  conceptualisation of 104
  cultural memory, and 109–11
  defining 103–4
  ethics, and 104
  film, using 227
  historical inquiry, and 111–13
  memorial obligation, and
    109–11
  moral 103
  multiculturalism, and 111
  nature of 103–4
  specific, choosing to teach 111
  teaching 106–13, 174–5
  'troubling questions', and 108–9
  values clarification 112–13
van Boxtel, Carla 61, 74
van Drie, Jannet 61, 74
VanSledright, Bruce 36, 62, 185
Verne, Jules 199
visible thinking 41–2
vocabulary xxvii
VoiceThread 251, 253, 256

Wake, Roy 6
Walker, David 313, 314
Ward, Elizabeth 14

websites
    classical model of online source analysis 240–1
    conceptual approach 241
    context-bounded credibility 232
    conventional sources 235–7
    'democratisation' of access 238–9
    evaluation and use of historical 231–3
    metadata, examining 237
    modelling website analysis 241–2
    raw material, using 238–40
    unconventional sources 237–8
    use of xxviii 231–42
    web literacy 240–2
Wells, H.G. 199, 200
    The Time Machine 200
Western novels 197
What is History? teaching kit 118
White Australia 314, 315

'white blindfold' history 75–6, 84, 305
White, Hayden 78, 84
Wikipedia 237–8
    credibility 231–2
    'Wikipedia test' 137
Willis, Connie 200
    Doomsday Book 200
Wiltshire, Kenneth 27
Windschuttle, Keith 283, 304–5, 305
    The Fabrication of Aboriginal History 283, 304
Wineburg, Sam 52, 174, 180–1, 222, 234
world history perspective 21, 22, 25
World War I *see* Great War
Wright, Clare 150

Yorta Yorta decision 305
Young, Carmel (Fahey) 8, 21, 53, 139
Yunupingu, Galarrwuy 292

For Product Safety Concerns and Information please contact our EU
representative GPSR@taylorandfrancis.com
Taylor & Francis Verlag GmbH, Kaufingerstraße 24, 80331 München, Germany

www.ingramcontent.com/pod-product-compliance
Lightning Source LLC
Chambersburg PA
CBHW071757300426
44116CB00009B/1110